LEARN TO
Ride

Crown copyright material has been reproduced by permission of the Driving
Standards Agency which does not accept any responsibility for the accuracy of
the reproduction.

First published in 2005
Revised and reprinted in 2006
Revised and reprinted in 2007
Second edition August 2008
Reprinted in 2009 & 2010
Third edition published 2011

Every effort has been made to ensure the accuracy of the information given
but the author and the publisher accept no responsibility for any injury, loss or
inconvenience sustained by anyone using this book.

A catalogue record for this book is available from the British Library

ISBN 978 0 85733 150 2

Published by Haynes Publishing,
Sparkford, Yeovil, Somerset BA22 7JJ, UK

Tel: +44 (0)1963 442030 Fax: +44 (0)1963 440001
E-mail: sales@haynes.co.uk
Website: www.haynes.co.uk

Haynes North America, Inc.,
861 Lawrence Drive, Newbury Park,
California 91320, USA

Printed in the USA by Odcombe Press LP,
1299 Bridgestone Parkway, La Vergne, TN 37086

contents

introduction

People come to motorcycling for any number of reasons – some attracted by the economy of a scooter for the urban commute, others by the challenge of mastering the massive performance of a sports bike. You may be learning to ride as a complete novice on the road, or you may already have a car licence. In either case, there's a lot to learn. Riding not only requires a unique set of technical skills, it also demands a rigorous and self-disciplined approach to staying safe. A poorly trained rider is a particularly vulnerable road user, and the testing system has been designed to ensure that riders have to earn the right to go out onto the road by putting in some serious preparation first.

That's where this book comes in. *Learn To Ride* brings together all the information you need to take you through Compulsory Basic Training and on to pass your theory and practical motorcycle tests. We've put all this information in one handy book because it's important to prepare for the theory and practical tests side by side. You won't get the most from your on-road preparation for the practical test without a thorough knowledge of riding theory, and you'll struggle to succeed in the theory test without plenty of practical riding experience under your belt.

One thing all motorcyclists agree on is that riding a bike should be fun – something few drivers can say about their cars. With the help of this book, we hope learning to pass your motorcycle test will be just as enjoyable too.

Safe riding!

1 first steps

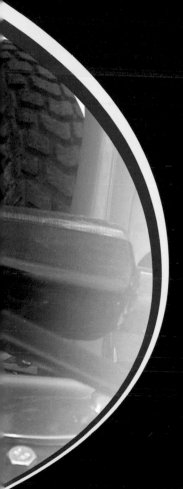

There are several routes to getting a motorcycle licence and the one you take will influence your choice of first bike. But whether you're aiming to ride a moped, a light motorcycle, or want to go straight to riding a larger bike through the Direct Access scheme, you first have to undertake Compulsory Basic Training (CBT). And before you even get on your bike you need to make sure it is taxed and insured, and that you are properly kitted out with protective clothing. You also need to check your fitness to ride, to ensure you are physically and mentally prepared to meet the challenge of riding a motorbike safely.

starting to ride

Riding a motorcycle may be many people's idea of freedom, but there's plenty of red tape to tie up before you can get on your bike. Be sure you understand the law as it relates to you before you start to ride.

Think also about the financial investment that motorcycling involves. Don't forget that as well as the cost of your motorbike, you have to budget for specialised clothing and helmet, as well as tax, insurance and the cost of the training you undertake.

rules and regulations

To start riding a motorcycle on a public road you must:

- ○ be at least 17 years old (16 years for mopeds)
- ○ be medically fit, with eyesight to the required standard (corrected with glasses or contact lenses if necessary)
- ○ hold a driving licence that gives provisional entitlement for motorcycles
- ○ undergo a course of Compulsory Basic Training (CBT)
- ○ wear a safety helmet
- ○ ensure that your bike is roadworthy, taxed, insured, and if it is over three years old has a current MOT certificate. (For more information about arranging insurance cover, as well as tax and MOT requirements, see p194.)

licence requirements

You need a driving licence which gives you provisional entitlement for motorcycles. If you hold a full car licence this automatically gives provisional motorcycle entitlement. A full moped licence gives provisional entitlement for motorcycles providing you are aged 17 or over.

If you do not already have one of these licences, you will need to apply for a provisional driving licence. Driving licences are issued by the Driver and Vehicle Licensing Agency (DVLA). Apply using form D1, which you can obtain from the post office. The fee for a provisional licence is currently £50. (In Northern Ireland the licensing authority is Driver and Vehicle Licensing Northern Ireland.)

All new provisional licences are valid until the holder's 70th birthday.

learners and the law

As a learner rider holding a provisional driving licence, these restrictions apply:

- ○ you cannot ride a motorcycle of more than 125cc (unless you are aged 21 or over and are training under the Direct Access scheme)

- ○ you must display L-plates to the front and rear of your motorcycle
- ○ you must not ride on motorways
- ○ you must not carry a pillion passenger
- ○ you may ride a motorcycle and sidecar outfit with a motorcycle of any capacity but the power-to-weight ratio of the outfit must not exceed 0.16kW/kg
- ○ you must not tow a trailer.

As a learner you are not allowed on motorways

L-plates

The size, shape and colour of L-plates is laid down by law, so don't try to economise by making your own. Make sure the plates are positioned on the front and rear of the motorcycle so they are clearly visible. In Wales a D-plate can take the place of an L-plate.

Fix L-plates to the front and back of the motorcycle in as vertical a position as possible

which licence?

Motorcycle licensing is extraordinarily complicated. In a nutshell, you can aim for a licence that restricts you to riding light motorcycles (under 125cc), or a licence that's valid for any bike. Understandably, most riders take the latter route. Even so, for two years after passing you are restricted to smaller bikes (under 25kW/33bhp) – unless you are aged 21 or over and you take the Direct Access route which lets you ride any size of bike. As this avoids having to wait and trade up from one bike to another, it is again understandably a popular route for those riders who are eligible to take it.

licence categories

Firstly you need to decide whether you want to aim for a licence that will allow you to ride any sort of motorcycle (category A) or one that restricts you to light motorcycles only (category A1).

category A

A category A licence entitles you to ride any size of motorcycle. You have to take the practical test for a category A licence on a learner motorcycle – one that is between 121–125cc and is capable of 100km/h (62mph) – unless you are taking your test under the Direct Access scheme (see below).

You are allowed to use motorways and carry a pillion passenger after getting a category A licence, but for the first two years you are restricted to a motorcycle of up to 25kW (33bhp) and with a power-to-weight ratio not exceeding 0.16kW/kg. Motorcycles producing less than 25kW are generally under 400cc, but there is no engine limit specified. This means it is permissible to ride a more powerful motorcycle as long as it has been modified to restrict it to 25kw. After two years, you can have the restrictor kit removed and restore the bike to its original power output.

category A1

A category A1 licence entitles you to ride a light motorcycle, of up to 125cc and with a power output of up to 11kW (14.6bhp). It allows you to ride on motorways and carry a pillion passenger. You can take the practical test for a category A1 licence on a motorcycle of 75–125cc.

Direct Access

Direct Access is an alternative route to obtaining a category A licence which is open only to riders aged 21 and above. It means that, after undergoing CBT (on a motorcycle of any size) and the theory test you take the practical test on a motorcycle with a power output of at least 35kW (46.6bhp). Having

passed, you are then permitted to ride a bike of any size.

You are permitted to practise for the practical test on any bike larger than the learner bike specification, provided that you:

- ◉ are accompanied at all times by a qualified instructor on another bike who is in radio contact with you
- ◉ wear fluorescent or reflective clothing
- ◉ follow all other provisional licence restrictions (ie display L-plates, do not carry pillion passengers and do not use motorways).

Accelerated Access

Accelerated Access is a similar scheme to Direct Access for riders who hold a category A licence and who reach the age of 21 before the end of their two-year restricted period. They can practise on a bike larger than 25kW (33bhp), under the same conditions as Direct Access riders, and take a test on a bike of at least 35kW (46.6bhp). Although the rider reverts to learner status while practising, failing the test will not affect their existing motorcycle licence entitlement.

Under Direct Access, riders over 21 can practise on a larger-engined bike under certain conditions

getting your licence

There are three steps to obtaining a full motorcycle licence. These are summarised in the chart overleaf.

step 1: CBT

All new riders must successfully complete a Compulsory Basic Training course before riding a moped or motorcycle on the road. The only exemptions are:

> riding a moped with the full entitlement automatically given by a full car licence obtained before February 1 2001

> learning to ride a motorcycle after having already obtained full moped entitlement as a result of passing a moped test on or after December 1 1990

> upgrading from one category of motorcycle licence to a higher category, eg full A1 to category A

> riders resident on certain offshore islands (see *It's the law* panel).

CBT is not a pass-or-fail examination, but you must demonstrate a basic level of skill and understanding of the topics covered in order to satisfy the instructor. On successfully completing CBT, you will be given a certificate of completion (DL196) which is valid for two years. You need to keep this safe as you have to show it when you apply for and take your practical test, and you may be required to produce it by a police officer. If you do not pass the practical test within two years of gaining your certificate of completion, you will have to re-take CBT and obtain a new certificate. A DL196 obtained on a moped is valid for a motorcycle when the rider reaches the age of 17.

See p18 for further details about booking and attending your CBT.

step 2: theory test

You must pass the theory test before you can take (or book) your practical test.

The theory test is split into two elements. First is a touch-screen multiple-choice exam which takes 57 minutes. This is followed by a video-clip based hazard perception test, which takes up to half an hour.

You are not required to take the theory test if you already hold a lower category of motorcycle licence or have passed a moped test since July 1 1996. However, if you hold a licence for a different type of vehicle, such as a car, you do still have to take a theory test. When you pass the theory test you will receive a pass certificate which is valid for two years: you must pass the practical test within this time or you have to retake the theory test.

See p226 for further details about booking and attending your theory test.

step 3: practical test

The practical test is divided into two modules. Module One involves completing a series of off-road exercises. Module Two is a ride on the road observed by an examiner who follows you by car or motorcycle. You also have to answer questions about basic motorcycle safety checks and carrying a pillion passenger.

You must take your practical test on a motorcycle of the appropriate size:

> **category A1:** a bike with engine capacity of 75cc to 125cc

> **category A:** a bike with engine capacity of 121cc to 125cc and capable of 100km/h (62mph)

> **category A (Direct Access/Accelerated Access):** a bike with a power output of at least 35kW (46.6bhp).

If you pass your practical test on an automatic motorcycle such as a scooter your licence will be valid only for riding automatics.

See p230 for further details about booking and attending your practical test.

mopeds

A moped is a motorcycle which:
- cannot go faster than 50km/h (31mph)
- has an engine no larger than 50cc
- can be moved by pedals (if the moped was first used before August 1 1977).

At age 16 you are able to apply for a driving licence that gives provisional moped entitlement. However, you must successfully complete a CBT course before going on the road, you must display L-plates and you cannot carry a pillion passenger. The CBT certificate is valid for two years and if you wish to continue riding a moped for longer than this you must take and pass the theory test and moped practical test and obtain a category P moped licence. Once you have this, you can discard your L-plates and are permitted to carry a pillion passenger (though not to ride on motorways, from which all mopeds are excluded).

There is an alternative route to riding a moped, and this is to acquire a full car licence. You then have to undergo CBT and obtain a DL196 certificate, upon which you are fully qualified, can ride without L-plates and carry a pillion passenger (a DL196 certificate obtained in this way lets you ride a moped indefinitely, but lasts the usual two years for motorcycles).

Drivers who passed their car test before February 1 2001 are automatically fully qualified to ride a moped, although taking a training course still makes a lot of sense.

A moped is the only form of motorised transport that you are permitted to ride at age 16

motorcycle and sidecar

Learners wishing to ride a motorcycle and sidecar can practise on an outfit with a power to weight ratio not exceeding 0.16kW/kg. On obtaining a category A licence, they are restricted to riding this size of outfit for two years. However, riders aged 21 and above may practise on a larger outfit, within the Direct Access or Accelerated Access provisions.

In any case all riders must take their test on a solo motorbike (except physically disabled riders, who may take their test using a motorcycle and sidecar, but on gaining their licence will be restricted to motorcycle and sidecar outfits only).

Direct Access provisions also apply to riders wishing to use a motorcycle and sidecar

it's the law

cbt exemptions

CBT must be completed by all learners resident on mainland Great Britain, islands that are connected to the mainland by a road, and the islands of Wight, North Uist, Lewis, South Uist, Harris, Benbecula, mainland Orkney and mainland Shetland. Residents of all other islands are exempt from the need to take CBT, but only if riding on roads on an exempted island.

how to get a moped licence

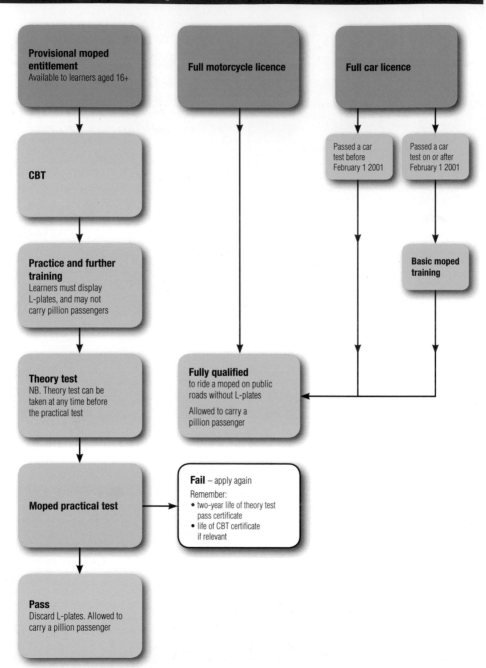

Provisional moped entitlement
Available to learners aged 16+

Full motorcycle licence

Full car licence

Passed a car test before February 1 2001

Passed a car test on or after February 1 2001

CBT

Basic moped training

Practice and further training
Learners must display L-plates, and may not carry pillion passengers

Theory test
NB. Theory test can be taken at any time before the practical test

Fully qualified
to ride a moped on public roads without L-plates

Allowed to carry a pillion passenger

Moped practical test

Fail – apply again
Remember:
• two-year life of theory test pass certificate
• life of CBT certificate if relevant

Pass
Discard L-plates. Allowed to carry a pillion passenger

how to get a motorcycle licence

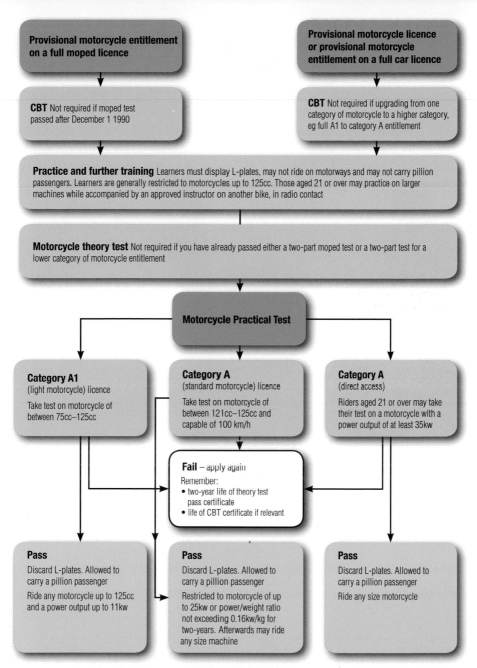

Provisional motorcycle entitlement on a full moped licence

CBT Not required if moped test passed after December 1 1990

Provisional motorcycle licence or provisional motorcycle entitlement on a full car licence

CBT Not required if upgrading from one category of motorcycle to a higher category, eg full A1 to category A entitlement

Practice and further training Learners must display L-plates, may not ride on motorways and may not carry pillion passengers. Learners are generally restricted to motorcycles up to 125cc. Those aged 21 or over may practice on larger machines while accompanied by an approved instructor on another bike, in radio contact

Motorcycle theory test Not required if you have already passed either a two-part moped test or a two-part test for a lower category of motorcycle entitlement

Motorcycle Practical Test

Category A1
(light motorcycle) licence

Take test on motorcycle of between 75cc–125cc

Category A
(standard motorcycle) licence

Take test on motorcycle of between 121cc–125cc and capable of 100 km/h

Category A
(direct access)

Riders aged 21 or over may take their test on a motorcycle with a power output of at least 35kw

Fail – apply again

Remember:
• two-year life of theory test pass certificate
• life of CBT certificate if relevant

Pass

Discard L-plates. Allowed to carry a pillion passenger

Ride any motorcycle up to 125cc and a power output up to 11kw

Pass

Discard L-plates. Allowed to carry a pillion passenger

Restricted to motorcycle of up to 25kw or power/weight ratio not exceeding 0.16kw/kg for two-years. Afterwards may ride any size machine

Pass

Discard L-plates. Allowed to carry a pillion passenger

Ride any size motorcycle

compulsory basic training

Since it was introduced in 1990, Compulsory Basic Training (CBT) has made a significant reduction to casualty rates among new riders. The course costs around £120 and generally takes a full day, although it can be spread over two days if desired. It provides a thorough grounding in the practical aspects of bike control, and lets you ask questions about any aspect of riding you are unsure about – as well as being an enjoyable opportunity to some fellow riders.

attending CBT

CBT courses can be given only by Approved Training Bodies (ATBs) whose instructors have been assessed by the DSA and who have sites approved by the DSA for off-road training.

Remember to take your driving licence. If you attend CBT with your own bike, you must also ensure you have all the bike's documentation for the trainer to check, including your insurance certificate, MOT certificate (if the bike is three or more years old), and a current tax disc fixed to the bike.

Most training centres can hire or loan bikes and helmets for use during CBT.

Be sure to wear suitable clothing for the course: this should include a stout pair of boots, a strong pair of gloves, and tough, warm and comfortable jacket and trousers – and if rain looks likely don't forget your waterproofs.

Your trainer will provide a high-visibility overjacket with the name of the ATB on it which you must wear during the course.

what CBT involves

The content of the CBT course is broken down into five elements: the first four take place at the training site, before heading out onto local roads for a session of practical riding under the guidance of the instructor.

Element A: introduction

Your instructor will take you through:
- the aims of the CBT course
- legal requirements, including a check of your documents
- the importance of wearing the correct helmet, visor and clothing
- eyesight test. You must be able to read the current style of numberplate in good daylight at a distance of 20m (66ft). You may wear glasses or contact lenses if necessary but in this case you must wear them for the rest of the course and at all other times while riding. If you fail the eyesight test then you will not be able to proceed with the course.

Your Compulsory Basic Training course will include some classroom instruction as well as practical training

Element B:
practical on-site training

Your instructor will show you round the motorcycle, making sure you understand:

- ➲ how the controls work
- ➲ how to carry out basic safety checks, including tyres, suspension, steering, electrics, fuel, oil and chain
- ➲ using the stand
- ➲ wheeling the motorcycle
- ➲ starting and stopping the engine.

Element C:
practical on-site riding

You will practise riding in the controlled conditions of the training site until you can demonstrate that you are competent at:

- ➲ clutch control
- ➲ slow riding
- ➲ changing gear
- ➲ riding in a figure of eight
- ➲ braking and emergency stops
- ➲ rear observation
- ➲ road junctions
- ➲ turning left and right
- ➲ U-turns.

After making sure everyone is familiar with how the motorbike operates, the instructor conducts a range of on-site exercises including road junctions, slow riding and the emergency stop (clockwise from top left)

Element D: practical on-road training

Your instructor will talk to you about:
- legal requirements for riding a motorcycle
- the *Highway Code*
- the importance of being clearly visible
- the vulnerability of riders as road users
- positioning on the road
- leaving space when following another vehicle
- weather conditions
- road surfaces
- use of speed
- observation and anticipation
- hazard perception
- how attitude affects safety
- the dangers of drink and drug-driving.

Element E: practical on-road riding

You will go out on to the road for a minimum two-hour session to demonstrate that you can ride safely and deal with a variety of different road situations, including:
- traffic lights
- roundabouts
- junctions
- pedestrian crossings
- hills
- bends
- obstructions in the road
- performing U-turns
- carrying out an emergency stop.

CBT ends with a session of practical riding on the public road under the instructor's supervision

after CBT

Although CBT covers a lot of ground, it should be regarded as only the first step in gaining your full motorcycle licence. Next you need to get in plenty of practice, and should arrange some further training to take you on to test standard.

choosing an instructor

Most ATBs are able to provide further instruction to practical test standard. You may be able to arrange this after completing your CBT. Training usually takes place with a group of learners – up to a maximum of four learners to one instructor.

practice makes perfect

Get in as much practice as you can in the run up to your practical test. Try to experience as many different riding situations as possible: ride in the country as well as in town, on dual carriageways with a 70mph limit, and don't neglect to go out in wet weather – it may be raining on your test day. Get plenty of practice of the essential exercises such as the U-turn and emergency stop (but remember not to obstruct other traffic, and don't repeat them endlessly in the same quiet back streets or you will irritate local residents).

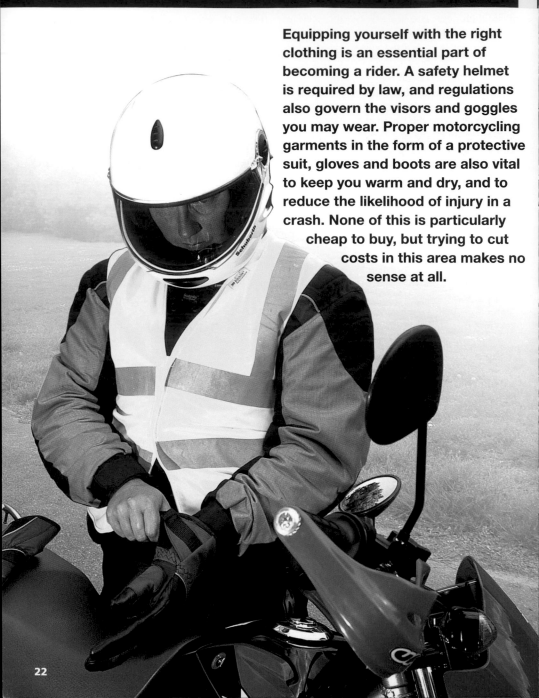

protective clothing

Equipping yourself with the right clothing is an essential part of becoming a rider. A safety helmet is required by law, and regulations also govern the visors and goggles you may wear. Proper motorcycling garments in the form of a protective suit, gloves and boots are also vital to keep you warm and dry, and to reduce the likelihood of injury in a crash. None of this is particularly cheap to buy, but trying to cut costs in this area makes no sense at all.

safety helmets

By law motorcyclists must wear an approved safety helmet (the exception is for members of the Sikh religion who wear a turban).

More than 75 per cent of motorcyclist deaths or serious injuries involve head injuries, and a helmet significantly reduces the risk of serious head injury and brain damage in a crash. Helmets also help to cut down wind noise which can be distracting and damaging to the hearing, as well as protecting your face and eyes from flying debris, cold and wind blast.

which helmet?

All helmets sold in the UK must comply with one of the following:

⊙ British Standard BS 6658:1985 and carry the BSI kitemark
⊙ UNECE Regulation 22.05 (look for the UN E-mark, with '05' as the first two digits of the approval number)
⊙ any standard accepted by a member of the European Economic Area (EEA) which offers the same safety standard as the British Standard, and which carries a mark equivalent to the BSI kitemark.

A helmet can be a life saver, so don't economise when buying one. Check its SHARP rating (one to five, the higher the better), an independent assessment of how much protection it will provide in an impact. And don't use a secondhand helmet: it may have sustained damage that can't be seen.

There are two types of helmet, open-face and full-face. The full-face has chin protection and a hinged visor, and is the better choice as it protects the face in a crash and gives fuller protection from the weather. Some riders prefer the more open feel of the open-face style, which lacks chin protection and can be worn with a visor or goggles.

The outer shell of a helmet may be made of polycarbonate, glassfibre or kevlar. Polycarbonate is lighter than glassfibre but less long-lasting. It is important not to paint or fix stickers to a polycarbonate helmet, and it must never be cleaned using solvents. Kevlar has the advantage of combining great strength with light weight, but kevlar helmets tend to be expensive.

Whichever type of helmet you buy, choose one which fits firmly but comfortably. The padding will bed down with wear so if it isn't a tight fit when new the helmet could later become loose, which means there's a risk of it coming off in a crash.

It also makes sense to go for a light-coloured helmet which helps to make you more visible to other road users.

By law a helmet must always be correctly fastened. There are two systems commonly in use – the double D-ring and quick release. Some helmets also have a velcro tab but this is intended solely to secure the strap and stop it flapping in the wind – it must never be used on its own to fasten the helmet.

Take good care of your helmet. Don't leave it on the seat of your bike, where it may fall off and be damaged, or let it roll around on the floor. If your helmet does ever suffer a serious impact, it should be discarded and replaced.

A full face helmet is the best choice because it provides the highest level of protection in a crash

visors and goggles

You should always wear a visor or a pair of goggles to protect your eyes from flying debris, insects, wind and rain. It must comply with British Standard BS 4110 Grade X, XA, YA or ZA, and display the BSI kitemark. Alternatively, it can comply with a European Standard which offers the same safety level as the British Standard, and which carries a mark (ECE 22-05) equivalent to the BSI kitemark. Goggles should comply with the EU Directive on personal protective equipment and carry the CE mark.

Never use a tinted visor or goggles in poor visibility or at night.

It is essential to keep your visor or goggles clean at all times. Use warm soapy water to wash off dirt and smears – never use solvents or petrol.

When riding in the cold or wet your visor or goggles may mist up on the inside, impairing your vision. If this happens, find somewhere safe to pull over and clear it with a clean moist cloth. You can buy anti-fog sprays and laminates which help to reduce misting in bad weather.

Avoid using a visor or goggles that has scratches or other damage. This will impair your view, and can cause glare when the sun is low in the sky, as well as dazzle from the lights of oncoming vehicles. Renew your visor or goggles as soon as you notice any damage that might affect your vision.

ear plugs

One medical problem motorcyclists are prone to is hearing impairment caused by excessive wind noise. You are strongly recommended to use ear plugs to reduce the risk of hearing damage. They can also help to reduce fatigue on a long journey.

protective clothing

Wearing the right clothing is vital at all times when riding a motorcycle, not only to keep you warm and dry but also to help protect you if you fall off. Specially designed motorcycling clothing may not be cheap but it is well worth the money for the extra comfort, weather protection and security it provides.

Leather is traditionally a popular choice as it gives a high degree of resistance to abrasion injuries. A one-piece leather suit offers more windproofing and better protection in a crash than a separate jacket and trousers, but most allow little room underneath for putting on extra layers in cold weather. They are also only showerproof so a rain suit will be needed in wet weather.

Alternatively, there is a wide choice of man-made fabrics available, some of which are fully waterproof without the need for a separate rain suit. Try on a good selection, paying particular attention to the fit around the neck, wrists and ankles where cold draughts can penetrate.

Whichever type you prefer, choose clothing which is fully reinforced with body armour, particularly on vulnerable points such as shoulders, elbows, knees and hips. This can play a vital role in cushioning the impact in a crash.

visibility

When choosing clothing, make it a priority to ensure you are as conspicuous as possible to other road users. For a motorcyclist, this is a vital element in staying safe on the road, so don't put fashion before common sense. For optimum visiblity, your outer garments (either your jacket or a specially designed high-visibilty vest designed to slip over your jacket) should be:

◉ fluorescent to give high visibility in all weathers

◉ include reflective belts or strips which will make you more easy to see at night.

A one-piece suit is more likely to keep out wind and cold than a jacket and trouser combination

Leather is still a popular choice as it provides a high level of protection from abrasion injuries

Wearing a fluorescent overjacket significantly improves your visiblity to other road users

Plenty of body armour is essential to protect vulnerable points such as knees and elbows

first steps

gloves

If you come off your bike, by instinct you'll put out your hands to try to stop your fall. That's why a strong pair of gloves or gauntlets is essential to help prevent serious injury to the hands.

Leather is still the best material for gloves, as it provides a high level of protection but remains supple enough to let you work the controls. Look for extra protection over the knuckles, a long wrist to help keep out the weather and a velcro strap to ensure the glove stays securely in place in a crash.

Leather gloves will quickly become sodden in bad weather, so you'll also need a pair of waterproof overmitts. Check before buying that you can operate the controls easily while wearing your gloves with the overmitts in place.

boots

Always wear a stout pair of over-the-ankle boots when riding. These help to keep your feet warm and also provide protection, both in the event of a fall and against inadvertent knocks and burns from your bike.

When choosing a pair of boots, look for a pair that offers plenty of protection for the shin and ankle. Remember to leave space for an extra pair of socks to keep your feet warm in cold weather. Most boots are made

of leather, which is strong and flexible, but not always fully waterproof in the worst conditions.

Whichever boots you buy, check that they are comfortable and that it is easy to operate the foot controls while wearing them.

weather conditions

Getting cold and wet while riding isn't just unpleasant – it can seriously reduce your concentration and slow your reaction times. Even in mild weather a rider can experience a wind-chill factor that makes it feel more like freezing, and this can quickly lead to the onset of hypothermia if you are inadequately dressed.

When riding in wintry conditions, don't underestimate the amount of extra clothing you will need to keep warm. Wear several layers, starting with thermal underwear and a thin balaclava under your helmet. If you plan to do a lot of riding in all weathers, there are more effective options to consider, such as investing in an electrically heated suit or vest, heated inner gloves or heated handlebar grips.

Waterproof overclothes are worth carrying in case of serious rain. Modern synthetic suits are breathable for comfort, and can be folded into a conveniently small package.

As well as wearing the right clothing, your bike's fairing plays an important part in keeping you protected from the worst of the weather too. If you plan to ride in all weathers, then a touring fairing is a better choice than a sports fairing as it gives much better wind protection to hands, legs and feet. Even fitting handlebar muffs can help to reduce the wind-chill factor.

In hot weather, you may feel overdressed wearing a motorcycle suit. But no matter how warm it is, never be tempted to ride in shorts, a t-shirt, training shoes or sandals – the abrasion injuries from even a slow speed spill onto the tarmac would be severe, extremely painful and could leave you permanently scarred.

Always wear a pair of sturdy over-the-ankle boots that offer adequate protection in a crash

Gloves should be strong but also supple enough to let you operate the controls easily

Wearing thermal underwear is an excellent way to help keep out the worst of the winter chill

A waterproof oversuit can be folded up small and carried on the bike in case the weather turrns wet

27

fit to ride

Riding a motorcycle demands a high degree of alertness, concentration, quick reactions and a sober, safety-conscious state of mind. Many forms of illness or disability, alcohol or drug use, or simply tiredness can affect your ability to the point where you are not safe to be on the road. Remember: it doesn't matter how important it seems to get to a job appointment or friend's party – if you're not fit to ride, stay off your bike.

You must by law contact the DVLA if you develop an illness which may affect your riding ability

Even everyday medicines can impair your ability to ride safely, so check the packet for warnings

health and safety

How you feel affects how safely you ride. If you develop a serious illness (see *It's the law* overleaf) then you must inform the DVLA. This won't necessarily mean you'll lose your licence, but the DVLA may ask you to undergo a medical check-up to ensure you are still fit to ride.

Less serious medical problems can also affect your safety on the road. Even a severe cold or flu can lower your concentration and reactions and make you unfit to ride. If you're feeling unwell enough to need medication, then ask yourself if you are really fit enough to get on your motorbike.

medicines

Many medicines can affect your ability to ride. Some of these are available without a prescription across the counter at a chemists.

Certain drugs prescribed to treat depression cause drowsiness and impair concentration. Riding should be avoided while taking these and for some months afterwards. Some tranquillisers and sleeping pills have similar side-effects.

Drugs available at a chemists without a prescription which impair driving include certain hayfever treatments and cold remedies. These can reduce concentration, slow reaction times and promote drowsiness, and they make riding particularly dangerous when taken with any amount of alcohol.

Whenever you take a medicine, carefully check the label for a warning – sometimes not as prominent as it might be – that you should not drive or ride while using it. If prescribed a drug by your doctor, always ask if it will affect your riding ability.

alcohol

Drinking doesn't mix with riding a motorcycle. The anti drink-drive message has been rammed home to all road users by endless publicity campaigns in the last 25 years, but still around one in five drivers and riders killed on the road is under the influence of alcohol.

When a rider has been drinking alcohol it makes them less in control of their machine, slows their reactions and impairs their ability to concentrate and judge speed accurately. It also gives them a false sense of confidence which can lead them to take dangerous risks. Researchers have even suggested that because riding a motorcycle demands a higher level of skill than driving a car, the legal blood-alcohol limit for riders should be lower than for drivers. By far the most sensible course is to drink no alcohol at all if you are planning to use your bike.

The police treat drink-driving very seriously. Drivers and riders involved in an accident are now routinely breathalysed; if

If you ride to the pub, either don't drink any alcohol at all, or arrange to go home by taxi

convicted they face at least a one-year ban. A conviction for riding under the influence of alcohol may invalidate your insurance, and also means you will pay much higher insurance premiums when you do get back on the road.

Remember:

⮑ you must not ride if your breath alcohol level is higher than 35µg per 100ml (equivalent to a blood-alcohol level of 80mg per 100ml)

⮑ alcohol takes time to be broken down by the body and if you have had a heavy night's drinking session the chances are that you will still be over the limit the next morning

⮑ any amount of alcohol impairs your ability to ride safely, even if you're still under the legal limit. So if you plan to drink anything at all, the safest option is to leave your bike at home.

Don't mix motorcycling with drugs or alcohol: it's dangerous, illegal and the penalties are severe

Pay a visit to an optician and get your eyesight checked before you start learning to ride

illegal drugs

Outlawed drugs such as cannabis, ecstasy, cocaine and heroin have the potential to impair your driving and it is an offence to drive under their influence. These drugs can have unpredictable effects and users may remain affected for up to 72 hours after taking them. The police are cracking down on drug-driving and introducing roadside tests to identify drivers who are under the influence of drugs.

eyesight

You must be able to read the current style of numberplate (introduced in September 2001) at a distance of 20 metres (66 feet). If you need to wear contact lenses or spectacles to do this then you must wear them at all times when riding (it makes sense to keep a spare pair with you too, in case you lose or damage your usual pair). Other eye defects such as tunnel vision can also affect your safety on the road so it's a good idea to take a full eye test before starting to ride, and again at the intervals recommended by your optician.

it's the law

fit to ride?

You must by law inform the DVLA if you suffer any of the following:

- epilepsy
- giddiness, fainting or blackouts
- a severe mental handicap
- diabetes
- heart pain while riding
- Parkinson's disease
- any chronic neurological condition
- a serious memory problem
- a stroke

- brain surgery, a brain tumour or a severe head injury
- severe psychiatric illness or mental disorder
- long-term problems with your arms or legs
- dependence on alcohol or drugs or chemical substances in the past three years
- any visual disability which affects both eyes (not short/long sightedness or colour blindness)
- have a pacemaker, defibrillator or anti-ventricular tachycardia device fitted.

2 in control

You've signed your provisional licence, your motorbike is roadworthy, taxed and insured, you've checked your eyesight and health and you can't wait to start the engine and ride off down the road. But try to be patient. A modern motorbike is a complex piece of machinery and before you go anywhere you need to understand exactly how all the controls work, what the various switches do and what the warning lights mean. Whenever you ride a different bike to the one you are used to, always take time to make certain you know how everything operates before moving off.

left-handlebar controls

On the left handlebar you'll usually find the:

◉ **clutch lever**

◉ **choke**

◉ **direction indicators**

◉ **horn**

◉ **headlight dip switch**

◉ **headlight flasher.**

clutch lever

Operating the clutch lever (*below*) disconnects the engine from the rear wheel. This allows the bike to come to a standstill without stalling the engine, and lets you change from one gear to another more easily.

The clutch itself consists of a pair of friction plates which are pulled apart when the clutch lever is operated.

As you let the clutch lever out, the two plates touch and power starts to be transmitted to the rear wheel. This is termed the 'biting point'. The further you release the lever, the more power is transmitted. Once the clutch lever is fully released the clutch plates lock together and all the power from the engine is delivered to the rear wheel.

When you hold the lever so that the clutch is only half engaged, it is called 'slipping the clutch' or 'clutch control'. Clutch control is useful when you want to ride very slowly – for instance when carrying out low-speed manoeuvres.

choke

The choke enriches the fuel mixture entering the engine and is used to start the engine from cold. Put the choke fully on before starting a cold engine. Gradually push the choke back in over the first mile or so of riding (the exact distance depends on the type of bike and the air temperature, but if you turn off the choke too early the engine may stall when you come to a halt).

Make sure the choke is pushed all the way back in as soon as the engine is warm, or it will cause the engine to run fast and make it difficult to control the motorcycle, particularly when slowing down. Leaving the choke on too long also wastes fuel and if done repeatedly can cause engine damage.

Some models, including many scooters, have an automatic choke fitted. Models with fuel injection do not have a choke but compensate automatically for the richer mixture needed on a cold start.

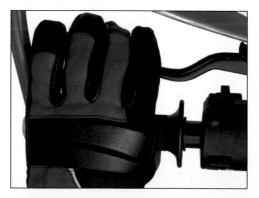

automatics

Some motorcycles (especially mopeds and scooters) are fitted with an automatic or semi-automatic gearbox.

◉ **fully automatic:** there is no clutch lever and no gear shift; when ready to move off you shift from neutral into drive. Often a lever operating the rear brakes is fitted instead of a clutch lever.

◉ **semi-automatic:** there is no clutch lever; you operate the gear shift as you would with a manual and the clutch works automatically.

headlight flasher

Use this for the same purpose as the horn, to warn other road users of your presence if you think they haven't seen you. A headlight flash is useful where the horn may not be audible, for instance at higher speeds.

headlight dip switch

This lowers your headlight beam from main beam to dipped beam to avoid dazzling other road users (*below*).

indicators

Flick the switch to the right to activate the right indicators, to the left for the left indicators. It is important to use your indicators to let other road users know that you intend to change direction. Unlike cars, few motorcycles have self-cancelling indicators so don't forget to cancel them once you have completed your manoeuvre.

horn

Used only to warn other road users that you are there. Make sure you know where the horn is before you have to use it in an emergency (*below*).

right handlebar controls

The right handlebar normally has fitted to it the:

- ➲ throttle
- ➲ front brake lever
- ➲ electric starter
- ➲ engine cut-out
- ➲ light switch.

throttle

Opening the throttle (*below*) by twisting it towards you increases the flow of fuel and air to the engine, giving extra power when you need to increase speed or ride uphill. The throttle automatically springs back to the closed position when released (in the fully closed position it still allows the engine to tick over). Light and gentle use of the throttle improves fuel economy and promotes a smooth riding style.

front brake lever

This lever (*below*) operates the front brake only (except on bikes which have a linked braking system – see p58). Operating this lever also illuminates the rear brake light, giving a warning to following traffic that you are slowing.

electric starter

Fitted on many bikes instead of (or as well as) the manual kick starter. (*See p51 for use.*)

engine cut-out

Used (*below*) to stop the engine in an emergency (the ignition switch should be used when stopping the engine normally).

lights

Many bikes do not have a separate light switch – the headlight comes on automatically whenever the ignition is switched on. Where a light switch is fitted, it usually has three settings:

⊘ off
⊘ parking lights (in this position the rear position light and numberplate light also illuminate). Parking lights must be displayed when parking at night on a road with a speed limit greater than 30mph (*see p139*)
⊘ headlight (plus rear position light and numberplate light). To maximise your visibility to other road users, use your headlight at all times when riding.

foot controls

On most motorcycles the right foot controls the rear brake pedal, and the left foot operates the gear selector. Most modern bikes have an electric starter, but there may also be a kick starter, used for starting the engine manually (*see p51*). Where fitted, this is usually on the right side of the engine in front of the footrest, and it should be securely folded away when not in use.

rear brake pedal

This is usually situated on the right side of the motorcycle, in front of the footrest (although some automatic bikes have a brake lever on the left handlebar that operates the rear brake). The brake pedal operates the rear brake only (except on bikes which have a linked braking system). Operating the pedal also illuminates the rear brake light, giving a warning to following traffic that you are slowing.

gear selector

Usually situated on the left side of the
motorcycle, in front of the footrest. Push
down on the selector with your left foot to
change to a lower gear, or lift it up with your
foot beneath it to change to a higher gear.
The number of gears varies from bike to bike,
though five or six is usual. In addition there is
a neutral position, where no gear is engaged.
In neutral the engine can tick over without
power being transmitted to the rear wheel.

instruments

On or around the instrument panel you'll find the:
- ignition switch
- speedometer
- odometer
- trip meter
- rev counter
- warning lights.

ignition switch

This turns on the motorbike's electrical systems in readiness to start the engine. The ignition switch usually has four positions:
- off
- on: this allows the engine to be started
- lock: in this position the steering locks into place if the handlebars are turned without the key in the ignition. It makes the bike more secure against theft
- park (P): this is used when the bike needs to be parked on the road at night with the parking light illuminated.

speedometer

The speedometer shows both miles per hour (mph) and kilometres per hour (km/h). The kilometre scale is marked in smaller figures on the inner ring of the dial and should be ignored unless the bike is ridden overseas. Some bikes have a digital speedometer – although these aren't always any easier to read at a glance. It is a legal requirement to have a working speedometer and it must not show a reading lower than the actual speed.

odometer

Shows the total mileage the motorcycle has covered from new (see top line of numbers within speedometer, *right*).

trip meter

Gives a mileage reading which can be reset. This is useful to show how many miles you have ridden since last refuelling (see lower line of numbers within speedometer, *right*).

rev counter

Most bikes are fitted with a rev counter (or tachometer) which shows the engine speed in revolutions per minute (rpm). The maximum engine speed permitted is usually indicated by a red line marked on the dial.

warning lights

Warning lights are fitted to alert you to serious faults and remind you about electrical items that are switched on.

Lights monitoring your motorcycle's systems (such as the ignition and oil pressure) should come on when you turn on the ignition, then extinguish. If they come on while you are riding, stop and investigate why.

Reminder lights (such as headlight main beam) remain illuminated whenever the item is in use.

neutral light

Glows when the gear selector is in neutral. Some bikes also have a digital gear position indicator to help you monitor which gear you are in.

temperature gauge

A temperature warning light and/or gauge is fitted to motorbikes with water-cooled engines. If the light illuminates or the needle of the gauge enters the red zone the engine is overheating and you should stop as soon as possible. When cold the engine does not operate so efficiently. Avoid working the engine hard until the gauge reaches its normal working temperature, or you will waste fuel and cause extra engine wear.

fuel gauge

The fuel gauge gives a rough indication of how much fuel remains in the fuel tank. On some bikes, as this reaches the lower limit a fuel warning light may illuminate, indicating that only a few litres (check the handbook for the exact amount) of fuel are left. Some bikes have a reserve fuel tank. If the main tank runs dry you need to turn the fuel tap to the reserve position to supply the engine with fuel from the reserve tank.

oil pressure

If this light comes on when riding it means the oil pressure is low. Stop as soon as possible and turn off the engine to avoid serious damage. Check the oil level and top up if necessary, but do not continue riding if the light stays on.

ignition

If lit when the engine is running this indicates there is a problem with the battery charging system.

ABS

If fitted, this should light up when you turn on the ignition and extinguish once you get underway. If it stays illuminated or comes on while riding it indicates a problem with the anti-lock braking system (see p59). Stop and consult the handbook to see if the bike is still safe to ride, and get the braking system checked immediately

left/right indicator

Shows that the indicators are operating.

headlamp main beam

Warns that the headlight is on main beam setting which may dazzle other road users.

3 basic skills

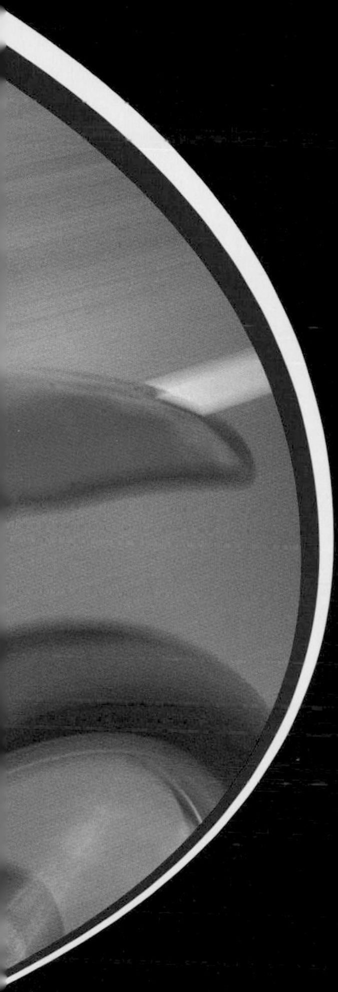

Riding a motorbike is a more physical task than driving a car. As well as controlling your bike at speed, you have to be able to take it on and off its stand, and wheel it with the engine off. If you already drive a car, you will be familiar with clutch control, but getting used to using your left hand instead of your left foot to find the biting point needs a little practice. Braking too is more complicated than with a car because on most bikes the front and rear brakes are operated by separate controls.

stands

For something that feels so agile when you're riding it, a bike can be a heavy and cumbersome object to manhandle when it's stationary. Bear this in mind when choosing your bike and don't buy one that you don't feel comfortable taking on and off its stand and wheeling about. In any exercise with a stationary bike, you should stand on the left-hand side of the bike, away from approaching traffic.

motorcycle stands

When parked, your motorcycle is supported on its stand. There are two types – the centre stand and side stand – and many bikes are fitted with both.

The side stand is quicker and easier to use, and relies for stability on the bike leaning onto the stand. However, take care that the surface is firm or the stand may sink into the ground, causing the bike to fall over. Care is also needed when leaning the bike against a slope: if the bike is too upright on the stand it will not be stable and may fall over.

The centre stand gives more stability, and can be used to support the bike while you are carrying out maintenance such as adjusting the drive chain. However, take care to use the centre stand on a flat, firm surface only.

Both the centre and side stands can pose a serious hazard if they are not fully retracted while the motorcycle is being ridden, as the stand may dig into the road when cornering, throw the bike off balance and cause an accident. For this reason, it is essential to double check that the stand is fully up before riding off. Some bikes feature an inhibitor switch which prevents them from being ridden when the side stand is down. If your bike is fitted with such a switch and the engine refuses to start, or starts but cuts out when you select a gear, check to make sure that the stand is in its fully retracted position.

using the centre stand

To put the motorbike on its stand:

➲ position yourself on the left of the bike, holding the left handlebar with your left hand and the frame near the saddle with your right hand (on some bikes there is a special handle to grab)
➲ push the stand down with your right foot (or left, if preferred)
➲ hold down the stand with your foot while pulling the bike backwards and upwards.

To take the motorbike off its stand:

➲ position yourself on the left of the bike, holding the left handlebar with your left hand and the frame near the saddle (or grab handle) with your right hand
➲ put your left foot (or right, if preferred) in front of the stand
➲ pull the bike forwards
➲ as the bike comes off the stand move your right hand on to the front brake lever to control it.

The centre stand gives better support than the side stand, so use it when carrying out maintenance

using the side stand

To put the motorbike on its stand:
◎ position yourself on the left of the bike, holding the left handlebar with your left hand
◎ holding the bike upright, push down the stand with your foot
◎ let the bike lean towards you until its weight is taken by the stand.

To take the motorbike off its stand:
◎ position yourself on the left of the bike, holding both handlebars
◎ push the motorbike upright
◎ pull the bike forwards
◎ push the stand up with your foot
◎ check that the stand has locked securely in its fully retracted position.

wheeling

It is important to be able to move your motorbike by wheeling it with the engine off and the gearbox in neutral. With the bike off its stand, position yourself on the left of the bike and hold both handlebars firmly, keeping your right hand on the brake to control the speed. Let the bike lean towards you, finding the angle which is most comfortable and easiest to balance, and practise wheeling it forwards and in circles left and right.

Take care to use the side stand on a firm, level surface; if it is used on a slope or on soft ground there is a danger of the bike toppling over

Wheeling your motorbike is an important skill; as part of the practical test your examiner will ask you to walk with your motorbike, usually in a U-turn

mounting and dismounting

Mount the motorcycle from the left-hand side, away from the traffic. As you get on, apply the front brake to prevent the bike from moving.

riding position

When sitting on the stationary bike you should be able to place both feet on the ground, and balance securely on one foot while using the other to work the foot controls. You should also be able to reach all the controls without stretching. If necessary, the main controls such as brake, clutch and gear levers can all be adjusted to give a more comfortable fit.

Make sure you apply the front brake lever to keep the motorbike steady as you mount it

You should be able to reach all the controls without stretching; if not, adjust them to fit

moving off

Turning a stationary motorbike into a moving one requires a fair degree of balance and coordination. You need to be able to modulate the clutch and throttle to move off in any road situation, whether on the level or a steep gradient, or if you have to pull out at an angle from a tight parking space. But at the same time it's essential you don't overlook the need for observation: when moving off you need to be fully aware of what is happening all around you and act on this information to stay safe.

starting the engine

Different motorcycles have different starting procedures. Some bikes will not start except in neutral, others won't unless the clutch lever is pulled in. On many scooters the brake must be applied before the engine will start. You should consult the handbook for advice on starting your particular bike. However, this is the general procedure:

⊃ check the gear selector is in neutral. If you try to start the motorcycle when it is in gear it will lurch forwards dangerously. The neutral light on the instrument panel should glow with the ignition turned on. If there is no neutral light fitted, push the motorcycle forward: if it is in neutral the rear wheel should turn freely

⊃ turn on the fuel tap (if fitted)

⊃ if starting a cold engine, put the choke on

⊃ check that the engine cut-out switch is in the on position

⊃ if an electric starter is fitted, press the starter button. Release the button as soon as the engine fires or the starter motor may be damaged. Open the throttle to help it catch until it settles to a steady tickover (tickover speed will be higher than usual when the choke is used)

⊃ if a kick starter is fitted, fold out the kick start lever (you may have to fold up the footrest first). Tread down briskly on the starter lever and allow it to return to its upright position. Repeat this until the engine fires, and open the throttle until it settles to a steady tickover. Fold the kick start lever back into its normal position

⊃ check that the ignition and oil pressure lights go out once the engine is running steadily

⊃ remember to move the choke to its off position as the engine warms up.

With an electric starter, release the button once the engine fires or the starter could be damaged

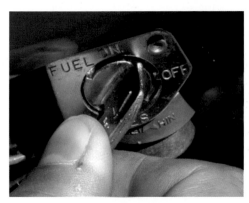

Don't forget to turn on the fuel tap, if one is fitted, before trying to start the engine

When starting a cold engine the choke is needed (on this bike it operates directly on the carburettor, but it is more usually situated on the left handlebar)

moving off

To get the motorbike underway:

⊙ apply the front brake and start the engine

⊙ squeeze the clutch lever in all the way

⊙ select first gear

⊙ take your weight on your left foot, place your right foot on the footrest and apply the rear brake. Take your right hand off the front brake ready to use the throttle

⊙ start to release the clutch lever until you feel the 'biting point' when the bike starts to move forward

⊙ open the throttle wider while smoothly continuing to release the clutch. As you move off let off the rear brake and put your left foot onto the footrest.

Moving off at an angle may be necessary when you have stopped behind a parked vehicle. It requires careful balance and clutch control. Be extra alert for traffic approaching from all directions, be ready to stop for pedestrians and leave plenty of room as you pull past the parked vehicle in case a door opens in front of you

avoiding stalls

If you release the clutch too quickly or don't apply enough power, the engine may cut out or 'stall'. Clutch control can be a difficult knack to acquire at first so be prepared to practice before you can move off seamlessly every time.

While learning you're most likely to stall when trying to move off uphill. You will need to use more throttle, and be precise about releasing the rear brake – too soon and the motorbike will roll back, too late and it will stall. Practise moving off uphill until you are confident you can carry out this manoeuvre even in tricky circumstances, such as when pulling out from behind a parked vehicle.

low-speed manoeuvres

Careful clutch control is also required when riding at low speeds. You may need to slip the clutch in order to keep the engine running smoothly. The front brake can be fierce at low speeds, so use the rear brake instead. When moving slowly a motorcycle can feel heavy and unwieldy, so practise to improve your balance when slow-riding. Looking well ahead can increase your stability: never look down at the front wheel when riding as this can seriously upset your sense of balance.

know the code

highway code rule 159

Before moving off you should

→ use all mirrors to check the road is clear

→ look round to check the blind spots (the areas you are unable to see in the mirrors)

→ signal if necessary before moving out

→ look round for a final check.

Move off only when it is safe to do so.

Performing a U-turn: you must check all around before starting the turn, and take a final look behind to ensure it is safe before moving off

U-turns

A U-turn is a useful way to turn around. It needs to be performed at low speed so practise until you are confident. You should only carry out a U-turn where it is safe and legal to do so, with no signs or road markings prohibiting this manoeuvre. Take special care to make sure the road is clear in both directions, and always look behind for a final check before starting the turn.

stopping

To bring the motorbike to a halt:
- close the throttle
- apply both front and rear brakes smoothly
- just before coming to a standstill pull in the clutch lever to prevent the engine from stalling
- as the bike stops put your left foot on the ground to support it
- keeping the front brake applied, take your right foot off the brake and put it on the ground so you are now supporting the bike with your right foot

- take your left foot off the ground and shift the gear selector to neutral
- release the clutch lever
- put both feet firmly on the ground.

At very low speeds you may need to pull in the clutch before you brake. However, avoid riding for longer than necessary with the clutch lever pulled in, as this reduces the control you have over the motorbike.

where to stop

When stopping at the side of the road always make sure you select somewhere safe to pull in: never stop where you would obstruct other road users or where road markings prohibit stopping. Don't stop or park:
- near a school entrance
- where you would prevent emergency access
- at or near a bus stop or taxi rank
- on the approach to a level crossing
- opposite or within ten metres of a junction
- near the brow of a hill or hump bridge
- opposite a traffic island
- opposite another parked vehicle if it would cause an obstruction
- where you would force other traffic to enter a tram lane
- where the kerb has been lowered to help wheelchair users
- in front of an entrance to a property
- on a bend.

turning off the engine

To stop the engine running:
- close the throttle
- check that the gear selector is in neutral
- turn the key to switch off the ignition (do not use the engine cut-out switch to turn off the engine – this is for emergency use only)
- turn off the fuel tap (if fitted).

changing gear

If you've ridden a bicycle fitted with gears you'll understand the effect that choice of gear has on speed and effort. Try to move off in too high a gear and you'll struggle to turn the pedals. Stay in a low gear on a level stretch of road and you'll find yourself pedalling furiously for no extra forward velocity. It's the same on a motorcycle, except that the engine does the work instead of the rider. The low gears provide lots of acceleration but run out of steam before the bike is travelling very quickly. Higher gears provide plenty of road speed, but not as much acceleration. Your job is to match the gears to the speed of the bike, moving up the gearbox as your speed rises, and to select a lower gear when more power is needed, for instance when overtaking or approaching a steep hill.

how to change gear

Changing gear requires careful coordination of foot and hand movements, so don't be surprised if your gear changes feel clumsy at first. To change gear:

◑ close the throttle and at the same time pull in the clutch lever to disengage the engine from the gearbox

◑ select the gear required with your left foot: to change up, put your toe under the selector and lift it up; to change down, press down on the selector

◑ release the clutch lever and simultaneously open the throttle.

To make even smoother changes going down the gearbox, keep the throttle slightly open as you shift the gear selector. This means the engine revs rise to match the new gear selected, and with practice you can make your changes down the gearbox almost seamless.

selecting the right gear

Listen to the engine to indicate when you should change gear. Don't race the engine unnecessarily, which simply wastes fuel, but also don't make it labour by riding in too high a gear for the conditions.

riding an automatic

Mopeds and scooters generally have automatic gearboxes which give an easy ride, especially in town. Simply engage drive, twist the throttle and away you go.

Even if you intend to ride an automatic motorcycle, it still makes a lot of sense to take your test on a manual bike, because passing on a manual qualifies you to ride both manual and automatic bikes, whereas if you pass on an automatic your licence restricts you to riding automatic bikes only.

Select a lower gear when you need more acceleration, for instance when gaining speed on a slip road to merge with fast-moving traffic

know the code

highway code rule 122

Coasting This term describes a vehicle travelling in neutral or with the clutch pressed down. It can reduce driver control because:

➔ engine braking is eliminated

➔ vehicle speed downhill will increase quickly

➔ increased use of the footbrake can reduce its effectiveness

➔ steering response will be affected, particularly on bends and corners

➔ it may be more difficult to select the appropriate gear when needed.

steering

The forces acting on a cornering motorcycle are highly complex but at speed a bike has a natural balance and most novice riders soon get the feel of leaning their bike through bends. At lower speeds a bike has less natural stability and the rider has to compensate by balancing and steering more actively. Low-speed riding is examined during the practical test and it is important to practise this element of bike control until you are thoroughly competent.

holding the bars

To be fully in control of your motorcycle you need to keep both hands firmly gripping the handlebars. Remove a hand from the handlebars only when absolutely necessary (for instance, to give a hand signal). Always replace both hands on the grips before starting any manoeuvre such as turning a corner. Never take both hands off the handlebars while you are riding.

steering technique

How you steer a motorcycle depends on how quickly you are riding.

⊙ **low-speed steering**
At low speeds you need to turn the handlebars in the direction of the turn as you would steer a bicycle. The motorbike will tend to fall inwards, so you need to shift your weight in the other direction to balance it and stay upright. Try to keep your movements as smooth and coordinated as possible and you will find it easy to stay in balance.

⊙ **high-speed steering**
At higher speeds more complex forces come into play. To change direction you need to shift your body weight so that you and your bike lean into the direction of the turn. On sharp bends or at higher speeds you will need a greater angle of lean to maintain your balance, but do not lean so far that you risk your tyres losing grip on the road. As you exit the turn, you need to progressively bring the bike back upright again.

counter-steering

This may not make sense until you experience it for yourself, but at higher speeds, if you try to steer a motorbike as you would at low speeds (that is, by turning the handlebars right to turn right) the bike will do the opposite – lean to the left and make a left turn.

Many riders actively use counter-steering

as an aid to turning into a corner. When approaching a left-hand curve, a gentle forward pressure on the left handlebar encourages the bike to start leaning towards the left. The rider then shifts his or her weight to balance the bike into the curve.

steering lock

When you turn the handlebars as far as they will go in either direction they are at full steering lock. Some bikes have a restricted steering lock which means you may have to allow more space when making slow manoeuvres such as U-turns.

To steer at low speed you need to move the handlebars in the direction you want to turn

The tighter the steering lock, the easier it is to manoeuvre the bike in and out of confined spaces

braking

Braking a motorcycle demands considerably more skill than using the brakes in a car. Firstly, most bikes have separate controls for front and rear brakes and you must learn to balance the two. And secondly, few bikes yet have anti-lock brakes which means extra care must be taken not to provoke a skid in an emergency. In everyday riding you should aim to use the brakes as little as possible by anticipating the need to slow down well in advance. Harsh, late braking is a sign of poor riding and it will not impress the examiner on your practical test.

using the brakes

Although a bike has front and rear brakes the two shouldn't be used evenly. Under braking the weight of the bike and rider is thrown forwards, over the front wheel. This presses the front tyre downwards, making it grip the road harder. It means that the front brake is capable of stopping the bike much more effectively than the rear brake.

You should apply the front brake slightly before the rear brake and, when road and weather conditions are good, use more force on the front brake. In poor weather you need to apply a more equal amount of force on front and rear brakes.

Apply the brakes gently at first, then progressively increase the pressure. Never brake harshly, or you risk making the wheels 'lock up' – stop rotating – and the bike will skid. Special care is needed when the roads are wet or icy as the risk of skidding becomes much higher.

Plan your braking well in advance of a hazard so you have to brake only when the bike is upright and travelling in a straight line. If you brake while leaning into a bend it will upset the balance of the bike and you may lose control. If you have no choice but to brake on a bend, try to use the rear brake only. If you have to use the front brake, do so very gently or the front wheel may skid. If possible, bring your bike back upright so you can apply the brakes normally.

emergency stop

By developing good observation and anticipation skills you should rarely have to stop in an emergency. However, emergency braking is a vital skill to master, and you will be required to carry out an emergency stop during your practical test.

To stop in an emergency, brake firmly but don't snatch violently at the brakes as this may cause the wheels to lock up and skid. Apply the front brake a fraction before the rear and progressively increase the braking

pressure. If a wheel does lock, ease off the appropriate brake until it starts to rotate again then reapply the brake less harshly. Pull in the clutch lever just before you come to a halt to prevent the engine stalling. Make sure emergency braking is carried out with the bike upright or you risk causing a skid and losing control. Always keep both hands firmly on the handlebars during an emergency stop.

engine braking

When you release the throttle the engine slows the bike even if you don't touch the brakes. Engine braking is hardly noticeable in top gear, but in the lower ratios it is much more effective. Make use of engine braking by selecting a lower gear to give more control over your bike when descending a steep hill.

linked brakes

Some bikes have a braking system which links the front and rear brakes so that whether you use the front brake lever or the rear brake pedal, braking force is apportioned to both front and rear wheels. The system varies between manufacturers so where fitted it is important to read the handbook. Not all riders are enthusiastic about linked brakes, but they do make it less likely that a skid will occur during emergency braking.

anti-lock brakes

An anti-lock braking system (ABS) works electronically to prevent the wheels from locking up under emergency braking. This means that in an emergency you can apply maximum pressure to the brakes without the risk of the wheels skidding. Anti-lock braking cannot, however, overcome the laws of physics: it will not necessarily make you stop any quicker, and it may not remove the risk of a skid if you brake while you are cornering or riding on a loose or slippery surface.

4 reading the road

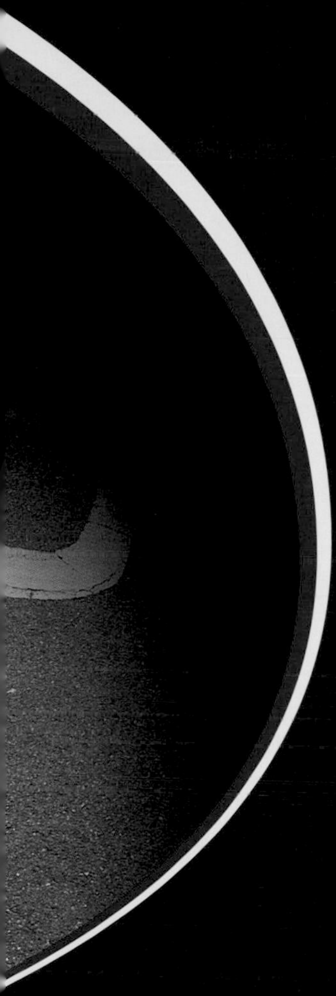

There's a vast amount of information on the road to help you ride safely – providing you see it and respond to it properly. Road markings and signs warn of a whole range of hazards as well as giving you instructions and information. Then there are the signals coming from other road users. Their indicators, brake lights and even how they position themselves on the road tell you a lot about what they are going to do. And at the same time you need to communicate to everyone else what you intend to do by giving clear and accurate signals yourself.

rear observation

It's as important to be aware of what's happening on the road behind you as it is to see what's going on ahead. Rear observation takes two forms: you need to keep checking your mirrors to monitor traffic movements behind, and you also need to turn your head and look behind to confirm everything is safe before making a manoeuvre.

adjusting mirrors

To get the best view behind, it makes sense to have mirrors fitted on both sides of your motorcycle

Make sure both mirrors are correctly adjusted to give the fullest view of the road behind. You may find that your elbows obscure the view, in which case you should add extensions to the mirror arms. Make sure you keep your mirrors clean at all times. On some bikes vibration may impair the image quality in the mirror – consult your dealer for advice on how to reduce this.

image distortion

Some mirrors are flat, giving an accurate view of traffic behind. Other mirrors are convex, or slightly curved. This has the advantage of giving a wider field of view but it also means that vehicles can look like they are further away than they really are. Take this into account before acting on information from your mirrors.

looking behind

Even with your mirrors perfectly adjusted there are blindspots – areas behind you which do not appear in the mirrors. This means there are times when it is essential to turn your head to get a full view of what's happening behind you. This rear glance is sometimes aptly called the lifesaver.

Looking behind gives a more accurate view of how fast traffic is approaching than you can get from your mirrors. It can also give an extra warning to following drivers that you are about to make a manoeuvre.

Of course while looking behind you have to take your eyes off the road ahead, which is in itself potentially dangerous. So use your judgement about when to look behind. Don't do it when there is a developing hazard ahead which requires all your concentration, or in the middle of making a hazardous manoeuvre such as overtaking, or when you are close behind another vehicle.

Adjust the mirrors so that you have a clear view of traffic approaching from behind

Some mirrors have curved glass which makes vehicles seem further away than they really are

Your mirrors can only tell you so much: before making a manoeuvre you should also look behind

using rear observation

You must always take adequate rear observation before carrying out any manoeuvre that affects your speed or position on the road. This includes:

⊘ **moving off**
  Check your mirrors, and look over your right shoulder to confirm that nothing is in your blind spot

⊘ **changing lanes**
  Use your mirrors plus a look behind to check for vehicles that are in your blind spot or moving into the lane you want to enter

⊘ **overtaking**
  Use your mirrors, and look behind if necessary, to check no one is about to overtake you before you begin your manoeuvre

⊘ **turning right**
  Check your mirrors as you approach the turn. Look over your right shoulder just before you make the turn to check no one is about to overtake you

⊘ **turning left**
  Check your mirrors as you approach the turn. Look over your left shoulder before you make the turn to check for a cyclist or other motorcyclist who could be about to pass you on the inside

⊘ **exiting a roundabout**
  Look over your left shoulder before you turn off to check for another vehicle passing you on the inside

⊘ **slowing down or stopping**
  A vehicle that is following you too closely may not be able to stop in time when you brake. Check your mirror in good time so you can lose speed more gently if necessary

⊘ **increasing speed**
  Check your mirrors before accelerating, for instance when leaving a lower speed limit, in case a following vehicle is about to overtake you.

Check over your right shoulder before changing lanes in case there's a vehicle in your blind spot

Look over your left shoulder before turning left in case someone is passing you on your nearside

observation–signal–manoeuvre

The observation-signal-manoeuvre (OSM) routine is fundamental to safe riding. Every time you intend to change your speed or position you must first take **observation** of what's happening in all directions around you. Next give a **signal** if it might help other road users. Only then can you begin to carry out the **manoeuvre**.

The manoeuvre itself involves three consecutive actions: this is called the position–speed–look (PSL) routine.

First you get into the correct **position** on the road to negotiate the hazard.

Next you adjust your **speed** to suit the hazard and select the appropriate gear.

Then you take a last good **look** all around, including taking rear observation, to check that it is safe for you to carry out the manoeuvre.

Only then can you make the manoeuvre if it is safe to do so.

Get into the habit of carrying out the OSM/PSL routine whenever you plan to make a manoeuvre. The sequence is the same for any type of manoeuvre: the diagram on the right illustrates how it works when making a right turn.

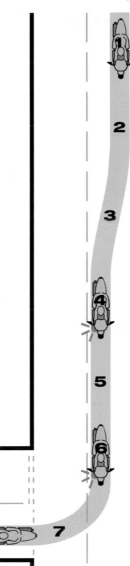

look all round and take rear observation

signal if necessary

change position towards the centre of the road

slow progressively to the required speed

select the appropriate gear

look all round including a last check over your right shoulder

make the turn if it is safe to do so

signals

It is essential to let other road users know what you intend to do well in advance. Giving clear and accurate signals cuts down misunderstandings which can lead to dangerous situations on the road. And fellow road users appreciate the courtesy of being given clear signals so they don't have to slow or stop for no reason and wait to see what you are going to do.

indicators

Use your indicators to signal that you intend to move off or change direction. Always:

- ⊙ give a signal in good time so other road users have time to react to it before you start changing your speed or position. If a road user shows no sign of reacting to your signal, don't carry out the manoeuvre until you're sure they have seen you

- ⊙ think before using your indicators. Identify who may benefit from a signal and make that signal as clear as possible. There's no point indicating if there is no one in the vicinity to see your signals

- ⊙ avoid making ambiguous signals. For instance, if you want to pull into the kerb just beyond a side road on the left, don't indicate until you are past the side road, or other road users may think you're turning left into it

- ⊙ make sure your indicator is cancelled after carrying out a manoeuvre, or you could mislead other road users.

Give a signal well in advance when you have to change lanes so that other road users have plenty of time to see and react to your signal

Don't signal where it might confuse other road users. For instance, if you want to pull into the kerb immediately after this junction, you should wait until you are past the junction before signalling. If you signal too early, the driver waiting to emerge might pull out in front of you, thinking you intend to turn into the side road

Your brake light gives a useful warning to other road users that you are slowing down or stopping

Use a headlight flash to alert another road user if you think they haven't seen you

brake signal

Each time you use the brakes, the brake warning light on the back of your motorcycle comes on, giving a signal to traffic behind that you are slowing down. You can use the brake controls very gently to illuminate the brake light and warn following drivers that you intend to slow for a hazard which they may not yet have noticed.

There are other situations where the brake lights can give a useful warning. For instance, holding on the brakes while you are stopped waiting to make a right turn, or when you are stationary at roadworks or traffic lights, can help to warn approaching drivers that your bike is stationary.

horn

The horn is one of the most misused signals on the road. Never sound the horn to tick off another road user who you think has behaved badly. This achieves nothing, and it may provoke an aggressive response. Use the horn only to alert another road user who you think may not have noticed that you are there. Give a short toot and consider raising your hand to show there was no aggressive intent on your part.

It is illegal to sound the horn when you are stationary, or in a built-up area between 11.30pm and 7.00am except when another moving vehicle poses a danger to you.

headlight flash

This signal has only one meaning, which is to alert another road user to your presence. A headlight flash is useful in situations where a horn may not be heard, such as at high speed on a motorway, or at night when horn use is not permitted.

Don't flash your headlight for the wrong reason. It must never be done to intimidate or give instructions to another road user – you might know what you mean when you flash your headlight, but the other road user may not, with potentially dangerous consequences.

The same reasoning applies if another vehicle flashes its headlights at you. Don't assume this is an invitation to ride on – the driver may intend it to mean 'stop, I'm coming through'. Always wait until you are certain what the other vehicle is doing before proceeding.

Treat signals from other drivers with caution; they may not necessarily mean what you think they do

Make sure you know where the horn button is so that you can use it instantly in an emergency

hazard warning lights

A few bikes have a hazard warning light facility. When in use all four indicators operate, giving a warning to other road users. Hazard warning lights should be used for the following purposes only:

- ⊘ when you have broken down
- ⊘ when your motorcycle is temporarily obstructing traffic
- ⊘ while riding on a dual carriageway or motorway, to alert other road users that there is a hazard ahead.

acting on signals

Imagine you are waiting to emerge from a T-junction. The road is clear to the left, and a car is approaching from the right with its left-hand indicator flashing. Does it mean that the driver is about to turn into your junction so it's safe for you to pull out ahead of it? Or does it mean that the driver:

- ⊘ is hard of hearing and has forgotten to cancel the indicator since their last manoeuvre
- ⊘ has knocked on the indicator by accident while reaching for the radio
- ⊘ intends to pull left into a driveway immediately past your junction
- ⊘ has a faulty indicator switch?

The answer, of course, is any of the above. Never assume another vehicle is about to do something simply because it is indicating. Always wait for some confirmation of the signal, for instance until you see the vehicle slow down or start to turn, before making any manoeuvre in front of it.

Be cautious if you see a driver signalling for no apparent reason. Never overtake a vehicle that is indicating right, even if you think that the driver has left on their indicator by mistake.

arm signals

There are certain situations when an arm signal can be really useful to confirm another signal given by your indicators or brake light, or to make your intentions certain if these lights cannot be seen. For instance:

⊃ a right turn arm signal can emphasise that you are about to make a right turn into a side road and are not just moving out to pass a parked car

⊃ a slowing down arm signal makes your intention clear when you want to show you are pulling in to the kerb, not turning left

⊃ an arm signal is clearly visible when your brake or indicator light is hard to see because of strong sunlight

⊃ pedestrians waiting at a crossing can't see your brake lights as you approach. Giving a slowing down arm signal tells them you are about to stop.

Never wave pedestrians across the road. You could put them in danger if they walk out without checking for themselves that the road is clear

Giving an arm signal means taking a hand off the handlebars, which reduces your control over your bike. Avoid giving arm signals at high speed, and if giving an arm signal before making a turn, make sure you return both hands securely to the handlebars before starting to make the turn.

Few car drivers give hand signals nowadays but you do need to learn to recognise them.

police directing traffic

When traffic lights fail or when traffic is unusually heavy, a police officer may use arm signals to direct the traffic flow.

You must by law obey arm signals given by any authorised persons – police officers and traffic wardens – as well as signs displayed by school crossing patrols.

arm signals given by riders and drivers

arm signals given by authorised persons

I intend to move to the left or turn left	I intend to move to the right or turn right	I intend to slow down or stop

Traffic coming from the front must stop	Traffic approaching from behind must stop	Traffic from both front and behind must stop

Traffic from the side may proceed	Traffic from the front may proceed	Traffic from behind may proceed

Keep your speed down when approaching a school crossing patrol: you must by law stop and wait when one signals you to do so

Consider making an arm signal where it would be helpful, for example to show waiting pedestrians you are slowing as you approach a zebra crossing

road signs

Road signs give vital information and you must obey them to stay safe and within the law. Many signs show simplified pictures instead of written instructions, which makes it easier to take in what they mean at a glance. You must be able to recognise and understand the meaning of all road signs. More importantly, you must act on the information given by signs. If a sign warns of a hazard ahead – such as an uneven road surface, no footway, slippery road or traffic queues – you should consider adjusting your speed and position on the road so that you are ready to deal safely with the hazard when you encounter it.

Give way to oncoming vehicles

shapes and colours

You'll know that some signs are round, some square and some triangular, and that they come in different colours, but you may not realise why. In fact, all these shapes and colours have distinct meanings.

Circular signs give orders. Those with a red border tell you what you must not do. For example:

Triangular signs warn of a hazard on the road ahead.

For example:

Blue rectangular signs give information.

For example:

no left turn *no overtaking*

children crossing *low bridge*

no through road *end of motorway*

Blue circular signs tell you what you must do. For example:

minimum speed 30 mph *turn left ahead*

unique shapes

Two particularly important traffic signs have unique shapes: the give way sign is an upside down triangle, and the stop sign is an octagon.

The reason? So that even if these signs are obscured by snow and can't be read, they can still be recognised by their shape alone.

give way sign is an inverted triangle

stop sign is octagonal

Direction signs use different colours depending on what sort of road they are on. Signs on motorways are blue, those on primary routes are green, those on other roads are white with a black border, diversion signs are yellow and signs showing local attractions are brown.

route finding

Route directions are generally clearly signposted, but it's not a good idea to rely on signs alone. Carry a map, and if you lose your way stop somewhere safe to consult it.

It's a good idea to plan your route before starting out. Use a map, or one of the route planning services available on the internet or from motoring organisations. Print off your route or write it down clearly, and plan an alternative route too, in case your first choice is blocked. Allow plenty of time for your journey, especially when travelling a long distance, and plan some rest breaks too. If you can avoid busy times you'll have an easier journey and be less likely to be delayed by heavy traffic – and you won't be adding to traffic congestion yourself.

motorways (blue signs)

left-hand lane leads to a different destination (the arrows pointing downwards mean 'get in lane')

inclined arrow indicates the destinations that can be reached by leaving motorway at next junction

sign placed at a junction leading onto a motorway

on approach to motorway junction ('25' is the junction number)

route confirmed after the junction

diversions (yellow signs)

when you encounter a diversion, follow the signs or the symbols that indicate the alternative route

non-primary and local routes (white signs)

signs on the approach to the junction. Route numbers on a blue background show the way to a motorway; those on green show the way to a primary road

sign at the junction

primary routes (green signs)

on the approach to the junction

at the junction (symbol warns of a hazard on this route)

blue panel indicates that the motorway starts at the next junction; motorways in brackets can also be reached along the route indicated

bilingual sign in Wales

route confirmed after junction

local attractions (brown signs)

tourist attraction *camp site* *picnic site*

other direction signs

ring road (by-passes town)

ring road (non-primary road)

holiday route

road markings

Road markings are a vital source of information. They are often placed alongside road signs, and have the advantage of being visible even when the signs are hidden by traffic. Or they may be used without other signs to give a continuous message along the road. Remember the general rule that the more paint there is on the road, the greater the danger. When you approach an area criss-crossed with white lines and warnings, take note, slow down and prepare to negotiate a serious hazard ahead.

types of road marking

There are a number of different types of road marking which each have distinct meanings. The main types are (with specific examples):

Lane arrows tell you in advance which lane you need to get into, and are often accompanied by road numbers or place names marked on the road.

traffic lane directions

Lines across the road separate traffic at road junctions, telling you where you must stop or give way to other vehicles.

give way

Written warnings on the road give specific commands or warnings of hazards ahead.

do not block entrance to side road

Lines along the road divide lanes of traffic and give information about hazards on the road ahead.

do not cross centre line

Parking restrictions are shown by yellow lines running alongside the kerb. They indicate that waiting restrictions are in force.

no waiting

Speed reduction lines are raised yellow lines across the road at the approach to a hazard such as a lower speed limit. They make road users aware of their speed so they slow down well in time. Rumble strips are red and give an audible warning too.

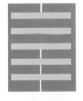

slow down for hazard ahead

know the code

highway code rule 132

Reflective road studs may be used with white lines.

→ white studs mark the lanes or the middle of the road
→ red studs mark the left edge of the road
→ amber studs mark the central reservation of a dual carriageway or motorway
→ green studs mark the edge of the main carriageway at lay-bys and slip roads.
→ green/yellow studs indicate temporary adjustments to lane layouts, e.g. where road works are taking place.

traffic lights

Traffic lights automatically control busy junctions. They ease traffic flow by switching priorities in sequence, allowing vehicles from one direction to flow freely while vehicles from another direction are held back to wait their turn. Approach junctions controlled by traffic lights with caution and be prepared for the lights to change.

approaching traffic lights

Use the observation–signal–manoeuvre routine as you approach a junction controlled by traffic lights. Slow down and be prepared to stop. Never speed up to try and get through while the lights are still green.

Remember that green means go only if the road is clear and it is safe to do so. Always check the road is clear before you proceed when the lights go green. Serious collisions occur at junctions controlled by traffic lights when one vehicle moves off through a green light at the same time as another from the other direction has left it too late to stop after the lights have changed.

When a green filter arrow is illuminated you may proceed only in the direction it indicates

traffic light sequence

1 RED means stop. Wait at the stop line.
2 RED AND **AMBER** also means stop. Do not start to move off until the lights change to green.
3 GREEN means go if it is clear and safe to do so. Give way to any pedestrians who are crossing.
4 AMBER means stop. You may only continue if the amber light appears after you have crossed the stop line or if you are so close to it that it might be dangerous to pull up. (Red then follows amber and the sequence repeats itself.)

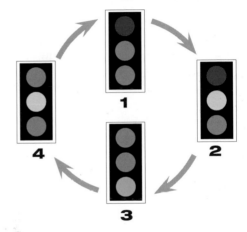

traffic light failure

If a set of traffic lights is not working, you should treat the intersection as an uncontrolled one where no one has priority. Be prepared to stop as traffic from other directions may assume they have right of way. If a police officer is controlling the junction, follow the signals you are given. When signalled to stop by a police officer, wait at the stop line.

Proceed with great care when traffic lights are out of order

5 in traffic

Learning how to control a motorcycle – making it start and stop and go round corners – is the easy bit. On today's busy roads, the real riding skill is interacting with other road users. Good riders blend in with the traffic flow, watch what other road users are doing, communicate their own intentions clearly, make good progress without needing to brake or accelerate harshly, and arrive at their destination relaxed and unruffled. Bad riders fail to observe what other road users are doing, get into misunderstandings, ride too close and too fast, and arrive feeling frustrated and tired. Learning to cope with traffic requires concentration and self-discipline, but it's a skill you must master to pass your motorcycle test.

5
positioning

As a motorcyclist you have the advantage that the narrow width of your bike allows you to position yourself to best advantage at all times. By always being in the right place on the road you will maximise your vision, make your intentions clearer to other road users and increase your margin of safety when approaching hazardous situations.

road position

Normally you should position your motorbike in the centre of your lane. You should ensure that your position makes you clearly visible to other traffic, especially vehicles emerging from junctions ahead, and that you can be seen in the mirror of any vehicle in front of you.

There are times when it is useful to move a little nearer to the kerb. For instance:
- ◗ to make space for oncoming traffic through a narrow gap
- ◗ to increase your vision and safety when approaching a right-hand bend.

But avoid getting too close to the kerb: the road surface is more loose and uneven near the gutter and if you accidentally clip the kerb you may lose control.

Conversely, you should move out towards the centre of the road, if it is safe to do so:
- ◗ when the pavement is busy with pedestrians
- ◗ when making a right-hand turn; this confirms your intentions to other road users and gives following vehicles space to overtake you on your left.

it's the law

crossing white lines

You are permitted to cross a central solid white line only if it is safe and necessary to do so in order to:

- ➔ enter or leave a side turning or driveway
- ➔ pass a stationary vehicle
- ➔ avoid an accident
- ➔ pass a working road maintenance vehicle displaying a keep left/right arrow and moving no faster than 10mph
- ➔ pass a pedal cycle or horse moving no faster than 10mph
- ➔ comply with the direction of a police constable or traffic warden.

lane markings

A broken white line marks the centre of the road

Longer broken white lines indicate a hazard ahead. Never cross a hazard warning line unless you are sure it is safe

Lane lines divide the lanes on dual carriageways and motorways; keep between them except when changing lane

You may cross the centre lines where there are double white lines and the line nearest to you is broken, if it is safe to do

You must not cross the centre lines where the line nearest to you is solid. You also must not park on a road with double white lines whether broken or solid

Where there are double solid white lines, vehicles from either direction are prohibited from crossing the lines

An edge line marks the left-hand side of the carriageway

Diagonal hatching is used to separate lanes of traffic and to protect vehicles waiting to turn off the road. If the area is bordered by a broken white line you can enter it, but only if it is necessary and safe to do so; if it is bounded by a solid white line then you must not enter it except in an emergency

Positioning yourself towards the nearside will improve your vision round a right-hand bend

Leave enough room for a door to open unexpectedly when passing parked vehicles

lane discipline

Always keep within the road markings indicating your lane unless you are changing lane or direction. Try to anticipate when lanes will have to split, and get ready to move across into the correct lane. Don't change lanes at the last moment if you find you have got into the wrong lane: instead carry on and find another way back onto your route. Never straddle lanes or weave in and out of lanes.

Get into the correct lane in good time when arrows indicate that lanes are changing direction

passing parked vehicles

When passing parked vehicles, leave plenty of space in case one of them starts pulling out, or a door opens unexpectedly. Making more space also helps you to see children coming out from between parked cars to cross the road. If you have to pass closer to parked cars, then reduce your speed and be ready to stop.

When passing a series of parked cars, don't weave in and out between them: maintain a straight course which clearly indicates your intentions to other road users.

know the code

highway code rule 143

One-way streets Traffic MUST travel in the direction indicated by signs. Buses and/or cycles may have a contraflow lane. Choose the correct lane for your exit as soon as you can. Do not change lanes suddenly. Unless road signs or markings indicate otherwise, you should use:

→ the left-hand lane when going left
→ the right-hand lane when going right
→ the most appropriate lane when going straight ahead. Remember – traffic could be passing on both sides.

Take care to observe lane markings in one-way streets, and beware of vehicles passing on your left

You must not ride in a bus lane except during the times indicated by the accompanying sign

one-way systems

In a one-way street select the most appropriate lane in good time before you have to turn at the end of the street.

It is legal to overtake on either the left or the right in a one-way street, so take particular care when changing lanes. If you ride down a one-way street by mistake, you must continue to the end of the road – don't try to turn round.

One-way streets may have contra-flow bus or cycle lanes, allowing these vehicles to proceed against the direction of traffic flow.

keep out

Remember that you must not drive in a bus lane, cycle lane, tram lane or high-occupancy vehicle lane unless signs specifically indicate that motorcyclists are permitted to share the lane.

You must also not ride on the pavement except to cross it when using a driveway into a property, or where signs specifically permit parking on the pavement.

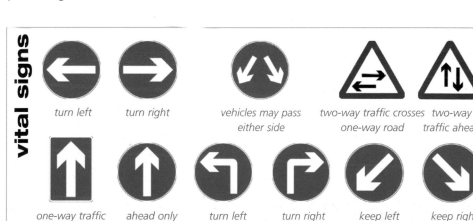

vital signs

turn left   turn right   vehicles may pass either side   two-way traffic crosses one-way road   two-way traffic ahead

one-way traffic   ahead only   turn left   turn right   keep left   keep right

On our busy roads we spend much of our time following the vehicle in front, yet far too many riders commit the serious error of following too closely. They get away with this until one day the vehicle ahead brakes unexpectedly and they end up careering into the back of it. Most serious collisions – such as motorway pile-ups – could be avoided if everyone left more space between their vehicles.

how close?

When you are following another vehicle, ask yourself: 'if it slams on its brakes without warning, have I left myself enough space to be able to react and stop without hitting it?'

If the answer is no, pull back until you have created a safe gap. A useful way to ensure you are keeping a safe distance in dry, bright conditions is to use the two-second rule. Watch as the vehicle in front goes by a lamp post or driveway, then count how long it takes for you to pass the same point. If you can slowly count 'one thousand – two thousand' (or repeat the apt phrase 'only a fool breaks the two-second rule') before you reach the marker then you are keeping a safe distance.

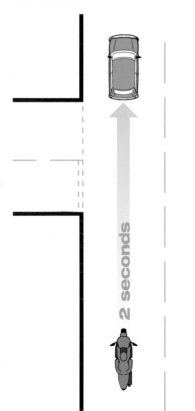

Use a fixed point on the road side to help measure a two-second gap from the vehicle in front

wet roads

On wet, greasy or icy roads you will take much longer to stop in an emergency. When it rains, double the two-second rule and leave a four-second gap. If the road is slippery or icy you should leave up to ten times the distance in which to stop.

Wet roads mean you will need further to stop in an emergency, so leave at least a four-second gap

large vehicles

Another time you need to leave extra space is when you're following a large truck or bus. If you are too close to it your view past will be obscured and you won't be able to anticipate what is happening on the road ahead. Keeping well back also means you don't have to breathe in the truck's diesel exhaust fumes, or get your visor smeared by spray thrown up from its rear wheels on a wet road.

Keep well back when following a bus or you won't be able to see past to overtake it when it stops

tailgating

This is the dangerous habit of following too closely behind the vehicle in front. If someone is tailgating you, it means that if you have to stop in an emergency they may not be able to avoid running into the back of your bike. Reduce this risk by easing off the throttle and increasing your following distance from the vehicle in front. Because you have created more space in front of yourself, you won't have to slow so abruptly in an emergency, which in turn gives the driver behind more time to react.

Often road users tailgate because they are impatient to get past. If this is the case, let them overtake at the first opportunity. Never try to retaliate to a tailgater by putting on your brakes or riding obstructively. The fact that they are behaving dangerously means that you have to take even more care to ride responsibly to help ensure everyone's safety.

queues

When in a slow-moving traffic queue, hold back if keeping up with the queue would mean obstructing the exit of a junction or straddling a pedestrian crossing or level crossing. Wait till the traffic in front has moved forward far enough for you to be able to clear the junction or crossing before proceeding.

Leave a gap when approaching side turnings in queuing traffic so you don't obstruct access to them

Filtering is a hazardous manoeuvre so ride slowly and don't expect others to see you coming

filtering

One advantage of the small size and manoeuvrability of a motorcycle is that it's possible to make progress in congested traffic by filtering past queuing vehicles. This is a potentially highly dangerous manoeuvre so do it only with great caution, remembering that other road users may not be expecting you to filter. Always:

- keep your speed low and be ready to brake
- be ready to use your horn to warn anyone who hasn't seen you
- identify the space where you intend to rejoin the queue *before* you move out
- be especially vigilant for pedestrians crossing between vehicles, vehicles emerging from junctions (especially where there is a gap in the queue at a 'keep clear' road marking), vehicles changing lanes or doing a U-turn without warning, and car doors opening
- take extra care if riding across road markings which may become slippery in wet weather
- look out for other motorbikes and bicycles which may also be filtering.

being overtaken

When you're in a line of traffic on the open road, remember that even if you don't intend to overtake, a rider or driver behind may want to overtake you. Leave enough space for them to do so safely.

If someone else is trying to overtake, you should help them get past quickly and safely. Keep a steady course, slow down if necessary and leave plenty of space from the vehicle in front for the overtaking vehicle to move into. But leave the decision to overtake to the other person – don't beckon them to pass, or indicate left, as there may be hazards which you haven't spotted.

Don't ever try to obstruct or prevent someone from overtaking, even if you are riding at the speed limit. Let the other vehicle get by and concentrate on ensuring your own safety. Slow down if someone overtakes where there is not enough forward vision for them to carry out the manoeuvre safely, or to assist a large vehicle which is taking a long time to pull past you.

Never be the cause of a tailback of traffic. If you are riding a slow-moving scooter and a queue forms behind you, pull over as soon as it is safe and let the traffic pass before resuming your journey.

When leaving a safe gap on a dual carriageway or motorway, you may find that other vehicles pull in too closely in front of you. Don't think of this as a problem – simply ease off the throttle and pull back until you open up a safe gap again. Even if ten vehicles pull in front of you during the course of a journey you'll still get where you're going only a few seconds later – and more importantly, you'll get there safely.

stopping in traffic

Avoid getting too close to the vehicle in front when it stops at traffic lights or a junction. Leave enough space so that if it stalls or breaks down you have plenty of room to manoeuvre safely past without getting stuck behind it. On a slope leaving this gap also gives room for the car in front to roll back if its driver performs a bad hill start.

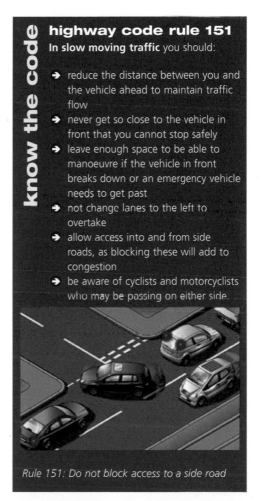

know the code

highway code rule 151

In slow moving traffic you should:

→ reduce the distance between you and the vehicle ahead to maintain traffic flow

→ never get so close to the vehicle in front that you cannot stop safely

→ leave enough space to be able to manoeuvre if the vehicle in front breaks down or an emergency vehicle needs to get past

→ not change lanes to the left to overtake

→ allow access into and from side roads, as blocking these will add to congestion

→ be aware of cyclists and motorcyclists who may be passing on either side

Rule 151: Do not block access to a side road

meeting

If you meet an oncoming vehicle where an obstruction such as a parked car reduces the width of the road so there is room for only one vehicle to proceed, one of you has to give way. Forward thinking and anticipation make all the difference when dealing with this sort of situation. You need to anticipate, and adjust your speed and position well in advance so that if it is necessary for you to give way you can do so smoothly and safely.

A hump bridge is a potentially dangerous meeting place because the brow of the bridge restricts your forward view. Hump bridges are often narrow so you may encounter oncoming vehicles or pedestrians in the middle of the road. Slow right down and consider sounding your horn to give a warning of your approach

giving way

Where the obstruction is on your side of the road you should be prepared to stop and give way to oncoming traffic. But don't assume you necessarily have priority if the obstruction is on the other side of the road. If an oncoming vehicle carries straight on through, you must be able to stop safely and give way to it. Thinking in terms of 'right of way' in this sort of situation isn't helpful: riders who insist on always taking what they see as their 'right of way' end up in a collision sooner or later.

judging the gap

As you approach a meeting situation use the observation–signal–manoeuvre routine. The oncoming vehicle may pull nearer to the kerb to create enough space for you to continue through the gap. But if you are not absolutely certain there is enough room, hold back until the other vehicle is through. Never pull past an obstruction expecting the oncoming vehicle to move over to make space for you.

hills

It's courteous to give way to vehicles, particularly large lorries and buses, which are coming towards you up a steep hill. If a heavily-laden truck loses momentum to give way on a hill it has to work hard to regain it.

Where parked vehicles cause an obstruction ahead, stop and give way to oncoming traffic

Use passing places to pull in and give way to oncoming vehicles on single track roads

vital signs

give way to vehicles from other direction *you have priority over oncoming vehicles*

road narrows on both sides *road narrows on right (left if symbol reversed)*

know the code

highway code rule 155

Single-track roads
These are only wide enough for one vehicle. They may have special passing places. If you see a vehicle coming towards you, or the driver behind wants to overtake, pull into a passing place on your left, or wait opposite a passing place on your right. Give way to vehicles coming uphill whenever you can. If necessary, reverse until you reach a passing place to let the other vehicle pass. Slow down when passing pedestrians, cyclists and horse riders.

overtaking

Many motorbikes are capable of rapid acceleration which makes it possible to exploit overtaking opportunities not open to most other vehicles. But overtaking is also one of the most potentially dangerous riding manoeuvres, and it demands careful judgement and a full assessment of the risks involved. Always remember the golden rule: if you're not absolutely sure it is safe to overtake, don't.

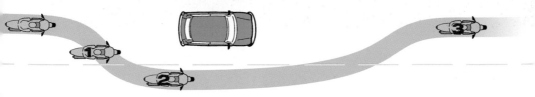

how to overtake

1 Maximise your observation of the road ahead before overtaking. Don't get too close or you will reduce your view past the vehicle you want to overtake. Position yourself towards the centre of the road so you can see past. (When following a large vehicle it can also be useful to move towards the kerb to get a view along its nearside.) Check your mirrors. Consider whether you need to look over your right shoulder and give a signal before pulling out. Make sure you are in a gear that gives enough power to get past quickly, but try to avoid having to change gear in the middle of an overtaking manoeuvre.

2 Move to the other side of the road to make a final check of the road ahead. If it is clear then overtake. You need to accelerate quickly to spend as little time as possible on the other side of the road, but take care not to accelerate too harshly, especially on a slippery road surface, or you may provoke a skid.

3 Don't cut in too early after overtaking. Take appropriate rear observation to ensure that it is safe to pull back in.

when to overtake

The only reason to overtake is when it will help you to make progress. There's no point overtaking when you are approaching a built-up area or if you intend to turn off the road soon.

Keep back and move towards the centre line to maximise your field of view past a slow vehicle

it's the law

no overtaking
It is illegal to overtake:

➜ if you would have to cross or straddle double white lines with a solid line nearest to you (apart from the exceptions mentioned on p83)

➜ if you would have to enter an area surrounded by a solid white line that is designed to divide traffic streams

➜ the nearest vehicle to a pedestrian crossing

➜ if you would have to enter a lane reserved for buses, trams or cycles during its hours of operation

➜ after a 'no overtaking' sign until you pass the sign cancelling it.

A white arrow in the middle of the road is warning you to move back to the left when overtaking. Never overtake where you see this marking

Don't try to squeeze past a cyclist or slower motorcyclist: hold back until it is safe to pass, and leave as much room as when overtaking a car

dangers from other vehicles

If you overtake at 60mph while an oncoming vehicle approaches at the same speed, it means you are closing at a combined speed of 120mph. This leaves little margin for error. Never overtake where you may force another vehicle to swerve or slow down.

While you are deciding whether to overtake, be aware that a driver or rider behind may be thinking about overtaking you. Take appropriate rear observation, and give a signal to indicate your intentions both to following traffic and to the vehicle you are overtaking.

Make sure there is no possibility that the vehicle you intend to overtake is about to make a right turn or swerve across the road to overtake a cyclist or pedestrian you haven't seen. Take care before overtaking at the start of a downhill stretch or when leaving a lower speed restriction in case the vehicle in front speeds up. If you are unsure that the vehicle you want to overtake is aware of your presence consider sounding your horn or flashing your headlamp briefly to warn that you are about to overtake.

If the driver in front waves or indicates left to encourage you to overtake, don't

rely on their judgement: overtake only if you can see to your own satisfaction that it is safe.

It is very dangerous to follow straight after another overtaking vehicle as your view ahead will be obscured and oncoming vehicles may not be able to see you. Hold back and make sure the road is clear before overtaking.

overtaking hazards

Overtaking is potentially dangerous because there are so many different hazards to assess before making the manoeuvre. Never overtake:

- ➲ where there are road junctions or driveways from which a vehicle may emerge in front of you
- ➲ where the road narrows
- ➲ where you cannot see the road ahead to be clear, such as on the approach to a bend, a hump bridge, the brow of a hill or a dip in the road
- ➲ when approaching a school crossing patrol
- ➲ between the kerb and a bus or tram when it is at a stop
- ➲ where traffic is queuing at junctions or road works
- ➲ at a level crossing.

Caution is required when overtaking on three-lane roads, especially where traffic from either direction is allowed to overtake on the same stretch

Overtaking on the left is legal in some situations, such as on a one-way street, but take extra care as other road users may not be expecting you to do so

three-lane roads

Take care when overtaking on a road with three lanes where vehicles from either direction may use the middle lane to overtake. Don't pull out unless you are certain there is no risk of an oncoming vehicle trying to overtake at the same time.

overtaking on the left

You must normally overtake on the right. However, there are a few situations where you are permitted to pass slower moving vehicles on the left-hand side:

- ◯ where a vehicle is signalling to turn right
- ◯ where traffic is moving slowly in queues on a multi-lane road
- ◯ in a one-way street
- ◯ in a lane turning left at a junction.

vital signs

*side winds:
take special care
when overtaking
cyclists, other
motorbikes or high-
sided vehicles*

*hidden dip in road:
don't overtake as
oncoming traffic
may be obscured*

Hidden dip

no overtaking

6 junctions

At a road junction two or more roads meet. Traffic has to merge and with this comes the risk that mistakes may lead to collisions. It's a fact that many serious accidents involving motorcyclists occur at junctions when drivers of other vehicles fail to see them. This means that you need to take extra care at junctions, whatever the weather conditions or time of day or night. Always signal clearly and position your bike accurately to give a clear indication to other road users of what you intend to do. Make sure you are as visible as possible, and never assume that other drivers are aware of your presence.

If no one knew who had priority where two roads meet the result would be chaos. To promote a smooth traffic flow, most junctions are organised so that traffic on the major road has priority and traffic on the minor road must wait until it is clear to proceed. Although there are few basic types of junctions, individual circumstances make each junction unique and they need to be negotiated with care. Assess each junction as you approach it by looking at such things as bends, visibility, obscured sightlines, the amount of traffic, road markings and signs.

types of junction

There are five main types of junction:

- T-junctions
- Y-junctions
- staggered junctions
- crossroads
- roundabouts.

priorities at junctions

Priorities at junctions are indicated by give way signs and markings, stop signs and markings, and traffic lights – or there may be no priority marked. Remember that even if you are on the road that has priority, you need to be ready to slow down or stop for vehicles which pull out in front of you, or for vulnerable road users such as cyclists or pedestrians who you may need to give priority to whatever the road signs say.

give way

A give way sign means you must stop at the line to give priority to traffic on the road you are joining. However, you do not need to stop if the road is clear and it is safe to proceed. A give way junction has double broken white lines across your half of the road, or a single broken white line at the entrance to a roundabout.

vital signs

STOP 100 yds

distance to stop line ahead

GIVE WAY 50 yds

distance to give way line ahead

give way to traffic on major road

side turning

T-junction (the road with priority is shown by the broader line)

stop and give way

roundabout

mini-roundabout

crossroads

staggered junction

stop sign

A stop sign is used instead of a give way sign where reduced visibility means it would be dangerous to proceed through a junction without stopping at all times. You must come to a complete halt at the line and check that the road is clear before proceeding. A stop junction has a single continuous white line across your side of the road. This type of line also shows where you should stop at traffic lights, level crossings, swing bridges and ferries.

uncontrolled junctions

On minor roads some junctions may not have road signs or markings. This means all vehicles approaching the junction have equal priority. Slow down, look for traffic coming from all directions and be prepared to stop and give way if necessary.

box junctions

Box junctions are designed to prevent the junction being blocked by queuing traffic. It is illegal to enter the area of yellow criss-cross lines marked on the road at a box junction unless your exit road is clear. But remember the important exception to this rule: you *can* enter a box junction when you want to turn right and your exit road is clear but you are prevented from proceeding by oncoming traffic or right-turning vehicles in front of you.

traffic lights

At junctions controlled by traffic lights the priorities change with the lights. See p79 to remind yourself of the sequence and meaning of traffic lights.

At a give way sign (left), if the junction is clear you may ride across it without coming to a halt; but at a stop sign (right) you must by law do just that – come to a complete standstill before moving off again

approaching junctions

All junctions should be approached using the observation–signal–manoeuvre and position–speed–look routines described on p65. In good time as you approach the junction:

- ➔ look all around including taking rear observation
- ➔ make a signal if it would assist other road users
- ➔ check your position on the road and adjust it if necessary
- ➔ check your speed and adjust it if necessary
- ➔ select the appropriate gear
- ➔ take one last good look all around, including rear observation into your blind spot, to check it is safe to proceed
- ➔ make the manoeuvre if it is safe to do so.

road markings at junctions

This marking appears on the road just before a give way sign

Give way to traffic on a major road

Stop line at stop sign

Give way to traffic from the right at a roundabout

Give way to traffic from the right at a mini-roundabout

Stop line at signals or police control

Stop line for pedestrians at a level crossing

highway code rule 174

know the code

Box junctions These have criss-cross yellow lines painted on the road. You MUST NOT enter the box until your exit road or lane is clear. However, you may enter the box and wait when you want to turn right, and are only stopped from doing so by oncoming traffic, or by other vehicles waiting to turn right. At signalled roundabouts you MUST NOT enter the box unless you can cross over it completely without stopping.

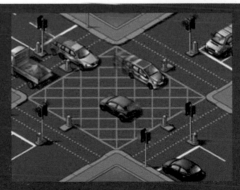

6

emerging from junctions

When you emerge from a junction you may have to join traffic which is heavy or fast-moving. If making a right turn there is the additional hazard of crossing the path of oncoming vehicles. This is a potentially dangerous situation and you must exercise careful judgement and continually monitor what is happening all around you.

Careful, all round observation is essential when you are emerging from a road junction

emerging left from a junction

Follow this general procedure:

- ◗ take rear observation as you approach the junction
- ◗ if other road users would benefit from a signal give it in good time
- ◗ position your bike to the left of the road, about one metre from the kerb
- ◗ slow down and be prepared to give way or stop at the junction
- ◗ look in all directions before pulling out. Check for bicycles or motorcycles which may be passing on your nearside
- ◗ pull onto the main road, cancel your indicator, take rear observation to check for following traffic and accelerate to a safe speed for the road you have joined.

emerging right from a junction

Carry out the same procedure, but position your bike as near to the centre of the road as possible (although if the road is narrow, you must leave enough space for other vehicles to turn into the junction). Take extra care when pulling out as you have to give way to traffic coming from both directions.

When stopping at a junction make sure that you pull right up to the give way or stop line (above). Do not stop short of the line (below) or you will restrict your view out of the junction

maximising your vision

Sometimes you will find that your view
out of a junction is obscured, for instance
by parked vehicles. If this is the case, stop
at the junction and then edge carefully
forward until you can get a good view
down the road in both directions.

Large vehicles may also obscure your
view. Before pulling out in front of a bus or
lorry, ask yourself if there might be a hidden
car or motorcycle overtaking it. Remember
that other motorcyclists and cyclists are
particularly vulnerable at junctions because
they are smaller and harder to see.

Take care if a vehicle approaching from
your right is signalling as though it intends
to turn into the road from which you are
emerging. Do not pull out until you are
absolutely certain that this what it is going
to do – the driver may intend pulling into
the side of the road after the junction,
or may simply have left on the indicator
by mistake.

staggered junctions

This is where two minor roads join a major
road not quite opposite each other. When
you are on a minor road and wish to pass
across the major road you should usually
treat this as two manoeuvres: first join the
major road, then make a second turn into
the minor road. If the junctions are very
close together you may proceed across
the major road in one manoeuvre, but
check carefully that the road is clear in
both directions.

When approaching a staggered junction
on the major road you should treat it with
caution. Be prepared to slow down and give
way to emerging vehicles.

Y-junctions

At a Y-junction the minor road meets the
major road at an angle. When turning right
at a Y-junction you may need to pull up
at a right angle to the major road to give
yourself a clearer view to your left.

*Where parked vehicles obstruct your view out of
a junction, edge cautiously forward until you can
see if the road is clear for you to pull out*

turning right onto a dual carriageway

Crossing a dual carriageway needs extra care because of the high speed of traffic. There are two types of right turn onto a dual carriageway:

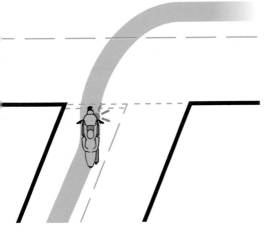

Pulling up at a right angle to the major road at a Y junction makes it easier to get a clear view in both directions

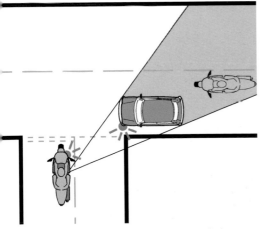

Be alert for overtaking vehicles – particularly other motorcycles – which can easily be hidden from view behind another vehicle at a junction

⊘ where there is a waiting area within the central reservation

You should cross the road in two stages. First, check that the road to your right is clear of oncoming traffic and ride into the waiting area. Stop here and check if the road is clear to the left before joining the carriageway. You must not not join the right-hand lane and expect approaching traffic to pass you on the left. Wait until both lanes are clear so you are able to cross safely to the left-hand lane.

Always check before carrying out this manoeuvre that there is enough space for your motorcycle to fit into the central reservation without obstructing traffic already on the dual carriageway.

⊘ where there is no waiting area within the central reservation

You must cross the dual carriageway in a single manoeuvre. This calls for careful observation in both directions before pulling out.

Where there is a central reservation wide enough to wait in, split a right turn across a dual carriageway into two separate manoeuvres

turning into side roads

Careful observation is needed when turning into a minor road. Try not to concentrate your attention on the danger from just one direction – for instance, oncoming traffic when you are turning right – as you may overlook other hazards, such as another motorcycle overtaking you, or pedestrians crossing the road you are turning into.

turning left

Follow this general procedure:

- ⊘ take rear observation as you approach the junction
- ⊘ if other road users would benefit from a signal give it in good time
- ⊘ position your bike to the left of the road, but don't move too far into the gutter or following drivers may think you are pulling up, not turning left
- ⊘ slow down, then select the appropriate gear. Your speed must reflect how sharp the corner is and how clearly you can see round it. Remember that a vehicle could be parked just round the corner out of sight, or an oncoming vehicle may be in the middle of the road passing parked cars
- ⊘ look all round. Check your mirrors again, and look over your left shoulder in case a cyclist or motorcyclist is passing on your nearside. Check that the road you are turning into is clear. You must stop and give way to any pedestrians who are crossing the road
- ⊘ turn the corner, making sure you stay well on your side of the road
- ⊘ cancel your indicator, take rear observation to check for following traffic and accelerate to a safe speed for the road you are now on.

Keep close in when turning left, but don't cut round so tightly that you risk clipping the kerb

know the code

highway code rule 182

Turning left Use your mirrors and give a left-turn signal well before you turn left. Do not overtake just before you turn left and watch out for traffic coming up on your left before you make the turn, especially if driving a large vehicle. Cyclists, motorcyclists and other road users in particular may be hidden from your view.

rule 183

When turning

- → keep as close to the left as is safe and practicable
- → give way to any vehicles using a bus lane, cycle lane or tramway from either direction.

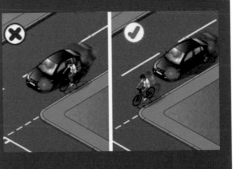

RULE 182: Do not cut in on cyclists

test tips

do

- ⊘ take care to check that the road you are riding into is clear before starting to turn
- ⊘ judge your positioning carefully when turning right on a road which has no centre line

don't

- → swing to the left before turning right, or swing out to the right before making a left turn
- → forget to check over your right shoulder immediately before making a right turn into a side road.

Continuous observation is vital when turning right. As well as checking for oncoming traffic, look for vehicles overtaking you and hazards – such as pedestrians – in the road you are turning into.

turning right

Follow this general procedure:

- ⟳ take rear observation as you approach the junction
- ⟳ if other road users would benefit from a signal give it in good time
- ⟳ position your bike towards the centre of the road, keeping as close as you can to the white line. This helps other road users see what you are intending to do, and also lets following traffic pass on your nearside while you are waiting to turn. If there is a waiting area marked on the road for traffic turning right, follow the road markings into this
- ⟳ slow down and be prepared to stop if you need to give way to oncoming traffic or if the entrance of the road you are turning into is blocked
- ⟳ look out for vehicles waiting to turn right from the road you are riding into – they may try to pull out ahead of you
- ⟳ check your mirrors and look over your right shoulder just before turning, in case a vehicle is overtaking you. Be particularly alert for other motorcycles
- ⟳ do not start to turn unless you are sure you can enter the side road and will not be forced to stop in a dangerous position halfway across the main road
- ⟳ if you have to wait for some time for oncoming traffic to clear, don't forget to repeat your rear observation just before starting to move
- ⟳ take care not to cut the corner as you make the turn
- ⟳ cancel your indicator, take rear observation to check for following traffic and accelerate to a safe speed for the road you are now on.

Never cut a corner like this as you risk colliding with a vehicle emerging from the junction

Move over to the white line when waiting to turn to allow other vehicles to get past on your inside

When waiting to make a right turn, don't turn the handlebars before you are ready to move off. If you were hit from behind while waiting in the middle of the road with your front wheel already turned, the impact could push you across the road into the path of oncoming traffic

vital signs

no motorcycles

no vehicles except bicycles being pushed

no entry for vehicular traffic

no left turn

no motor vehicles

no right turn

The above signs all mean that you must not ride into a road. Sometimes there will be a plate giving exceptions – for instance, you may be able to enter outside certain hours, or if you need to gain access to a property in the road.

However, you may enter a road showing this sign, which means 'no motor vehicles except motorcycles without sidecars'

no U-turns

no through road

crossroads

At a crossroads there are two T-junctions opposite each other. Serious collisions can occur at crossroads when one vehicle crosses in front of another travelling at high speed. Take special care when you are on a major road and see a crossroads ahead. Slow down and be prepared to give way in case a driver proceeds straight across without seeing you.

turning right

When turning right at a crossroads at the same time as an oncoming vehicle wants to turn right across you, you have two choices:

◆ **turn right side to right side**

This is the safer option. It has the advantage of giving you a clear view of approaching traffic.

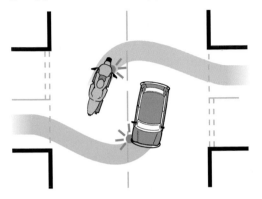

◆ **turn left side to left side**

This method can be useful when turning against a long vehicle, or where the side roads are slightly offset. But because the other vehicle is passing in front of you, it blocks your view of oncoming traffic, so take extra care.

Sometimes there are road markings which direct which course you should take. Where there are no markings, watching the course of the other vehicle and establishing eye contact with its driver may help you decide.

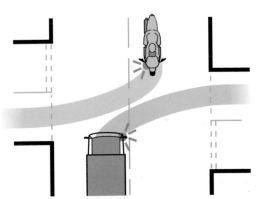

emerging

When you are emerging from one minor road at a crossroads and another vehicle is waiting to emerge from the minor road opposite, what you should do depends on the circumstances:

◆ if you are turning right and the other vehicle is turning left or going ahead, you should wait for the other vehicle to proceed before you emerge, otherwise you would be cutting across its path

◆ if you are turning left or going ahead you should proceed with caution in case the other vehicle emerges and cuts across your path

◆ if you are turning right and the other driver is turning right, neither of you has priority and you should proceed with extra care.

In practice you will find that many road users are unfamiliar with the priorities described above. It is usually helpful to establish eye contact with the other driver to help determine what they intend to do. The other driver may gesture you to come out first – but do so only if you are completely certain that their meaning is clear and it is safe to do so. You should not wave or flash at someone across a crossroads – it could be dangerous if they pull out without checking for themselves that the road is clear.

Extra caution is needed when emerging from a crossroads at the same time as another vehicle

roundabouts

Roundabouts are designed to allow vehicles to merge smoothly and so keep the overall traffic stream flowing. A rider who is looking well ahead and anticipating traffic movements may be able to traverse a string of roundabouts safely and smoothly without once having to come to a complete halt. But negotiating roundabouts correctly does demand a high degree of concentration, anticipation and accurate signalling.

roundabout safety

Fewer serious crashes occur on roundabouts than at crossroads. That's because roundabouts slow down the traffic flow so when accidents happen they tend to be less severe. But the give and take nature of roundabouts means that these minor shunts are more common – and, of course, they can have more serious consequences for the motorcyclist than for a driver coccooned in a car. Careful observation, anticipation and signalling are needed to stay out of trouble.

Take care when anticipating what other road users intend to do on roundabouts. Some drivers have strange ideas about the correct lane or signalling to use, others don't bother signalling at all and some may simply be lost and unsure of which exit to take. So look out for vehicles:

⊘ turning right without indicating
⊘ indicating right but going straight on
⊘ using the right-hand lane to go straight ahead even if the left lane is clear
⊘ making a U-turn at the roundabout.

Take extra care also around cyclists, horse riders and long vehicles, all of which may take an unusual course at roundabouts.

Signal clearly at roundabouts to let other road users know which direction you intend to take

At roundabouts you should look carefully for warning signs that the road surface may be slippery. Tyre rubber can accumulate on the road at roundabouts, and diesel can spill from trucks when they corner with a full tank of fuel. There's also likely to be a lot of paint on the road, and poorly sited metal inspection covers: all these can make the road treacherous for motorcyclists, especially in wet conditions.

negotiating roundabouts

As you approach the roundabout, scan all the approach roads to spot vehicles which may arrive there at the same time as you do. Aim to make progress by adjusting your speed so you can join the traffic flow, but be prepared to stop and give way if necessary. Use the observation–signal–manoeuvre routine on the approach to a roundabout, and always look over your left shoulder before taking your exit road in case someone is trying to pass on your left.

lanes and signalling

On some roundabouts, particularly larger roundabouts with multiple exits, white arrows painted on the approach road indicate which lane you should get into for the exit you intend to take. Where there are no arrows or signs indicating which lane to take, follow these guidelines:

Turning left:
- ➲ indicate left as you approach
- ➲ take the left-hand lane
- ➲ keep left on the roundabout
- ➲ continue to indicate left until you have exited the roundabout.

Turning right:
- ➲ indicate right as you approach
- ➲ take the right-hand lane
- ➲ keep right on the roundabout
- ➲ after passing the exit before the one you intend to take, indicate left
- ➲ continue to indicate left until you have exited the roundabout.

Going straight ahead:
- ➲ do not indicate on approach
- ➲ take the left-hand lane
- ➲ keep left on the roundabout
- ➲ after passing the exit before the one you intend to take, indicate left
- ➲ continue to indicate left until you have exited the roundabout.

It is also acceptable to use the right-hand lane when going straight ahead if the left-hand lane of the roundabout is blocked, for instance by vehicles turning left. In this case you should stay in the right-hand lane as you ride through the roundabout. Don't forget to check over your left shoulder before moving over towards your exit, in case a vehicle is coming up on your nearside.

It is perfectly legal to carry out a U-turn by going all the way round a roundabout, but other road users may not be expecting you to do this so take special care and signal your intentions clearly.

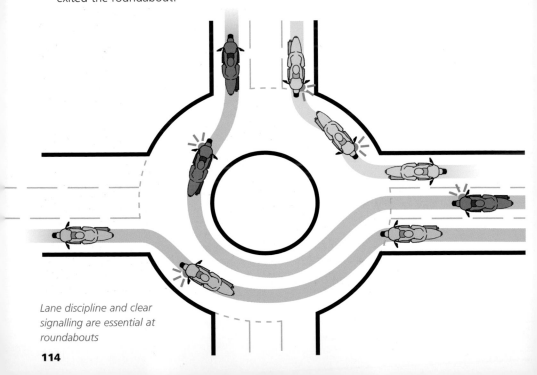

Lane discipline and clear signalling are essential at roundabouts

Where there are mini-roundabouts close together, you must treat them as separate junctions

Get into the correct lane for your exit as soon as possible on the approach to a roundabout

Avoid riding alongside large vehicles on roundabouts as they may need to take up more than one lane to make their turn

mini-roundabouts

Treat mini-roundabouts in the same way as larger roundabouts. You must ride around, not over, the white central circle for two reasons: firstly, because that's the law, and secondly, because such an expanse of white paint can be dangerously slippery when wet. Do however watch out for other road users who may cut straight across mini-roundabouts without slowing down.

When turning right at a mini-roundabout you should indicate right as you approach but the small size of the roundabout means it is usually not practical to indicate left before exiting.

Some junctions consist of a series of mini-roundabouts. Treat each separately and give way if necessary as you approach each one in turn.

test tips

do

➲ give special caution to cyclists: they can find it difficult to pull across the traffic stream and may stay in the left-hand lane even when they want to turn right

➲ take extra care in the wet, as the road surface on roundabouts can become polished and slippery, increasing the risk of a skid if you brake or accelerate harshly

don't

➜ creep forward when waiting to join the roundabout. Drivers on the roundabout may think you are about to pull out in front of them. It could also lead to someone driving into the back of your bike because they think you are pulling onto the roundabout

➜ neglect to take proper rear observation, including a check over your left shoulder before exiting the roundabout.

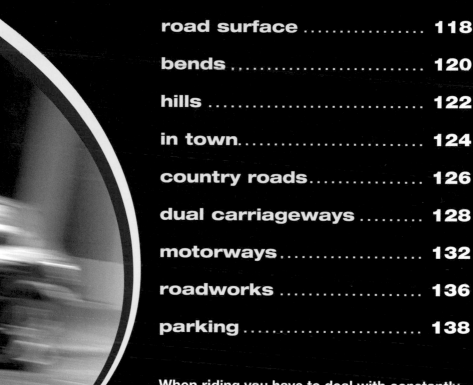

7 on the road

When riding you have to deal with constantly changing situations. In a single journey you could find yourself negotiating busy city back streets, cruising on an empty motorway, tackling a twisting country lane and queuing in head to tail traffic at roadworks. You need to be ready to adapt your riding style to meet these changing conditions, and be aware of the specific hazards you are likely to encounter in different situations on the road.

7

road surface

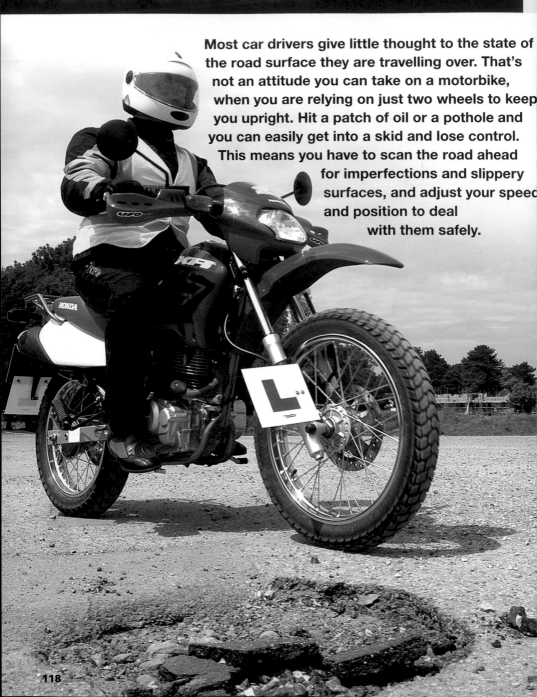

Most car drivers give little thought to the state of the road surface they are travelling over. That's not an attitude you can take on a motorbike, when you are relying on just two wheels to keep you upright. Hit a patch of oil or a pothole and you can easily get into a skid and lose control. This means you have to scan the road ahead for imperfections and slippery surfaces, and adjust your speed and position to deal with them safely.

poor road conditions

Many roads are in a poor state of repair. Look out for potholes so you can slow down well in advance and steer around them. Avoid having to swerve to avoid obstacles at the last second – on a poor road surface this is itself likely to provoke a skid.

Take into account seasonal factors, such as winter mud and autumn leaves, and reduce your speed, particularly when cornering.

Weather conditions have a significant effect on tyre adhesion (this is covered in Chapter 10). Remember that as well as the more obvious dangers of icy conditions, hot weather can make tarmac roads soft and affect braking and cornering, and rain after a hot spell can make it slippery where rubber coats the surface of the road, especially at junctions and roundabouts.

If you do find you are riding on a slippery surface, don't brake abruptly: instead ease off the throttle and lose speed gradually to reduce the risk of skidding.

road repairs

Rough surfaces encountered at roadworks need to be negotiated with caution. After resurfacing, loose chippings may be left on the road and these will greatly reduce tyre grip. Reduce your speed and take care when braking, accelerating and changing direction.

Look out also for chippings thrown up by other vehicles. Keep well back from the vehicle in front to avoid injury or damage to your bike, and always keep your visor down or goggles on through roadworks.

Also keep your eyes peeled for tar banding – the shiny black lines left around road repairs. These become dangerously slippery when wet.

metal surfaces

Items made of metal such as inspection covers (manholes) and tram lines are likely to be slippery, especially in wet conditions, and you should avoid riding over them wherever possible.

road markings

Although the road markings painted on the road serve an important purpose they have the unfortunate property of getting slippery when wet. Try not to brake, accelerate or change direction when passing over road markings, and avoid taking a course which means both your wheels pass over road markings at the same time.

diesel spills

Diesel can spill from a truck when it corners with a full fuel tank, as the fuel sloshes about and overflows. The resulting slick of oil is hazardous for riders in any weather, and on a wet road it can be as slippery as black ice. Take care wherever diesel spills are likely, especially at junctions, roundabouts and bends. Look out for the rainbow-coloured sheen on a wet road which indicates the presence of a diesel spill; if you see this, slow down but don't brake or steer harshly or you could provoke a skid.

Oil patches are also left by buses while stationary at bus stops, and can be slippery in wet weather. Slow down and ease out away from the kerb while passing bus stops to reduce the risk of a skid.

vital signs

falling or fallen rocks

uneven road

loose chippings

SLOW WET TAR

temporary hazard at roadworks

bends

A major element in the enjoyment of riding is the agility and responsiveness of a motorbike on a twisting road. Many bikes have impressive cornering abilities, but you should never forget that ultimately all that gets your bike round a bend is the contact of two patches of tyre tread – no bigger than your handprints – on the tarmac.

cornering

Road signs and markings give advance warning to slow down when you approach a bend, but not all sharp bends have warning signs. Remember that the bend sign not only warns you to slow down, it also shows you which direction the road turns.

On a right-hand bend, position your bike a little nearer to the kerb to improve your view through the bend. But avoid moving towards the centre of the road at the start of a left-hand bend: this could put you in danger from oncoming traffic, particularly if an oncoming vehicle cuts the corner.

If you need to change down a gear do this before you enter the bend. Lean with the bike through the bend, and apply a little power to maintain a constant speed. Once the bend starts to open out and your bike returns to the upright, progressively apply more power and build back up to an appropriate speed.

speed and grip

The golden rule when riding through a bend is that you must be able to stop, on your side of the road, in the distance you can see to be clear. Most bends are blind — your view through them is obscured by hedges or walls. At every bend ask yourself what might be hidden from your view halfway round. A horse rider? Stationary traffic? A fallen branch? Some riders get into the habit of cornering a little too fast because experience tells them that most of the time there is nothing hidden round a bend. Until one day their luck runs out and they have a serious accident.

Corner at a speed that keeps you well within the grip of your tyres on the road. On a damp or greasy road the amount of grip you have is greatly reduced. If you try to take a corner too fast, the tyres will start to slide, putting you in danger of skidding off the road or into the path of another vehicle.

Remember that it is much more difficult to carry out emergency braking while cornering, so you will not be able to stop

as quickly as if you can while riding on a straight road. Always avoid harsh braking while cornering or you may provoke a skid.

Take into account the camber of the road when cornering. Camber is the slope built into a road to allow rainwater to drain off it, and most roads slope downwards from the centre to the kerbs. On an adverse camber – such as when taking a right-hand bend on a steeply cambered road – your tyres will start to lose grip at a lower speed.

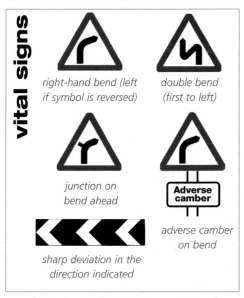

vital signs

right-hand bend (left if symbol is reversed)

double bend (first to left)

junction on bend ahead

Adverse camber

adverse camber on bend

sharp deviation in the direction indicated

Slow down when approaching a bend and be ready to stop in the distance you can see to be clear

On hills you have to take into account the force of gravity. Going uphill, a motorbike needs more power to maintain its speed, so you may have to change down the gearbox. Downhill, the bike will pick up speed and you may need to use the brakes and select a lower gear to restrain it. Hills affect the feel of the controls: harder braking is needed to slow a bike going downhill, and in a high gear it may lose speed up a steep hill even with the throttle fully open.

hill warnings

Steep hills often have warning signs shown as a percentage: 25% indicates a steep one-in-four gradient, where the road rises one metre for every four metres travelled horizontally; 10% means a less severe one-in-ten slope.

In hilly country look out for crests and dips in the road: taking a crest at speed can make your bike unstable, while dips in the road can hide other vehicles and make overtaking hazardous.

riding uphill

You will need to apply more power when climbing a hill, and your motorbike will slow more quickly than when riding on the level. When approaching an uphill gradient don't wait until the engine starts to labour before changing down. Anticipate the need for more power and select the appropriate gear before the bike starts losing momentum.

Look out for slow-moving heavy vehicles going uphill. If you want to overtake, remember that your bike will feel more sluggish than on the level, and you will need more space to get past safely.

On motorways look out for special crawler lanes provided for the use of slow vehicles on uphill sections.

riding downhill

You need to prevent your bike picking up unwanted speed when going downhill. Making use of engine braking by engaging a lower gear to help slow the bike gives more control than relying on the brakes alone. The steeper the descent, the lower the gear you should select: as a rule of thumb, you should use the same gear to go down a hill as you would to come up it.

Always apply the brakes carefully when riding downhill as harsh use may provoke a skid, especially if the road is wet or slippery.

Leave extra space between your bike and the vehicle in front when going downhill, as you will need a greater distance to stop in an emergency. On very steep hills an escape lane is sometimes provided, filled with loose gravel which will bring a vehicle to a halt if its brakes fail.

vital signs

steep hill upwards
(1-in-5 gradient)

steep hill downwards
(1-in-10 gradient)

lane for slow-moving vehicles
(uphill)

escape lane on steep hill
(downhill)

When riding downhill change down the gears for extra engine braking, which makes it easier to control your bike than relying on the brakes alone

in town

Riding in a built-up area poses an extra challenge because of the sheer number of hazards. You are sharing the road with vulnerable road users such as cyclists, pedestrians and children, there are numerous traffic signs and speed limits to observe, and your view of the road ahead is often obscured by parked vehicles. It means that extra concentration, anticipation and observation is required to ride safely.

speed

Because they are so hazardous, town streets have low speed limits – usually 30mph. Remember that there is no requirement for 30mph repeater signs to be displayed on roads which have street lighting. Where buildings are less dense a 40mph limit is often posted, while in town centres 20mph zones are becoming common. Take special care:

○ on busy high streets where people may not have their mind on traffic

○ in zones with a 20mph speed limit where there are pedestrians or children playing

○ near schools, especially around school opening and closing times. Roads outside schools can become chaotic when parents are dropping off and picking up their children so slow down and give way to manoeuvring vehicles. Parking or stopping to drop off passengers is not permitted where road markings indicate a school entrance.

traffic calming

Features designed to slow down traffic such as humps, road narrowings and mini-roundabouts are becoming more common in urban streets, often in conjunction with a 20mph speed limit.

Ride smoothly and slowly through these areas. Don't accelerate and then brake harshly between humps, and don't try to overtake a slower-moving vehicle. Not all humps are of uniform size so be prepared to slow to a walking pace to pass over them without discomfort.

Road narrowings will be accompanied by warning signs showing which side the road narrows and from which direction vehicles have priority. You must give way to oncoming vehicles at road narrowings where signs and road markings indicate.

congestion charging

Riding a bike is a great way to get around town. In London it can also be much cheaper than driving a car because motorcyclists are exempt from the congestion charge which is levied on vehicles entering central London.

The 'twist-and-go' ease of scooter riding makes them an increasingly popular choice for city dwellers

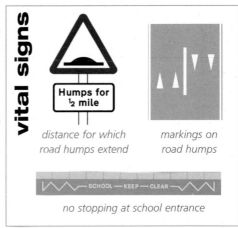

vital signs

distance for which road humps extend

markings on road humps

no stopping at school entrance

Take special care in residential zones which have a 20mph speed limit and traffic calming measures

country roads

Country roads may look open, traffic free and safe, but appearances can be deceptive. That country bend could hide a horse and rider, a slick of mud left by a tractor, or a sudden sharp turn onto a narrow hump bridge. Although you should make progress where it is safe to do so on country roads, always be ready to encounter slow-moving vehicles, cyclists and pedestrians.

narrow lanes

On country roads wide enough for only one vehicle, be prepared to pull over where there is a passing place to let an oncoming vehicle through, or to let a following vehicle overtake. If the passing place is on your right-hand side then wait opposite it. Never park in a passing place.

Use extreme caution when approaching a blind bend on a single-track road. In this situation you should be able to stop in half the distance you can see to be clear, which allows space for any approaching vehicle to stop too.

special hazards

Take care when overtaking slow-moving agricultural vehicles as the driver may have difficulty seeing or hearing you.

Look out for horse riders and cyclists, and for pedestrians who may be approaching on your side of the road.

Animals – both domestic and wild – are another hazard you may encounter on country roads (see p164).

Leaves, mud and hedge clippings on the road can all be hazardous for motorcyclists. Take heed of the unofficial signs that farmers put up as a warning when agriculture vehicles are depositing large quantities of mud on the road.

Be prepared to stop and give way to oncoming vehicles when riding on narrow county roads

Look out for slow-moving agricultural vehicles – and for the slippery mud they leave on the road

vital signs

agricultural vehicles

hump bridge

opening or swing bridge ahead

quayside or river bank

know the code

highway code rule 154

Country roads Take extra care on country roads and reduce your speed at approaches to bends, which can be sharper than they appear, and at junctions and turnings, which may be partially hidden. Be prepared for pedestrians, horse riders, cyclists, slow-moving farm vehicles or mud on the road surface. Make sure you can stop within the distance you can see to be clear. You should also reduce your speed where country roads enter villages.

dual carriageways

On dual carriageways the lanes in either direction are separated by a central reservation. Riding on a dual carriageway is similar to riding on a motorway, with a speed limit of 70mph unless otherwise signed, but there can be extra hazards such as slow-moving vehicles and right turns across the carriageway which would not be encountered on a motorway.

joining a dual carriageway

At many dual carriageway junctions you join by using a slip road. The purpose of the slip road is to let vehicles build up speed so they can merge smoothly with the traffic on the main carriageway.

As you ride onto the slip road try to assess the speed at which traffic in the inside lane of the dual carriageway is moving and accelerate to match it. Use the observation–signal–manoeuvre routine, signal right to show that you intend moving across from the slip road and glance over your right shoulder just before you join the main carriageway to make sure there is nothing in your blind spot.

Don't expect traffic to make space for you and be prepared to use the full length of the slip road to merge safely. You should not have to stop and wait at the end of the slip road unless traffic on the main dual carriageway is very slow moving.

Where there is no slip road you join the dual carriageway as you would a normal road at a stop or give way junction. Be sure to take into account the higher speed of vehicles on the dual carriageway before moving out.

leaving a dual carriageway

Where there is a long slip road at the exit to a dual carriageway you can use this to lose speed. But some slip roads are short and end in a sharp bend, so be prepared to start losing speed before you leave the main carriageway. Where no slip road is provided you should start signalling and slowing early to give following traffic plenty of warning that you are turning off.

When joining from a slip road you must be prepared to give way to vehicles already on the dual carriageway. Always check your blind spot before moving across into the inside lane

Exit slip roads may be short and busy so watch your speed when leaving a dual carriageway

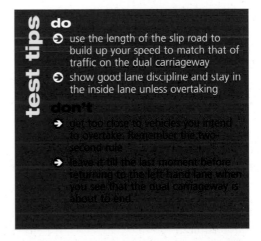

test tips

do
➔ use the length of the slip road to build up your speed to match that of traffic on the dual carriageway
➔ show good lane discipline and stay in the inside lane unless overtaking

don't
➔ get too close to vehicles you intend to overtake. Remember the two-second rule
➔ leave it till the last moment before returning to the left-hand lane when you see that the dual carriageway is about to end

right turns

Keep in the left lane of the dual carriageway unless you are overtaking slower-moving traffic or turning right. If you want to carry out a right turn, you need to consider the high speed of traffic and start planning your turn at an early stage. Take rear observation and signal well in advance, and consider a gentle pressure on the brakes at an early stage to signal to following traffic that you are slowing. Position your bike accurately inside the turning bay in the central reservation, and take care to check that the road you are entering is clear before turning across the right-hand carriageway.

Take extra care when overtaking large vehicles as you may be obscured in the driver's blind spot

dual carriageway ends

When you see the 'dual carriageway ends' sign, check your speed because, unless signposted otherwise, the speed limit is about to drop back from 70mph to 60mph – the national speed limit for single carriageway roads. If you are overtaking, make sure you get back into the left-hand lane in good time before the dual carriageway ends. Be alert for other vehicles cutting past to pull in front of you at the last moment, and leave plenty of room from the vehicle in front so they have space to pull in safely.

Keep in the left-hand lane of the dual carriageway except when overtaking or making a right turn

Finish overtaking and return to the inside lane in good time when you see the dual carriageway ends sign

overtaking

On dual carriageways you need to plan your overtaking manoeuvres well in advance and give clear signals in good time because other vehicles may be coming up fast behind you.

1 Carry out the observation–signal–manoeuvre routine and look down the road to check for hazards in front of the vehicle you will be overtaking. Let the indicator flash at least three times before you start to move out to give other road users time to respond to your signal. Take a final glance over your right shoulder before changing lanes to check for vehicles in your blind spot.

2 When you have confirmed it is safe to do so, pull across into the right-hand lane of the dual carriageway. This should be carried out as a smoothly flowing manoeuvre – don't steer harshly or change lanes abruptly. (Remember that on a dual carriageway you may overtake only on the right, unless traffic is moving slowly in queues and your queue is quicker than the one in the right-hand lane.)

3 Accelerate and overtake briskly, always keeping within the speed limit. Avoid lingering in the blind spot of the vehicle you are overtaking where the driver may not be able to see you, especially when you are overtaking a large vehicle.

4 Don't cut in sharply once you're past the front of the vehicle you've overtaken – you mustn't leave it with less than a two-second separation distance once you've pulled back in. Take rear observation to make sure you've left enough room before pulling back into the inside lane.

motorways

You aren't permitted to ride on motorways until you get your full motorcycle licence (and no bike under 50cc is allowed on the motorway) but the theory test includes lots of questions about motorways, so don't overlook this section. Motorways are useful for covering long distances quickly, but using them demands discipline and responsibility. Although motorways are statistically the safest of all roads, because of their higher speeds and volume of traffic, when accidents do occur they are often serious ones.

planning your journey

Always make sure you are prepared before setting out, because long high-speed journeys put an extra strain on both motorbike and rider. Check your bike's lights, fluid levels and tyre pressures.

Many motorbikes have a limited range so keep an eye on signs advising distances to service stations and make sure you have enough fuel to avoid running out before the next one. If you do break down, recovery from a motorway is expensive so it pays to be a member of a recovery service.

lane discipline

Keep in the left-hand lane unless you need to overtake slower-moving vehicles. Where there is a stream of slower-moving traffic, don't weave in and out of the left-hand lane. It's better to stay in the middle lane until the left-hand lane clears (but do keep an eye on your mirrors and be prepared to move over to let faster-moving vehicles pass).

Use the outer lane to overtake when the inner and middle lanes are occupied with slower traffic, but again be ready to move back as soon as it is clear to do so.

If a vehicle which is clearly exceeding the speed limit comes up behind you, never try to make it slow down or hold it up: pull over at the first safe opportunity and let it overtake. If you are held up by a slower vehicle, never try to intimidate your way past: wait patiently until it pulls over.

Large goods vehicles, buses, coaches and vehicles towing a trailer or caravan are not allowed to use the outer lane of a motorway, so take care not to block their progress by neglecting to pull back into the left-hand lane as soon as you are able to do so.

anticipation

Anticipating what is happening far ahead is vital when riding at high speed on the motorway. Leave at least a two-second following distance from the vehicle in front – more in wet weather or poor visibility. Keep looking well ahead and ease off the throttle if you see brake lights in the distance. Be ready to slow down or stop if you see hazard warning lights flashing ahead. Don't be distracted if you see an accident in the opposite carriageway: concentrate on what's happening ahead of you.

junctions

As you approach a junction be prepared for vehicles exiting the motorway to cut across in front of you at the last moment.

There is usually a slip road joining the motorway immediately after you pass an exit. Anticipate that vehicles may be joining here. If there is space to do so then pull into the middle lane to give vehicles joining the motorway room to move across from the slip road into the inside lane.

It is illegal (except in an emergency) to ride into the triangular area of chevrons within a solid white line which separates a motorway slip road from the main carriageway

it's the law

no access
Motorways must not be used by:

→ learner drivers and riders
→ pedestrians
→ cyclists
→ horse riders
→ motorcycles under 50cc
→ slow-moving vehicles, agricultural vehicles and invalid carriages.

stopping

Stopping is permitted on a motorway only in an emergency, or if you are directed to stop by a sign with flashing red lights or by the police. (Highways Agency traffic officers also work alongside police officers on motorways to manage incidents and keep traffic moving and it is an offence not to comply with any directions they give.) The hard shoulder is reserved for emergency use only – If you need to take a break then ride on to the next exit or service station.

joining and leaving

When joining a motorway, use the slip road as when joining a dual carriageway. Once you have joined, keep in the left-hand lane until you have adjusted to traffic conditions.

Motorway exits are marked with signs at one mile and half a mile, and then countdown markers at 300, 200 and 100

yards (270, 180 and 90m) before the slip road. Don't pull across to the exit at the last moment, but aim to be in the left-hand lane by the half-mile warning sign. Where other traffic might benefit from a signal, start indicating left at the 300 yard marker. Take special care when entering service stations as slip roads can be shorter than normal.

If you go past your junction by mistake you must continue to the next junction to turn around.

Keep an eye on your speedometer after leaving a motorway, as it may seem you are riding more slowly than you really are.

bad weather

Because of the high traffic speeds it is essential to make yourself visible on the motorway. Use your headlight at all times.

In wet conditions, beware of spray thrown up from the road, particularly as you overtake large vehicles. Look out also for the effect of crosswinds on exposed stretches.

Fog patches are a special danger on motorways as you may enter them at high speed without warning. Reduce your speed in conditions where fog patches may be likely to form and take heed of fog warning signs, even if it is clear where you are.

ATM schemes

Active Traffic Management (ATM) schemes are in place on some motorways to reduce congestion. They use variable mandatory speed limits to promote a more constant traffic flow and reduce delays. In congested conditions the hard shoulder comes into use as an extra traffic lane. Emergency refuge areas are provided every 500m and should be used in the event of a breakdown, whether or not the hard shoulder is open to traffic. When the ATM is operating, speed limits are shown in red circles on electronic overhead signs: a speed limit shown above the hard shoulder means it is open to traffic; a red cross or a blank sign means the hard shoulder is to be used in emergencies only.

know the code

highway code rules 255–58
Motorway signals

255. Motorway signals are used to warn you of a danger ahead. For example, there may be an incident, fog, a spillage or road workers on the carriageway which you may not immediately be able to see.
256. Signals situated on the central reservation apply to all lanes. On very busy stretches, signals may be overhead with a separate signal for each lane.
257. Amber flashing lights. These warn of a hazard ahead. The signal may show a temporary maximum speed limit, lanes that are closed or a message such as 'Fog'. Adjust your speed and look out for the danger until you pass a signal which is not flashing or one that gives the 'All clear' sign and you are sure it is safe to increase your speed.
258. Red flashing lights. If red lights on the overhead signals flash above your lane and a red 'X' is showing, you MUST NOT go beyond the signal in that lane. If red lights flash on a signal in the central reservation or at the side of the road, you MUST NOT go beyond the signal in any lane.

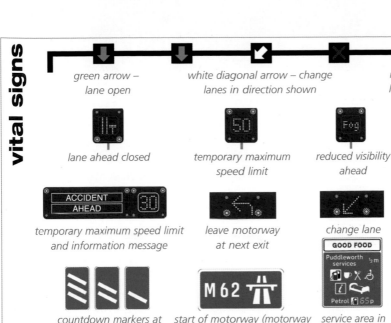

vital signs

green arrow –
lane open

white diagonal arrow – change
lanes in direction shown

red cross –
lane closed

lane ahead closed

temporary maximum
speed limit

reduced visibility
ahead

end of
restriction

temporary maximum speed limit
and information message

leave motorway
at next exit

change lane

do not proceed
further in this lane

countdown markers at
exit from motorway

start of motorway (motorway
regulations now apply)

service area in
half a mile

end of
motorway

emergency telephone
box on motorway (use
the number to tell the
operator your location)

direction to nearest
emergency telephone
shown on marker post
on hard shoulder

tunnel ahead

direction to
emergency
pedestrian exit in
tunnel

tunnels

Take extra care by observing all road signs and signals on the approach to a tunnel. Always use your dipped headlight in a tunnel, and if you are wearing sunglasses stop and remove them before you enter it.

Leave a generous separation distance from the vehicle in front, especially if you have to stop in a tunnel in congested traffic. Follow any instructions given on variable message signs.

Breaking down in a tunnel can be particularly hazardous. If you break down in a tunnel, switch off the engine, put on your hazard warning lights (if fitted) and telephone for help.

If fire breaks out and you cannot continue out of the tunnel, pull over, switch offf the engine and put the bike on its stand. Try to extinguish the fire with your own extinguisher or an emergency fire extinguisher situated in the tunnel, but if you cannot put it out or in the case of a serious fire developing, make your way to the nearest emergency exit and safety.

roadworks

Roadworks are an occupational hazard for any road user, and the delays they cause can be frustrating. For safety's sake, stay calm and follow all signs to the letter. You may have to merge with other traffic where lanes are closed off, follow a deviation over an uneven temporary road surface, and give way to workmen and machinery crossing in front of you. Take particular care on motorway contraflows.

WHEN RED LIGHT SHOWS WAIT HERE

WN54 ZRC

roadwork precautions

- take care when you see a 'roadworks ahead' sign, and look out for more signs
- temporary speed limits posted at roadworks are mandatory and you must obey them, even if there is no work taking place
- if one or more lanes are closed, carry out the observation–signal–manoeuvre routine and get into the correct lane in good time. Leave plenty of space and be alert for vehicles cutting across at the last moment
- when queuing in lines of traffic, obey merge-in-turn signs where posted
- use the hard shoulder if signs direct you
- be prepared to stop where traffic at roadworks is controlled by a stop-go board, a police officer or temporary traffic lights. At roadworks with temporary traffic lights, you must obey the lights even if the road ahead appears to be clear
- do not enter areas cordoned off by cones
- try not to be distracted by work going on around you, but be prepared to give way to works vehicles or staff
- slow down for ramps, rough road surfaces or loose chippings
- at the end of motorway roadworks there may be a national speed limit sign or an end of roadworks sign: both indicate that the speed limit has returned to 70mph
- where the pavement is closed due to street repairs, look out for pedestrians walking in the road.

contraflows

On motorway contraflows vehicles from both directions share the same carriageway. Lanes are separated by temporary red and white marker posts, and may be narrower than usual. You may need to select a lane some way in advance if you intend leaving at the next junction. Make sure you:

- reduce speed in good time and obey any speed limit signposted
- get into an appropriate lane early
- keep a generous separation distance.

vital signs

roadworks | manually operated temporary stop and go signs

roadworks one mile ahead | lane restrictions at roadworks ahead

temporary lane closure | one lane crossover at contraflow roadworks

Mandatory reduced speed limit ahead | end of roadworks and any temporary restrictions

When minor roadworks are carried out on motorways and dual carriageways these signs may be shown on the back of a slow-moving or stationary works vehicle blocking a traffic lane. The four amber lamps flash in alternate horizontal pairs. Pass the vehicle in the direction shown by the arrow. Where a lane is closed there will be no cones to separate it off

parking

When you need to park your motorcycle you must make sure you find a safe and legal place. Parking regulations can be complicated, so if you plan to leave your bike check road markings and signs to make sure that it is permitted. Sadly, motorcycles are a popular target for thieves, so invest in an effective security device and make sure you use it every time you leave your bike.

where to park

When looking for somewhere to leave your motorbike, try to use a secure off-street parking site. If you have to park in the street use a marked parking bay wherever possible. When parking on the road, always dismount on your nearside, away from passing traffic. Do not park on the pavement unless there are signs which specifically permit this.

You must by law switch off the engine and headlight (and foglight if fitted) when leaving your bike on the roadside, even just for a couple of minutes.

parking at night

When leaving your motorbike at night, remember the following rules:

- ◯ you are not allowed to leave your motorbike facing against the direction of traffic flow on a road at night
- ◯ motorbikes must display parking lights when parked on a road (or a lay-by on a road) with a speed limit over 30mph
- ◯ motorbikes may be parked without lights on a road (or a lay-by on a road) with a speed limit of 30mph or less as long as they are at least ten metres away from any junction, close to the kerb and facing in the direction of the traffic flow, or in a recognised parking place or lay-by
- ◯ trailers must not be left on a road at night without lights.

signs and markings

Whenever you park your motorbike, check signs and road markings to ensure you are legally entitled to do so.

On a clearway you may not stop at any time. On an urban clearway, you may stop only to set down or pick up a passenger.

Double yellow lines along the edge of the road mean no waiting at any time (although in places such as seaside towns this restriction may be eased out of season). A single yellow line indicates no waiting during the times shown on the nearby yellow plate. If no days are shown on the plate, then the restrictions are in force every day including Sundays and bank holidays.

You may stop on yellow lines for a short time to load and unload, or to let a passenger on and off, unless yellow lines on the kerb and accompanying black and white plates indicate that no loading is allowed.

Red routes have been introduced in some cities to improve the traffic flow. These have red lines in place of yellow lines along the side of the road. You must not stop even to unload or drop off passengers on a red route except in marked bays or at the times indicated by accompanying signs.

disabled parking

Disabled parking spaces are reserved for disabled motorists displaying the blue or orange disabled badge. Leave extra space if you park next to a car displaying a disabled badge. The driver may need room to get a wheelchair alongside the car.

it's the law

no parking

It is illegal to stop or park on:

- → the carriageway or hard shoulder of a motorway (except in an emergency)
- → a pedestrian crossing (including the area marked by zig-zag lines)
- → a clearway
- → an urban clearway, or a bus stop clearway within its hours of operation (except to pick up or set down passengers)
- → a road marked with centre double white lines (except to pick up or set down passengers)
- → a bus, tram or cycle lane during its hours of operation
- → a cycle track
- → red routes, unless otherwise indicated by signs
- → school entrance markings.

parking hazards

Parking areas are full of hazards such as manoeuvring vehicles, pedestrians walking to and from their cars and excited children running around. The golden rule is to ride dead slow. Observe what is going on all around and look out for children running out from between parked cars. Show courtesy when parking – don't leave your bike so close to another vehicle that it will be difficult for its driver or passengers to get in or out.

beat the bike thief

A motorcycle is vulnerable to theft: even if it can't be started, the determined thief can haul it into a van and make off with it. To keep your bike safe:

- if you have a garage always keep your bike locked inside it overnight
- if you don't have a garage, park your bike where a thief would draw attention to himself. Leave it under a lamp post on the main road and not in a dark side street where the thief could work uninterrupted
- lock your bike and remove the key, even if you are leaving it for just a few seconds outside your home or at a petrol station

- always ensure the steering column lock is engaged by twisting the handlebar until it clicks
- fit an additional lock whenever you leave your bike. There are locks available that fit on the front brake disc or forks to immobilise the front wheel, but these won't stop a determined thief lifting your bike into a van. A better option is a lock and chain that can be used to fasten your bike to an immovable object. Be sure to take out any slack so the chain doesn't rest on the ground where it could be attacked with a hammer, and don't thread it through a removable part of your bike. Stow the lock and chain safely when not in use – never ride with it carried around your waist or shoulder
- choose a model of motorbike that has an engine immobiliser and alarm, and make sure they are always activated when leaving your bike
- look after your motorbike keys. Don't leave them near the front door at night where they are vulnerable to theft by an intruder.

Take extra care in car parks: ride very slowly and look out for cyclists, pedestrians and children

Get a lock and chain and use it to secure your motorbike whenever you leave it parked

vital signs

no stopping
(clearway)

no waiting

no stopping at times shown
(except to set down or pick up
passengers)

controlled
parking zone
(pay at meter at
times shown)

end of
controlled
parking zone

distance to
parking place
ahead

vehicles may
park fully on
the verge or
footway

parking place
for solo
motorbikes

parking
restricted to
permit holders

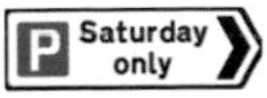

direction
to parking
place

direction to
park and ride
site

No loading at
any time

no loading at
times shown

no waiting
at any time

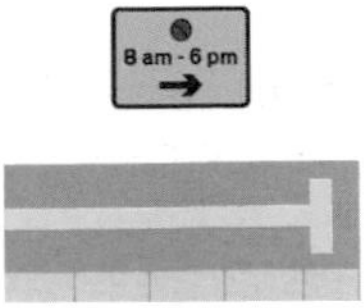

no waiting at times
shown

loading allowed only
at times shown

parking limited as
indicated by sign

no stopping
at any time

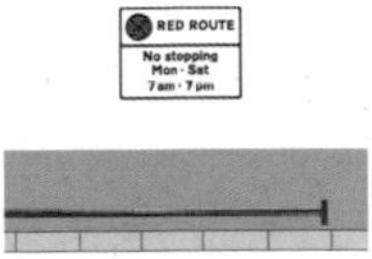

no stopping
at times shown

waiting limited as
indicated by sign

loading bay

parking space reserved
for vehicles named

141

8 road sense

Every second you are riding your motorbike, you need to concentrate one hundred per cent. Not only do you need to observe what is happening on the road all around you, you need to think hard about what you're seeing, identifying hazards and assessing what sort of risk they represent. That way you will be able to anticipate dangers before they happen, instead of reacting to them at the last moment. You must also watch your speed on the road: speeding is both illegal and responsible for many serious road accidents involving motorcyclists.

hazard perception

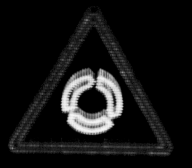

SLOW DOWN

One reason why inexperienced riders have a higher accident rate is that they take more time to recognise a hazard as it is developing on the road ahead. Hazard perception is tested in a special video-clip based exam that forms part of the theory test. Get into the habit of trying to identify potential hazards as you ride and ask yourself what action you need to take to deal with them safely.

what is a hazard?

A hazard is simply any potential danger you encounter on the road which may cause you to change your speed or direction.

There are three types of hazard:

static hazards

These are stationary features such as bends, junctions, traffic lights and crossings. They are the easiest type of hazard to recognise, as they do not change as you approach them, but you often have to deal with them while concentrating on what other road users – such as pedestrians using a zebra crossing – are doing as well

moving hazards

These may be pedestrians, cyclists, animals, horse riders, cars and large vehicles as well as other motorcyclists. Each type of road user is likely to react differently to situations on the road, and you need to understand why this is in order to anticipate how they are likely to react and share the road safely with them

road and weather hazards

Rain, ice or snow, mud or loose gravel on the road all make it more likely that harsh steering, braking or acceleration will cause a skid. Bright sunshine can dazzle you, and darkness makes it harder to spot hazards. Fog dangerously reduces visibility and high winds are especially hazardous to motorcyclists as well as cyclists and high-sided vehicles.

prioritising hazards

Hazards on the road don't come neatly one at a time. It's important to assess how serious each hazard is so you can decide which one takes priority. For instance, a parked car on a wide road with no oncoming traffic is a minor hazard. But if you spot that there is a driver sitting in the car and exhaust fumes show that the engine is running, then it becomes a more serious hazard, and you must anticipate that the driver might pull out in front of you.

The sooner you recognise a hazard, the sooner you are able to take the action needed to negotiate it safely. If ever you have to take emergency action to avoid a collision on the road, ask yourself whether you could have recognised and anticipated the hazard earlier, and what steps could you take to avoid the same thing happening again in the future.

observation

Effective observation is a vital skill that you need to develop. You can only react to hazards that you see, and the sooner you see a hazard, the more time you will be able to give yourself to deal with it safely.

looking or seeing?

If you let your attention wander you may find you are looking at hazards without really seeing them. It is surprisingly easy to ride straight past a road sign without taking in what it means. It's important to train your sense of observation so you really are seeing and thinking about everything on the road around you.

scanning

Keep your eyes moving, so you are seeing what is happening in all directions. Scan to the left and right of the road, then shift the focus of your eyes into the far distance. By looking well ahead of the vehicle in front you can see any hazards that it may have to react to, and anticipate in advance when you will need to slow down. Don't wait till you see the brake lights of the vehicle in front come on before starting to take action.

Keep your eyes constantly moving and shifting focus from the foreground into the far distance

Use effective rear observation so you are aware at all times of what is happening behind you too. Check your mirrors whenever you encounter a hazard, as you need to judge how your response to it will affect the traffic behind you.

improve your view

- ⊘ following closely behind the vehicle in front drastically reduces your view. Keep well back, especially when following a large vehicle, so you can see past it
- ⊘ scan to your left and right as you approach a crossroads or roundabout to see if you can spot other vehicles which will arrive there at the same time you do
- ⊘ look at rows of trees or lamp posts along the road ahead to see if they curve to indicate a bend in the road
- ⊘ look underneath parked cars to spot the feet of pedestrians who may be about to cross the road
- ⊘ don't rely just on your eyes. In fog or where high hedges or walls obscure a junction, listen for the sound of approaching vehicles.

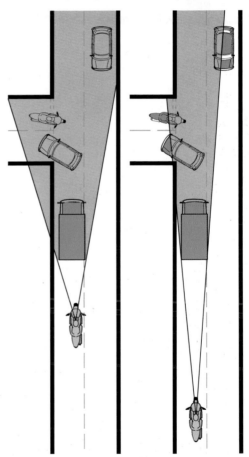

Keeping well back from the vehicle in front can dramatically improve your view and give you earlier warning of any hazards ahead

anticipation

Some people think that a good rider is one who has the quick reactions to get out of trouble. This isn't true. The good rider is the one who anticipates trouble and avoids getting into it in the first place. Constantly ask yourself 'what if?' as you drive along the road. What if that pedestrian walks onto the zebra crossing? What if that taxi does a U-turn? What if that driver waiting to pull out hasn't seen me? If you always anticipate the worst that may happen, you won't be taken unawares when it does.

anticipating hazards

Hazards on the road come in all sorts, shapes and sizes. The situations pictured opposite illustrate the sort of questions you need to ask yourself in order to anticipate what hazards might develop on the road ahead.

Approaching a pedestrian crossing
Scan the pavements on either side of the road and ask yourself whether any pedestrians may be about to use the crossing ahead

Approaching a busy junction
Ask yourself if the drivers waiting to join the road ahead of you have seen you. Slow down and be prepared to stop if one pulls out

Approaching a school entrance
Extra care is needed at school opening and closing hours in term time. Ask yourself if there are likely to be children about whenever you approach a school

Car following slow truck on motorway
Ask yourself if the driver is likely to pull out in front of you in order to overtake the slow truck, with or without giving a signal beforehand

Stationary vehicle on hard shoulder
Ask yourself whether this vehicle may start to move out without warning, or if the driver may open the door and jump out without looking. This situation needs particular care as most of your attention is focused on joining the motorway

vital signs

stationary traffic is likely ahead (always make sure that you can stop in the distance you can see to be clear)

danger ahead

REDUCE SPEED NOW

reduce speed warning shown beneath some signs

concentration

Riding is a serious business. If you walk along a footpath not concentrating on where you're stepping, you may trip on a fallen branch and stub your toe. It's irritating but no disaster. But if you're riding along daydreaming about your next holiday, and you fail to anticipate a car pulling out in front of you, then the outcome could be devastating.

staying alert

To maintain your concentration:

○ never ride when you are feeling distracted or emotional. Delay setting out until you have calmed down, or take a cab instead

○ keep your eyes on the road. At 70mph you are travelling over 30 metres (100ft) every second – so if you glance away for just three seconds, you have covered nearly 100 metres (330ft) without looking where you are going

○ if you need to consult a map, find a safe place to pull over. Never try to read a map and ride at the same time

○ if you need to use a mobile phone, stop and park in a safe place first

○ don't ride when you are tired or unwell – even a cold can seriously impair your ability to concentrate

○ never ride when under the influence of alcohol or drugs.

fatigue

Tiredness is a major cause of death on the road. Don't start a journey if you are already feeling tired. Monotonous roads, such as motorways, can increase boredom and make it harder to concentrate. If you start to feel drowsy and lose concentration you should:

○ pull over as soon as you can into a lay-by or service area (but not the hard shoulder of a motorway) and take a break

○ have a drink high in caffeine, such as two cups of strong coffee.

You can reduce the risk of becoming seriously sleepy while you are riding by:

○ avoiding long journeys during your body's natural sleep periods (the early hours of the morning and just after lunch)

○ taking regular breaks during a long journey. Stop for at least 15 minutes for every two hours you are on the road

○ not riding a long distance after a poor or interrupted night's sleep.

warm and dry

You'll start to lose concentration if you get cold or wet. Always wear adequate clothing for the prevailing conditions and be prepared to meet bad weather on your journey.

Noise can also affect your concentration. Wearing ear plugs to reduce sound levels is a good idea, both to help you concentrate better and to prevent your hearing from being damaged.

Getting cold and wet can badly affect your ability to concentrate, so always wear appropriate clothing

Take regular breaks when riding long distances to avoid getting tired and losing concentration

151

Most motorbikes are capable of rapid acceleration which can quickly take you above the speed limit. Many could easily double the maximum speed permitted on the motorway. With so much power on tap it takes discipline to keep your speed under control. But using speed safely is one of the most vital riding skills. The stark truth is that if you have to stop in an emergency and you are riding too quickly then you will crash. The higher your speed, the more serious that crash will be.

speed limits

You must always keep your speed below the maximum speed limit for the road and vehicle you are driving. These general rules govern speed limits for motorcycles:

- ➲ the national speed limit on single carriageway roads is 60mph
- ➲ the national speed limit on dual carriageways and motorways is 70mph
- ➲ the speed limit on roads with street lighting is 30mph.

These speed limits apply at all times unless signs indicate otherwise. There will not necessarily be repeater signs to remind you that one of these speed limits is in force.

These limits are overridden if there are signs which indicate a different speed limit, such as 50mph on a dual carriageway. Some stretches of motorway have variable speed limits, which allow a lower speed limit to be set during congested periods to smooth traffic flow and prevent vehicles bunching.

Where different speed limits apply there will be regular speed limit repeater signs placed along the road.

safe speeds

Speed limits represent the maximum speed permitted. They are not targets to be achieved at all costs. There are many occasions where it is not safe to ride as fast as the speed limit. For instance, when riding past children running along the pavement, or where parked cars obscure your vision on either side, 30mph could be recklessly fast.

national speed limits

Type of vehicle	Built-up area	Single carriageway	Dual carriageway	Motorway
Cars & motorcycles	30	60	70	70
Cars & motorcycles towing a trailer	30	50	60	60
Buses & coaches	30	50	60	70
Goods vehicles * 60 if articulated or towing a trailer	30	50	60	70 *
Goods vehicles (exceeding 7.5 tonnes maximum laden weight)	30	40	50	60

In busy town centres (above) or on narrow country lanes (below) you may need to keep your speed well below the speed limit to stay safe

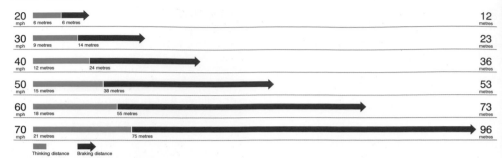

20 mph	6 metres · 6 metres	12 metres
30 mph	9 metres · 14 metres	23 metres
40 mph	12 metres · 24 metres	36 metres
50 mph	15 metres · 38 metres	53 metres
60 mph	18 metres · 55 metres	73 metres
70 mph	21 metres · 75 metres	96 metres

Thinking distance Braking distance

stopping distances

The diagram above gives typical stopping distances from varying speeds. There are a number of important points to bear in mind when you are considering these stopping distances:

- ⊙ it takes a long way to come to a complete halt even from a low speed – 23m is needed from just 30mph
- ⊙ it takes time to react and put on the brakes before you even start to slow down. At 40mph you will travel 12m during the time it takes you to react. This assumes that it takes you about 0.7 seconds to react before braking, a time that could easily treble if you aren't concentrating
- ⊙ stopping distance doesn't increase uniformly with speed: double your speed from 30mph to 60mph, and you need not twice but three times the distance in which to stop
- ⊙ these are stopping distances on a dry road in good weather: in the wet, allow twice the distance to stop; on icy roads, ten times further may be needed
- ⊙ a motorbike with worn brakes or tyres may take much further to stop, particularly on a wet road, even if the tyre tread depth is still above the legal minimum
- ⊙ if you are carrying a load, or a pillion passenger, or have a sidecar, the extra weight will increase your stopping distances

- ⊙ don't expect your bike to brake as effectively as the car you're following. This is partly down to physics – four wheels give more braking grip than two – and partly because the car is likely to be fitted with anti-lock brakes which can be more effective in an emergency than the non-ABS brakes fitted to most bikes
- ⊙ always remember the rule which cannot be repeated too often: you must always be able to stop in the distance you can see to be clear.

how fast?

Sometimes your senses can trick you into thinking you are riding more slowly than you really are. A speed of 40mph feels much slower on an open road than it does through an avenue of trees, because the objects flashing past on the edge of your vision give you a sensation of speed. This means it is particularly difficult to judge your speed when the reference points around you are obscured, for instance at night or in foggy weather.

Take particular care to monitor your speed at times when you may feel you are going more slowly than you really are, such as:

- ⊙ at night or in poor visibility
- ⊙ on long, open stretches of road, especially motorways
- ⊙ when you enter a speed limit after a spell of fast riding on the open road
- ⊙ when riding an unusual motorbike, particularly if it is quieter and more powerful than the one you are used to.

Don't race up to hazards and brake at the last moment: anticipate them and lose speed smoothly

It's good riding to make progress when it is safe to do so, but you must stay within the speed limit

minimum speed limits

Minimum speed limits aren't common, but are sometimes posted on roads where it is important to keep traffic flowing smoothly.

acceleration sense

Never accelerate towards a hazard. If you spot brake lights coming on ahead, or see advance warning for a give way sign, ease off the throttle. The sooner you start to lose speed as you approach a hazard, the more time you give yourself to deal with it. Accelerating up to a hazard and braking at the last moment also wastes fuel and causes unnecessary brake wear.

making progress

Speeding is bad for safety, but conversely you do need to make progress on the road, to keep traffic flowing and avoid holding up other road users. Where it is safe to ride at the indicated speed limit, then it is good practice to do just that.

other vehicles

Remember that other vehicles are not necessarily permitted to travel as quickly as you are. Make allowance for this and don't get frustrated when you are following, for instance, a car towing a caravan at 50mph on an A-road – it's going as fast as the law allows.

 **vital signs**

maximum speed limit

national speed limit applies

end of 20 mph zone

maximum speed limit within traffic calming scheme

minimum speed limit

end of minimum speed limit

area with traffic enforcement cameras

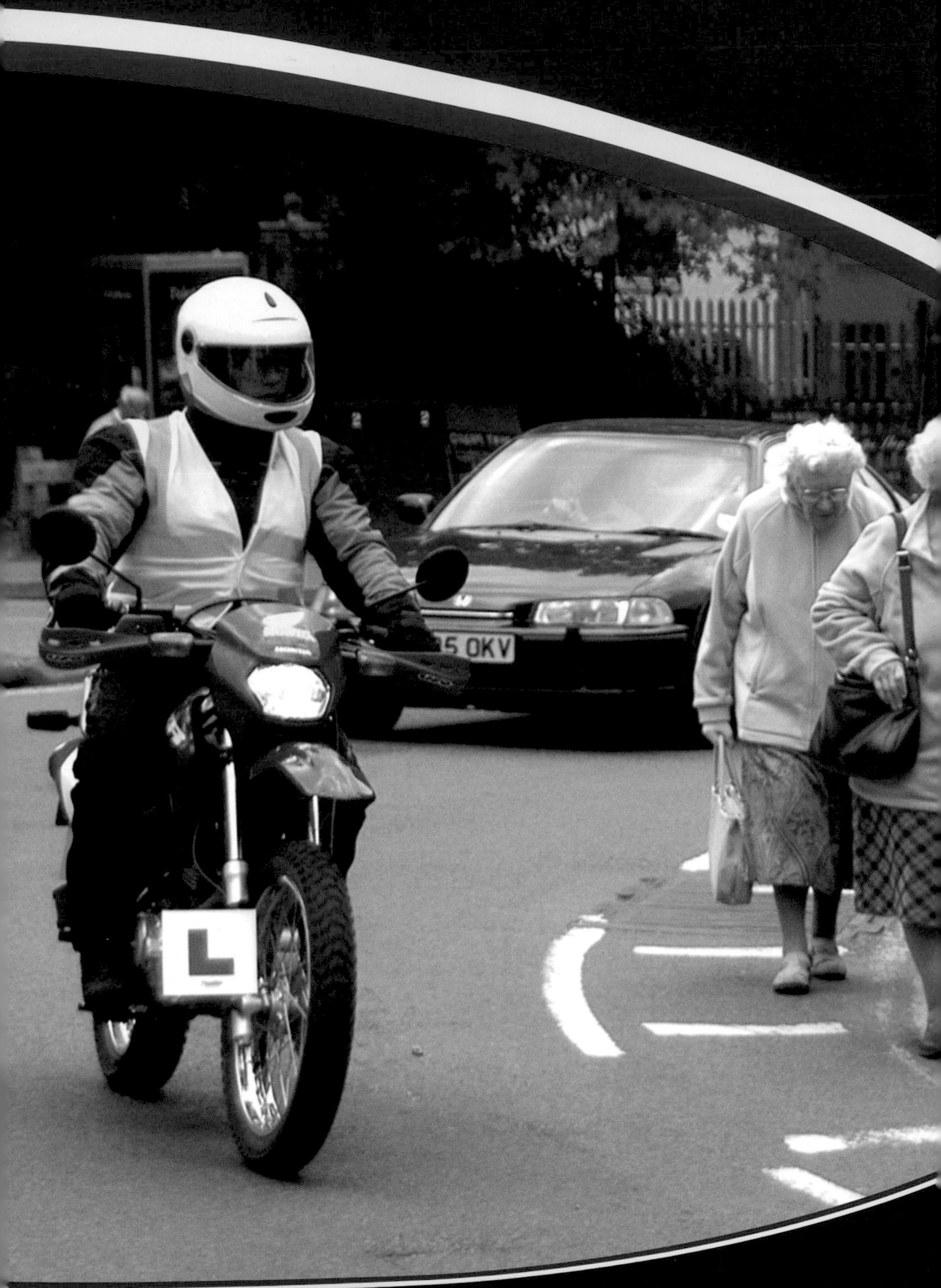

9 other road users

Other road users may view road conditions differently to you as a motorcyclist, and this can affect how they react. So try to put yourself in their position to anticipate what they are about to do. Are those pedestrians hurrying to get home through blinding rain likely to look as they cross the road? Will the cyclist swerve to avoid that broken drain cover? How will that nervous-looking horse react as you approach? You should never forget that your motorcycle is a potentially lethal weapon and it is your responsibility to look out for the safety of more vulnerable road users.

pedestrians

For a pedestrian a speeding motorbike is a potentially lethal missile. You simply cannot take risks where pedestrians are around. That means slowing down when there are people on the pavement and always being prepared to give way to pedestrians crossing the road.

vulnerable people

Take special care around pedestrians who may fail to be aware of your presence, such as:

○ the elderly, who can find it harder to judge the speed of an approaching bike

○ children, who may run into the road unexpectedly

○ blind and deaf pedestrians, who may be unaware of your approach. If a person is holding a white stick, or leading a guide dog on a harness, it means they are blind. If the white stick has a red band around it, they are deaf as well. There are guide dogs for the deaf too, and these usually wear a burgundy-coloured coat

○ wheelchair users. Be patient when a wheelchair user needs to cross the road, and don't obstruct them by parking your bike where the kerb is lowered to allow wheelchair access.

Look out for powered vehicles used by disabled people. These small vehicles travel at a maximum speed of 8mph. When used on a dual carriageway they must by law have a flashing amber light, but on other roads you may not be given any such warning of their presence

pedestrian crossings

Pedestrian crossings are points designed to allow pedestrians to cross the road in safety. Always be prepared to stop when approaching a crossing, and take special care if your view as you approach the crossing is obscured by queuing traffic or badly parked vehicles.

Treat pedestrians using a crossing courteously. Consider giving a slowing down arm signal as you approach to let waiting pedestrians know you are stopping, but do not beckon them to cross – this may be dangerous if other vehicles are approaching. Wait patiently while they are crossing, especially for elderly or disabled pedestrians who may not be able to get across before the lights change.

Never park your bike on a crossing or in the area marked by zig-zag lines. When approaching a crossing in a slow-moving queue, hold back so you do not stop where you would obstruct the crossing. It is illegal to overtake the moving vehicle nearest to a pedestrian crossing or a vehicle which has stopped to give way to pedestrians at the crossing.

Pedestrians don't always use crossings, so ride with extra care wherever there are people on foot

know the code

highway code rule 5

Organised walks Large groups of people walking together should use a pavement if available; if one is not, they should keep to the left. Look-outs should be positioned at the front and back of the group, and they should wear fluorescent clothes in daylight and reflective clothes in the dark. At night, the look-out in front should show a white light and the one at the back a red light. People on the outside of large groups should also carry lights and wear reflective clothing.

Approach zebra crossings with caution and be prepared to stop and give way to pedestrians

zebra crossings

Be ready to slow down or stop as you approach a zebra crossing. You must by law give way when someone has stepped on to a crossing, but you should also be prepared to stop and let waiting pedestrians cross. Scan the pavements as you approach for anyone who looks like they might want to cross and slow down well before you get to the crossing. If a pedestrian does not cross immediately, be patient and remain stationary until they do. Be prepared for pedestrians to change their mind halfway across and walk back in front of you.

Where the zebra crossing is divided by a central island you should treat each half as a separate crossing.

pelican crossings

Pelican crossings are controlled by lights. Unlike normal traffic lights, these have a flashing amber phase in between red and green. When the amber light is flashing, you must give way to pedestrians who are on the crossing. If there are no pedestrians on the crossing when the amber light is flashing, you may proceed across it with caution. If pedestrians are still crossing after the lights have changed to green you should continue to give way to them.

Pelican crossings which go straight across the road are one crossing, even when there is a central island. This means you must wait for pedestrians who are crossing from the other side of the island. However, if the crossings are staggered on either side of the central island they should be treated as separate crossings.

Pelican crossings (above), toucan crossings and puffin crossings are all controlled by traffic lights

Take care around children: you must by law obey the signals given by a school crossing patrol

toucan crossings

Cyclists as well as pedestrians are permitted to use a toucan crossing. They are operated by push buttons and follow the normal traffic light sequence, with no flashing amber phase. Take care when preparing to move off when the lights turn green, in case a pedestrian has left it late to cross or an elderly person is crossing slowly.

school crossings

You must stop when a school crossing patrol shows a stop for children sign. Always be courteous to school crossing patrols.

There may be a flashing amber signal below a school crossing sign as a warning at times that children are crossing the road ahead. Ride very slowly until you are clear of the area. Be cautious also when passing a stationary bus showing a school bus sign. You may have to give way to children running across the road to and from the bus.

puffin crossings

These have automatic sensors which detect when pedestrians are on the crossing and delay the green light until they have safely reached the other side. Like the toucan crossing, puffins have a normal traffic light sequence with no flashing amber.

vital signs

pedestrian crossing

elderly people (or blind or disabled as shown) crossing road

STOP

stop at school crossing patrol

Patrol

school crossing patrol ahead

No footway for 400 yds

no footway (there may be pedestrians walking in the road)

horse riders

Horses are easily alarmed and unpredictable.
When you encounter a horse rider on the
road, slow right down and be prepared to
stop. Don't become irritated with horse
riders for slowing your journey – they aren't
riding on the road for the fun of it, but usually
have no other option to get to and from local
bridleways.

passing horses

Treat all horses as a potential hazard. Slow to a walking pace as you approach a horse rider and give them plenty of space. Be prepared to stop and wait if other vehicles are approaching, as you will need to move well onto the other side of the road to pass a horse rider. Never try to squeeze by when a vehicle is coming the other way. Remember that horses are easily startled and may shy into the middle of the road if surprised by something – even just a rustling crisp packet – in the hedge.

Slow right down when passing horse riders and always leave them plenty of space

avoid noise

The extra noise of a motorbike can alarm horses, so don't rev your engine or accelerate harshly in their vicinity. Never sound your horn while approaching a horse. If the horse looks skittish, stop and turn off your engine until it has gone by.

Caution is also needed in wet weather when your tyres make more noise, and you need to avoid startling the horse by splashing it with spray.

inexperienced riders

Be particularly careful when horses are being ridden by children, or where there is a line of inexperienced riders. Riders may be in double file when escorting a young or inexperienced horse rider. Look out for signals from horse riders, and always heed a request to slow down or stop.

Take special care when you encounter horse riders who may be young or inexperienced

right turns

Take care when following a horse and rider at the approach to a right-hand turn or roundabout. The rider may signal right but stay on the left of the road at the approach to the turn, so slow down and be prepared to stop and wait to let the rider cross the road in front of you and make the right turn.

know the code

highway code rule 215

Horse riders and horse-drawn vehicles. Be particularly careful of horse riders and horse-drawn vehicles especially when overtaking. Always pass wide and slowly. Horse riders are often children, so take extra care and remember riders may ride in double file when escorting a young or inexperienced horse or rider. Look out for horse riders' and horse drivers' signals and heed a request to slow down or stop. Take great care and treat all horses as a potential hazard; they can be unpredictable, despite the efforts of their rider/driver.

animals

Animals – both wild and domestic – are unpredictable and represent a serious hazard when they stray onto the road. Observe signs warning of animals, and keep your speed down, especially where there are no fences to keep cattle, sheep or ponies off the road.

domestic animals

In country areas, especially moorland, there may be no fences keeping cattle, sheep and horses from straying onto the road. Exercise great caution in these areas and keep your speed down, especially at night or in misty conditions. Where there are animals on or near the road, ride past them at a walking pace. Do not sound your horn, flash your lights, or rev your engine loudly as this may cause them to panic. Bear in mind that if an animal such as a sheep crosses the road in front of you then several others may follow it, and that young animals will run to their mother if they feel threatened, even if that means darting in front of you.

Sometimes sheep or cattle have to be led across the road. If your way is blocked by a herd of animals, stop, switch off your engine and wait until they have left the road.

wild animals

Colliding with a large wild animal like a deer could be potentially life threatening both to it and you. Keep your speed down wherever there is likely to be wildlife near the road, and slow down when you see warning signs. Take special care at dawn and dusk when deer are most active.

Cattle grids are often placed at the entrance to areas of open country: vehicles can cross them but cattle cannot. Slow right down when riding across a grid as they can be loose and the metal will be slippery when wet

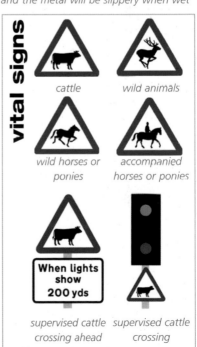

vital signs

cattle

wild animals

wild horses or ponies

accompanied horses or ponies

When lights show 200 yds

supervised cattle crossing ahead

supervised cattle crossing

cyclists

If you have ever cycled on a busy road you'll know how intimidating it is when vehicles speed by leaving only a couple of feet to spare. Cyclists have every much right to use the road as motorcyclists, so treat them with courtesy, and be conscious of their extra vulnerability.

overtaking cyclists

Leave as much room when overtaking a cyclist as you would when overtaking a car. Remember that a cyclist may swerve to avoid something you may not see, such as a pothole or rubbish in the road. Never try to squeeze past a cyclist when another vehicle is coming towards you, and slow right down when passing a cyclist on a narrow road.

Be prepared for cyclists to do the unexpected. Although most cyclists are responsible road users, remember that no training is needed to ride a bicycle and riders of any age are allowed to use the road. Situations where you should be particularly alert for cyclists include:

Always take care when approaching cyclists and leave plenty of space when overtaking them

◉ **slow-moving traffic**
Cyclists may try to filter through narrow gaps where even motorcyclists have to queue, so when moving slowly in traffic check your nearside mirror before pulling into the kerb or turning left

◉ **junctions and roundabouts**
Cyclists can find it daunting to pull across the road to turn right in busy traffic, and may feel safer keeping to the left when turning right at a roundabout. Be cautious whenever you see a cyclist looking over their shoulder as they could be about to turn right. Give them time and space to do so safely

◉ **left turns**
Never overtake a cyclist just before a left turn so you have to cut in front to make the turn. Slow down and hold back until the cyclist has passed the turning

◉ **country lanes**
In rural areas you may encounter slow-moving cyclists around any bend

◉ **at night or dusk**
Cyclists may not be showing lights, or their lights may be hard to spot among other vehicle lights

◉ **windy weather**
In strong winds cyclists may find it hard to keep a straight course and you should leave more space when overtaking.

vital signs

cycle route ahead

no cycling

route for cycles only

route for pedestrians and cyclists

recommended route for cycles

with-flow cycle lane

know the code

highway code rule 140

Cycle lanes These are shown by road markings and signs. You MUST NOT drive or park in a cycle lane marked by a solid white line during its times of operation. Do not drive or park in a cycle lane marked by a broken white line unless it is unavoidable. You MUST NOT park in any cycle lane whilst waiting restrictions apply.

large vehicles

Drivers of large articulated vehicles demonstrate some impressive skills as they thread their vehicles through narrow streets and reverse into tight spaces. But LGV drivers can't work miracles, and there are times when they need extra space and consideration from other road users.

caution needed

Situations where you need to take extra care around large vehicles include:

- ○ **left turns**: a long vehicle may need to pull onto the right side of the road to be able to make a sharp left turn without cutting the corner. Don't overtake until it has completed the manoeuvre
- ○ **roundabouts**: a long vehicle may not be able to keep entirely inside its own lane markings on a tight roundabout. Don't pull alongside it or you may get squashed
- ○ **low bridges**: a high lorry or bus may have to pull into the middle of the road to squeeze under a low bridge. Slow down and be prepared to stop at a bridge with a height restriction
- ○ **overtaking**: it can be difficult to see past large vehicles to overtake. Keep well back to improve your view, and look down the nearside of the vehicle as well as the offside. Remember you will need extra space to overtake a long vehicle. Be cautious about overtaking a truck after it crests a hill – it may pick up speed quickly as it starts heading downhill
- ○ **blind spots**: you may be hidden in the driver's blind spot while riding past a truck or coach, particularly if it's a left-hand drive vehicle. Remember – if you cannot see the driver's eyes in their offside mirror, they cannot see you. Don't linger in this blind spot: get past trucks on multi-lane roads briskly. You will also be hidden from the driver's view if you get too close behind a large vehicle, so always maintain a generous separation distance
- ○ **bad weather**: in the wet take care to avoid being blinded by spray thrown up by large vehicles. Be careful when passing high vehicles in windy weather as wind gusting around them may cause your bike to wobble alarmingly.

vital signs

no goods vehicles over maximum weight shown in tonnes

risk of grounding

markers displayed on a vehicle with an overhanging load

low bridge – beware of oncoming high vehicles in middle of road

vehicles more than 13 metres long must display these warnings to the rear. The vertical markings are also required to be fitted to builders' skips left in the road

know the code

highway code rule 221

Large vehicles. These may need extra road space to turn or to deal with a hazard that you are not able to see. If you are following a large vehicle, such as a bus or articulated lorry, be aware that the driver may not be able to see you in the mirrors. Be prepared to stop and wait if it needs room or time to turn.

buses

One thing you know for certain when you are following a bus is that it's soon going to stop to let down or pick up passengers. Keep well back so when the bus does pull in you are not held up behind it but are in a position to see beyond and overtake it if it is safe to do so.

bus stops

Exercise great care when passing a stationary bus as passengers getting on or off may walk into the road without checking for traffic. Take care even when a bus has stopped on the other side of the road: passengers may run across to it, and oncoming vehicles may pull onto your side of the road to overtake it.

As you approach a bus at a bus stop try to assess whether it is about to move off. If there is a long queue waiting, it will probably be stopped for a while; if no-one is queuing, it may have loaded its passengers and be ready to leave. Be ready to slow down and give way to a bus which indicates that it wants to pull out.

Take care and position your motorcycle towards the middle of the road when riding past a bus stop as oil deposits can make the road surface there slippery. Do not park at or near a bus stop.

bus lanes

These are special lanes at the side of the road which only buses (and taxis or cycles if indicated) are permitted to use. Check if there is a sign showing times of operation because the lane may be restricted to rush hours only; outside the times indicated, you are allowed to ride in the lane. Where there are no signs it means the lane is reserved for buses 24 hours a day.

In some areas, bus lanes may be used by motorcyclists if indicated on the sign.

If you have to turn across a bus or cycle lane to enter a side road or driveway, always give way to vehicles using it.

Slow down and give way when you see a bus at a bus stop with its right-hand indicator flashing

vital signs

school bus: take extreme care passing a stationary school bus as children may run from or towards it without looking

bus lane on road at junction ahead

with-flow bus and cycle lane

other vehicles may use this bus lane outside the times shown

no buses (over eight passenger seats)

bus lane road markings

bus stop road markings

buses and cycles only

contra-flow bus lane

other road users

trams

Trams or Light Rapid Transit (LRT) systems have been established in several cities. They are an environmentally efficient public transport system which runs on electricity and helps to reduce noise and traffic congestion in town. For a motorcyclist trams represent a special hazard: not only do you have to look out for the trams, which move quickly and quietly, and cannot steer to avoid you, but you also have to take care to avoid losing control on bumpy and slippery tram lines.

tram lanes

Do not enter a lane reserved for trams and indicated by white lines, yellow dots or a different colour or texture of road surface.

Always give way to trams and do not try to overtake a moving tram – wait until it is stationary at a tram stop. Take care where a tram track crosses from one side of the road to the other and where the road narrows and the tracks come close to the kerb. Where a tram line crosses the road, treat it in the same way as a railway level crossing.

Tram lines are a special hazard for cyclists and motorcyclists. They can be slippery when wet so where possible avoid riding on them and do not brake or steer as you cross them.

traffic signals

Tram drivers usually have their own traffic signals. These may give a different instruction to the signal for other road users, and a tram may be permitted to move when other vehicles are not. Diamond-shaped road signs give instructions to tram drivers only.

tram stops

Follow the route indicated by signs and road markings where the tram stops at a platform, either in the middle or at the side of the road. Do not ride between a tram and the left-hand kerb when it has stopped to pick up passengers at a stop with no platform. Look out for pedestrians, especially children, running to catch a tram which is at or approaching a stop.

vital signs

trams crossing ahead

give way to trams

route for trams only

speed limit for tram drivers

at traffic lights the right-hand signal gives instructions to tram drivers

stop   *proceed ahead*   *proceed left*   *proceed right*   *stop if safe*

Extra care is needed near a tramway, especially where trams are stopping or crossing the road

level crossings

Level crossings are situated where a railway line crosses the road. Trains approach them at high speed, which means accidents involving vehicles on a crossing are serious ones. Never take risks when approaching a level crossing, and make sure you do not get stranded on a level crossing when a train is approaching. Only ride onto a crossing if you can see the exit is clear on the other side, and never stop or park on or near the crossing.

controlled crossings

Most crossings have traffic light signals with a steady amber light, twin flashing red stop lights and an audible alarm for pedestrians. They may have full, half or no barriers. Never try to zig-zag around half-barriers or ride over a crossing without barriers when the lights show.

When a train approaches, the amber light will show, followed by the red lights. If the amber light comes on after you have passed the stop line you should keep going. Otherwise, stop and wait at the line. Turn off your engine as you may be waiting for a few minutes. If a train goes by and the red lights continue to flash, or the alarm changes tone, you must carry on waiting as this means another train is approaching. Only cross when the lights go out and the barriers open.

Some crossings do not have warning lights. In this case you should stop and wait at the barrier or gate when it begins to close, and wait until it opens again before crossing.

user-operated crossings

These crossings have stop signs and small red and green lights. Only cross if the green light is on, and wait when the red light shows. To cross, open the gates or barriers on both sides of the crossing, check that the green light is still on and ride quickly across. Then pull up well clear of the crossing, walk back and close the gates or barriers.

If there are no lights, stop, look both ways and listen before you cross. If there is a railway telephone, use it to contact the signal operator to make sure it is safe to cross. Inform the signal operator again when you are clear of the crossing.

open crossings

These require special care as they have no gates, barriers, attendant or traffic lights (but do have a give way sign). Look both ways, listen and make sure there is no train coming before crossing.

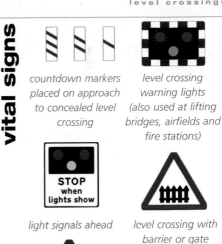

vital signs

countdown markers placed on approach to concealed level crossing

level crossing warning lights (also used at lifting bridges, airfields and fire stations)

light signals ahead

level crossing with barrier or gate

level crossing without barrier or gate

level crossing without barrier

accidents and breakdowns

If your motorcycle breaks down or you have an accident on a level crossing you should get yourself and any passengers or occupants of other vehicles clear of the crossing immediately.

If there is a railway telephone then use it to tell the operator what has happened. Follow any instructions you are given. If there is time before a train arrives then try to move your bike clear of the crossing. If the alarm sounds, or the amber light comes on, leave the bike and get clear of the crossing immediately.

emergency vehicles

It's easy to panic when you see an emergency vehicle bearing down on you with lights flashing and siren blaring. In this situation it's important to stay calm and do your best to help the driver of the emergency vehicle get past quickly and safely.

Stop in a safe place and give way when you see or hear an emergency vehicle approaching

warning lights

In an emergency, drivers of police, fire and ambulance vehicles are permitted to use flashing blue lights and sirens. They are also exempt from certain road regulations and may lawfully exceed the speed limit and drive through red traffic lights.

Certain other organisations, including mountain rescue, coastguard, mines rescue, bomb disposal, blood transfusion, lifeboat and medical transplant services are also permitted to drive under blue lights. A doctor answering an emergency call may display a flashing green beacon.

(A flashing amber beacon indicates a slow-moving vehicle.)

giving way

When you see an emergency vehicle it's important to keep your cool and not simply slam on the brakes. This will only make it more difficult for the driver to get by quickly. Look ahead and find a safe space where you can pull over, and signal clearly to let the driver of the emergency vehicle know what you are doing.

If you see an emergency vehicle coming from the other direction, pull over to make room for it to drive on your side of the road

if it needs to. If you are approaching a junction and can hear the emergency vehicle but are uncertain where it is coming from, hold back till you can see it.

Remember that several vehicles may attend the same emergency. Don't pull straight out after letting an emergency vehicle pass without checking there isn't another one following it.

stop – police

You must by law stop your motorbike if signalled to do so by a police officer. The officer will usually signal you to stop by flashing their vehicle headlights and indicating and pointing to the left. Stop in the first safe place you come to, then switch off your engine. Stay calm and courteous, listen carefully to what the officers have to say, and be prepared to produce your documents for inspection (see p192).

Vehicle & Operator Services Agency officers and Highways Agency traffic officers are also empowered to stop vehicles. They will direct you to pull over with flashing amber lights. It is an offence not to comply with their directions.

177

10 adverse conditions

Riding is easiest – and most enjoyable – in clear, bright weather on dry roads. Once night falls, or it starts to rain, or the thermometer drops below zero, the hazards start to multiply alarmingly. You need to slow down, concentrate harder and sharpen your anticipation skills to stay safe. Unlike a car driver you are exposed to the elements, and a cold, wet, miserable rider trying to get home as quickly as possible can make poor judgements that compromise safety. Recognise that in bad weather it can be best to avoid riding altogether. If you wake up to icy roads or torrential rain, ask yourself whether your journey is really worth risking an accident to accomplish, and stay at home instead until conditions improve. There's no shame in taking the course that many riders follow and restricting your motorcycling to the summer months, using alternative modes of transport in winter.

riding at night

Riding at night can feel strange and a little unnerving at first. Get your first experience of night riding in clear weather on quiet roads you know well. In busy traffic, drivers may find it hard to pick out your headlight from so many other distracting lights, so take extra care to check that drivers have seen you before crossing their path, and always wear reflective clothing at night.

night vision

On unlit roads at night, what you can see is limited to the range of your headlight. Reduce speed to compensate, and never ride so fast that you are unable to stop within the distance your headlight shows to be clear.

Keep your helmet visor spotlessly clean for night riding as smears and dirt can blur the lights of other vehicles. A scratched visor also causes dazzle at night, so replace yours as soon as it shows signs of deterioration. Never wear sunglasses, or use a tinted visor or goggles at night.

If you find riding at night particularly difficult this can be a sign that your eyesight needs checking, so see an optician.

using lights

By law you must use your headlight at night (except on town roads with a 30mph speed limit and street lighting) and whenever visibility falls below 100 metres (328ft). But because a motorbike is more easily overlooked than larger vehicles, it is strongly advisable to keep your dipped headlight lit at all times, even in bright daylight. Wear bright, clothing too, with reflective strips that show up at night.

Use the headlight's main beam setting whenever you ride on unlit roads at night. But remember that main beam will dazzle oncoming drivers, so dip your headlight when you see another vehicle approaching. Road users such as cyclists or pedestrians will also be dazzled by main beam so dip your headlight for them too.

Just before you dip your headlight look along the left-hand verge to check that there is nothing on the road ahead. Immediately the oncoming vehicle has passed, switch back to main beam. If there is a stream of traffic approaching you will need to leave your headlight dipped until the road clears.

Main beam headlights can cause discomfort for drivers in vehicles you are following, so switch to dipped beam when you approach a vehicle ahead.

overtaking at night

Exercise great caution when overtaking at night. Switch to main beam as soon as you have pulled past the vehicle you are overtaking so you get the maximum view of the road ahead. Beware of bends and dips in the road ahead which may hide an oncoming vehicle.

If another road user wants to overtake you, help them see the road ahead by keeping your headlight on main beam while they are preparing to overtake, and dip it only as the overtaking vehicle comes level with you.

avoiding dazzle

- don't stare at oncoming headlights, or you may be dazzled. Look slightly towards the left-hand side of the road. Slow down and if necessary stop if you cannot see
- anticipate when your vision may be reduced by oncoming lights. When a car approaches round a bend, slow down in advance if you think that you may be dazzled by its lights
- if an oncoming vehicle is blinding you with main beam headlights, give a short flash of main beam to remind the driver that they need to dip their lights. But never try to retaliate by leaving your light on main beam as this will leave both of you dangerously dazzled
- when you are carrying a pillion passsenger the altered weight distribution can cause your headlight beam to rise so it dazzles oncoming traffic even when dipped. If necessary adjust the headlight angle to compensate.

noise at night

Remember that people are trying to sleep at night so avoid revving your engine.

It is illegal to use your horn in a built-up area between 11.30pm and 7.00am, except in an emergency. Flash your headlight instead if you need to give a warning.

bad weather

Bad weather makes riding more difficult in many ways. Winter is a time to be especially cautious on the road, as it brings a number of hazards including icy roads, snow, fog, heavy rain and high winds. When bad weather threatens check the forecast before leaving and if possible postpone your journey until conditions improve.

riding in winter

Make sure you and your bike are prepared for wintry conditions before setting out. You need to:

- get your battery checked, especially if your bike has an electric starter
- inspect your tyres to ensure they have plenty of tread: to be sure of staying safe on winter roads you need at least double the legal 1.0mm minimum
- keep your headlight and indicators clean
- wear plenty of warm clothing under a proper weatherproof motorcycling suit
- use sunglasses or an approved tinted visor in bright weather, as during the winter the sun is low in the sky and is particularly likely to dazzle you.

In bad wintry conditions, if possible stay off the roads. If you do have to make a journey, keep to main roads which are more likely to be gritted to keep them free of ice. Remember that falling snow is likely to build up on your headlight and indicators and obscure them, so stop frequently to wipe them clear.

Be extremely cautious in freezing conditions. You need to slow right down, steer and brake very gently and leave a much greater stopping distance – up to ten times further than normal.

Be alert for ice forming on roads whenever you ride on a winter evening with clear skies. Look for signs of frost forming on verges or parked cars. Take special care where the road is exposed, such as on motorway bridges, because ice often forms here first.

Beware of rain falling in freezing conditions and forming black ice, which is particularly treacherous because it is invisible. If it is very cold and the road looks wet but you cannot hear the usual noise caused by tyres on a wet road, black ice may be the cause. Slow down, and keep in as high a gear as possible.

As the air temperature rises, look out for

Snow makes the roads extremely hazardous, so unless you have no choice postpone your journey and stay off your bike until conditions improve

areas where ice may linger, such as shady patches behind trees or buildings, and dips in the road where pockets of cold air settle.

highway code rule 230

When driving in icy or snowy weather:

- → drive with care, even if the roads have been treated
- → keep well back from the vehicle in front as stopping distances can be ten times greater than on dry roads
- → take care when overtaking vehicles spreading salt or other de-icer, particularly if you are riding a motorcycle or cycle
- → watch out for snowploughs which may throw out snow on either side. Do not overtake them unless the lane you intend to use has been cleared
- → be prepared for the road conditions changing over relatively short distances
- → listen to travel bulletins and take note of variable message signs that may provide information about weather, road and traffic conditions ahead

know the code

wet weather

Riding is more dangerous when it's raining for several reasons:

◯ reduced vision

Rain makes it more difficult to see, and other road users may find it harder to see you too. When the roads are wet the reflections from wet surfaces can make it harder to see unlit objects.

Your visor and goggles become obscured by raindrops, and they may mist up too. Carry a cloth and when necessary stop and use it. It's a good idea to use an anti-misting spray on your visor and also on your mirrors.

◯ slippery roads

Water on the road acts as a lubricant which reduces tyre grip, making it easier to skid and lose control. Emergency braking distances are increased in the wet, even if your bike has anti-lock brakes. On wet surfaces it's even more important than usual to anticipate the need to brake and make sure any braking is done while your bike is upright and moving in a straight line. Reduce your speed and increase your separation distance from the vehicle in front, leaving at least a four-second gap. Be careful when cornering, especially where the road surface is worn or greasy, such as on roundabouts. Be vigilant for hazards such as manhole covers and road markings, which become dangerously slippery when wet. Where possible steer around such

hazards and avoid taking a cornering line which will cause your tyres to pass over them. Look out for the rainbow film on the road which indicates a slippery patch of spilt diesel.

◯ spray

In wet weather vehicles send up spray from their tyres which can drastically reduce your vision. Keep well back from other vehicles, particularly large vehicles which can throw up huge quantities of spray, and take special care when overtaking.

◯ standing water

Aquaplaning can occur on standing water when tyres surf on the water and lose their grip. The higher your speed on a wet road, the more likely you are to aquaplane, so slow down in conditions where aquaplaning is likely. Try to anticipate where puddles of standing water are likely to form in dips in the road and slow down well in advance. If you feel your bike begin to aquaplane don't attempt to steer or brake as this could cause loss of control. Ease off the throttle, and as the bike loses speed the tyres will regain contact with the road surface. If you do experience aquaplaning, check your tyres as the better condition the treads are in, the more effectively they resist aquaplaning.

If your visor mists up while riding, stop as soon as possible and clean it with a soft cloth

vital signs

risk of ice   slippery road

Ride through a ford only if you are certain the water level is low enough to allow safe passage

◯ flooding

You may have to ride through water either where the road has flooded, or at a ford (where a river runs across the road). If possible, try to take a route which avoids any flooded roads, as riding through deep water can cause your engine to stall if water blocks the exhaust, and if water enters the engine it can cause serious damage.

Fords may be slippery and uneven with loose gravel. There may be a strong current which could throw you off balance. They may get much deeper than usual after heavy rain or in winter and become unsafe to cross. Never attempt to ride through water unless you are certain how deep it is. Watch another vehicle make the attempt first, or check the depth on the gauge located beside many fords. If the water is too deep, turn round and find another route.

When you ride through standing water, try to choose the shallowest route. This is usually the middle of the road, because the camber makes the edges slope away. Proceed slowly and steadily in a low gear and keep the engine revs high by slipping the clutch if necessary (this helps prevent water entering the exhaust).

Once out the other side, ride slowly while applying the brakes gently to make sure they are dry and working properly.

know the code

highway code rule 227

Wet weather In wet weather, stopping distances will be at least double those required for stopping on dry roads. This is because your tyres have less grip on the road. In wet weather

→ you should keep well back from the vehicle in front. This will increase your ability to see and plan ahead

→ if the steering becomes unresponsive, it probably means that water is preventing the tyres from gripping the road. Ease off the accelerator and slow down gradually

→ the rain and spray from vehicles may make it difficult to see and be seen

→ be aware of the dangers of spilt diesel that will make the surface very slippery

→ take extra care around pedestrians, cyclists, motorcyclists and horse riders.

Riding in fog is hazardous, so slow down and leave plenty of extra time to complete your journey

Be careful when riding with the sun low in the sky, as it can dazzle you and obscure other vehicles

fog

Fog is a major road hazard. Serious motorway pile-ups occur because road users go too fast and too close in foggy conditions. If you can avoid making your journey, stay off the road when it is foggy.

If you do have to ride in fog:

- ⊖ leave more time for your journey as you will have to reduce your speed
- ⊖ make sure your lights – including your foglight (if fitted) – are clean and working properly
- ⊖ check your visor or goggles are clean, and carry a cloth in case you need to demist them during the journey
- ⊖ use your dipped headlight, plus foglight (if fitted) when visibility falls below 100 metres (328 ft). Avoid using your headlight on main beam as the light reflecting back off the fog can make it harder to see. Don't leave a foglight switched on once visibility has improved – this is illegal, it makes your brake light less easy to see and it dazzles and annoys other road users

- ⊖ leave more space between the vehicle in front of you, and always make sure you can stop in the distance you can see to be clear. With all usual reference points obscured by thick fog it can be harder to gauge how quickly you're travelling, so keep an eye on your speedometer
- ⊖ don't overtake unless you can be absolutely sure nothing is coming
- ⊖ when waiting to emerge at a junction it can help to listen for the sound of approaching vehicles which may not be visible till the last moment. Use your brake light while stationary at the junction to give an extra warning to vehicles approaching from behind, and consider using your horn as a signal before pulling out
- ⊖ keep to the centre of your lane; riding along the central lane marking to find your way in thick fog is extremely dangerous; keeping to the gutter is also hazardous as you could suddenly encounter hazards such as pedestrians or a parked car
- ⊖ beware of other vehicles which may not have switched on their lights despite the reduced visibility

○ remember that in dense fog the reflective studs separating lanes on a motorway can help you tell which lane you are in:
red studs to left, white studs to right mean you are in the left-hand lane
white studs to both left and right mean you are in a middle lane
white studs to left, amber studs right mean you are in the right-hand lane
green studs to left mean you are passing a slip road

○ avoid parking your bike on the road on a foggy day. If you have to do this, then leave the parking lights on

○ be alert to the possibility of encountering unexpected fog patches. Slow down in conditions where fog might occur, and anticipate that fog may form on higher ground, or in valleys on cold winter mornings. Always slow down on the motorway when you see a fog warning sign, even if it is clear where you are.

high winds

Motorcycles are particularly vulnerable to windy conditions. Keep your speed down and take particular care where crosswinds may gust across the road, such as on exposed open sections of road, and as you pass gaps in fences, hedges or buildings. In windy weather expect to encounter fallen branches or even trees in the road.

Take care around other vehicles which are vulnerable to high winds, such as high-sided vehicles, caravans and trailers. Leave plenty of space when overtaking other motorcyclists and cyclists who could be blown in front of you by a fierce gust. Choose a sheltered place to pass high-sided vehicles, and as you pass anticipate that you may need to correct your steering to compensate for eddying wind currents.

hot weather

Although most bikers would agree that warm, sunny weather is best for motorcycling, it can bring its own problems. A full set of protective clothing can get uncomfortably warm in summer, but never be tempted to compromise your safety by riding with legs or arms uncovered or in skimpy footware.

Glare from the sun can make riding tiring and compromise your vision. Use an approved tinted visor, or sunglasses (if you need corrective lenses to ride, make sure your sunglasses are made up to match your prescription). Slow down or if necessary stop if you are dazzled by sunlight and cannot properly. When riding with the sun setting behind you, be aware that oncoming drivers may find it harder to see you, although from your perspective you can still see clearly. Use your dipped headlight to make yourself more visible.

When it's very hot the road surface becomes soft, reducing the grip of the tyres, so take extra care particularly when steering and braking.

Be cautious also when it rains after a period of dry weather: the water can combine with the film of grease, rubber and oil deposited on the road to make the road surface treacherous.

know the code
highway code rules 232-3

Windy weather High-sided vehicles are most affected by windy weather, but strong gusts can also blow a car, cyclist, motorcyclist or horse rider off course. This can happen on open stretches of road exposed to strong crosswinds, or when passing bridges or gaps in hedges.

In very windy weather your vehicle may be affected by turbulence created by large vehicles. Motorcyclists are particularly affected, so keep well back from them when they are overtaking a high-sided vehicle.

skidding

Skidding is more likely in bad weather, but it's important to understand that in the majority of cases when a motorbike skids the fundamental cause is bad riding. Most skids occur only because the bike is being ridden too fast for the conditions, or control is compromised by harsh steering, braking or acceleration. Ride smoothly and sensibly at all times and you will dramatically reduce your risk of experiencing a skid.

avoiding skids

Skids can be avoided by never asking your
bike to do more than it can with the grip
available from its tyres in the prevailing road
conditions. Skidding is more likely:
- in bad weather when roads are damp,
  flooded, icy or snow-covered
- on poor surfaces such as loose chippings
- where there are slippery features on the
  road such as road markings, tar banding
  and metal inspection covers
- if you have worn tyres

Wherever there is an increased risk of
skidding you must:
- slow down
- increase your stopping distance, so if the
  vehicle in front of you stops unexpectedly
  you have enough space to brake to a halt
  without skidding
- take extra care when approaching a bend
  which may be slippery
- be gentle and progressive when changing
  direction, accelerating and braking.

skidding when accelerating

If you accelerate too harshly when moving
off, especially on a slippery road, the rear
wheel will spin and the rear of the bike may
slide sideways. High-performance bikes may
skid at higher speeds if the throttle is opened
too abruptly.

To counteract a skid caused by harsh
acceleration, ease off the throttle and steer
in the same direction that the bike is sliding.
If you experience wheelspin on a slippery or
icy road, use a higher gear for moving off
and riding at low speed.

Traction control systems are becoming
more common on motorcycles. These detect
electronically when the rear wheel is starting
to spin and reduce the power going to
it. This reduces the risk of skidding under
acceleration. However, it is still best to use
the throttle smoothly to ensure that traction
control never needs to intervene.

skidding when braking

If you brake hard on a slippery surface the
wheels may lock up. Because of forward
weight transfer under braking, the rear
wheel has less grip and locks up more
readily. If you feel the rear wheel locking up,
release the brake pedal and reapply it more
gently and progressively.

If the front wheel locks up, keep a
firm grip on the handlebars, release the
brake lever and reapply it more gently and
progressively.

If your motorcycle has ABS fitted it
will prevent the wheels locking up under
braking (see p59). But even ABS can't
work miracles on greasy or icy roads. You
still need to allow a much longer stopping
distance than you would if you were riding
on dry tarmac.

Whenever road conditions are poor,
anticipate the effect it is likely to have on
your bike's braking performance. Slow down
for hazards earlier, make more use of engine
braking, and when you use the brakes do so
smoothly and progressively.

Be extra cautious when heading downhill
on a slippery road. Engage a lower gear and
approach the incline slowly, as you may find
it particularly difficult to slow down without
risking a skid.

skidding when cornering

A skid can be provoked by a sudden change
of direction (such as a swerve to avoid
something in the road) or by leaning over
too far while cornering.

If the rear wheel loses grip during
cornering the rear of the bike will swing
to the outside of the curve. If you feel the
rear starting to slide, ease off the throttle
or brake, and steer in the direction that the
rear of the bike is sliding. Keep your feet
on the footrests, as putting a foot on the
ground is more likely to make you
lose balance.

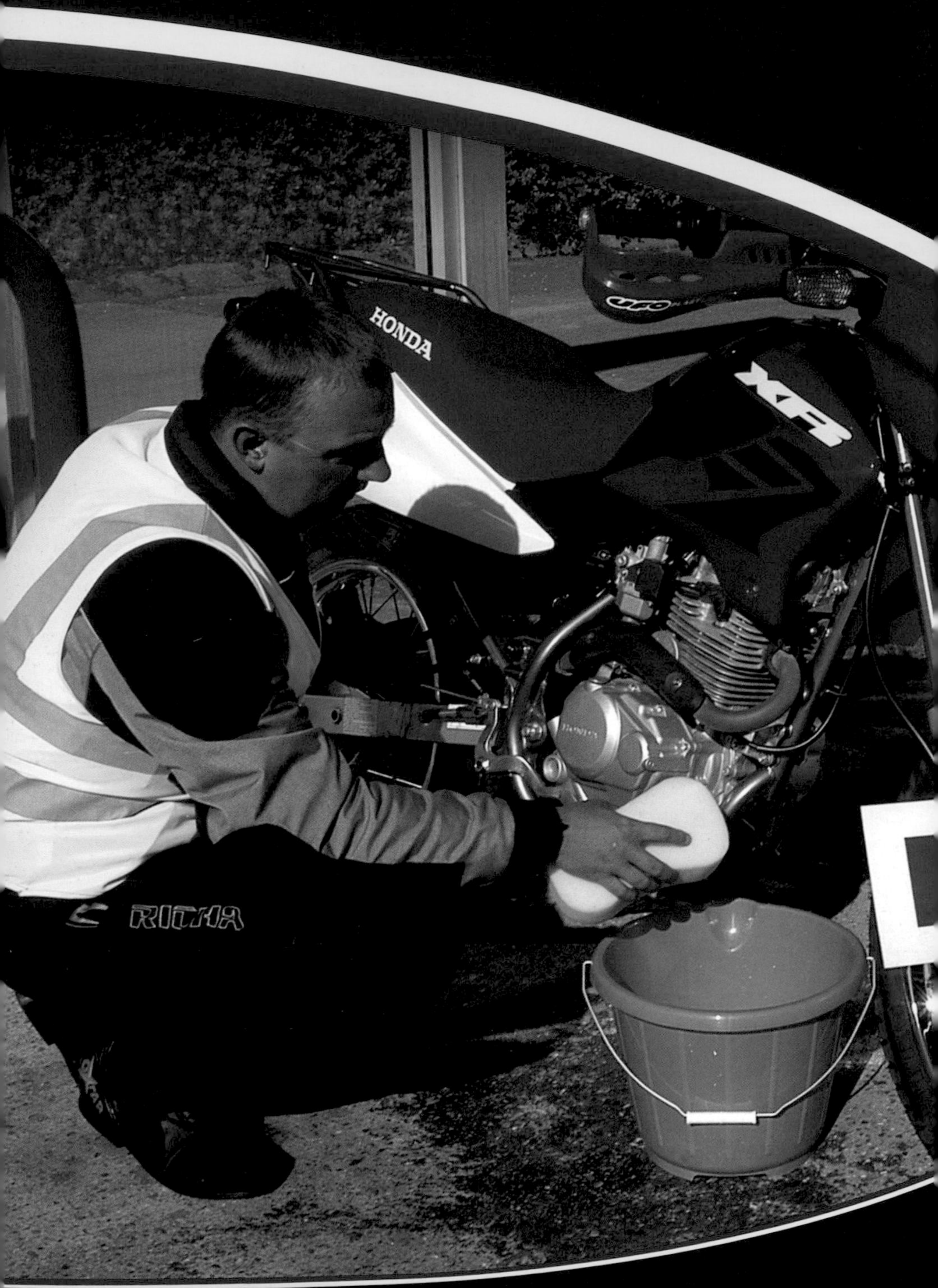
HONDA
XR
RITHA

11 you and your bike

As a motorcyclist you have legal responsibilities. You must ensure that you have a valid signed driving licence, that you are insured for the bike you are riding, and that it is properly registered and taxed. It is also your responsibility to keep your bike properly maintained in a roadworthy condition at all times. You must take care that it is never overloaded, and if you carry a pillion passenger you must make sure they understand what they must and must not do while they are on your bike. You should also take whatever steps you can to minimise the impact of your bike on the environment.

documents

There are a number of documents required to keep you and your bike lega
on the road. You must by law produce your driving licence and counterpar
a valid insurance certificate and (if appropriate) a valid **MOT** certificate if
requested to do so by the police. If you can't produce these documents or
the spot, you will be asked to take them to a police station of your choice
within seven days. You must also ensure your motorcycle is taxed and the
tax disc clearly displayed.

driving licence

You must have a valid signed driving licence which allows you to ride your category of motorcycle.

The photocard driving licence consists of a photo ID card and a counterpart. You must be able to show both parts if you are asked to produce your licence by a police officer. You must by law inform the Driver and Vehicle Licensing Agency (DVLA) if you change your name or address – there is a section on the licence to fill in and return to the DVLA to do this.

The photograph on your photocard licence is valid for ten years, after which you need to renew it. You can renew online, providing you have a valid UK passport issued within the last five years.

registration document

Every motorcycle has its own registration document (sometimes called a logbook or V5C) which lists identification details including the name and address of its registered keeper, the make, model, engine size and number, and year of first registration.

As the registered vehicle keeper, you must by law notify the DVLA if you change any of the details listed on the V5C, including your name or your permanent address. When a motorcycle is sold, both buyer and seller must complete the top part of the V5C and the seller must forward this immediately to the DVLA.

The V5C is not proof of ownership of a motorcycle – which is something worth bearing in mind when you are buying a second-hand bike privately.

insurance certificate

There are three types of motor insurance:

⊘ **third party insurance** is the minimum legal requirement. It means that if you injure or cause damage to the property of a third party (that is, another person), your insurance will cover the cost of their repairs and medical treatment – but you will receive nothing for your own injuries or damage to your own motorcycle

⊘ **third party, fire and theft insurance** means that in addition to having third party cover you will be compensated if your motorcycle is stolen or if it is damaged by fire

⊘ **comprehensive insurance** means that your costs, as well as those of any third party, will be covered if you have an accident, even if it is your own fault. Comprehensive is the most expensive sort of insurance cover but it is well worth the extra cost.

You must notify the DVLA of any changes to your motorcycle on the registration document (V5)

By law you must keep your motorbike insured at all times. If you ever want to keep your bike uninsured off the road, then you must make a SORN (Statutory Off Road Notification), using the reference number shown on your V5C registration certificate.

When you take out motorcycle insurance you will be given a detailed policy document, plus an insurance certificate which acts as legal confirmation of your insurance cover (you may initially receive a cover note, which is legally recognised as a substitute for your certificate until this is sent to you).

You must always inform your insurer of any changes to your circumstances, or modifications to your motorcycle, otherwise you may invalidate your insurance policy.

If you intend to carry a pillion passenger check that the terms of your insurance cover permits this; some policies give a discount if you agree not to carry a pillion.

Always check that you are properly insured before riding another person's bike; most policies give a reduced level of cover or no cover at all when you are not on your own bike.

You will need to produce your insurance certificate when taxing your motorcycle and at its MOT.

Various factors influence the cost of motorcycle insurance. You will pay more:
- to insure a high-performance bike
- if you live in a high-risk area such as an inner city
- if you are a younger rider
- if you get penalty points on your licence – insurance is particularly difficult to get after a drink-driving conviction.

You may cut your insurance premium by:
- avoiding accidents – every year that you don't claim on your insurance earns you a no-claims bonus, which knocks a percentage off your insurance premium (usually up to a five-year maximum). If you have to make a claim you lose a year's no-claims bonus, and your next premium may also rise
- opting for a higher excess (this is an amount you have to pay when you make a claim. If you have an excess of £100, it means you have to pay the first £100 of any claim you make).
- taking the Enhanced Rider Scheme after your test, which qualifies you for insurance discounts

Vehicle Excise Duty

This is better known as road tax. You must by law clearly display a tax disc on the left-hand side of any motorcycle which is used or parked on the public road (on a motorcycle with sidecar, the disc must be displayed on the left-hand side of the

riding abroad

If you take your motorcycle overseas, be sure to carry with you all necessary documentation, including your full valid UK driving licence, the registration document and MOT certificate (if applicable). If the bike is on hire or lease you need written authorisation that you are permitted to ride it. Check also with your insurance company that you are fully covered.

Unless it is fitted with a europlate (which show the letters GB below the Euro symbol) you must affix a GB sticker to the rear of your bike. You should also fit headlight convertors so your lights do not dazzle other road users when riding on the right-hand side of the road. Be alert for different speed limits and laws – in most European countries it is a legal requirement for motorbikes to use their headlight at all times.

*For further advice and information on motoring laws overseas, see the Haynes book **Driving Abroad** by Robert Davies*

handlebars or on the left-hand side of the sidecar). You can apply for a tax disc at a post office or online. You will need to take along your motor insurance certificate, MOT certificate (if applicable) and either the DVLA road tax reminder form V11, or the registration document (V5C). Applications can be made from the 15th day of the month in which the current tax is due to expire.

Tax discs are available for one year for bikes up to 600cc, and for either six months or one year for larger-engined bikes. The cost varies depending on the engine size, in the following classes:
- 150cc and under
- 151cc to 400cc
- 401cc to 600cc
- 601cc and over.

If you intend to keep your motorcycle off the road you must use the road tax reminder form (V11) to make a Statutory Off Road Notification (SORN) declaration at the post office. This must be renewed annually if the bike is kept off the road for more than a year.

Motorcycles first registered before 1973 are exempt from road tax but must still display a current nil tax disc.

There is an automatic fine for failing to display a valid tax disc; in addition your motorcycle may be wheelclamped, or seized and scrapped

MOT certificate

All motorcycles, mopeds and scooters must take an MOT test three years after the date they were first registered. The MOT test checks that the bike is safe to use on the road, and that exhaust noise and emissions are within specified limits. Items examined include suspension, steering, brakes, lighting, tyres, indicators and horn.

If your bike passes you will be given an MOT certificate which shows the bike's registration number and chassis number. This is valid for one year. You can get your bike tested up to one month before its current MOT expires, and the new certificate will still run from the original expiry date. You need to produce your MOT certificate when renewing your road tax disc.

Remember that an MOT certificate shows only that the items examined were found to be satisfactory on the day the test was carried out – it is no guarantee of roadworthiness, and possession of a current MOT is no defence against a charge of riding an unroadworthy motorcycle.

You are breaking the law if you ride a motorcycle without a current MOT certificate when it requires one (the only exception is if you are riding it to an MOT test which you have already booked). If you ride a motorcycle without a current MOT it could invalidate your insurance cover.

motoring law

The consequences of breaking the law on the road can be severe. Serious offences result in automatic disqualification or even a jail sentence – up to ten years for causing death by dangerous driving. Being convicted of even a minor motoring offence is an unpleasant and expensive experience. It's worth remembering that it is easy to avoid ever coming into conflict with the law, simply by riding in a safe, sensible and responsible manner.

penalty table

OFFENCE	Imprisonment	Fine	Disqualification	Penalty points
Causing death by dangerous driving	14 years	Unlimited	Obligatory 2 years minimum	3–11 (if exceptionally not disqualified)
Dangerous driving	2 years	Unlimited	Obligatory	3–11 (if exceptionally not disqualified)
Causing death by careless driving under the influence of drink or drugs	14 years	Unlimited	Obligatory 2 years minimum	3–11 (if exceptionally not disqualified)
Careless or inconsiderate driving	–	£5000	Discretionary	3–9
Driving while unfit through drink or drugs or with excess alcohol; or failing to provide a specimen for analysis	6 months	£5000	Obligatory	3–11 (if exceptionally not disqualified)
Failing to stop after an accident or failing to report an accident	6 months	£5000	Discretionary	5–10
Driving when disqualified	6 months (12 months in Scotland)	£5000	Discretionary	6
Driving after refusal or revocation of licence on medical grounds	6 months	£5000	Discretionary	3–6
Driving without insurance	–	£5000	Discretionary	6–8
Speeding	–	£1000 (£2500 for motorway offences)	Discretionary	3–6 or 3 (fixed penalty)
Traffic light offences	–	£1000	Discretionary	3
No MOT certificate	–	£1000	–	–

MAXIMUM PENALTIES

it's the law

motoring offences

Some examples of motoring offences and their maximum penalties are shown in the table above. For serious offences, the courts can impose a range of penalties including imprisonment, a fine, disqualification and endorsing the offender's driving licence with penalty points. Minor offences, such as speeding slightly in excess of the limit, may be dealt with by a fixed penalty fine and licence endorsement which can be settled without a court hearing.

penalty points

Under the penalty point system, a motorcyclist who breaks the law has their licence endorsed with points, the number depending on the severity of the offence. A rider who accumulates 12 or more penalty points within a three-year period will be disqualified for a minimum of six months.

For every offence which carries penalty points the court has a discretionary power to order the licence holder to be disqualified. This may be for any period the court thinks fit, but is usually between one week and a few months. For serious offences there is a mandatory period of disqualification – 12 months in the case of drink-driving. Serious or repeat offenders may face longer periods of disqualification, and in some cases the offender has to take and pass an extended motorcycle test before being allowed back on the road.

New Driver Act

Special rules apply to all riders and drivers for the first two years after passing their driving test. If they get six or more penalty points on their licence as a result of offences they commit before the two years are over (including any they committed before passing their test) their licence is revoked. Riders revert to learner status and must reapply for a provisional licence and retake CBT and theory and practical tests to regain their full licence.

maintenance

Your motorcycle needs regular attention to function safely and efficiently. Running a bike with worn or wrongly inflated tyres, or which is low on oil or brake fluid, is dangerous and illegal. Although it can be satisfying and save money to carry out your own routine maintenance, if you have any doubts about tackling a job yourself take the bike to your dealer instead. You will be asked questions about basic safety checks as part of your practical test (see p232). Your answers should refer specifically to the bike you are riding, so consult your own bike's handbook in addition to the advice in this section.

regular checks

Every time you ride your bike you should ensure that it is roadworthy, with lights, brakes and tyres in good condition. Its lights and numberplate must by law be kept clean. Be alert for any indications that a mechanical fault is developing, for instance:

- ⊙ poor braking performance suggesting a fault in the braking system – get the bike checked as soon as possible
- ⊙ a smell of petrol or burning rubber. Stop and investigate immediately to avoid any risk of fire
- ⊙ loud or unusual knocking or rubbing noises. Any noise indicates that wear is taking place and it needs to be checked
- ⊙ poor handling which may point to worn steering or shock absorbers.

refuelling

Check your fuel level whenever you start a journey and anticipate when you may need to fill up. Many bikes have a fuel gauge with a warning light that comes on when the tank is getting low, but if yours does not you will have to remove the petrol filler cap to check how much fuel remains. Resetting the trip

If your bike has a two-stroke engine it needs a special lubricant in addition to unleaded petrol

meter after refuelling will help you to judge when you need to stop and refill.

Some bikes have a reserve fuel supply. When the main tank runs dry the engine splutters and loses power, and you need to turn the fuel tap to the reserve position to restore fuel supply. Clearly, losing power could be dangerous during manoeuvres such as overtaking, so it's always preferable to fill up before the main tank runs dry.

When you visit a fuel station, remember that petrol is highly flammable. Smoking is strictly forbidden on fuel station forecourts. You must also never use a mobile phone in the vicinity of a fuel station.

There are two types of motorcycle engine:

- ⊙ a two-stroke engine runs on a mixture of petrol and oil, typically in a 20:1 ratio (see your handbook for the ratio recommended for your bike). You will either need to add two-stroke oil directly to the fuel tank when refuelling, or, more usually these days, add it to a separate oil tank where it feeds automatically into the engine.
- ⊙ a four-stroke engine does not need extra oil. Modern bikes run on unleaded fuel, and if your bike is fitted with a catalytic converter you must not use leaded fuel or you will damage it.

horn

Test the horn at regular intervals, but do so where it will not affect other road users and remember that it is illegal to sound the horn while your bike is stationary on the road.

lights

Check regularly that all the lights, including brake light and indicators, are working properly. The indicators should flash between one and two times per second. Make sure your headlight beam is properly adjusted so it doesn't dazzle other road users. You may need to adjust the beam when you carry a pillion passenger or a heavy load on the rear of your bike.

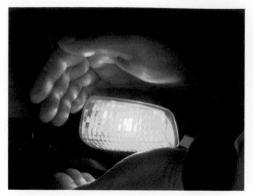

Check regularly that all the lights are working, including indicators and brake light

Controls such as the clutch which are operated by a cable need to be lubricated to work smoothly

brakes

Check brake pads and shoes regularly for wear and replace as necessary. Two types of braking system are commonly fitted:

◆ **mechanically operated**
These need regular adjustment to allow for stretching of the brake cables and wear of the brake pads or shoes. Cables and pivots also need oiling regularly to ensure they move freely

◆ **hydraulically operated**
These use pipes filled with brake fluid to work the brakes. If the brake fluid is allowed to run low then braking efficiency can be seriously impaired and an accident may result. Look out for brake fluid weeping from joints and couplings, and check flexible hoses regularly for damage. Never let the fluid in the brake fluid reservoir drop below the minimum mark. Get a garage to investigate if there is any loss of fluid. Brake fluid becomes contaminated with age and must be replaced at the intervals stated in your bike's service schedule.

clutch

As with the brakes, the clutch may be mechanically or hydraulically operated. If cable-operated, inspect the cable regularly for fraying or chafing, adjust it if the amount of free play exceeds that specified in the handbook and keep it oiled so it moves freely. If hydraulic, check for leaking joints and couplings, damaged flexible hoses and monitor the fluid level in the reservoir.

throttle

The throttle should operate smoothly and return to the fully closed position when released. Check that throttle cables (many bikes have two, an accelerator and a decelerator) are not chafing or fraying and that they aren't stretched when turning the handlebars from lock to lock. Keep them lubricated to prevent stiff operation caused by friction inside the casing.

battery

Most batteries are sealed and need no maintenance other than keeping the terminals secure, clean and greased. If there is a filler cap, remove it and check the fluid level – it should just cover the plates in each cell. Use distilled water to top up if necessary. Dispose of a battery only by taking it to a local authority site or garage.

Keep the drive chain correctly adjusted and make sure it never runs short of oil or it will wear rapidly

Any grinding or crunching sounds when you turn the handlebars must be investigated without delay

chain

It is important that the drive chain is in good condition, properly lubricated and correctly adjusted (around 3 to 4cm of slack is normal, but refer to your motorbike's handbook for the exact specification).

A loose or worn drive chain is potentially dangerous: it can cause a noisy rattle, affect gear changing and ultimately cause the rear wheel to lock, leading to an accident. After adjusting the drive chain tension, you should also check the alignment of the rear wheel.

Special lubricants are available for oiling the chain; it must not be allowed to run dry as this will cause rapid wear.

Some bikes use a shaft final drive in place of a chain. These have their own oil reservoir on the rear wheel hub. Make sure the bike is upright when you check the oil level. You must use the correct hypoid-type EP oil specified in the handbook.

steering

Before riding, check that the handlebars are free to move smoothly from full lock to lock without any control cables being stretched, trapped or pinched and without any snagging between moving and fixed parts.

If the steering head bearings become worn or out of adjustment, it may cause the bike to weave and wobble. Check for steering wear by turning the handlebars left and right with the bike stationary to make sure there is no grinding or crunching, or signs of excessive free play.

suspension

Shock absorbers must be in good condition or the bike's handling will be impaired. It's important to check for oil leaking from your front shock absorber as this could run onto your front tyre or brakes and cause an accident: if you see signs of an oil leak, don't ride the bike until it has been repaired.

wheels

With the motorbike on its centre stand, spin each wheel in turn and check that they are running true with no wobble from side to side. Look for cracks or other damage, and on spoked wheels check for loose or broken spokes. Always make sure your wheels are balanced after fitting a new tyre or having a puncture repaired.

The rear wheel needs to be precisely aligned behind the front or your bike could be unstable on bends and tyre wear will increase. Always recheck the wheel alignment to the manufacturer's specification after adjusting the drive chain or refitting the rear wheel.

engine oil

Check the engine oil regularly, especially before setting out on a long journey. If the engine runs short of oil expensive wear may result.

To check the oil level, first make sure the bike is level and upright on its centre stand. Your bike will be fitted with either a dipstick or a sight glass:

- **dipstick**: take out the dipstick, wipe it clean with a rag, reinsert it and then remove it again. Check that the oil is above the minimum marked on the stick.
- **sight glass**: first wipe the glass with a rag to make sure it is clean. The level should be between the minimum and maximum marks.

If necessary, undo the oil filler cap and add more oil of the grade recommended in the handbook (add a little at a time so you do not overfill, which could overpressurise the system and cause oil leaks). If changing your own oil, never pour old engine oil down the drain – take it to a local authority waste disposal site.

engine coolant

You should check whether your bike's engine is air-cooled or liquid-cooled.

If liquid-cooled, it is important not to let the coolant level fall below the minimum indicated on the coolant reservoir or the engine may overheat and be damaged. The engine cooling system is pressurised when hot, so never try to take off the filler cap straight after the engine has been running or you could be scalded. Don't add cold water to an overheated engine: let it cool down first. Ask a garage to investigate if you have to keep topping up the coolant level. Don't use water on its own in the cooling system. Anti-freeze should be added at the recommended concentration: this helps prevent corrosion as well as stopping the system from freezing in winter and causing expensive damage.

Check the engine oil at regular intervals – and always before setting out on a long journey

tyre care

Your tyres are your only contact with the road, so don't skimp on their maintenance or you could regret it. Get in the habit of glancing at your tyres every time you use your bike to check for obvious defects such as cuts or bulges.

At least every two weeks check that the tyres are correctly inflated to the pressures laid down in the handbook. Do this before a journey, when the tyres are cold, as warm tyres would give an inaccurate reading. Having underinflated tyres affects the braking and steering, and causes increased fuel consumption and tread wear. Overinflated tyres also affect steering and cause increased tread wear.

Tyre pressures may need increasing when carrying a pillion passenger or a heavy load, or when riding at sustained high speeds.

Replace any tyres which are worn or damaged. You must not use recut tyres or a tyre which:

◯ has a cut longer than 25mm or 10% of the width of the tyre, whichever is greater, and which is deep enough to reach the ply
◯ has a lump, bulge or tear
◯ shows exposed ply or cord
◯ has less than the legal minimum tread depth remaining. Tyres must have a tread depth of at least 1.0mm, forming a continuous band across at least three quarters of the width of the tyre and all the way around the tyre. Motorcycles under 50cc may have a tread depth of under 1.0mm, provided that the base of all the original tread grooves still show clearly. But you should regard these as the absolute legal minimum requirements. Worn tyres greatly reduce roadholding on damp, flooded or icy roads, and for safety's sake you should start thinking about replacing a tyre well before it approaches the legal limit, especially if you intend riding throughout the winter.

Excessive or uneven tyre wear may indicate that there is a fault with the brakes, wheel alignment or suspension.

When replacing a tyre, make sure you buy the correct type (this may vary between front and back wheels) and ensure it is fitted in the direction of travel as indicated by an arrow on the tyre. If your bike has tubed tyres fitted as standard, the tube should be replaced with each change of tyre.

Replacement tyres will not provide their usual level of grip when they are brand new, so ride carefully until the shiny surface has worn off them.

It's essential to check tyre pressures regularly to keep your bike safe on the road and to prevent unnecessary tyre wear and fuel consumption

203

loads and passengers

There are a number of ways to make your motorcycle a more practical load carrier, including fitting a sidecar or trailer, but you must always take into account the effect of the extra weight. It is your responsibility to ensure that your bike is never overloaded, which could seriously affect its steering and handling. You also have responsibilities when carrying a pillion passenger, and must ensure that anyone you carry is fully aware of what they need to do to be safe while they are on your bike.

load carrying

If you want to carry items on your motorcycle you have several options:

panniers

These come as either a pair of rigid boxes fixed to either side of the rear of the bike, or a bag which throws over the saddle. In either case, it is important that when loading panniers you make sure you distribute the weight evenly either side or your stability may be affected.

When using panniers it is important to make sure that the load is distributed evenly on both sides

top box

This fastens onto a rack behind the seat. A top box is convenient to use, but there are disadvantages with carrying loads so high up on the bike. Avoid carrying heavy loads in a top box or you may cause instability, low-speed wobble and high-speed weave.

tank bag

This fastens on to the top of the fuel tank. Be careful that a tank bag doesn't interfere with your control of the steering.

A top box is convenient to use, but avoid carrying too heavy a load in it or it can cause instability

luggage rack

Items can be strapped straight on to the rear luggage rack. Make sure they are securely fastened and that there are no dangling straps that could get caught in the wheel or chain.

When carrying extra weight on your bike you may have to adjust its tyre pressures, suspension and headlight beam (see the section on pillion passengers overleaf, and check your handbook for advice specific to your bike).

Ride cautiously until you get used to the effect of the extra weight on your bike's handling. If it feels unbalanced, stop and rearrange the load more evenly.

Make sure any load is securely fastened with no dangling straps to get caught in the chain or wheel

205

pillion passengers

To carry a pillion passenger you must have a full licence for the category of motorcycle you are riding. Your bike must be fitted with rear footrests and a proper passenger seat, and you must not carry a child who isn't big enough to use the footrests and handholds safely.

The suspension and tyres have to work harder to cope with the extra weight of a passenger. The change in weight distribution can also raise the angle of the headlight. Check your handbook and follow the advice it gives on how to set up your bike for carrying a passenger. You may need to:
- inflate the tyres to a higher pressure
- adjust the rear shock absorber pre-load setting
- adjust the headlight aim to avoid dazzling oncoming drivers
- adjust your mirrors.

Make sure your passenger is properly attired, with:
- an approved, correctly fastened motorcycle helmet
- weatherproof, protective clothing, which is brightly coloured (and reflective if you are riding at night)
- no loose or dangling items such as a scarf which might get caught in the wheel or chain.

If your passenger has little or no experience of riding as a pillion, make sure you give instructions before setting out. Tell your passenger to:
- sit properly over the saddle – never ride side-saddle
- keep both feet on the footrests
- hold on securely to your waist, or to the passenger grab handle, if fitted
- lean with you when going round bends (but don't lean to the side to see ahead, which could affect your stability).

Carrying a pillion passenger requires extra care on your part. Your acceleration will be slower than you are used to with the extra weight on board, so take this into account when pulling out into a traffic stream or overtaking. Braking will be less effective, so leave extra space when following another vehicle. It will also be more difficult to balance, especially at low speeds, the steering will feel lighter, and the bike may lean more into corners than you expect. Be prepared too for the weight of your pillion passenger to be thrown forwards against you when you are braking.

Remember that you and only you are responsible for riding your motorbike. Don't ask your passenger to look behind or signal for you, and don't rely on your passenger to tell you the road is clear – always look and check for yourself.

Talk to your pillion passenger before setting off to make sure they know what is expected of them

sidecars

Motorcycle and sidecar outfits are a rare sight nowadays – for most people, the comfort, safety and convenience of a car is a better option.

If you wish to fit a sidecar you should first check with your dealer that your motorcycle is suitable. Sidecars must by law be fitted to the left side of the motorbike (except for bikes first registered before August 1 1981). The sidecar must be correctly fixed to the mounting points, and it must be properly aligned or the outfit will be hard to control and unsafe.

Riding with a sidecar attached requires special techniques:

❍ when steering, because the outfit can't be leaned into bends, it must be steered with a deliberate turn of the handlebars
❍ special care is needed on left-hand bends as the sidecar wheel may lift off the ground if they are taken too quickly
❍ under heavy braking the outfit will pull to the right unless the sidecar wheel has its own brake. The extra weight of the sidecar will increase stopping distances, so keep your speed down and leave longer following distances
❍ when parking on a hill, leave your motorcycle and sidecar in a low gear to prevent it rolling away.

A motorcycle and sidecar outfit has very different handling characteristics to a solo motorcycle

towing a trailer

A motorcycle is not ideally designed for towing a trailer, and if you need to transport larger loads a car may be a better option. However, it is legal to tow a trailer behind a bike, providing that:

❍ you have a full motorcycle licence
❍ the motorcycle's engine size is over 125cc
❍ the trailer is less than 1 metre wide
❍ there is less than 2.5 metres between the rear of the trailer and the motorcycle's rear axle
❍ the laden weight of the trailer is not greater than 150kg or two-thirds of the kerbside weight of the motorcycle (whichever is less)
❍ the motorcycle is clearly marked with its kerbside weight
❍ the trailer is clearly marked with its unladen weight
❍ the load in the trailer is securely fastened
❍ you tow no more than one trailer
❍ you do not carry a passenger in the trailer
❍ you obey the lower speed limits that apply to all vehicles towing trailers: 50mph on single carriageways, 60mph on dual carriageways and motorways
❍ you do not use the right-hand lane of a motorway that has more than two lanes.

Take great care when towing as your stopping distances will increase, the handling of your bike will be compromised, braking distances will be longer and you will need to leave more space when manoeuvring to take your greater width and length into account. If a trailer swerves or snakes when you are towing it, ease off the throttle and reduce your speed to bring it back under control.

Remember that a trailer must never be left on the road at night without lights.

environment

In the last hundred years motor vehicles have transformed the way we live. They allow us to go where we want when we want, and to travel long distances for work and leisure. The downside is that this mobility has been achieved at a considerable cost to the environment we live in.

environmental issues

The growth in traffic has had wide-ranging effects on the environment, including:

⊘ production of carbon dioxide (CO_2), which contributes to global warming: road transport accounts for about 20% of the UK's CO_2 emissions

⊘ depletion of natural resources such as oil reserves

⊘ air pollution which causes health problems and damages historic buildings

⊘ road building which degrades the natural landscape

⊘ traffic congestion

⊘ noise pollution.

eco-safe riding

Eco-safe riding is about applying good, safe riding techniques such as anticipation and smoothness to help reduce your fuel consumption and emissions. Follow these tips when riding, and not only will you minimise your impact on the environment, you will also save money by cutting fuel consumption and wear and tear on your motorcycle.

⊘ **keep your bike maintained**
An unserviced engine can waste fuel and produce unnecessary emissions

⊘ **stick to the speed limit**
The higher your speed, the more fuel your bike uses. At 70mph fuel consumption is up to 30% higher than at 50mph

⊘ **accelerate gently**
Racing the engine in the lower gears wastes fuel

⊘ **avoid short journeys**
Short journeys on a cold engine cause a disproportionate amount of pollution. Walking or cycling these short journeys cuts pollution – and is better for your health

⊘ **check tyre pressures**
Wrongly inflated tyres can cause fuel consumption and tread wear to increase

⊘ **travel light**
Improve fuel consumption by not carrying unnecessary heavy items

⊘ **plan your journey**
Work out your best route in advance, make sure you know the way so you don't waste time and fuel by getting lost, and try to travel off-peak to avoid traffic congestion

⊘ **cut the choke**
Using the choke for longer than necessary wastes fuel – and can cause engine damage

⊘ **use public transport**
If more people took the train or bus, traffic congestion would be reduced

⊘ **don't idle**
Switch off your engine if you have to wait in a traffic queue, and never leave it idling while parked

⊘ **anticipate**
Planning ahead avoids the need for unnecessary braking and acceleration

⊘ **choose an efficient motorcycle**
A motorcycle fitted with a catalytic converter produces significantly cleaner exhaust emissions

⊘ **ride sensibly off-road**
If you ride off-road, respect the countryside, its livestock and wildlife

⊘ **dispose of oil and batteries properly**
Take them to a local authority site or garage for safe and environmentally-friendly disposal.

Avoid revving your engine unnecessarily, as this increases fuel consumption and mechanical wear

Hidden
dips
for 2 miles

WN54
ZRC
L

12 staying safe

Taking to the road is such an everyday thing to do that few people pause to think how dangerous it can be. Each of us has about a 1 in 200 chance of being killed in a road accident. For motorcyclists, lacking the protective cocoon of a car's bodyshell, the risks are even greater. And when riding you don't just put yourself at risk. A speeding bike can be a lethal weapon and every time you take to the road you have the capability to kill or maim. But crashes don't happen for no reason. In the overwhelming majority of road accidents human error is the cause. If you become a rider who always puts safety first, there is no reason why you should not enjoy an accident-free riding career.

Riding a motorcycle is considerably more risky than driving a car: for motorcyclists the risk of being killed or seriously injured on the road is over 16 times greater than for car users. Many crashes involving motorcyclists are caused by riding inappropriately for the conditions; others result when other road users do not show enough awareness for motorcyclists. In either case, there are strategies you can follow to reduce your risk on the road.

causes of accidents

Motorcyclists tend to have different sorts of serious accident than other road users. In particular, motorcyclists have more crashes involving:

◆ excessive speed
◆ losing control on bends
◆ collisions at junctions
◆ manoeuvres that only motorcycles can perform, such as filtering between queues of traffic.

Accidents vary according to the age of the rider too. Young riders tend to have more crashes caused by poor judgement of other traffic, particularly at junctions. They are also likely to be overconfident in their own ability, liable to take unnecessary risks and to show off or act competitively when riding. If you are a young rider, you need to identify how these issues may influence you and address them before they affect your safety.

If you are coming to motorcycling after some years of driving, you also have some readjustments to make. As a rider rather than a car driver, you need to be much more aware of how weather conditions affect your safety. You also need to pay more attention to the quality of the road surface and anticipate how it will affect your ability to accelerate, brake and change direction.

Mature riders tend to ride more powerful bikes and are over-represented in crashes that don't involve another vehicle. These are likely to involve excessive speed or losing control on bends – even when road and weather conditions are good. If you want to find out what it's like to ride a high-performance motorbike at its limits, doing so on the public road is asking for trouble. Go to a track day at a racing circuit where you can ride quickly without putting anyone at unnecessary risk.

Riders are particularly at risk at junctions (above) where drivers sometimes seem to look without registering that a motorcyclist is there; filtering (below) is another hazardous manoeuvre and great care must be taken to anticipate the actions of other road users who may not be aware of you

defensive riding

You might think that the way to avoid accidents is to have highly developed bike control skills. This is actually not the case. The sort of abilities that make a good racer – quick reactions, the ability to corner a bike at its limits of grip, skid control and so on – are of little value when it comes to staying safe on the road. What really counts is having the right mental attitude. On the road good riders are those who put safety first. They always ride within their limits and do not let their emotions influence their behaviour.

Most car drivers expect to go through their driving career having the occasional knock resulting in a minor insurance claim. This attitude just doesn't work when you're riding a motorcycle. The kind of bump that results in a dented door on a car means a broken leg – or worse – for a rider. You must have an attitude of zero tolerance to risk. Train yourself to imagine the worst that might develop in any road scenario and plan your riding to neutralise the danger before it occurs.

Too many road users think no further ahead than the rear bumper of the vehicle in front. As a motorcyclist, you must make much better use of your anticipation skills to stay safe. Look as far up the road as you can see, and anticipate the events that will unfold around you two or three moves in advance – just as in a game of chess.

Recognise how your mood can affect your riding. If you've just fallen out with a friend, or are anxious because you're running behind schedule, this may cloud your judgement and make you aggressive towards other road users. It's important to realise when your mood is being affected and try to stay cool on the road at all times.

other drivers

Many car drivers are alert, conscientious and safety minded. Equally, there are those who put little active thought or effort into their driving. They drive on autopilot, minds busy with talking to their passenger or chatting on their mobile phone. When you are riding, as well as avoiding making your own mistakes, you need to anticipate and compensate for these drivers' mistakes too.

Most bike crashes involve a collision with another vehicle. Many of these happen at junctions where the driver simply fails to perceive that the bike is there – the 'sorry mate, I didn't see you' accident so familiar to riders. It's all too common for car drivers to fail to notice motorcyclists, even when they are in clear view. It is, of course, no comfort to be able to say from your hospital bed that the other driver was at fault. Take steps to prevent this sort of accident by:

- ⬦ using visibility aids such as daytime running lights and high-visibility clothing
- ⬦ never putting yourself in a situation where you are dependent on another person's reactions or alertness to stay safe
- ⬦ never assuming that another road user has seen you. Always look for confirmation of what they are about to do before putting yourself in their path.

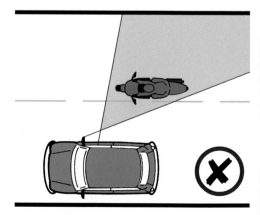

Don't ride in another driver's blind spot – always make sure you are clearly visible in their mirrors

bad habits

When a rider does something wrong and gets away with it they may do it again and again until it becomes a habit. They may get too close to the car in front on the motorway, or filter past queueing traffic at high speed. They keep doing this and getting away with it until it becomes part of their normal riding. Then one day the car in front slams on its brakes unexpectedly, or a queuing van changes lanes without warning.

To prevent yourself developing bad habits, you need to:

⊙ be critical about your own riding. If you have to slam on the brakes to avoid another vehicle, or have a close shave when overtaking, ask yourself what you could do to avoid such a situation happening again in the future

⊙ put your imagination to work when you are riding. Continually ask yourself 'what if?' What if a car pulls out of that driveway? What if there's a queue of stationary traffic round this bend? What if a child runs out between those two cars? If the answer is that there would be a nasty accident, then you're going too fast for the conditions and you need to slow down

⊙ realise that riding is a skill which you can never stop trying to improve. Don't fall into the trap of getting two or three years' experience and thinking you have no room for improvement. The best riders – including professional police motorcyclists – recognise that however well trained they are, they are not perfect and are always working to improve their riding. Consider taking an advanced riding course such as that offered by the Institute of Advanced Motorists (see p241).

Always ask yourself 'What if' as you ride: for instance, 'What if there is a broken down truck just around this blind bend? Could I stop in time?'

know the code

highway code rule 69

Daylight riding Make yourself as visible as possible from the side as well as the front and rear. You could wear a light or brightly coloured helmet and fluorescent clothing or strips. Dipped headlights, even in good daylight, may also make you more conspicuous. However, be aware that other vehicle drivers may still not have seen you, or judged your distance or speed correctly, especially at junctions.

sharing the road

There are some 27 million vehicles on our congested roads, and whenever you get on your motorcycle you need to interact with other road users. As in any other sphere of life, you can't expect these people to think or act exactly like you do – but you should make it your aim to get along with them courteously and harmoniously.

staying calm

Losing your cool on the road can seriously impair your ability to ride safely. If you find yourself getting angry or impatient with other road users:

● recognise that when on the road you are not able to communicate with other people face to face and this prevents you from reacting to them as you would normally. In your daily life you meet all sorts of people, and even when they seem difficult you make an effort to get along with them and create a pleasant atmosphere. Aim to do the same when you are on the road

● remember that if someone seems to be getting in your way, it's almost certain they're not doing it on purpose. Other people get distracted, or lose their way, or make a mistake – just as we do ourselves on occasion

● don't get into stressful situations where you're more likely to lose control over your emotions. Plan your journey in advance and leave plenty of time so you don't find yourself running late and getting tense

● recognise that getting upset over someone else's bad driving serves no useful purpose. You can't control how other people behave on the road, so let them get on with it and concentrate on what you *can* control – your own riding. If you think someone is driving dangerously, let them get on their way and have their accident somewhere else, not near you

● remind yourself that however important your appointment may be, it's not worth having a crash because you're rushing to get there on time

● never use hand signals or your horn or lights to rebuke another road user. It will have no positive effect whatsoever, but it could provoke them to retaliate, putting you and other road users at risk

● be patient with elderly drivers who seem slow and hesitant behind the wheel.

They may hate driving and share your wish that they weren't on the road, but for many older people without access to public transport driving is their only way of staying in touch with friends and family and getting to the shops

● give learner drivers and riders plenty of space to do something unpredictable, and don't hassle a learner who is holding you up – they may just get more nervous and take even longer to move out of your way

● always take particular care around children, whether they are on foot or riding bicycles, and anticipate that they may act unpredictably and not follow the rules of the road.

know the code

highway code rule 147

Be considerate Be careful of and considerate towards other road users, especially those requiring extra care.

You should:

➔ try to be understanding if other drivers cause problems; they may be inexperienced or not know the area well

➔ be patient; remember that anyone can make a mistake

➔ not allow yourself to become agitated or involved if someone is behaving badly on the road. This will only make the situation worse. Pull over, calm down and, when you feel relaxed, continue your journey

➔ slow down and hold back if a road user pulls out into your path at a junction. Allow them to get clear. Do not over-react by driving too close behind to intimidate them

➔ not throw anything out of a vehicle, for example, cigarette ends, cans, paper or carrier bags. This can endanger other road users, particularly motorcyclists and cyclists.

breakdowns

Motorcycles rarely break down unless they have been poorly maintained or abused. Never ignore any faults which your bike develops. Be alert for unusual noises or smells, and stop immediately to investigate. And consider joining a breakdown service: even if you are a competent home mechanic you will not want to try fixing your bike on the side of a busy road in bad weather, and the membership fee is worth paying for peace of mind alone.

safety first

If your motorbike breaks down, your first responsibility is to ensure that it is not causing a hazard for other road users. Try to get it right off the road if possible. If it is on the road, keep the parking lights on at night or in poor visibility. Put on the hazard warning lights if fitted.

Never stand between your broken-down bike and oncoming traffic, or stand where you might prevent other road users seeing your lights.

When riding, be prepared for the possibility of your bike suffering a breakdown. This can include:

◯ engine failure

If the engine cuts out while you are riding, it may be because the fuel supply needs switching to the reserve tank. Try to avoid this happening by filling up in good time before the tank runs dry.

◯ tyre blow-out

If a tyre deflates while you are riding, grip the handlebars firmly and allow the bike to roll gently to a stop at the side of the road. Try to avoid using the brakes or steering, which may cause you to lose control.

◯ overheating

If your engine overheats, stop and let it cool down before investigating further. Only when it is cool should you remove the filler cap and top up the coolant level if required.

◯ fire

Reduce the risk of fire by always stopping and checking for the cause if you smell petrol fumes while riding. If your bike catches fire, get everyone well clear and call the fire brigade.

motorway breakdowns

The motorway is a hazardous place to break down, so if your bike develops a fault, move to the inside lane and try to carry on to the next exit or service station. If you do have to stop on the motorway:

◯ pull on to the hard shoulder and stop as far to the left as possible. Keep your parking lights on at night or in poor visibility, and switch on hazard warning lights if fitted

◯ do not try to make even a simple repair

◯ phone the emergency services. Use an emergency phone rather than your own mobile, as this allows the police (in some areas, the Highways Agency) control operator to pinpoint your location. The direction of the nearest emergency telephone is given on marker posts situated every 100 metres along the hard shoulder. Face the oncoming traffic while you are using the phone so you can see danger approaching. The operator will ask you for the number of the telephone you are using, details of yourself and your motorbike, and whether you belong to a motoring organisation. Tell the operator if you are a woman on her own

◯ if you do decide to use your mobile phone to call for help, take note of the number on the nearest marker post as this can also help to identify your location

◯ wait near your motorbike on the embankment away from the carriageway and hard shoulder

◯ when you rejoin the carriageway, build up speed on the hard shoulder before pulling into a safe gap in the traffic

◯ If you (or another motorist) drop something on the motorway, don't attempt to retrieve it yourself: stop on the hard shoulder and use an emergency telephone to call the police

◯ If you see a vehicle with a 'help' pennant displayed, it indicates a disabled motorist who needs assistance.

accidents

If you are involved in a road accident you must meet your legal obligations, and you should also try to gather as much information as possible for insurance purposes. Where you come across the scene of an accident involving other vehicles, you should stop to give assistance. It is useful to carry a basic first aid kit and take some training in how to use it in case you ever have to give emergency first aid to road casualties.

getting information

Even a minor accident may involve an
insurance claim. You should gather as much
information on the spot as you can. Draw
a sketch map of the scene, and if you are
carrying a camera take some photographs.
Make a note of:

- the other driver's name, address and
  telephone number
- whether the driver owns the other
  vehicle
- the make, model and registration number
  of the other vehicle
- details of the other driver's insurance
- names and addresses of witnesses
- road and weather conditions
- what vehicles were doing at the time of
  the accident (such as whether their lights
  were on and if they were signalling)
- what other people say to you
- identification numbers of police officers
  attending the accident.

accident scenes

If other people have already stopped to
give assistance, try not to let yourself be
distracted by an accident scene. Where
an incident has occurred on the other
side of a motorway or dual carriageway,
keep your attention on the road ahead
as further accidents are often caused by
'rubbernecking' at accidents.

If you need to stop to give assistance:

- first stop and warn other traffic
- switch on your hazard warning lights if
  fitted
- make sure someone telephones for an
  ambulance if people are badly injured
- get people who are not injured clear of
  the scene
- place a warning triangle on the road at
  least 45 metres behind the crash scene
- switch off all engines
- make sure no one is smoking
- do not put yourself at unnecessary risk.

*If your motorbike is involved in a accident, use the
engine cut-off switch to turn off the engine and
reduce the risk of fire breaking out*

it's the law

in an accident

If you are involved in an accident
which causes damage or injury to
any other person, vehicle, animal or
property, you must by law:

→ stop

→ give your own and (if different) your
   vehicle owner's name and address,
   and the registration number of your
   vehicle, to anyone having reasonable
   grounds for requiring them

→ if you do not give your name and
   address at the time of the accident,
   report the accident to the police as
   soon as reasonably practicable, and in
   any case within 24 hours

→ if another person is injured and
   you do not produce your insurance
   certificate at the time of the accident
   to a police officer or to anyone having
   reasonable grounds to request it, you
   must report the accident to the police
   as soon as possible (and in any case
   within 24 hours), and produce your
   insurance certificate for the police
   within seven days.

If a vehicle catches fire, stand well clear and call for the fire brigade to deal with it

first aid

Carry a first aid kit in your car and take some training in how to use it so you are prepared if you ever have to help accident casualties.

At an accident scene do not move injured people out of their vehicles unless you have to do so to protect them from further danger (moving them could aggravate a back injury). Do not remove a motorcyclist's helmet unless it is essential to clear their airway as it could make their injury worse. If a casualty is unconscious, first check that they are still breathing (monitor their breathing for at least 10 seconds) before dealing with any heavy bleeding or burns.

◗ resuscitation

If the casualty is not breathing you will need to begin the ABC of resuscitation: this means checking the Airway, Breathing and Circulation. Clear away any obstruction to the airway and loosen tight clothing. If breathing does not restart when the airway has been cleared, give mouth-to-mouth resuscitation. Lift the chin and tilt the head backwards. Pinch the casualty's nostrils and blow into the mouth (gently in the case of a child) until the chest rises. Repeat every four seconds until the casualty can breathe without assistance. If there is no pulse (circulation), start external chest compression. Press down firmly by about 4–5cm with the heel of your hand in the middle of the casualty's chest at a rate of 100 compressions per minute. Give two breaths after every 30 compressions.

◗ recovery position

If a casualty is unconscious but breathing, putting them in the recovery position will maintain an open airway and ensure they do not swallow their tongue: place them on their side, supported by one leg and one arm, and open the airway (after checking that it is clear) by tilting the head and lifting the chin.

◗ bleeding

Where there is heavy bleeding, apply firm hand pressure over the wound, preferably using some clean material. Don't press on any foreign body in the wound. Secure a pad with a bandage or length of cloth. Raise the limb or wound (if there are no fractures) to lessen the bleeding.

◗ burns

Douse burns with cool liquid and continue to cool them for at least ten minutes. But do not put any creams on a burn and do not remove anything sticking to it.

◗ shock

Casualties may be suffering from shock. Symptoms include sweating; rapid shallow breathing; clammy, grey skin and blue lips; faintness, nausea and dizziness. Keep them warm and comfortable, give them constant reassurance and make sure they are not left alone. Do not give them anything to eat, drink or smoke. Stay at the scene until the emergency services arrive.

hazard warning plates

hazard information panel displayed by tanker carrying dangerous goods (in this case flammable liquid)

diamond symbols indicating other hazardous substances include:

toxic substance

oxidising substance

non-flammable compressed gas

radioactive substance

spontaneously combustible substance

corrosive substance

panel displayed by vehicle carrying dangerous goods in packages

dangerous goods

Learn to recognise the markings displayed on vehicles carrying hazardous goods. If an accident involves a vehicle containing dangerous goods, it is essential that all engines are switched off and no one smokes. Do not use a mobile phone nearby. Keep well clear of the vehicle and stay away from any liquids, dust or vapours. Call the emergency services and give as much information as possible about the labels and markings on the vehicle.

Keep at a safe distance if a tanker carrying a dangerous substance is involved in an accident

vital signs

temporary police warning signs at scene of accident or other danger

hospital with accident and emergency facilities

hospital without accident and emergency facilities

13 taking your test

The motorcycle test consists of a theory test and a practical test. The theory test includes a multiple-choice examination, plus a hazard perception test based on video clips. The practical test is split into two modules: the first consists of a series of off-road exercises while the second is an observed ride on the road. It includes an eyesight test plus questions on vehicle safety checks and carrying a pillion passenger. You cannot book a practical test until you have passed the theory test, and you must complete both practical test modules within two years of passing the theory test. The test is administered by the Driving Standards Agency (DSA) and you'll find useful information about applying for and taking theory and practical tests on their website: www.direct.gov.uk/drivingtest.

The theory test consists of two elements. Firstly, there's a multiple-choice examination in which you have to answer correctly 43 out of 50 questions covering all aspects of driving on a touch-screen computer. Secondly, you have to identify the road hazards shown on 14 video clips by clicking a mouse button.

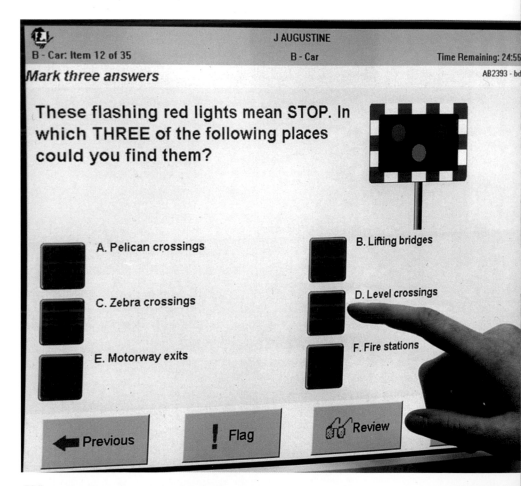

B - Car: Item 12 of 35

J AUGUSTINE

B - Car

Time Remaining: 24:56

AB2393 - bd

Mark three answers

These flashing red lights mean STOP. In which THREE of the following places could you find them?

A. Pelican crossings

B. Lifting bridges

C. Zebra crossings

D. Level crossings

E. Motorway exits

F. Fire stations

Previous

Flag

Review

booking your test

You can book your theory test by telephone, post, or on-line.

The cost of the theory test is currently £31. Weekday, evening and saturday test sessions are available as well as daytime appointments. If you need to cancel your theory test appointment, you must give at least three whole working days notice, or you forfeit your theory test fee. If you have hearing difficulties, dyslexia or light-sensitive epilepsy then let the DSA know at the time of making your booking and special arrangements will be made for you.

In Northern Ireland, driving tests are administered by the Driver and Vehicle Agency. The tests follow the same format.

what to take with you

At the test centre you will need to show both parts of your photocard driving licence. If you have one of the older style driving licences which doesn't include a photograph, you also need to take a passport with you. No other form of photographic ID will be accepted.

If you forget to bring the correct documents with you on the day, you won't be able to take your test and you will lose your fee.

Arrive in plenty of time for your theory test so that you don't feel rushed or stressed.

multiple-choice test

The theory test begins with a multiple-choice exam. To pass this you must answer correctly at least 43 out of 50 multiple-choice questions within the 57 minutes allowed (candidates with special needs can apply for additional time when they are booking their test).

Some questions will be presented as a case study. This shows a short scenario based on a real life situation that you could experience while riding. You will be asked five questions based on the scenario.

You select your answers by touching the button on the screen beside the answer you want to select. You will be given the opportunity to practise this before starting the test.

If you think you have selected the wrong answer you can change it by touching the screen again. If you are unsure which answer is correct you can mark questions with a flag to help you go back to them. The system also prompts you to go back to questions you have not answered fully.

After the multiple-choice exam, you have a break of up to three minutes before taking the hazard perception test.

preparing for the multiple-choice test

The 50 questions in the multiple-choice test are selected from a bank of questions similar to those listed at the end of this book. Use these questions to practise taking the multiple-choice section of the theory test. If you are not sure of an answer, read the explanatory text alongside each question for more information, or refer to the relevant section of this book.

If you have read and made sure you thoroughly understand all the preceding chapters of this book, then you will know everything you need to answer any of the questions you may be asked in your test.

contact details

Driving Standards Agency (DSA)
Customer Enquiry Unit
PO Box 280
Newcastle-Upon-Tyne
NE99 1FP

telephone: 0300 200 1122
website: www.direct.gov.uk/drivingtest

Driver and Vehicle Agency (DVA) (Northern Ireland)
Customer Services, DVA, County Hall, Castlerock Rd, Coleraine BT51 3HS

telephone: 0845 601 4094
website: www.dvtani.gov.uk

hazard perception test

Before you sit the hazard perception test you will be shown a short tutorial video demonstrating how it works.

The test consists of 14 video clips, each about one minute long, showing road situations involving other road users. You should press your mouse button as soon as you see a hazard which may require you to change speed or direction. The earlier you spot the potential danger and respond, the higher the score you receive. The video will not stop or slow down when you respond but a red flag appears at the bottom of the screen each time you press the mouse button to show your response has been recorded. You can click the right or left button on the mouse to show you have identified the hazard.

There are a total of 15 scoreable hazards: 13 clips contain one scoreable hazard and one clip contains two of them. You can score up to five marks for each hazard depending on how quickly you identify it. Unlike the multiple-choice test, in this section you are not able to go back or change your response. You will not lose points for identifying non-scoring hazards.

It is not possible to pass the test by clicking the mouse button continuously: this will score zero points.

You must score at least 44 out of 75 points to pass the hazard perception test.

what is a hazard?

Imagine the video clip shows a car parked at the side of the road. It's a potential hazard, but at the moment it's not doing anything that will affect you. So if you clicked the mouse button at this point you wouldn't score anything (though you wouldn't lose any points either).

Then the car's right-hand indicator starts to flash. This means the driver is thinking of pulling out. This is now a developing hazard and you should click to show you have identified it.

preparing for the hazard perception test

The video clips you will see show real-life hazards of the sort you come across on the road every day. Test yourself whenever you are on the road, even as a passenger in a car, by scanning the road ahead and identifying potential hazards. Read through this book carefully, paying special attention to Chapter 8 which deals with hazard perception, observation and anticipation. You may also find it useful to talk through some practice video sessions with an instructor.

pass or fail?

After completing both sections of the theory test you should receive your results, and feedback, within 30 minutes.

You must pass both the multiple-choice and hazard perception elements to pass your theory test. If you fail one element but pass the other, you still have to take the whole test over again.

If you have failed you can book another theory test straight away, but you must leave three clear working days before the date of your new test.

When you pass the theory test you will receive a pass certificate which is valid for two years. This means that if you don't pass your practical test within two years you will have to retake the theory test.

test tips

do
- prepare properly beforehand by studying and making sure you understand the answers to all the theory questions listed in the back of this book
- listen carefully to all the instructions you are given before and during the theory test

don't
- arrive at the test centre late and feeling flustered
- forget to take along your driving licence and appointment card

video clip example 1

The hazard is the school crossing patrol with children ready to cross the road. You should click on the mouse button as soon as you realise that the patrol might walk into the road to stop traffic in front of you and let the children cross

video clip example 2

The hazard is the small child on a bicycle who cycles across the road. You should click on the mouse button as soon as you realise that the child might ride across the road, causing the motorcyclist in front of you to brake

13
practical test

The practical test isn't as daunting as you may think. But to make your test modules go as smoothly as possible, you do need to get plenty of practice beforehand. Taking either before you are properly prepared will certainly result in a costly and confidence-denting failure.

booking your test

The practical test includes two separate modules. Module one involves a series of off-road exercises and costs £15.50. Module two is an observed ride on the public road and costs £75 (£88.50 on weekday evenings, weekends and bank holidays). You must pass module one before you can take module two.

You can book your practical test by post, by telephone, or on-line. If for any reason you need to postpone or cancel your test, you must give the DSA at least three working days notice (not counting the day of the test and day of notification) or you will lose your fee. You can book both modules at the same time, but leave enough time in between them so that you can give the necessary three days' notice in the event of your failing module one and having to cancel module two, otherwise you will lose your fee for module two.

If you have hearing difficulties, dyslexia or any other disability which may affect your ability to take the test then you should let the DSA know at the time of booking.

what to take with you

Before taking your test you need to show:
- ◯ both parts of your signed photocard driving licence
- ◯ your theory test pass certificate
- ◯ your CBT certificate (DL196).

If you have one of the older style driving licences without a photograph, you must bring a passport too. If you do not bring the right documents with you, your test will be cancelled and you will lose your fee.

Make sure you wear suitable clothing for both modules of the practical test. You will not be permitted to take the test wearing lightweight clothing, gloves or shoes that do not offer adequate protection. You must use an approved safety helmet, properly fastened, throughout both modules.

your test motorcycle

The motorcycle you intend to take your test on must be legally roadworthy and have a current MOT certificate (if applicable). It must be insured for you to ride and you will be asked to sign a declaration that your insurance is in order (contact your insurance company in advance to let them know you will be taking your test on your bike).

If you are planning to take your test on a hired bike, you should check with the hire company that you are authorised to do so.

You must take your practical test on a motorcycle of the appropriate size, ie:

- ◯ **category P**: a moped with engine capacity under 50cc, weight under 250kg, and top speed of no more than 50km/h (31mph)
- ◯ **category A1**: a motorcycle with engine capacity of 75cc to 125cc
- ◯ **category A**: a motorcycle with engine capacity of 121cc to 125cc and capable of 100km/h (62mph)
- ◯ **category A (Direct Access)**: a motorcycle with a power output of at least 35kW (46.6bhp).

Your test motorcycle must have a valid tax disc and L-plates (or D-plates, if taking your test in Wales) displayed front and rear.

If you pass your practical test on an automatic motorcycle your licence will be valid for automatics only.

Only physically disabled riders may take their test using a motorcycle and sidecar, and on passing their licence they will be restricted to motorcycle and sidecar outfits only.

coping with nerves

Of course you'll be nervous during your motorcycle test – everyone is. A reasonable degree of nervousness isn't necessarily a bad thing as it sharpens up your senses and concentration. But you will feel a lot happier if you have put in plenty of practice and have reached the stage where you are fluent and confident in your riding.

Make sure that you arrive at the test centre for each of the test modules in good time to avoid any last minute panics. Look out all the documents you'll need the day before, and get an early night.

module one

Module one of the practical test is conducted at a specially-designed multi-purpose test centre (MPTC). The examiner will require you to perform a series of off-road exercises around a circuit marked out with coloured cones.

Once you have successfully completed module one you can take module two, which involves a ride of around 30 minutes on the public road under the observation of an examiner.

In addition to the off- and on-road riding assessments, as part of the practical test you will be asked two safety check questions relating to your bike, plus a question about carrying a passenger, and you will be required to pass a simple eyesight test.

eyesight examination

An eyesight examination takes place at the start of module two. You must be able to read the current style of numberplate from a distance of 20 metres. You can wear spectacles or contact lenses to do so, but if so you must keep them on when you are riding.

The examiner will select a parked vehicle probably a little further away than 20 metres and ask you to read the numberplate. If you cannot read it, the examiner will measure the distance exactly and ask you to repeat

the test. If you are still unable to read it, you have failed and the examiner will end your test at this point.

safety check questions

Candidates are required to answer two questions about motorcycle safety checks.

These are 'tell me' and 'show me' questions. For a 'tell me' question, you will be required to tell the examiner how you would carry out a procedure such as checking the engine oil.

For a 'show me' question, you need to show the examiner how you would carry out a safety check, such as inspecting the indicator lights to make sure they are working. You will not be required to touch any hot engine parts, but you may have to switch on the ignition.

Your answers should refer specifically to the motorcycle you are taking your test on, so practise these maintenance checks on your bike and study its handbook before you take your test.

The questions you will be asked are set out below. If you fail to answer one or both of the safety check questions correctly it counts as one minor fault.

'show me' questions

Q *show me how you would check that the horn is working on this machine*
A press the horn button to sound the horn (turn on the ignition first if necessary).

Q *show me how you would check the operation of the engine cut-out switch*
A operate the switch (without the engine being started).

Q *show me how you would check the operation of the front brake on this machine*
A wheel the machine forward and apply the front brake to test that it is working.

You will be asked to show how you would carry out basic checks on your bike such as checking that the brake light is working (left) or that the emergency cut-out switch is operating correctly (right)

Q *show me how you would check that the brake lights are working*
A operate the brake and check that the brake light is working by cupping your hand around the light, or observing its reflection in a surface such as a nearby window or garage door, or asking someone to help you check it.

Q *show me how you would check the operation of the brakes on this machine*
A check for excessive travel on the brake lever and the brake pedal and for unusual play or sponginess.

Q *show me what checks you would make on the steering movement before using the machine*
A check that the handlebars are free to move smoothly from full left lock to full right lock without any control cables being stretched, trapped or pinched and without any snagging between moving and fixed parts.

Q *show me how you would switch on the rear fog light and explain when you would use it (if fitted)*
A operate the fog light switch (with the ignition or engine on if necessary). Check warning light is on. Explain the conditions in which you would use it (see p186).

Q *show me how to switch your headlight from dipped to main beam*
A operate switch (with ignition or engine on if necessary) and check that the main beam warning light illuminates.

'tell me' questions

Q *tell me how you would check the condition of the chain on this machine*
A explain that you would check for chain wear, correct tension and rear wheel alignment. Tension should be adjusted as specified in the motorcycle's handbook. The drive chain should be kept lubricated to ensure excessive wear does not occur.

❓ *tell me how you would check your tyres to ensure that they are correctly inflated, have sufficient tread depth and that their general condition is safe to use on the road*

🅐 explain that you would find the correct tyre pressure settings in the owner's manual. Pressures should be checked using a reliable gauge. Tread must be at least 1mm deep, forming a continuous band across at least three-quarters of the width of the tyre and all the way around it (on a bike over 50cc). There should be no lumps, bulges or tears in the tyre.

❓ *identify where you would check the engine oil level and tell me how you would check that the engine has sufficient oil*

🅐 indicate where to check the oil level, on the sight glass or dipstick. Explain that the sight glass should be clean before checking and that the oil level should be between the maximum and minimum marks. A dipstick should be removed and wiped clean, returned then removed again, before checking the level against the maximum and minimum marks.

❓ *identify where the brake fluid reservoir is and tell me how you would check that you have a safe level of hydraulic fluid*

🅐 indicate the reservoir and explain how to check the brake fluid level against the maximum and minimum markings.

❓ *tell me how you would check that the lights and reflectors are clean and working*

🅐 explain that you would operate the light switch (turning on the ignition if necessary). Identify the reflectors and say that you would check lights and reflectors visually to ensure they are clean and operating correctly.

pillion question

Your examiner will ask you a straightforward question on the topic of 'balance when carrying a passenger'. There is no set list of questions to revise, but typical questions you may be asked include:

⊙ what problems could arise from carrying a pillion passenger?

⊙ how should a passenger be carried on the pillion seat?

⊙ how would the balance of the machine be affected if you carried a pillion passenger?

Refer to p206 where you will find full details about carrying a pillion passenger. Make sure you know:

⊙ what you should tell an inexperienced pillion passenger that they need to do when riding on a bike

⊙ how the extra weight of a pillion passenger may affect the way your bike handles

⊙ what adjustments you may need to make to your bike to compensate for the extra weight of a pillion passenger.

As part of your test you will be asked one question about carrying a pillion passenger

Module one of the practical test involves completing a series of off-road exercises

off-road exercises

The off-road exercises in module one are designed to test your manoeuvring and slow riding skills. The exercises are not difficult but you will be much more likely to pass if you practise them thoroughly beforehand.

Although these exercises take place on a safe area away from traffic, you are required to carry out observation in the same way as if you were riding on the road, and if your observation is inadequate you will fail.

Blue, green, red and yellow cones are laid out to form a left or a right circuit (*see diagram overleaf*). The examiner will decide which layout to use and you will not know in advance whether you will have a left or right circuit.

For some exercises minimum speeds are specified and measured by a speed detector. You must reach 30km/h (19mph) during the circuit ride and 50km/h (32mph) before the emergency stop and avoidance exercises. If you do not ride within five per cent of these speeds you will incur a riding fault (you are permitted to make up to five riding faults before failing module one). If you fail the emergency stop then you will

not be permitted to continue to the hazard avoidence exercise.

For mopeds the speed requirement is 30km/h (19mph) for all exercises.

After successfully completing module one of the practical test you will be able to go on to take module two, which depending on your location may not necessarily be conducted from the same test site.

If you fail module one then you will be required to wait three working days before retaking it.

The examiner will brief you on what you need to do before you start the off-road exercises

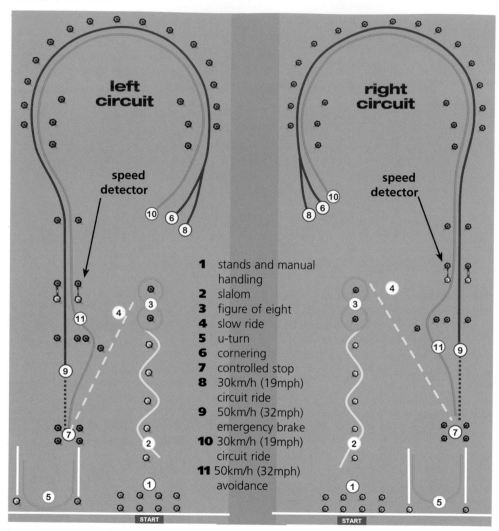

left circuit

speed detector

right circuit

speed detector

1 stands and manual handling
2 slalom
3 figure of eight
4 slow ride
5 u-turn
6 cornering
7 controlled stop
8 30km/h (19mph) circuit ride
9 50km/h (32mph) emergency brake
10 30km/h (19mph) circuit ride
11 50km/h (32mph) avoidance

START

START

off-road exercises
The examiner will ask you to perform the following off-road exercises:

⊘ manual handling
Park your bike on its stand in one of the coned-off parking bays. Take the bike off its stand, wheel it (1) into the other parking bay and place it back on its stand. Don't forget to take observation as though you were in a car park or on the road.

❂ slalom & figure of eight

Ride between the yellow cones (2); when you reach the blue cones (3), ride around them in a figure of eight for two complete circuits.

❂ slow riding

Ride slowly, as though in a queue of traffic, from where you have carried out the figure of eight manoeuvre to the U-turn area (4).

❂ U-turn

Make a turn between the two lines (5) and come to a halt facing the other way. Remember your observation and do not touch the lines, which represent kerbs.

❂ controlled stop

Ride around the bend (6) between the red and blue cones (there is no minimum speed requirement) and stop with your front wheel in the box formed by the blue cones (7).

❂ emergency stop

Enter the bend between the red and blue cones, taking the corner at a minimum 30km/h (8). When you pass the speed detector you must be doing at least 50km/h. When the examiner signals, stop immediately and under full control (9).

❂ hazard avoidance

Enter the bend between the red and blue cones and take the corner at a minimum 30km/h (10). When you pass the speed detector you must be doing at least 50km/h. Steer through the blue cones (11) and come to a controlled stop near the final blue cones.

Module two

In module two of the practical test your examiner will assess your ability to ride on the road and interact with other road users. The test takes in a wide range of the riding situations covered in this book, although it excludes motorways.

The examiner will follow you round the test route, either on a motorcycle or in a car. During the ride the examiner will give you instructions and route directions via a radio receiver.

You will be expected to keep riding ahead, unless the examiner specifically asks you to turn or traffic signs direct you otherwise. So if you receive no other instruction at a roundabout, take the exit straight ahead. If a road sign instructs you to turn left or right ahead, the examiner will expect you to obey this without being told to do so.

independent riding

For around ten minutes during your test you will be required to ride independently. This means that the examiner will ask you to follow traffic signs towards a destination, or follow a series of directions. He may show you a diagram to make these instructions clearer.

The purpose of the independent riding exercise is to assess that you are able to ride safely on your own and make your own decisions. It is not a test of your ability to navigate – you won't lose marks if you go the wrong way (unless you commit a fault in doing so), and if you need a reminder of the directions you can ask the examiner. If you do take a wrong turning then the examiner will help you get back on the right route so you can continue with the independent riding.

Your examiner will not tell you to turn where a road sign indicates the direction you must take

You will be required to make an angle start from behind a parked vehicle during the on-road test

special exercises

During the test you will be required to perform two moving-off exercises:

⊙angle start

You will be asked to pull up just behind a parked vehicle, then move off again at an angle. The examiner will be watching your balance and control and that you carry out full all-round observation for traffic coming from ahead and behind.

⊙hill start

You will be asked to stop on an uphill gradient and move off again. You must take into account your bike's reduced acceleration and move off without obstructing other traffic.

If you do an angle or hill start while you are riding the test route it may not be necessary for the examiner to ask you to perform one as a separate exercise.

Remember that whenever you are asked to stop at the side of the road for an exercise the examiner will expect you to select somewhere safe and legal to stop.

fault assessment

The examiner assesses faults committed during both modules of the practical test according to three categories:

⊙dangerous faults

This is when a fault committed during the test has resulted in actual danger. Committing one dangerous fault is a test failure. An examiner who considers that a candidate is riding dangerously may stop the test on the spot

⊙serious faults

This is when a potentially dangerous incident occurs, or the candidate reveals a habitual riding fault. Committing one serious fault results in failure

⊙rider faults

These are minor faults. You can make up to five rider faults in module one, and up to ten rider faults in module two, before failing your test.

if you fail

Don't be too disheartened. If you fail module two of your practical test there's no reason why you shouldn't go on to pass next time. The most common reason why applicants fail is lack of preparation. If you've tried to prepare for the test on your own and failed, now would be a good time to consider signing up for some lessons with a qualified instructor.

The examiner will give you a riding test report showing all the faults you have made, plus a short debrief, running through the reasons why you failed. Pay attention to improving the weak points revealed by your test, but don't concentrate only on the items where you failed, or you may find yourself getting out of practice in other areas.

If you fail module two of the practical test you must wait at least 10 working days before you can retake it.

Signing up for lessons will boost your chances of success when you retake your practical test

after the test

Those few seconds as you wait for the examiner's verdict at the end of your test will be as nerve-racking as any in your life. Being told you've passed comes as a massive relief. But passing doesn't mean you should stop thinking about learning to ride. Your career as a motorcyclist is only just beginning, and for a good rider the learning never stops.

UNIPART

passing your test

If you pass and have a photocard driving licence issued after March 1 2004, your examiner will ask if you want your full motorcycle licence issued to you automatically. If you do, the examiner will scan the details of your provisional licence and send them electronically to the DVLA. You will then be given a pass certificate to prove you have passed your test and the DVLA will send you a full licence by post within three weeks.

If you have an older licence, you will be given a pass certificate which you must exchange for a full licence within two years. You will need to complete form D1 (available from the post office) and send it to the DVLA with all the supporting documentation required and the appropriate fee.

moving up

Now that you have a full licence you can use a motorway and carry a pillion passenger. Try both for the first time under good conditions, not when you're in a hurry, the weather is poor or the traffic heavy. Some extra training may help you to cope safely with these new situations.

If you passed the category A test on a 125cc motorcycle, you are restricted for two years to a bike with a maximum power output of 25kW (33bhp). Once the two years is up, you can ride any type of bike.

If you reach the age of 21 during the two years, you can elect to take a further test under the Accelerated Access scheme. Passing this qualifies you to ride any motorcycle.

If you passed your test under the Direct Access scheme you are immediately qualified to ride any bike.

For many riders, moving up to high-performance bike is a tempting prospect – but don't try to take on too much too soon. Top sports bikes are capable of astonishing

acceleration and you need to build up your experience and bike handling skills over a number of years on less powerful machines before graduating to one of these.

Guard against overconfidence in the early months and years after passing your test. Motorcycling is a complex skill which takes a considerable time to master and you must never forget your vulnerabilty compared with road users in larger vehicles.

advanced riding

The best riders know that no matter how much experience you have, you can never stop learning to be a better rider. Treat your riding seriously and continuously assess how you are performing on the road.

Taking further training once you have passed your test makes excellent sense. The Enhanced Rider Scheme gives you a chance to address any weak points there may be in your riding, and once you have successfully completed the course it also entitles you to a discount on your insurance premium.

You should also consider taking an advanced riding test, such as those organised by RoSPA and the Institute of Advanced Motorists.

If you want to get the most out of your riding, consider going on to take an advanced test

14 theory questions

To pass your theory test you will need to answer correctly 43 out of 50 questions on all aspects of riding. The following question bank shows examples of the types of question you will be asked. Test your knowledge by answering these questions and checking to see if you have answered correctly. If you don't understand one of the answers, refer to the accompanying explanatory text for extra information.

alertness

1.1 Mark one answer

You are about to turn right. What should you do just before you turn?

☐ Give the correct signal
☐ Take a 'lifesaver' glance over your shoulder
☐ Select the correct gear
☐ Get in position ready for the turn

When you are turning right, plan your approach to the junction. Signal and select the correct gear in good time. Just before you turn, take a 'lifesaver' glance for a final check behind and to the side of you.

1.2 Mark one answer

What is the 'lifesaver' when riding a motorcycle?

☐ A certificate every motorcyclist must have
☐ A final, rearward glance before changing direction
☐ A part of the motorcycle tool kit
☐ A mirror fitted to check blind spots

This action makes you aware of what's happening behind and alongside you. The 'lifesaver' glance should be timed so that you still have time to react if it isn't safe to perform the manoeuvre.

1.3 Mark one answer

You see road signs showing a sharp bend ahead. What should you do?

☐ Continue at the same speed
☐ Slow down as you go around the bend
☐ Slow down as you come out of the bend
☐ Slow down before the bend

Always look for any advance warning of hazards, such as road signs and hazard warning lines. Use this information to plan ahead and to help you avoid the need for late, harsh braking. Your motorcycle should be upright and moving in a straight line when you brake. This will help you to keep maximum control when dealing with the hazard.

1.4 Mark one answer

You are riding at night and are dazzled by the headlights of an oncoming car. You should

☐ slow down or stop
☐ close your eyes
☐ flash your headlight
☐ turn your head away

If you are dazzled by lights when riding, slow down or stop until your eyes have adjusted. Taking a hand off the handlebars to adjust your visor while riding could lead to loss of control. A dirty or scratched visor could cause dazzle and impair vision further.

1.5 Mark one answer

When riding, your shoulders obstruct the view in your mirrors. To overcome this you should

☐ indicate earlier than normal
☐ fit smaller mirrors
☐ extend the mirror arms
☐ brake earlier than normal

It's essential that you have a clear view all around. Adjust your mirrors to give you the best view of the road behind. If your elbows obscure the view try fitting mirrors with longer stems.

1.6 Mark one answer

On a motorcycle you should only use a mobile telephone when you

☐ have a pillion passenger to help
☐ have parked in a safe place
☐ have a motorcycle with automatic gears
☐ are travelling on a quiet road

It's important that you're in full control at all times. Even using a hands-free kit can distract your attention from the road. Don't take the risk. If you need to use a mobile phone stop at a safe and convenient place.

1.7   Mark one answer

You are riding at night. You have your headlight on main beam. Another vehicle is overtaking you. When should you dip your headlight?

☐ When the other vehicle signals to overtake
☐ As soon as the other vehicle moves out to overtake
☐ As soon as the other vehicle passes you
☐ After the other vehicle pulls in front of you

At night you should dip your headlight to avoid dazzling oncoming drivers or those ahead of you. If you're being overtaken, dip your headlight as the other vehicle comes past. When you switch to dipped beam your view of the road ahead will be reduced, so look ahead for hazards on your side of the road before you do so.

1.8   Mark one answer

To move off safely from a parked position you should

☐ signal if other drivers will need to slow down
☐ leave your motorcycle on its stand until the road is clear
☐ give an arm signal as well as using your indicators
☐ look over your shoulder for a final check

Before you move off from the side of the road on a motorcycle you must take a final look around over your shoulder. There may be another road user who is not visible in your mirrors.

1.9   Mark one answer

Riding a motorcycle when you are cold could cause you to

☐ be more alert
☐ be more relaxed
☐ react more quickly
☐ lose concentration

It can be difficult to keep warm when riding a motorcycle. Although it isn't cheap, proper motorcycle clothing will help to keep you warm and is essential. It also helps to protect you if you fall off or are involved in a crash.

1.10   Mark one answer

You are riding at night and are dazzled by the lights of an approaching vehicle. What should you do?

☐ Switch off your headlight
☐ Switch to main beam
☐ Slow down and stop
☐ Flash your headlight

If your view of the road ahead is restricted because you are being dazzled by approaching headlights, slow down and if you need to, pull over and stop.

1.11   Mark one answer

You should always check the 'blind areas' before

☐ moving off
☐ slowing down
☐ changing gear
☐ giving a signal

These are the areas behind and to either side of you which are not covered by your mirrors. You should always check these areas before moving off or changing direction.

1.12   Mark one answer

The 'blind area' should be checked before

☐ giving a signal
☐ applying the brakes
☐ changing direction
☐ giving an arm signal

The areas not covered by your mirrors are called blind spots. They should always be checked before changing direction. This check is so important that it is called the 'lifesaver'.

1.13   Mark one answer

It is vital to check the 'blind area' before

☐ changing gear
☐ giving signals
☐ slowing down
☐ changing lanes

Other vehicles may be hidden in the blind spots that are not covered by your mirrors.
   Always make sure it is safe before changing lanes by taking a 'lifesaver' check.

1.14   Mark one answer

Why can it be helpful to have mirrors fitted on each side of your motorcycle?

☐ To judge the gap when filtering in traffic
☐ To give protection when riding in poor weather
☐ To make your motorcycle appear larger to other drivers
☐ To give you the best view of the road behind

When riding on the road you need to know as much about following traffic as you can.
   A mirror fitted on each side of your motorcycle will help give you the best view of the road behind.

1.15   Mark one answer

In motorcycling, the term 'lifesaver' refers to

☐ a final rearward glance
☐ an approved safety helmet
☐ a reflective jacket
☐ the two-second rule

Mirrors on motorcycles don't always give a clear view behind. There will be times when you need to look round to see the full picture.

1.16   Mark one answer

You are about to emerge from a junction. Your pillion passenger tells you it's clear. When should you rely on their judgement?

☐ Never, you should always look for yourself
☐ When the roads are very busy
☐ When the roads are very quiet
☐ Only when they are a qualified rider

Your passenger may be inexperienced in judging traffic situations, have a poor view and not have seen a potential hazard. You are responsible for your own safety and your passenger. Always make your own checks to be sure it is safe to pull out.

1.17   Mark one answer

You are about to emerge from a junction. Your pillion passenger tells you it's safe to go. What should you do?

☐ Go, if you are sure they can see clearly
☐ Check for yourself before pulling out
☐ Take their advice and ride on
☐ Ask them to check again before you go

You must rely on your own judgement when making decisions. Only you know your own capabilities and the performance of your machine.

1.18   Mark one answer

What must you do before stopping normally?

☐ Put both feet down
☐ Select first gear
☐ Use your mirrors
☐ Move into neutral

Check your mirrors before slowing down or stopping as there could be vehicles close behind you. If necessary, look behind before stopping.

1.19   Mark two answers

You want to change lanes in busy, moving traffic. Why could looking over your shoulder help?

☐ Mirrors may not cover blind spots
☐ To avoid having to give a signal
☐ So traffic ahead will make room for you
☐ So your balance will not be affected
☐ Drivers behind you would be warned

Before changing lanes make sure there's a safe gap to move into. Looking over your shoulder allows you to check the area not covered by your mirrors, where a vehicle could be hidden from view. It also warns following drivers that you want to change lanes.

1.20   Mark one answer

You have been waiting for some time to make a right turn into a side road. What should you do just before you make the turn?

☐ Move close to the kerb
☐ Select a higher gear
☐ Make a 'lifesaver' check
☐ Wave to the oncoming traffic

Remember your 'lifesaver' glance before you start to turn. If you've been waiting for some time and a queue has built up behind you, a vehicle further back may try to overtake. It is especially important to look out for other motorcycles in this situation which may be approaching at speed.

1.21   Mark one answer

You are turning right onto a dual carriageway. What should you do before emerging?

☐ Stop, and then select a very low gear
☐ Position in the left gutter of the side road
☐ Check that the central reservation is wide enough
☐ Check there is enough room for vehicles behind you

Before emerging right onto a dual carriageway make sure that the central reservation is wide enough to protect your vehicle. If it's not, you should treat it as one road and check that it's clear in both directions before pulling out. Otherwise, you could obstruct part of the carriageway and cause a hazard, both for yourself and other road users.

1.22 Mark one answer

When riding a different motorcycle you should

☐ ask someone to ride with you for the first time
☐ ride as soon as possible as all controls and switches are the same
☐ leave your gloves behind so switches can be operated more easily
☐ be sure you know where all controls and switches are

Before you ride any motorcycle make sure you're familiar with the layout of all the controls and switches. While control layouts are generally similar, there may be differences in their feel and method of operation.

1.23 Mark one answer

You are turning right at a large roundabout. Before you leave the roundabout you should

☐ take a 'lifesaver' glance over your left shoulder
☐ give way to all traffic from the right
☐ put on your right indicator
☐ cancel the left indicator

You need to be aware of what's happening behind and alongside you. Looking left, just before you move across gives you time to react if it isn't safe to make the manoeuvre.

1.24 Mark one answer

You are turning right at a large roundabout. Before you cross a lane to reach your exit you should

☐ take a 'lifesaver' glance over your right shoulder
☐ put on your right indicator
☐ take a 'lifesaver' glance over your left shoulder
☐ cancel the left indicator

On busy roundabouts traffic may be moving very quickly and changing lanes suddenly. You need to be aware of what's happening all around you. Before crossing lanes to the left make sure you take a 'lifesaver' glance to the left. This gives you time to react if it's not safe to make the manoeuvre.

1.25 Mark one answer

You are positioned to turn right on a multi-lane roundabout. What should you do before moving to a lane on your left?

☐ Take a 'lifesaver' glance over your right shoulder
☐ Cancel the left signal
☐ Signal to the right
☐ Take a 'lifesaver' glance over your left shoulder

Beware of traffic changing lanes quickly and at the last moment on these roundabouts. Be aware of all signs and road markings so that you can position correctly in good time. Your life could depend on you knowing where other vehicles are.

1.26 Mark one answer

You are turning right on a multi-lane roundabout. When should you take a 'lifesaver' glance over your left shoulder?

☐ After moving into the left lane
☐ After leaving the roundabout
☐ Before signalling to the right
☐ Before moving into the left lane

The 'lifesaver' is essential to motorcyclists and is exactly what it says. It could save your life. It's purpose is to check the blind spot that is not covered by your mirrors.
   Understand and learn how and when you should use it.

1.27 Mark one answer

You are on a motorway. You see an incident on the other side of the road. Your lane is clear. You should

☐ assist the emergency services
☐ stop, and cross the road to help
☐ concentrate on what is happening ahead
☐ place a warning triangle in the road

Always concentrate on the road ahead. Try not to be distracted by an incident on the other side of the road. Many motorway collisions occur due to traffic slowing down. This is because drivers are looking at something on the other side of the road.

1.28 Mark one answer

Before you make a U-turn in the road, you should

☐ give an arm signal as well as using your indicators
☐ signal so that other drivers can slow down for you
☐ look over your shoulder for a final check
☐ select a higher gear than normal

If you want to make a U-turn, slow down and ensure that the road is clear in both directions. Make sure that the road is wide enough to carry out the manoeuvre safely.

1.29 Mark three answers

As you approach this bridge you should

☐ move into the middle of the road to get a better view
☐ slow down
☐ get over the bridge as quickly as possible
☐ consider using your horn
☐ find another route
☐ beware of pedestrians

This sign gives you a warning. The brow of the hill prevents you seeing oncoming traffic so you must be cautious. The bridge is narrow and there may not be enough room for you to pass an oncoming vehicle at this point. There is no footpath, so pedestrians may be walking in the road. Consider the hidden hazards and be ready to react if necessary.

1.30 Mark one answer

In which of these situations should you avoid overtaking?

☐ Just after a bend
☐ In a one-way street
☐ On a 30 mph road
☐ Approaching a dip in the road

As you begin to think about overtaking, ask yourself if it's really necessary. If you can't see well ahead stay back and wait for a safer place to pull out.

1.31 Mark one answer

This road marking warns

☐ drivers to use the hard shoulder
☐ overtaking drivers there is a bend to the left
☐ overtaking drivers to move back to the left
☐ drivers that it is safe to overtake

You should plan your overtaking to take into account any hazards ahead. In this picture the marking indicates that you are approaching a junction. You will not have time to overtake and move back into the left safely.

1.32 Mark one answer

Your mobile phone rings while you are

☐ stop immediately
☐ answer it immediately
☐ pull up in a suitable place
☐ pull up at the nearest kerb

The safest option is to switch off your mobile phone before you set off, and use a message service. Even hands-free systems are likely to distract your attention. Don't endanger other road users. If you need to make a call, pull up in a safe place when you can, you may need to go some distance before you can find one. It's illegal to use a hand-held mobile or similar device when driving or riding, except in a genuine emergency.

1.33 Mark one answer

Why are these yellow lines painted across the road?

☐ To help you choose the correct lane
☐ To help you keep the correct separation distance
☐ To make you aware of your speed
☐ To tell you the distance to the roundabout

These lines are often found on the approach to a roundabout or a dangerous junction. They give you extra warning to adjust your speed. Look well ahead and do this in good time.

1.34 Mark one answer

You are approaching traffic lights that have been on green for some time. You should

☐ accelerate hard
☐ maintain your speed
☐ be ready to stop
☐ brake hard

The longer traffic lights have been on green, the greater the chance of them changing. Always allow for this on approach and be prepared to stop.

1.35 Mark one answer

Which of the following should you do before stopping?

☐ Sound the horn
☐ Use the mirrors
☐ Select a higher gear
☐ Flash your headlights

Before pulling up check the mirrors to see what is happening behind you. Also assess what is ahead and make sure you give the correct signal if it helps other road users.

1.36 Mark one answer

When following a large vehicle you should keep well back because this

☐ allows you to corner more quickly
☐ helps the large vehicle to stop more easily
☐ allows the driver to see you in the mirrors
☐ helps you to keep out of the wind

If you're following a large vehicle but are so close to it that you can't see the exterior mirrors, the driver can't see you.
Keeping well back will also allow you to see the road ahead by looking past either side of the large vehicle.

1.37 Mark one answer

When you see a hazard ahead you should use the mirrors. Why is this?

☐ Because you will need to accelerate out of danger
☐ To assess how your actions will affect following traffic
☐ Because you will need to brake sharply to a stop
☐ To check what is happening on the road ahead

You should be constantly scanning the road for clues about what is going to happen next. Check your mirrors regularly, particularly as soon as you spot a hazard. What is happening behind may affect your response to hazards ahead.

1.38 Mark one answer

You are waiting to turn right at the end of a road. Your view is obstructed by parked vehicles. What should you do?

☐ Stop and then move forward slowly and carefully for a proper view
☐ Move quickly to where you can see so you only block traffic from one direction
☐ Wait for a pedestrian to let you know when it is safe for you to emerge
☐ Turn your vehicle around immediately and find another junction to use

At junctions your view is often restricted by buildings, trees or parked cars. You need to be able to see in order to judge a safe gap. Edge forward slowly and keep looking all the time. Don't cause other road users to change speed or direction as you emerge.

attitude

2.1 Mark one answer

You are riding towards a zebra crossing. Pedestrians are waiting to cross. You should

☐ give way to the elderly and infirm only
☐ slow down and prepare to stop
☐ use your headlight to indicate they can cross
☐ wave at them to cross the road

Look for people waiting to cross and be ready to slow down or stop. Some pedestrians may be hesitant. Children can be unpredictable and may hesitate or run out unexpectedly.

2.2 Mark one answer

You are riding a motorcycle and following a large vehicle at 40 mph. You should position yourself

☐ close behind to make it easier to overtake the vehicle
☐ to the left of the road to make it easier to be seen
☐ close behind the vehicle to keep out of the wind
☐ well back so that you can see past the vehicle

You need to be able to see well down the road and be ready for any hazards. Staying too close to the vehicle will reduce your view of the road ahead and the driver of the vehicle in front may not be able to see you either. Without a safe separation gap you do not have the time and space necessary to react to any hazards.

2.3 Mark one answer

You are riding on a country road. Two horses with riders are in the distance. You should

☐ continue at your normal speed
☐ change down the gears quickly
☐ slow down and be ready to stop
☐ flash your headlight to warn them

Animals are easily frightened by moving motor vehicles. If you're approaching horses keep your speed down and watch to see if the rider has any difficulty keeping control. Always be ready to stop if necessary.

2.4 Mark one answer

You are approaching a red light at a puffin crossing. Pedestrians are on the crossing. The red light will stay on until

☐ you start to edge forward on to the crossing
☐ the pedestrians have reached a safe position
☐ the pedestrians are clear of the front of your motorcycle
☐ a driver from the opposite direction reaches the crossing

The electronic device will automatically detect when the pedestrians have reached a safe position. Don't proceed until the green light shows it is safe to do so.

2.5 Mark one answer

You are riding a slow-moving scooter on a narrow winding road. You should

☐ keep well out to stop vehicles overtaking dangerously
☐ wave vehicles behind you to pass, if you think they can overtake quickly
☐ pull in safely when you can, to let vehicles behind you overtake
☐ give a left signal when it is safe for vehicles to overtake you

Try not to hold up a queue of traffic. This might lead to other road users becoming impatient and attempting dangerous manoeuvres.
   If you're riding a slow-moving scooter or small motorcycle on a narrow road and a queue of traffic has built up behind you, look out for a safe place to pull in.

2.6 Mark two answers

When riding a motorcycle your normal road position should allow

☐ other vehicles to overtake on your left
☐ the driver ahead to see you in their mirrors
☐ you to prevent vehicles behind from overtaking
☐ you to be seen by traffic that is emerging from junctions ahead
☐ you to ride within half a metre (1 foot 8 ins) of the kerb

Aim to ride in the middle of your lane. Avoid riding in the gutter or in the centre of the road, where you might obstruct overtaking traffic or put yourself in danger from oncoming traffic. Riding in this position could also encourage other traffic to overtake you on the left.

2.7 Mark one answer
Young, inexperienced and newly qualified motorcyclists can often be involved in crashes. This is due to

☐ being too cautious at junctions
☐ riding in the middle of their lane
☐ showing off and being competitive
☐ wearing full weather protection

Over-confidence, lack of experience and poor judgement can lead to disaster. No matter what anyone says, don't do anything that could endanger lives. It's not worth the risk.

2.8 Mark one answer
At a pelican crossing the flashing amber light means you MUST

☐ stop and wait for the green light
☐ stop and wait for the red light
☐ give way to pedestrians waiting to cross
☐ give way to pedestrians already on the crossing

Pelican crossings are signal-controlled crossings operated by pedestrians. Pushbutton controls change the signals. Pelican crossings have no red-and-amber stage before green. Instead, they have a flashing amber light, which means you MUST give way to pedestrians already on the crossing, but if it is clear, you may continue.

2.9 Mark one answer
You should never wave people across at pedestrian crossings because

☐ there may be another vehicle coming
☐ they may not be looking
☐ it is safer for you to carry on
☐ they may not be ready to cross

It people are waiting to use a pedestrian crossing, slow down and be prepared to stop. Don't wave them across the road since another driver may not have seen them, not have seen your signal and may not be able to stop safely.

2.10 Mark one answer
'Tailgating' means

☐ using the rear door of a hatchback car
☐ reversing into a parking space
☐ following another vehicle too closely
☐ driving with rear fog lights on

'Tailgating' is used to describe this dangerous practice, often seen in fast-moving traffic and on motorways. Following the vehicle in front too closely is dangerous because it

• restricts your view of the road ahead

• leaves you no safety margin if the vehicle in front slows down or stops suddenly.

2.11 Mark one answer
Following this vehicle too closely is unwise because

☐ your brakes will overheat
☐ your view ahead is increased
☐ your engine will overheat
☐ your view ahead is reduced

Staying back will increase your view of the road ahead. This will help you to see any hazards that might occur and allow you more time to react.

2.12 Mark one answer
You are following a vehicle on a wet road. You should leave a time gap of at least

☐ one second
☐ two seconds
☐ three seconds
☐ four seconds

Wet roads will reduce your tyres' grip on the road. The safe separation gap of at least two seconds in dry conditions should be doubled in wet weather.

2.13　Mark one answer

A long, heavily-laden lorry is taking a long time to overtake you. What should you do?

☐ Speed up
☐ Slow down
☐ Hold your speed
☐ Change direction

A long lorry with a heavy load will need more time to pass you than a car, especially on an uphill stretch of road. Slow down and allow the lorry to pass.

2.14　Mark three answers

Which of the following vehicles will use blue flashing beacons?

☐ Motorway maintenance
☐ Bomb disposal
☐ Blood transfusion
☐ Police patrol
☐ Breakdown recovery

When you see emergency vehicles with blue flashing beacons, move out of the way as soon as it is safe to do so.

2.15　Mark three answers

Which THREE of these emergency services might have blue flashing beacons?

☐ Coastguard
☐ Bomb disposal
☐ Gritting lorries
☐ Animal ambulances
☐ Mountain rescue
☐ Doctors' cars

When attending an emergency these vehicles will be travelling at speed. You should help their progress by pulling over and allowing them to pass. Do so safely.
　　Don't stop suddenly or in a dangerous position.

2.16　Mark one answer

When being followed by an ambulance showing a flashing blue beacon you should

☐ pull over as soon as safely possible to let it pass
☐ accelerate hard to get away from it
☐ maintain your speed and course
☐ brake harshly and immediately stop in the road

Pull over in a place where the ambulance can pass safely. Check that there are no bollards or obstructions in the road that will prevent it from doing so.

2.17　Mark one answer

What type of emergency vehicle is fitted with a green flashing beacon?

☐ Fire engine
☐ Road gritter
☐ Ambulance
☐ Doctor's car

A green flashing beacon on a vehicle means the driver or passenger is a doctor on an emergency call. Give way to them if it's safe to do so. Be aware that the vehicle may be travelling quickly or may stop in a hurry.

2.18　Mark one answer

A flashing green beacon on a vehicle means

☐ police on non-urgent duties
☐ doctor on an emergency call
☐ road safety patrol operating
☐ gritting in progress

If you see a vehicle with a flashing green beacon approaching, allow it to pass when you can do so safely. Be aware that someone's life could depend on the driver making good progress through traffic.

2.19　Mark one answer

Diamond-shaped signs give instructions to

☐ tram drivers
☐ bus drivers
☐ lorry drivers
☐ taxi drivers

These signs only apply to trams. They are directed at tram drivers but you should know their meaning so that you're aware of the priorities and are able to anticipate the actions of the driver.

2.20 Mark one answer

On a road where trams operate, which of these vehicles will be most at risk from the tram rails?

☐ Cars
☐ Cycles
☐ Buses
☐ Lorries

The narrow wheels of a bicycle can become stuck in the tram rails, causing the cyclist to stop suddenly, wobble or even lose balance altogether. The tram lines are also slippery which could cause a cyclist to slide or fall off.

2.21 Mark one answer

What should you use your horn for?

☐ To alert others to your presence
☐ To allow you right of way
☐ To greet other road users
☐ To signal your annoyance

Your horn must not be used between 11.30 pm and 7 am in a built-up area or when you are stationary, unless a moving vehicle poses a danger. Its function is to alert other road users to your presence.

2.22 Mark one answer

You are in a one-way street and want to turn right. You should position yourself

☐ in the right-hand lane
☐ in the left-hand lane
☐ in either lane, depending on the traffic
☐ just left of the centre line

If you're travelling in a one-way street and wish to turn right you should take up a position in the right-hand lane. This will enable other road users not wishing to turn to proceed on the left. Indicate your intention and take up your position in good time.

2.23 Mark one answer

You wish to turn right ahead. Why should you take up the correct position in good time?

☐ To allow other drivers to pull out in front of you
☐ To give a better view into the road that you're joining
☐ To help other road users know what you intend to do
☐ To allow drivers to pass you on the right

If you wish to turn right into a side road take up your position in good time. Move to the centre of the road when it's safe to do so. This will allow vehicles to pass you on the left. Early planning will show other traffic what you intend to do.

2.24 Mark one answer

At which type of crossing are cyclists allowed to ride across with pedestrians?

☐ Toucan
☐ Puffin
☐ Pelican
☐ Zebra

A toucan crossing is designed to allow pedestrians and cyclists to cross at the same time. Look out for cyclists approaching the crossing at speed.

2.25 Mark one answer

You are travelling at the legal speed limit. A vehicle comes up quickly behind, flashing its headlights. You should

☐ accelerate to make a gap behind you
☐ touch the brakes sharply to show your brake lights
☐ maintain your speed to prevent the vehicle from overtaking
☐ allow the vehicle to overtake

Don't enforce the speed limit by blocking another vehicle's progress. This will only lead to the other driver becoming more frustrated. Allow the other vehicle to pass when you can do so safely.

2.26 Mark one answer

You should ONLY flash your headlights to other road users

☐ to show that you are giving way
☐ to show that you are about to turn
☐ to tell them that you have right of way
☐ to let them know that you are there

You should only flash your headlights to warn others of your presence. Don't use them to greet others, show impatience or give priority to other road users. They could misunderstand your signal.

2.27 Mark one answer

You are approaching unmarked crossroads. How should you deal with this type of junction?

☐ Accelerate and keep to the middle
☐ Slow down and keep to the right
☐ Accelerate looking to the left
☐ Slow down and look both ways

Be extra-cautious, especially when your view is restricted by hedges, bushes, walls and large vehicles etc. In the summer months these junctions can become more difficult to deal with when growing foliage may obscure your view.

2.28 Mark one answer

You are approaching a pelican crossing. The amber light is flashing. You must

☐ give way to pedestrians who are crossing
☐ encourage pedestrians to cross
☐ not move until the green light appears
☐ stop even if the crossing is clear

While the pedestrians are crossing don't encourage them to cross by waving or flashing your headlights: other road users may misunderstand your signal. Don't harass them by creeping forward or revving your engine.

2.29 Mark one answer

The conditions are good and dry. You could use the 'two-second rule'

☐ before restarting the engine after it has stalled
☐ to keep a safe gap from the vehicle in front
☐ before using the 'Mirror–Signal–Manoeuvre' routine
☐ when emerging on wet roads

To measure this, choose a fixed reference point such as a bridge, sign or tree. When the vehicle ahead passes the object, say to yourself 'Only a fool breaks the two-second rule.' If you reach the object before you finish saying this, you're TOO CLOSE.

2.30 Mark one answer

At a puffin crossing, which colour follows the green signal?

☐ Steady red
☐ Flashing amber
☐ Steady amber
☐ Flashing green

Puffin crossings have infra-red sensors which detect when pedestrians are crossing and hold the red traffic signal until the crossing is clear. The use of a sensor means there is no flashing amber phase as there is with a pelican crossing.

2.31 Mark one answer

You are in a line of traffic. The driver behind you is following very closely. What action should you take?

☐ Ignore the following driver and continue to travel within the speed limit
☐ Slow down, gradually increasing the gap between you and the vehicle in front
☐ Signal left and wave the following driver past
☐ Move over to a position just left of the centre line of the road

It can be worrying to see that the car behind is following you too closely. Give yourself a greater safety margin by easing back from the vehicle in front.

2.32 Mark one answer

A vehicle has a flashing green beacon. What does this mean?

☐ A doctor is answering an emergency call
☐ The vehicle is slow-moving
☐ It is a motorway police patrol vehicle
☐ The vehicle is carrying hazardous chemicals

A doctor attending an emergency may show a green flashing beacon on their vehicle. Give way to them when you can do so safely as they will need to reach their destination quickly. Be aware that they might pull over suddenly.

2.33 Mark one answer

A bus has stopped at a bus stop ahead of you. Its right-hand indicator is flashing. You should

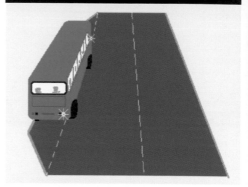

☐ flash your headlights and slow down
☐ slow down and give way if it is safe to do so
☐ sound your horn and keep going
☐ slow down and then sound your horn

Give way to buses whenever you can do so safely, especially when they signal to pull away from bus stops. Look out for people leaving the bus and crossing the road.

safety and your motorcycle

3.1 Mark one answer

A loose drive chain on a motorcycle could cause

☐ the front wheel to wobble
☐ the ignition to cut out
☐ the brakes to fail
☐ the rear wheel to lock

Drive chains are subject to wear and require frequent adjustment to maintain the correct tension. Allowing the drive chain to run dry will greatly increase the rate of wear, so it is important to keep it lubricated. If the chain becomes worn or slack it can jump off the sprocket and lock the rear wheel.

3.2 Mark one answer

What is the most important reason why you should keep your motorcycle regularly maintained?

☐ To accelerate faster than other traffic
☐ So the motorcycle can carry panniers
☐ To keep the machine roadworthy
☐ So the motorcycle can carry a passenger

Whenever you use any motorcycle on the road it must be in a roadworthy condition.
  Regular maintenance should identify any faults at an early stage and help prevent more serious problems.

3.3 Mark one answer

How should you ride a motorcycle when NEW tyres have just been fitted?

☐ Carefully, until the shiny surface is worn off
☐ By braking hard especially into bends
☐ Through normal riding with higher air pressures
☐ By riding at faster than normal speeds

New tyres have a shiny finish which needs to wear off before the tyre will give the best grip. Take extra care if the road surface is wet or slippery.

3.4 Mark one answer

When riding and wearing brightly coloured clothing you will

☐ dazzle other motorists on the road
☐ be seen more easily by other motorists
☐ create a hazard by distracting other drivers
☐ be able to ride on unlit roads at night with sidelights

For your own safety you need other road users to see you easily. Wearing brightly coloured or fluorescent clothing will help you to achieve this during daylight. At night, wearing clothing that includes reflective material is the best way of helping others to see you.

3.5 Mark one answer

You are riding a motorcycle in very hot weather. You should

☐ ride with your visor fully open
☐ continue to wear protective clothing
☐ wear trainers instead of boots
☐ slacken your helmet strap

Always wear your protective clothing, whatever the weather.
  In very hot weather it's tempting to ride in light summer clothes. Don't take the risk. If you fall from your motorcycle you'll have no protection from the hard road surface.

3.6 Mark one answer

Why should you wear fluorescent clothing when riding in daylight?

☐ It reduces wind resistance
☐ It prevents injury if you come off the machine
☐ It helps other road users to see you
☐ It keeps you cool in hot weather

Motorcycles are smaller and therefore harder to see than most other vehicles on the road. You need to make yourself as visible as possible to other road users.
  Fluorescent and reflective clothing will help achieve this. You must be visible from all sides.

3.7   Mark one answer
Why should riders wear reflective clothing?

☐ To protect them from the cold
☐ To protect them from direct sunlight
☐ To be seen better in daylight
☐ To be seen better at night

Fluorescent clothing will help others to see you during the day. At night, however, you should wear clothing that reflects the light.
   This allows other road users to see you more easily in their headlights. Ask your local motorcycle dealer about fluorescent and reflective clothing.

3.8   Mark one answer
Which of the following fairings would give you the best weather protection?

☐ Handlebar
☐ Sports
☐ Touring
☐ Windscreen

Fairings give protection to the hands, legs and feet. They also make riding more comfortable by keeping you out of the wind.

3.9   Mark one answer
Your visor becomes badly scratched. You should

☐ polish it with a fine abrasive
☐ replace it
☐ wash it in soapy water
☐ clean it with petrol

Your visor protects your eyes from wind, rain, insects and road dirt. It's therefore important to keep it clean and in good repair. A badly scratched visor can, obscure your view and cause dazzle from lights of oncoming vehicles.

3.10   Mark one answer
The legal minimum depth of tread for motorcycle tyres is

☐ 1 mm
☐ 1.6 mm
☐ 2.5 mm
☐ 4 mm

The entire original tread should be continuous. Don't ride a motorcycle with worn tyres. Your tyres are your only contact with the road so it's very important that you ensure they are in good condition.

3.11   Mark three answers
Which of the following makes it easier for motorcyclists to be seen?

☐ Using a dipped headlight
☐ Wearing a fluorescent jacket
☐ Wearing a white helmet
☐ Wearing a grey helmet
☐ Wearing black leathers
☐ Using a tinted visor

Many incidents and collisions involving motorcyclists occur because another road user didn't see them. Do what you can to make yourself more visible to others. Be aware that you are vulnerable and ride defensively.

3.12   Mark one answer
Your oil light comes on as you are riding. You should

☐ go to a dealer for an oil change
☐ go to the nearest garage for their advice
☐ ride slowly for a few miles to see if the light goes out
☐ stop as quickly as possible and try to find the cause

If the oil pressure warning light comes on when the engine is running you may have a serious problem. Pull over as soon as you can, stop the engine and investigate the cause.

3.13   Mark two answers
Motorcycle tyres MUST

☐ have the same tread pattern
☐ be correctly inflated
☐ be the same size, front and rear
☐ both be the same make
☐ have sufficient tread depth

Your safety and that of others may depend on the condition of your tyres. Before you ride you must check they are correctly inflated and have sufficient tread depth.
   Make sure these checks become part of a routine.

3.14   Mark one answer
Riding your motorcycle with a slack or worn drive chain may cause

☐ an engine misfire
☐ early tyre wear
☐ increased emissions
☐ a locked wheel

Check your drive chain regularly; adjust and lubricate it if necessary. It needs to be adjusted until the free play is as specified in the vehicle handbook.

3.15 Mark one answer

You forget to switch the choke off after the engine warms up. This could

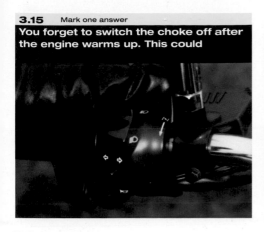

- ☐ flatten the battery
- ☐ reduce braking distances
- ☐ use less fuel
- ☐ cause much more engine wear

Leaving the choke on for too long will cause unnecessary engine wear and waste fuel.

3.16 Mark one answer

When riding your motorcycle a tyre bursts. What should you do?

- ☐ Slow gently to a stop
- ☐ Brake firmly to a stop
- ☐ Change to a high gear
- ☐ Lower the side stand

If a tyre bursts, close the throttle smoothly and slow gently to a stop, holding the handlebars firmly to help you keep a straight course.

3.17 Mark one answer

A motorcycle engine that is properly maintained will

- ☐ use much more fuel
- ☐ have lower exhaust emissions
- ☐ increase your insurance premiums
- ☐ not need to have an MOT

A badly maintained engine can emit more exhaust fumes than one that is correctly serviced. This can be damaging to the environment and also cost you more in fuel.

3.18 Mark one answer

What should you clean visors and goggles with?

- ☐ Petrol
- ☐ White spirit
- ☐ Antifreeze
- ☐ Soapy water

It is very important to keep your visor or goggles clean. Clean them using warm soapy water. Do not use solvents or petrol.

3.19 Mark one answer

You are riding on a quiet road. Your visor fogs up. What should you do?

- ☐ Continue at a reduced speed
- ☐ Stop as soon as possible and wipe it
- ☐ Build up speed to increase air flow
- ☐ Close the helmet air vents

In cold and wet weather your visor may fog up. If this happens when you are riding choose somewhere safe to stop, and wipe it clean with a damp cloth. Special anti-fog products are available at motorcycle dealers.

3.20 Mark one answer

You are riding in hot weather. What is the safest type of footwear?

- ☐ Sandals
- ☐ Trainers
- ☐ Shoes
- ☐ Boots

It is important to wear good boots when you ride a motorcycle. Boots protect your feet and shins from knocks, and give some protection in a crash. They also help keep you warm and dry in cold or wet weather.

3.21 Mark one answer

Which of the following should not be used to fasten your safety helmet?

☐ Double D ring fastening
☐ Velcro tab
☐ Quick release fastening
☐ Bar and buckle

Some helmet straps have a velcro tab in addition to the main fastening, which is intended to secure the strap so that it does not flap in the wind. It should NOT be used on its own to fasten the helmet.

3.22 Mark one answer

After warming up the engine you leave the choke ON. What will this do?

☐ Discharge the battery
☐ Use more fuel
☐ Improve handling
☐ Use less fuel

Leaving the choke on for too long could waste fuel and cause unnecessary pollution.

3.23 Mark two answers

You want to ride your motorcycle in the dark. What could you wear to be seen more easily ?

☐ A black leather jacket
☐ Reflective clothing
☐ A white helmet
☐ A red helmet

When riding in the dark you will be easier to see if you wear reflective clothing and a white helmet. A light-coloured helmet contrasts starkly with the surrounding darkness, while reflective clothing reflects the light from other vehicles and makes the rider much more visible.

3.24 Mark one answer

Your motorcycle has a catalytic converter. Its purpose is to reduce

☐ exhaust noise
☐ fuel consumption
☐ exhaust emissions
☐ engine noise

Catalytic converters reduce the toxic and polluting gases given out by the engine.
    Never use leaded or lead replacement petrol in a vehicle with a catalytic converter, as even one tankful can permanently damage the system.

3.25 Mark one answer

Refitting which of the following will disturb your wheel alignment?

☐ front wheel
☐ front brakes
☐ rear brakes
☐ rear wheel

When refitting the rear wheel or adjusting the drive chain it is possible to disturb the wheel alignment. Incorrect alignment can cause instability, especially when cornering, and increased tyre wear.

3.26 Mark one answer

After refitting your rear wheel what should you check?

☐ Your steering damper
☐ Your side stand
☐ Your wheel alignment
☐ Your suspension preload

After refitting the rear wheel or adjusting the drive chain you should check your wheel alignment. Incorrect alignment will result in excessive tyre wear and poor road holding.

3.27 Mark one answer

You are checking your direction indicators. How often per second must they flash?

☐ Between 1 and 2 times
☐ Between 3 and 4 times
☐ Between 5 and 6 times
☐ Between 7 and 8 times

You should check that all your lights work properly before every journey. Make sure that any signals you give can be clearly seen.
    If you're not sure whether your signals can be seen you can use arm signals as well to make your intentions clear. Only do this if you're going slowly.

3.28 Mark one answer

After adjusting the final drive chain what should you check?

☐ The rear wheel alignment
☐ The suspension adjustment
☐ The rear shock absorber
☐ The front suspension forks

Always check the rear wheel alignment after adjusting the chain tension. Marks on the chain adjuster may be provided to make this easy. Incorrect alignment can cause instability and increased tyre wear.

3.29 Mark one answer

Your steering feels wobbly. Which of these is a likely cause?

☐ Tyre pressure is too high
☐ Incorrectly adjusted brakes
☐ Worn steering head bearings
☐ A broken clutch cable

Worn bearings in the steering head can make your motorcycle very difficult to control. They should be checked for wear and correct adjustment.

3.30 Mark one answer

You see oil on your front forks. Should you be concerned about this?

☐ No, unless the amount of oil increases
☐ No, lubrication here is perfectly normal
☐ Yes, it is illegal to ride with an oil leak
☐ Yes, oil could drip onto your tyre

Oil leaking from your forks could get on to your tyre or brake disc. This could result in your tyre losing grip, or your brakes being less effective. A loss of front fork oil will also affect handling and stability.

3.31 Mark one answer

You have a faulty oil seal on a shock absorber. Why is this a serious problem?

☐ It will cause excessive chain wear
☐ Dripping oil could reduce the grip of your tyre
☐ Your motorcycle will be harder to ride uphill
☐ Your motorcycle will not accelerate so quickly

Leaking oil could affect the grip of your tyres and also the effectiveness of your brakes. This could result in a loss of control, putting you and other road users in danger.

3.32 Mark one answer

Oil is leaking from your forks. Why should you NOT ride a motorcycle in this condition?

☐ Your brakes could be affected by dripping oil
☐ Your steering is likely to seize up
☐ The forks will quickly begin to rust
☐ The motorcycle will become too noisy

Oil dripping from forks and shock absorbers is dangerous if it gets onto brakes and tyres. Replace faulty oil seals immediately.

3.33 Mark one answer

You have adjusted your drive chain. If this is not done properly, what problem could it cause?

☐ Inaccurate speedometer reading
☐ Loss of braking power
☐ Incorrect rear wheel alignment
☐ Excessive fuel consumption

After carrying out drive chain adjustment, you should always check the rear wheel alignment. Many motorcycles have alignment guides stamped onto the frame to help you do this correctly.

3.34 Mark one answer

You have adjusted your drive chain. Why is it also important to check rear wheel alignment?

☐ Your tyre may be more likely to puncture
☐ Fuel consumption could be greatly increased
☐ You may not be able to reach top speed
☐ Your motorcycle could be unstable on bends

Rear wheel alignment can be disturbed by adjustments to the drive chain. It's very important to make sure that the wheel is still properly aligned after doing this.

3.35 Mark one answer

There is a cut in the sidewall of one of your tyres. What should you do about this?

☐ Replace the tyre before riding the motorcycle
☐ Check regularly to see if it gets any worse
☐ Repair the puncture before riding the motorcycle
☐ Reduce pressure in the tyre before you ride

A cut in the side-wall can be very dangerous. The tyre is in danger of blowing out if you ride the motorcycle in this condition.

3.36 Mark one answer

You need to put air into your tyres. How would you find out the correct pressure to use?

☐ It will be shown on the tyre wall
☐ It will be stamped on the wheel
☐ By checking the vehicle owner's manual
☐ By checking the registration document

Tyre pressures should be checked regularly. Use your vehicle manual to find advice on the correct pressures to use.

3.37 Mark one answer

You can prevent a cable operated clutch from becoming stiff by keeping the cable

☐ tight
☐ dry
☐ slack
☐ oiled

Keeping the cable oiled will help it to move smoothly through its outer casing. This will extend the life of the cable and assist your control of the motorcycle.

3.38 Mark one answer

When adjusting your chain it is important for the wheels to be aligned accurately. Incorrect wheel alignment can cause

☐ a serious loss of power
☐ reduced braking performance
☐ increased tyre wear
☐ reduced ground clearance

If a motorcycle's wheels are incorrectly aligned tyres may wear unevenly and the motorcycle can become unstable, especially when cornering.

3.39 Mark one answer

What problem can incorrectly aligned wheels cause?

☐ Faulty headlight adjustment
☐ Reduced braking performance
☐ Better ground clearance
☐ Instability when cornering

Wheels should be aligned accurately after refitting your rear wheel. Incorrect wheel alignment can cause uneven tyre wear and poor handling. Most motorcycles have wheel alignment guides stamped onto the swinging arm.

3.40 Mark one answer

What is most likely to be affected by incorrect wheel alignment?

☐ Braking performance
☐ Stability
☐ Acceleration
☐ Suspension preload

It is important that your wheels are aligned accurately. It will be necessary to do this after removing your rear wheel or adjusting the chain. Incorrect alignment can cause instability, especially when cornering. It can also increase tyre wear.

3.41 Mark one answer

Why should you wear specialist motorcycle clothing when riding?

☐ Because the law requires you to do so
☐ Because it looks better than ordinary clothing
☐ Because it gives best protection from the weather
☐ Because it will reduce your insurance

If you become cold and wet when riding, this can have a serious effect on your concentration and control of your motorcycle.
  Proper riding gear can help shield you from the weather, as well as giving protection in the event of a crash.

3.42 Mark one answer

When leaving your motorcycle parked, you should always

☐ remove the battery lead
☐ pull it onto the kerb
☐ use the steering lock
☐ leave the parking light on

When leaving your motorcycle you should always use the steering lock. You should also consider using additional locking devices such as a U-lock, disc lock or chain. If possible fasten it to an immovable post or another motorcycle.

3.43 Mark one answer

You are parking your motorcycle. Chaining it to an immovable object will

☐ be against the law
☐ give extra security
☐ be likely to cause damage
☐ leave the motorcycle unstable

Theft of motorcycles is a very common crime. If you can, secure your vehicle to a lamp post or other such object, to help reduce the chances of it being stolen.

3.44 Mark one answer

You are parking your motorcycle and sidecar on a hill. What is the best way to stop it rolling away?

☐ Leave it in neutral
☐ Put the rear wheel on the pavement
☐ Leave it in a low gear
☐ Park very close to another vehicle

To make sure a sidecar outfit doesn't roll away when parking you should leave it in a low gear, and wedge it against the kerb or place a block behind the wheel.

3.45 Mark one answer

An engine cut-out switch should be used to

☐ reduce speed in an emergency
☐ prevent the motorcycle being stolen
☐ stop the engine normally
☐ stop the engine in an emergency

If you are involved in a collision or crash, using the engine cut-out switch will help to reduce any fire hazard. When stopping the engine normally, use the ignition switch.

3.46 Mark one answer

You enter a road where there are road humps. What should you do?

☐ Maintain a reduced speed throughout
☐ Accelerate quickly between each one
☐ Always keep to the maximum legal speed
☐ Ride slowly at school times only

The humps are there for a reason; to reduce the speed of the traffic. Don't accelerate harshly between them, as this means you will only have to brake sharply to negotiate the next hump.

Harsh braking and acceleration uses more fuel as well as causing wear and tear to your vehicle.

3.47 Mark one answer

When should you especially check the engine oil level?

☐ Before a long journey
☐ When the engine is hot
☐ Early in the morning
☐ Every 6000 miles

As well as the oil you will also need to check other items. These include, fuel, water and tyres.

3.48 Mark one answer

You service your own motorcycle. How should you get rid of the old engine oil?

☐ Take it to a local authority site
☐ Pour it down a drain
☐ Tip it into a hole in the ground
☐ Put it into your dustbin

Never pour the oil down any drain. The oil is highly pollutant and could harm wildlife.

Confine it in a container and dispose of it properly at an authorised site.

3.49 Mark one answer

What safeguard could you take against fire risk to your motorcycle?

☐ Keep water levels above maximum
☐ Check out any strong smell of petrol
☐ Avoid riding with a full tank of petrol
☐ Use unleaded petrol

The fuel in your motorcycle can be a dangerous fire hazard. DON'T use a naked flame if you can smell fuel, or smoke when refuelling.

3.50 Mark one answer

Which of the following would NOT make you more visible in daylight?

☐ Wearing a black helmet
☐ Wearing a white helmet
☐ Switching on your dipped headlight
☐ Wearing a fluorescent jacket

Wearing bright or fluorescent clothes will help other road users to see you. Wearing a white or brightly coloured helmet can also make you more visible.

3.51 Mark one answer

It would be illegal to ride with a helmet on when

☐ the helmet is not fastened correctly
☐ the helmet is more than four years old
☐ you have borrowed someone else's helmet
☐ the helmet does not have chin protection

A helmet that is incorrectly fastened or not fastened at all is likely to come off in a crash. It will provide little or no protection.

By law, you must wear a helmet when riding on the road and it must be correctly fastened (members of the Sikh religion who wear a turban are exempt).

3.52 Mark three answers

When may you have to increase the tyre pressures on your motorcycle?

☐ When carrying a passenger
☐ After a long journey
☐ When carrying a load
☐ When riding at high speeds
☐ When riding in hot weather

Read the manufacturer's handbook to see if they recommend increasing tyre pressures under certain conditions.

3.53 Mark two answers

Which TWO of these items on a motorcycle MUST be kept clean?

☐ Number plate
☐ Wheels
☐ Engine
☐ Fairing
☐ Headlight

Maintenance is a vital part of road safety.

Lights, indicators, reflectors and number plates MUST be kept clean and clear.

3.54 Mark one answer

You should use the engine cut-out switch on your motorcycle to

☐ save wear and tear on the battery
☐ stop the engine for a short time
☐ stop the engine in an emergency
☐ save wear and tear on the ignition

Only use the engine cut-out switch in an emergency. When stopping the engine normally, use the ignition switch. This will remind you to take your keys with you when parking. It could also prevent starting problems if you forget you've left the cut-out switch in the 'off' position. When returning to your motorcycle make sure someone has not done this as a trick.

3.55 Mark one answer

You have adjusted the tension on your drive chain. You should check the

☐ rear wheel alignment
☐ tyre pressures
☐ valve clearances
☐ sidelights

Drive chains wear and need frequent adjustment and lubrication. If the drive chain is worn or slack it can jump off the sprocket and lock the rear wheel. When you have adjusted the chain tension, you need to check the rear wheel alignment.

Marks by the chain adjusters may be provided to make this easier.

3.56 Mark one answer

A friend offers you a second-hand safety helmet for you to use. Why may this be a bad idea?

☐ It may be damaged
☐ You will be breaking the law
☐ You will affect your insurance cover
☐ It may be a full-face type

A second-hand helmet may look in good condition but it could have received damage that is not visible externally. A damaged helmet could be unreliable in a crash. Don't take the risk.

3.57 Mark four answers

You are riding a motorcycle of more than 50 cc. Which FOUR would make a tyre illegal?

☐ Tread less than 1.6 mm deep
☐ Tread less than 1 mm deep
☐ A large bulge in the wall
☐ A recut tread
☐ Exposed ply or cord
☐ A stone wedged in the tread

When checking tyres make sure there are no bulges or cuts in the side walls. Always buy your tyres from a reputable dealer to ensure quality and value for money.

3.58 Mark two answers

You should maintain cable operated brakes

☐ by regular adjustment when necessary
☐ at normal service times only
☐ yearly, before taking the motorcycle for its MOT
☐ by oiling cables and pivots regularly

Keeping your brakes in good working order is vital for safety. Cables will stretch with use and need checking and adjusting regularly. They will also need lubricating to prevent friction and wear of the cables and pivots.

3.59 Mark two answers

A properly serviced motorcycle will give

☐ lower insurance premiums
☐ a refund on your road tax
☐ better fuel economy
☐ cleaner exhaust emissions

When you purchase your motorcycle, check at what intervals you should have it serviced. This can vary depending on model or manufacturer. Use the service manual and keep it up to date.

3.60 Mark one answer

A loosely adjusted drive chain could

☐ lock the rear wheel
☐ make wheels wobble
☐ cause a braking fault
☐ affect your headlight beam

A motorcycle chain will stretch as it wears. It needs frequent checking, and adjustment if necessary, to keep the tension correct. In extreme cases a loose chain can jump off the sprocket and become wedged in the rear wheel. This could cause serious loss of control and result in a crash.

3.61 Mark one answer

Your motorcycle is NOT fitted with daytime running lights. When MUST you use a dipped headlight during the day?

☐ On country roads
☐ In poor visibility
☐ Along narrow streets
☐ When parking

It's important that other road users can see you clearly at all times. It will help other road users to see you if you use a dipped headlight during the day. You MUST use a dipped headlight during the day if visibility is seriously reduced, that is, when you can't see for more than 100 metres (328 feet).

3.62 Mark one answer

Tyre pressures should usually be increased on your motorcycle when

☐ riding on a wet road
☐ carrying a pillion passenger
☐ travelling on an uneven surface
☐ riding on twisty roads

Sometimes manufacturers advise you to increase your tyre pressures for high-speed riding and when carrying extra weight. This information can be found in the handbook.

3.63 Mark one answer

You have too much oil in your engine. What could this cause?

☐ Low oil pressure
☐ Engine overheating
☐ Chain wear
☐ Oil leaks

Too much oil in the engine will create excess pressure and could damage engine seals and cause oil leaks. Any excess oil should be drained off.

3.64 Mark one answer

You are leaving your motorcycle unattended on a road. When may you leave the engine running?

☐ When parking for less than five minutes
☐ If the battery is flat
☐ When in a 20 mph zone
☐ Not on any occasion

When you leave your motorcycle parked and unattended on a road, switch off the engine, use the steering lock and remove the ignition key. Also take any tank bags, panniers or loose luggage with you, set the alarm if it has one, and use an additional lock and chain or cable lock.

3.65 Mark one answer

You are involved in a crash. To reduce the risk of fire what is the best thing to do?

☐ Keep the engine running
☐ Open the choke
☐ Turn the fuel tap to reserve
☐ Use the engine cut-out switch

The engine cut-out switch is used to stop the engine in an emergency. In the event of a crash this may help to reduce any fire risk.

3.66 Mark two answers
When riding at night you should

☐ ride with your headlight on
☐ wear reflective clothing
☐ wear a tinted visor
☐ ride in the centre of the road
☐ give arm signals

At night you should wear clothing that includes reflective material to help other road users see you. This could be a vest, tabard or reflective body strap. Use your headlight on dipped or main beam as appropriate without dazzling other road users.

3.67 Mark two answers
Which TWO are badly affected if the tyres are under-inflated?

☐ Braking
☐ Steering
☐ Changing gear
☐ Parking

Your tyres are your only contact with the road so it is very important to ensure that they are free from defects, have sufficient tread depth and are correctly inflated.
Correct tyre pressures help reduce the risk of skidding and provide a safer and more comfortable drive or ride.

3.68 Mark one answer
You must NOT sound your horn

☐ between 10 pm and 6 am in a built-up area
☐ at any time in a built-up area
☐ between 11.30 pm and 7 am in a built-up area
☐ between 11.30 pm and 6 am on any road

Vehicles can be noisy. Every effort must be made to prevent excessive noise, especially in built-up areas at night. Don't

• rev the engine

• sound the horn unnecessarily.

It is illegal to sound your horn in a built-up area between 11.30 pm and 7 am, except when another vehicle poses a danger.

3.69 Mark three answers
The pictured vehicle is 'environmentally friendly' because it

☐ reduces noise pollution
☐ uses diesel fuel
☐ uses electricity
☐ uses unleaded fuel
☐ reduces parking spaces
☐ reduces town traffic

Trams are powered by electricity and therefore do not emit exhaust fumes. They are also much quieter than petrol or diesel engined vehicles and can carry a large number of passengers.

3.70 Mark one answer
Supertrams or Light Rapid Transit (LRT) systems are environmentally friendly because

☐ they use diesel power
☐ they use quieter roads
☐ they use electric power
☐ they do not operate during rush hour

This means that they do not emit toxic fumes, which add to city pollution problems. They are also a lot quieter and smoother to ride on.

3.71 Mark one answer
'Red routes' in major cities have been introduced to

☐ raise the speed limits
☐ help the traffic flow
☐ provide better parking
☐ allow lorries to load more freely

Traffic jams today are often caused by the volume of traffic. However, inconsiderate parking can lead to the closure of an inside lane or traffic having to wait for oncoming vehicles. Driving slowly in traffic increases fuel consumption and causes a build-up of exhaust fumes.

3.72 Mark one answer
Road humps, chicanes, and narrowings are

☐ always at major road works
☐ used to increase traffic speed
☐ at toll-bridge approaches only
☐ traffic calming measures

Traffic calming measures help keep vehicle speeds low in congested areas where there are pedestrians and children. A pedestrian is much more likely to survive a collision with a vehicle travelling at 20 mph than at 40 mph.

3.73 Mark one answer
The purpose of a catalytic converter is to reduce

☐ fuel consumption
☐ the risk of fire
☐ toxic exhaust gases
☐ engine wear

Catalytic converters are designed to reduce a large percentage of toxic emissions. They work more efficiently when the engine has reached its normal working temperature.

3.74 Mark one answer
Catalytic converters are fitted to make the

☐ engine produce more power
☐ exhaust system easier to replace
☐ engine run quietly
☐ exhaust fumes cleaner

Harmful gases in the exhaust system pollute the atmosphere. These gases are reduced by up to 90% if a catalytic converter is fitted. Cleaner air benefits everyone, especially people who live or work near congested roads.

3.75 Mark one answer
It is essential that tyre pressures are checked regularly. When should this be done?

☐ After any lengthy journey
☐ After travelling at high speed
☐ When tyres are hot
☐ When tyres are cold

When you check the tyre pressures do so when the tyres are cold. This will give you a more accurate reading. The heat generated from a long journey will raise the pressure inside the tyre.

3.76 Mark one answer
When should you NOT use your horn in a built-up area?

☐ Between 8 pm and 8 am
☐ Between 9 pm and dawn
☐ Between dusk and 8 am
☐ Between 11.30 pm and 7 am

By law you must not sound your horn in a built-up area between 11.30 pm and 7.00 am. The exception to this is when another road user poses a danger.

3.77 Mark one answer
You will use more fuel if your tyres are

☐ under-inflated
☐ of different makes
☐ over-inflated
☐ new and hardly used

Check your tyre pressures frequently – normally once a week. If pressures are lower than those recommended by the manufacturer, there will be more 'rolling resistance'. The engine will have to work harder to overcome this, leading to increased fuel consumption.

3.78 Mark two answers
How should you dispose of a used battery?

☐ Take it to a local authority site
☐ Put it in the dustbin
☐ Break it up into pieces
☐ Leave it on waste land
☐ Take it to a garage
☐ Burn it on a fire

Batteries contain acid which is hazardous and must be disposed of safely.

3.79 Mark one answer
What is most likely to cause high fuel consumption?

☐ Poor steering control
☐ Accelerating around bends
☐ Staying in high gears
☐ Harsh braking and accelerating

Accelerating and braking gently and smoothly will help to save fuel, reduce wear on your vehicle and is better for the environment.

3.80 Mark one answer

The fluid level in your battery is low. What should you top it up with?

☐ Battery acid
☐ Distilled water
☐ Engine oil
☐ Engine coolant

Some modern batteries are maintenance-free. Check your vehicle handbook and, if necessary, make sure that the plates in each battery cell are covered.

3.81 Mark one answer

You are parked on the road at night. Where must you use parking lights?

☐ Where there are continuous white lines in the middle of the road
☐ Where the speed limit exceeds 30 mph
☐ Where you are facing oncoming traffic
☐ Where you are near a bus stop

When parking at night, park in the direction of the traffic. This will enable other road users to see the reflectors on the rear of your vehicle. Use your parking lights if the speed limit is over 30 mph.

3.82 Mark three answers

Motor vehicles can harm the environment. This has resulted in

☐ air pollution
☐ damage to buildings
☐ less risk to health
☐ improved public transport
☐ less use of electrical vehicles
☐ using up of natural resources

Exhaust emissions are harmful to health. Together with vibration from heavy traffic this can result in damage to buildings. Most petrol and diesel fuels come from a finite and non-renewable source. Anything you can do to reduce your use of these fuels will help the environment.

3.83 Mark three answers

Excessive or uneven tyre wear can be caused by faults in which THREE of the following?

☐ The gearbox
☐ The braking system
☐ The accelerator
☐ The exhaust system
☐ Wheel alignment
☐ The suspension

Regular servicing will help to detect faults at an early stage and this will avoid the risk of minor faults becoming serious or even dangerous.

3.84 Mark one answer

You need to top up your battery. What level should you fill to?

☐ The top of the battery
☐ Half-way up the battery
☐ Just below the cell plates
☐ Just above the cell plates

Top up the battery with distilled water and make sure each cell plate is covered.

3.85 Mark one answer

You are parking on a two-way road at night. The speed limit is 40 mph. You should park on the

☐ left with parking lights on
☐ left with no lights on
☐ right with parking lights on
☐ right with dipped headlights on

At night all vehicles must display parking lights when parked on a road with a speed limit greater than 30 mph. They should be close to the kerb, facing in the direction of the traffic flow and not within a distance as specified in *The Highway Code*.

3.86 Mark one answer

Before starting a journey it is wise to plan your route. How can you do this?

☐ Look at a map
☐ Contact your local garage
☐ Look in your vehicle handbook
☐ Check your vehicle registration document

Planning your journey before you set out can help to make it much easier, more pleasant and may help to ease traffic congestion. Look at a map to help you to do this. You may need different scale maps depending on where and how far you're going. Printing or writing out the route can also help.

3.87 Mark one answer   NI EXEMPT

It can help to plan your route before starting a journey. You can do this by contacting

☐ your local filling station
☐ a motoring organisation
☐ the Driver Vehicle Licensing Agency
☐ your vehicle manufacturer

Most motoring organisations will give you a detailed plan of your trip showing directions and distance. Some will also include advice on rest and fuel stops. The Highways Agency website will also give you information on roadworks and incidents and gives expected delay times.

3.88 Mark one answer

How can you plan your route before starting a long journey?

☐ Check your vehicle's workshop manual
☐ Ask your local garage
☐ Use a route planner on the internet
☐ Consult your travel agents

Various route planners are available on the internet. Most of them give you various options allowing you to choose the most direct, quickest or scenic route. They can also include rest and fuel stops and distances. Print them off and take them with you.

3.89 Mark one answer

Planning your route before setting out can be helpful. How can you do this?

☐ Look in a motoring magazine
☐ Only visit places you know
☐ Try to travel at busy times
☐ Print or write down the route

Print or write down your route before setting out. Some places are not well signed so using place names and road numbers may help you avoid problems en route. Try to get an idea of how far you're going before you leave. You can also use it to re-check the next stage at each rest stop.

3.90 Mark one answer

Why is it a good idea to plan your journey to avoid busy times?

☐ You will have an easier journey
☐ You will have a more stressful journey
☐ Your journey time will be longer
☐ It will cause more traffic congestion

No one likes to spend time in traffic queues. Try to avoid busy times related to school or work travel. As well as moving vehicles you should also consider congestion caused by parked cars, buses and coaches around schools.

3.91 Mark one answer

Planning your journey to avoid busy times has a number of advantages. One of these is

☐ your journey will take longer
☐ you will have a more pleasant journey
☐ you will cause more pollution
☐ your stress level will be greater

Having a pleasant journey can have safety benefits. You will be less tired and stressed and this will allow you to concentrate more on your driving or riding.

3.92 Mark one answer

It is a good idea to plan your journey to avoid busy times. This is because

☐ your vehicle will use more fuel
☐ you will see less road works
☐ it will help to ease congestion
☐ you will travel a much shorter distance

Avoiding busy times means that you are not adding needlessly to traffic congestion.
   Other advantages are that you will use less fuel and feel less stressed.

3.93 Mark one answer

By avoiding busy times when travelling

☐ you are more likely to be held up
☐ your journey time will be longer
☐ you will travel a much shorter distance
☐ you are less likely to be delayed

If possible, avoid the early morning and, late afternoon and early evening 'rush hour'. Doing this should allow you to travel in a more relaxed frame of mind, concentrate solely on what you're doing and arrive at your destination feeling less stressed.

3.94 Mark one answer

It can help to plan your route before starting a journey. Why should you also plan an alternative route?

☐ Your original route may be blocked
☐ Your maps may have different scales
☐ You may find you have to pay a congestion charge
☐ Because you may get held up by a tractor

It can be frustrating and worrying to find your planned route is blocked by roadworks or diversions. If you have planned an alternative you will feel less stressed and more able to concentrate fully on your driving or riding. If your original route is mostly on motorways it's a good idea to plan an alternative using non-motorway roads. Always carry a map with you just in case you need to refer to it.

3.95 Mark one answer

As well as planning your route before starting a journey, you should also plan an alternative route. Why is this?

☐ To let another driver overtake
☐ Your first route may be blocked
☐ To avoid a railway level crossing
☐ In case you have to avoid emergency vehicles

It's a good idea to plan an alternative route in case your original route is blocked for any reason. You're less likely to feel worried and stressed if you've got an alternative in mind. This will enable you to concentrate fully on your driving or riding. Always carry a map that covers the area you will travel in.

3.96 Mark one answer

You are making an appointment and will have to travel a long distance. You should

☐ allow plenty of time for your journey
☐ plan to go at busy times
☐ avoid all national speed limit roads
☐ prevent other drivers from overtaking

Always allow plenty of time for your journey in case of unforeseen problems. Anything can happen, punctures, breakdowns, road closures, diversions etc. You will feel less stressed and less inclined to take risks if you are not 'pushed for time'.

3.97 Mark one answer

Rapid acceleration and heavy braking can lead to

☐ reduced pollution
☐ increased fuel consumption
☐ reduced exhaust emissions
☐ increased road safety

Using the controls smoothly can reduce fuel consumption by about 15% as well as reducing wear and tear on your vehicle.

Plan ahead and anticipate changes of speed well in advance. This will reduce the need to accelerate rapidly or brake sharply.

3.98 Mark one answer

What percentage of all emissions does road transport account for?

☐ 10%
☐ 20%
☐ 30%
☐ 40%

Transport is an essential part of modern life but it does have environmental effects. In heavily populated areas traffic is the biggest source of air pollution. Eco-safe driving and riding will reduce emissions and can make a surprising difference to local air quality.

3.99 Mark one answer

Which of these, if allowed to get low, could cause you to crash?

☐ Anti-freeze level
☐ Brake fluid level
☐ Battery water level
☐ Radiator coolant level

You should carry out frequent checks on all fluid levels but particularly brake fluid. As the brake pads or shoes wear down the brake fluid level will drop. If it drops below the minimum mark on the fluid reservoir, air could enter the hydraulic system and lead to a loss of braking efficiency or complete brake failure.

safety margins

4.1 Mark one answer
Your overall stopping distance will be longer when riding

☐ at night
☐ in the fog
☐ with a passenger
☐ up a hill

When carrying a passenger on a motorcycle the overall weight will be much more than when riding alone. This additional weight will make it harder for you to stop quickly in an emergency.

4.2 Mark one answer
On a wet road what is the safest way to stop?

☐ Change gear without braking
☐ Use the back brake only
☐ Use the front brake only
☐ Use both brakes

Motorcyclists need to take extra care when stopping on wet road surfaces. Plan well ahead so that you're able to brake in good time. You should ensure your motorcycle is upright and brake when travelling in a straight line.

4.3 Mark one answer
You are riding in heavy rain when your rear wheel skids as you accelerate. To get control again you must

☐ change down to a lower gear
☐ ease off the throttle
☐ brake to reduce speed
☐ put your feet down

If you feel your back wheel beginning to skid as you pull away, ease off the throttle.
This will give your rear tyre the chance to grip the road and stop the skid.

4.4 Mark one answer
It is snowing. Before starting your journey you should

☐ think if you need to ride at all
☐ try to avoid taking a passenger
☐ plan a route avoiding towns
☐ take a hot drink before setting out

Do not ride in snowy or icy conditions unless your journey is essential. If you must go out, try and keep to main roads which are more likely to be treated and clear.

4.5 Mark one answer
Why should you ride with a dipped headlight on in the daytime?

☐ It helps other road users to see you
☐ It means that you can ride faster
☐ Other vehicles will get out of the way
☐ So that it is already on when it gets dark

Make yourself as visible as possible, from the side as well as from the front and rear.
Having your headlight on, even in good daylight, can help make you more conspicuous.

4.6 Mark one answer
Motorcyclists are only allowed to use high-intensity rear fog lights when

☐ a pillion passenger is being carried
☐ they ride a large touring machine
☐ visibility is 100 metres (328 feet) or less
☐ they are riding on the road for the first time

If your motorcycle is fitted with high-intensity rear fog lights you must only use them when visibility is seriously reduced, that is, when you can see no further than 100 metres (328 feet). This rule also applies to all other motor vehicles using these lights.

4.7 Mark three answers
You MUST use your headlight

☐ when riding in a group
☐ at night when street lighting is poor
☐ when carrying a passenger
☐ on motorways during darkness
☐ at times of poor visibility
☐ when parked on an unlit road

Your headlight helps you to see in the dark and helps other road users to see you. You must also use your headlight at any time when visibility is seriously reduced.

4.8 Mark one answer
You are riding in town at night. The roads are wet after rain. The reflections from wet surfaces will

☐ affect your stopping distance
☐ affect your road holding
☐ make it easy to see unlit objects
☐ make it hard to see unlit objects

If you can't see clearly, slow down and stop. Make sure that your visor or goggles are clean. Be extra-cautious in these conditions and allow twice the normal separation distance.

4.9 Mark two answers

You are riding through a flood. Which TWO should you do?

☐ Keep in a high gear and stand up on the footrests
☐ Keep the engine running fast to keep water out of the exhaust
☐ Ride slowly and test your brakes when you are out of the water
☐ Turn your headlight off to avoid any electrical damage

Take extra care when riding through flood water or fords. Ride through with high engine revs while partly slipping the clutch to prevent water entering the exhaust system. Try your brakes as soon as you are clear.

4.10 Mark one answer

You have just ridden through a flood. When clear of the water you should test your

☐ starter motor
☐ headlight
☐ steering
☐ brakes

If you have ridden through deep water your brakes may be less effective. If they have been affected, ride slowly while gently applying both brakes until normal braking is restored.

4.11 Mark one answer

When going through flood water you should ride

☐ quickly in a high gear
☐ slowly in a high gear
☐ quickly in a low gear
☐ slowly in a low gear

If you have to go through a flood, ride slowly in a low gear. Keep the engine running fast enough to keep water out of the exhaust. You may need to slip the clutch to do this.

4.12 Mark one answer

When riding at night you should NOT

☐ switch on full beam headlights
☐ overtake slower vehicles in front
☐ use dipped beam headlights
☐ use tinted glasses, lenses or visors

Do not use tinted glasses, lenses or visors at night because they reduce the amount of available light reaching your eyes. It's also important to keep your visor or goggles clean to give a clear view of the road at all times.

4.13 Mark two answers

Which of the following should you do when riding in fog?

☐ Keep close to the vehicle in front
☐ Use your dipped headlight
☐ Ride close to the centre of the road
☐ Keep your visor or goggles clear
☐ Keep the vehicle in front in view

You must use your dipped headlight when visibility is seriously reduced. In fog a film of mist can form over the outside of your visor or goggles. This can further reduce your ability to see. Be aware of this hazard and keep your visor or goggles clear.

4.14 Mark one answer

You are riding in heavy rain. Why should you try to avoid this marked area?

☐ It is illegal to ride over bus stops
☐ The painted lines may be slippery
☐ Cyclists may be using the bus stop
☐ Only emergency vehicles may drive over bus stops

Painted lines and road markings can be very slippery, especially for motorcyclists.
Try to avoid them if you can do so safely.

4.15 Mark one answer

When riding at night you should

☐ wear reflective clothing
☐ wear a tinted visor
☐ ride in the middle of the road
☐ always give arm signals

You need to make yourself as visible as possible, from the front and rear and also from the side. Don't just rely on your headlight and tail light. Wear clothing that uses reflective material as this stands out in other vehicles' headlights.

4.16 Mark one answer

When riding in extremely cold conditions what can you do to keep warm?

☐ Stay close to the vehicles in front
☐ Wear suitable clothing
☐ Lie flat on the tank
☐ Put one hand on the exhaust pipe

Motorcyclists are exposed to the elements and can become very cold when riding in wintry conditions. It's important to keep warm or your concentration could be affected. The only way to stay warm is to wear suitable clothing. If you do find yourself getting cold then stop at a suitable place to warm up.

4.17 Mark two answers

You are riding at night. To be seen more easily you should

☐ ride with your headlight on dipped beam
☐ wear reflective clothing
☐ keep the motorcycle clean
☐ stay well out to the right
☐ wear waterproof clothing

Reflective clothing works by reflecting light from the headlights of the other vehicles. This will make it easier for you to be seen.
 Fluorescent clothing, although effective during the day, won't show up as well as reflective clothing at night.

4.18 Mark one answer

Your overall stopping distance will be much longer when riding

☐ in the rain
☐ in fog
☐ at night
☐ in strong winds

Extra care should be taken in wet weather.
 Wet roads will affect the time it takes you to stop. Your stopping distance could be at least doubled.

4.19 Mark four answers

The road surface is very important to motorcyclists. Which FOUR of these are more likely to reduce the stability of your motorcycle?

☐ Potholes
☐ Drain covers
☐ Concrete
☐ Oil patches
☐ Tarmac
☐ Loose gravel

Apart from the weather conditions, the road surface and any changes in it can affect the stability of your motorcycle. Be on the lookout for poor road surfaces and be aware of any traffic around you, in case you need to take avoiding action.

4.20 Mark two answers

You are riding in very hot weather. What are TWO effects that melting tar has on the control of your motorcycle?

☐ It can make the surface slippery
☐ It can reduce tyre grip
☐ It can reduce stopping distances
☐ It can improve braking efficiency

If the tarmac road surface has softened in the heat, take extra care when braking and cornering. You should also look out for loose chippings where roads have been resurfaced. These will reduce your tyres' grip and can fly up, causing injury and damage.

4.21 Mark one answer

You are riding past queuing traffic. Why should you be more cautious when approaching this road marking?

☐ Lorries will be unloading here
☐ School children will be crossing here
☐ Pedestrians will be standing in the road
☐ Traffic could be emerging and may not see you

When riding past queuing traffic look out for 'keep clear' road markings that will indicate a side road or entrance on the left.
 Vehicles may emerge between gaps in the traffic.

4.22 Mark one answer

What can cause your tyres to skid and lose their grip on the road surface?

☐ Giving hand signals
☐ Riding one handed
☐ Looking over your shoulder
☐ Heavy braking

You can cause your motorcycle to skid by heavy or uncoordinated braking, as well as excessive acceleration, swerving or changing direction too sharply, and leaning over too far.

4.23 Mark one answer

When riding in heavy rain a film of water can build up between your tyres and the road surface. This may result in loss of control.
What can you do to avoid this happening?

☐ Keep your speed down
☐ Increase your tyre pressures
☐ Decrease your tyre pressures
☐ Keep trying your brakes

There is a greater risk of aquaplaning when riding at speed. Keeping your speed down will help prevent aquaplaning.
   If you can do so safely, try to avoid pools of water on the road.

4.24 Mark one answer

When riding in heavy rain a film of water can build up between your tyres and the road. This is known as aquaplaning. What should you do to keep control?

☐ Use your rear brakes gently
☐ Steer to the crown of the road
☐ Ease off the throttle smoothly
☐ Change up into a higher gear

If your vehicle starts to aquaplane ease off the throttle smoothly. Do not brake or turn the steering until tyre grip has been restored.

4.25 Mark one answer

After riding through deep water you notice your scooter brakes do not work properly. What would be the best way to dry them out?

☐ Ride slowly, braking lightly
☐ Ride quickly, braking harshly
☐ Stop and dry them with a cloth
☐ Stop and wait for a few minutes

You can help to dry out brakes by riding slowly and applying light pressure to the brake pedal/lever. DO NOT ride at normal speeds until they are working normally again.

4.26 Mark two answers

You have to ride in foggy weather. You should

☐ stay close to the centre of the road
☐ switch only your sidelights on
☐ switch on your dipped headlights
☐ be aware of others not using their headlights
☐ always ride in the gutter to see the kerb

Only travel in fog if your journey is absolutely necessary. Fog is often patchy and visibility can suddenly reduce without warning.

4.27 Mark one answer

Only a fool breaks the two-second rule refers to

☐ the time recommended when using the choke
☐ the separation distance when riding in good conditions
☐ restarting a stalled engine in busy traffic
☐ the time you should keep your foot down at a junction

It is very important that you always leave a safe gap between yourself and any vehicle you're following. In good conditions you need to leave at least one metre for every mile per hour of your speed or a two-second time interval.

4.28 Mark one answer

At a mini roundabout it is important that a motorcyclist should avoid

☐ turning right
☐ using signals
☐ taking 'lifesavers'
☐ the painted area

Avoid riding over the painted area as these can become very slippery, especially when wet. Even on dry roads only a small part of the motorcycle's tyre makes contact with the road. Any reduction in grip can therefore affect the stability of your machine.

4.29 Mark two answers

You are riding on a motorway in a crosswind. You should take extra care when

☐ approaching service areas
☐ overtaking a large vehicle
☐ riding in slow-moving traffic
☐ approaching an exit
☐ riding in exposed places

Take extra care when overtaking large vehicles as they can cause air turbulence and buffeting. Beware of crosswinds when riding on exposed stretches of road, which can suddenly blow you off course. Bear in mind that strong winds can also affect the stability of other road users.

4.30 Mark one answer

Why should you try to avoid riding over this marked area?

☐ It is illegal to ride over bus stops
☐ It will alter your machine's centre of gravity
☐ Pedestrians may be waiting at the bus stop
☐ A bus may have left patches of oil

Try to anticipate slippery road surfaces.
    Watch out for oil patches at places where vehicles stop for some time, such as bus stops, lay-bys and busy junctions.

4.31 Mark one answer

Your overall stopping distance comprises thinking and braking distance. You are on a good, dry road surface with good brakes and tyres. What is the typical BRAKING distance at 50 mph?

☐ 14 metres (46 feet)
☐ 24 metres (79 feet)
☐ 38 metres (125 feet)
☐ 55 metres (180 feet)

Different factors can affect how long it takes you to stop, such as weather and road conditions, vehicle condition and loading. You also need to add reaction time to this. The overall stopping distance at 50 mph includes 15 metres thinking distance (the reaction time before braking starts) plus your braking distance of 38 metres, giving a typical overall stopping distance of 53 metres (175 feet) in good conditions.

4.32 Mark one answer

You are riding at speed through surface water. A thin film of water has built up between your tyres and the road surface. To keep control what should you do?

☐ Turn the steering quickly
☐ Use the rear brake gently
☐ Use both brakes gently
☐ Ease off the throttle

Riding at speed where there is surface water can cause it to build up between your tyres and the road. This is known as aquaplaning and results in serious loss of steering and braking control, and can cause you to crash. The faster you are going, the more likely it is to happen. If it does, ease off the throttle smoothly.

4.33 Mark one answer

Braking distances on ice can be

☐ twice the normal distance
☐ five times the normal distance
☐ seven times the normal distance
☐ ten times the normal distance

In icy and snowy weather, your stopping distance will increase by up to ten times compared to good, dry conditions.
    Take extra care when braking, accelerating and steering, to cut down the risk of skidding.

4.34 Mark one answer

Freezing conditions will affect the distance it takes you to come to a stop. You should expect stopping distances to increase by up to

☐ two times
☐ three times
☐ five times
☐ ten times

Your tyre grip is greatly reduced on icy roads and you need to allow up to ten times the normal stopping distance.

4.35 Mark one answer

In windy conditions you need to take extra care when

☐ using the brakes
☐ making a hill start
☐ turning into a narrow road
☐ passing pedal cyclists

You should always give cyclists plenty of room when overtaking. When it's windy, a sudden gust could blow them off course.

4.36 Mark one answer

When approaching a right-hand bend you should keep well to the left. Why is this?

☐ To improve your view of the road
☐ To overcome the effect of the road's slope
☐ To let faster traffic from behind overtake
☐ To be positioned safely if you skid

Doing this will give you an earlier view around the bend and enable you to see any hazards sooner.
    It also reduces the risk of collision with an oncoming vehicle that may have drifted over the centre line while taking the bend.

4.37 Mark one answer

You have just gone through deep water. To dry off the brakes you should

☐ accelerate and keep to a high speed for a short time
☐ go slowly while gently applying the brakes
☐ avoid using the brakes at all for a few miles
☐ stop for at least an hour to allow them time to dry

Water on the brakes will act as a lubricant, causing them to work less efficiently. Using the brakes lightly as you go along will dry them out.

4.38 Mark two answers

In very hot weather the road surface can become soft. Which TWO of the following will be most affected?

☐ The suspension
☐ The grip of the tyres
☐ The braking
☐ The exhaust

Only a small part of your tyres is in contact with the road. This is why you must consider the surface on which you're travelling, and alter your speed to suit the road conditions.

4.39 Mark one answer

Where are you most likely to be affected by a side wind?

☐ On a narrow country lane
☐ On an open stretch of road
☐ On a busy stretch of road
☐ On a long, straight road

In windy conditions, care must be taken on exposed roads. A strong gust of wind can blow you off course. Watch out for other road users who are particularly likely to be affected, such as cyclists, motorcyclists, high-sided lorries and vehicles towing trailers.

4.40 Mark one answer

In good conditions, what is the typical stopping distance at 70 mph?

☐ 53 metres (175 feet)
☐ 60 metres (197 feet)
☐ 73 metres (240 feet)
☐ 96 metres (315 feet)

Note that this is the typical stopping distance. It will take at least this distance to think, brake and stop in good conditions. In poor conditions it will take much longer.

4.41 Mark one answer

What is the shortest overall stopping distance on a dry road at 60 mph?

☐ 53 metres (175 feet)
☐ 58 metres (190 feet)
☐ 73 metres (240 feet)
☐ 96 metres (315 feet)

This distance is the equivalent of 18 car lengths. Try pacing out 73 metres and then look back. It's probably further than you think.

4.42 Mark one answer

You are following a vehicle at a safe distance on a wet road. Another driver overtakes you and pulls into the gap you have left. What should you do?

☐ Flash your headlight as a warning
☐ Try to overtake safely as soon as you can
☐ Drop back to regain a safe distance
☐ Stay close to the other vehicle until it moves on

Wet weather will affect the time it takes for you to stop and can affect your control.
    Your speed should allow you to stop safely and in good time. If another vehicle pulls into the gap you've left, ease back until you've regained your stopping distance.

4.43 Mark one answer

You are travelling at 50 mph on a good, dry road. What is your typical overall stopping distance?

☐ 36 metres (118 feet)
☐ 53 metres (175 feet)
☐ 75 metres (245 feet)
☐ 96 metres (315 feet)

Even in good conditions it will usually take you further than you think to stop. Don't just learn the figures, make sure you understand how far the distance is.

4.44 Mark one answer

You are on a good, dry, road surface. Your brakes and tyres are good. What is the typical overall stopping distance at 40 mph?

☐ 23 metres (75 feet)
☐ 36 metres (118 feet)
☐ 53 metres (175 feet)
☐ 96 metres (315 feet)

Stopping distances are affected by a number of variable factors. These include the type, model and condition of your vehicle, road and weather conditions, and your reaction time. Look well ahead for hazards and leave enough space between you and the vehicle in front. This should allow you to pull up safely if you have to, without braking sharply.

4.45 Mark one answer

What should you do when overtaking a motorcyclist in strong winds?

☐ Pass close
☐ Pass quickly
☐ Pass wide
☐ Pass immediately

In strong winds riders of two-wheeled vehicles are particularly vulnerable. When you overtake them allow plenty of room.
    Always check to the left as you pass.

4.46 Mark one answer

You are overtaking a motorcyclist in strong winds. What should you do?

☐ Allow extra room
☐ Give a thank you wave
☐ Move back early
☐ Sound your horn

It is easy for motorcyclists to be blown off course. Always give them plenty of room if you decide to overtake, especially in strong winds. Decide whether you need to overtake at all. Always check to the left as you pass.

4.47 Mark one answer

Overall stopping distance is made up of thinking and braking distance. You are on a good, dry road surface with good brakes and tyres. What is the typical BRAKING distance from 50 mph?

☐ 14 metres (46 feet)
☐ 24 metres (80 feet)
☐ 38 metres (125 feet)
☐ 55 metres (180 feet)

Be aware this is just the braking distance.
   You need to add the thinking distance to this to give the OVERALL STOPPING DISTANCE. At 50 mph the typical thinking distance will be 15 metres (50 feet), plus a braking distance of 38 metres (125 feet), giving an overall stopping distance of 53 metres (175 feet). The distance could be greater than this depending on your attention and response to any hazards.
   These figures are a general guide.

4.48 Mark one answer

In heavy motorway traffic the vehicle behind you is following too closely. How can you lower the risk of a collision?

☐ Increase your distance from the vehicle in front
☐ Operate the brakes sharply
☐ Switch on your hazard lights
☐ Move onto the hard shoulder and stop

On busy roads traffic may still travel at high speeds despite being close together. Don't follow too closely to the vehicle in front. If a driver behind seems to be 'pushing' you, gradually increase your distance from the vehicle in front by slowing down gently. This will give you more space in front if you have to brake, and lessen the risk of a collision involving several vehicles.

4.49 Mark one answer

You are following other vehicles in fog. You have your lights on. What else can you do to reduce the chances of being in a collision?

☐ Keep close to the vehicle in front
☐ Use your main beam instead of dipped headlights
☐ Keep up with the faster vehicles
☐ Reduce your speed and increase the gap in front

When it's foggy use dipped headlights. This will help you see and be seen by other road users. If visibility is seriously reduced consider using front and rear fog lights.
   Keep a sensible speed and don't follow the vehicle in front too closely. If the road is wet and slippery you'll need to allow twice the normal stopping distance.

4.50 Mark three answers

To avoid a collision when entering a contraflow system, you should

☐ reduce speed in good time
☐ switch lanes at any time to make progress
☐ choose an appropriate lane in good time
☐ keep the correct separation distance
☐ increase speed to pass through quickly
☐ follow other motorists closely to avoid long queues

In a contraflow system you will be travelling close to oncoming traffic and sometimes in narrow lanes. You should obey the temporary speed limit signs, get into the correct lane at the proper time and keep a safe separation distance from the vehicle ahead. When traffic is at a very low speed, merging in turn is recommended if it's safe and appropriate.

hazard awareness

5.1 Mark two answers

You get cold and wet when riding. Which TWO are likely to happen?

- ☐ You may lose concentration
- ☐ You may slide off the seat
- ☐ Your visor may freeze up
- ☐ Your reaction times may be slower
- ☐ Your helmet may loosen

When you're riding a motorcycle make sure you're wearing suitable clothing. If you become cold and uncomfortable this could cause you to lose concentration and could slow down your reaction time.

5.2 Mark one answer

You are riding up to a zebra crossing. You intend to stop for waiting pedestrians. How could you let them know you are stopping?

- ☐ By signalling with your left arm
- ☐ By waving them across
- ☐ By flashing your headlight
- ☐ By signalling with your right arm

Giving the correct arm signal would indicate to approaching vehicles, as well as pedestrians, that you are stopping at the pedestrian crossing.

5.3 Mark one answer

You are about to ride home. You cannot find the glasses you need to wear. You should

- ☐ ride home slowly, keeping to quiet roads
- ☐ borrow a friend's glasses and use those
- ☐ ride home at night, so that the lights will help you
- ☐ find a way of getting home without riding

Don't be tempted to ride if you've lost or forgotten your glasses. You must be able to see clearly when riding. If you can't you will be endangering yourself and other road users.

5.4 Mark three answers

Which THREE of these are likely effects of drinking alcohol?

- ☐ Reduced co-ordination
- ☐ Increased confidence
- ☐ Poor judgement
- ☐ Increased concentration
- ☐ Faster reactions
- ☐ Colour blindness

Alcohol can increase confidence to a point where a rider's behaviour might become 'out of character'. Someone who normally behaves sensibly suddenly takes risks and could endanger themselves and others.

Never drink and ride, or accept a ride from anyone who's been drinking.

5.5 Mark one answer

You find that you need glasses to read vehicle number plates at the required distance. When MUST you wear them?

- ☐ Only in bad weather conditions
- ☐ At all times when riding
- ☐ Only when you think it necessary
- ☐ Only in bad light or at night time

Have your eyesight tested before you start your practical training. Then, throughout your riding life, have periodical checks to ensure that your eyesight hasn't deteriorated.

5.6 Mark three answers

Drinking any amount of alcohol is likely to

- ☐ slow down your reactions to hazards
- ☐ increase the speed of your reactions
- ☐ worsen your judgement of speed
- ☐ improve your awareness of danger
- ☐ give a false sense of confidence

Never drink if you are going to ride. It's always the safest option not to drink at all.

Don't take risks, it's not worth it.

5.7 Mark one answer

Which of the following types of glasses should NOT be worn when riding at night?

☐ Half-moon
☐ Round
☐ Bi-focal
☐ Tinted

If you are riding at night or in poor visibility, tinted lenses or a tinted visor will reduce the amount of available light reaching your eyes, making you less able to see clearly.

5.8 Mark one answer

For which of these may you use hazard warning lights?

☐ When riding on a motorway to warn traffic behind of a hazard ahead
☐ When you are double parked on a two way road
☐ When your direction indicators are not working
☐ When warning oncoming traffic that you intend to stop

Hazard warning lights are an important safety feature. Use them when riding on a motorway to warn following traffic of danger ahead. You should also use them if your motorcycle has broken down and is causing an obstruction.

5.9 Mark one answer

When riding how can you help to reduce the risk of hearing damage?

☐ Wearing goggles
☐ Using ear plugs
☐ Wearing a scarf
☐ Keeping the visor up

Using ear plugs can help prevent hearing damage and fatigue caused by noise.

5.10 Mark one answer

When riding long distances at speed, noise can cause fatigue. What can you do to help reduce this?

☐ Vary your speed
☐ Wear ear plugs
☐ Use an open-face helmet
☐ Ride in an upright position

Wearing ear plugs can help prevent hearing damage and also fatigue caused by noise.

5.11 Mark one answer

Why should you wear ear plugs when riding a motorcycle?

☐ To help to prevent ear damage
☐ To make you less aware of traffic
☐ To help to keep you warm
☐ To make your helmet fit better

The use of ear plugs is recommended to reduce the effect of noise levels and protect your hearing.

5.12 Mark one answer

You are going out to a social event and alcohol will be available. You will be riding your motorcycle shortly afterwards. What is the safest thing to do?

☐ Stay just below the legal limit
☐ Have soft drinks and alcohol in turn
☐ Don't go beyond the legal limit
☐ Stick to non-alcoholic drinks

The legal limit of alcohol is 80 milligrams per 100 millilitres of blood. However, drinking even the smallest amount of alcohol can affect your judgement and reactions. The safest and best option is to avoid any alcohol at all when riding or driving.

5.13 Mark one answer

You are convicted of riding after drinking too much alcohol. How could this affect your insurance?

☐ Your insurance may become invalid
☐ The amount of excess you pay will be reduced
☐ You will only be able to get third party cover
☐ Cover will only be given for riding smaller motorcycles

Riding while under the influence of drink or drugs can invalidate your insurance. This also endangers yourself and others. It's not a risk worth taking.

5.14 Mark one answer

Why should you check over your shoulder before turning right into a side road?

☐ To make sure the side road is clear
☐ To check for emerging traffic
☐ To check for overtaking vehicles
☐ To confirm your intention to turn

Take a last check over your shoulder before committing yourself to a manoeuvre. This is especially important when turning right, as other road users may not have seen your signal or may not understand your intentions.

5.15 Mark two answers

You are not sure if your cough medicine will affect you. What TWO things should you do?

☐ Ask your doctor
☐ Check the medicine label
☐ Ride if you feel alright
☐ Ask a friend or relative for advice

If you're taking medicine or drugs prescribed by your doctor, check to ensure that they won't make you drowsy. If you forget to ask when you're at the surgery, check with your pharmacist.

5.16 Mark one answer

When should you use hazard warning lights?

☐ When you are double-parked on a two-way road
☐ When your direction indicators are not working
☐ When warning oncoming traffic that you intend to stop
☐ When your motorcycle has broken down and is causing an obstruction

Hazard warning lights are an important safety feature and should be used if you have broken down and are causing an obstruction. Don't use them as an excuse to park illegally, such as when using a cash machine or post box. You may also use them on motorways to warn following traffic of danger ahead.

5.17 Mark one answer

It is a very hot day. What would you expect to find?

☐ Mud on the road
☐ A soft road surface
☐ Roadworks ahead
☐ Banks of fog

In very hot weather the road surface can become soft and may melt. Take care when braking and cornering on soft tarmac, as this can lead to reduced grip and cause skidding.

5.18 Mark one answer

You see this road marking in between queuing traffic. What should you look out for?

☐ Overhanging trees
☐ Roadworks
☐ Traffic wardens
☐ Traffic emerging

'Keep clear' markings should not be obstructed. They can be found in congested areas to help traffic waiting to emerge onto a busy road.

5.19 Mark two answers

Where would you expect to see these markers?

☐ On a motorway sign
☐ At the entrance to a narrow bridge
☐ On a large goods vehicle
☐ On a builder's skip placed on the road

These markers must be fitted to vehicles over 13 metres long, large goods vehicles, and rubbish skips placed in the road. They are reflective to make them easier to see in the dark.

279

5.20 Mark one answer

What is the main hazard shown in this picture?

☐ Vehicles turning right
☐ Vehicles doing U-turns
☐ The cyclist crossing the road
☐ Parked cars around the corner

Look at the picture carefully and try to imagine you're there. The cyclist in this picture appears to be trying to cross the road. You must be able to deal with the unexpected, especially when you're approaching a hazardous junction. Look well ahead to give yourself time to deal with any hazards.

5.21 Mark one answer

Which road user has caused a hazard?

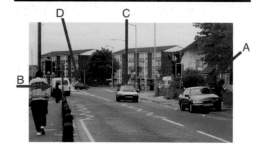

☐ The parked car (arrowed A)
☐ The pedestrian waiting to cross (arrowed B)
☐ The moving car (arrowed C)
☐ The car turning (arrowed D)

The car arrowed A is parked within the area marked by zigzag lines at the pedestrian crossing. Parking here is illegal. It also

• blocks the view for pedestrians wishing to cross the road

• restricts the view of the crossing for approaching traffic.

5.22 Mark one answer

What should the driver of the car approaching the crossing do?

☐ Continue at the same speed
☐ Sound the horn
☐ Drive through quickly
☐ Slow down and get ready to stop

Look well ahead to see if any hazards are developing. This will give you more time to deal with them in the correct way. The man in the picture is clearly intending to cross the road. You should be travelling at a speed that allows you to check your mirror, slow down and stop in good time. You shouldn't have to brake harshly.

5.23 Mark three answers

What THREE things should the driver of the grey car (arrowed) be especially aware of?

☐ Pedestrians stepping out between cars
☐ Other cars behind the grey car
☐ Doors opening on parked cars
☐ The bumpy road surface
☐ Cars leaving parking spaces
☐ Empty parking spaces

You need to be aware that other road users may not have seen you. Always be on the lookout for hazards that may develop suddenly and need you to take avoiding action.

5.24 Mark one answer

You see this sign ahead. You should expect the road to

☐ go steeply uphill
☐ go steeply downhill
☐ bend sharply to the left
☐ bend sharply to the right

Adjust your speed in good time and select the correct gear for your speed. Going too fast into the bend could cause you to lose control.

Braking late and harshly while changing direction reduces your vehicle's grip on the road, and is likely to cause a skid.

5.25 Mark one answer

You are approaching this cyclist. You should

☐ overtake before the cyclist gets to the junction
☐ flash your headlights at the cyclist
☐ slow down and allow the cyclist to turn
☐ overtake the cyclist on the left-hand side

Keep well back and allow the cyclist room to take up the correct position for the turn.

Don't get too close behind or try to squeeze past.

5.26 Mark one answer

Why must you take extra care when turning right at this junction?

☐ Road surface is poor
☐ Footpaths are narrow
☐ Road markings are faint
☐ There is reduced visibility

You may have to pull forward slowly until you can see up and down the road. Be aware that the traffic approaching the junction can't see you either. If you don't know that it's clear, don't go.

5.27 Mark one answer

When approaching this bridge you should give way to

☐ bicycles
☐ buses
☐ motorcycles
☐ cars

A double-deck bus or high-sided lorry will have to take up a position in the centre of the road so that it can clear the bridge. There is normally a sign to indicate this.

Look well down the road, through the bridge and be aware you may have to stop and give way to an oncoming large vehicle.

5.28 Mark one answer

What type of vehicle could you expect to meet in the middle of the road?

☐ Lorry
☐ Bicycle
☐ Car
☐ Motorcycle

The highest point of the bridge is in the centre so a large vehicle might have to move to the centre of the road to allow it enough room to pass under the bridge.

5.29 Mark one answer

At this blind junction you must stop

☐ behind the line, then edge forward to see clearly
☐ beyond the line at a point where you can see clearly
☐ only if there is traffic on the main road
☐ only if you are turning to the right

The 'stop' sign has been put here because there is a poor view into the main road. You must stop because it will not be possible to assess the situation on the move, however slowly you are travelling.

5.30 Mark one answer

A driver pulls out of a side road in front of you. You have to brake hard. You should

☐ ignore the error and stay calm
☐ flash your lights to show your annoyance
☐ sound your horn to show your annoyance
☐ overtake as soon as possible

Where there are a number of side roads, be alert. Be especially careful if there are a lot of parked vehicles because they can make it more difficult for drivers emerging to see you. Try to be tolerant if a vehicle does emerge and you have to brake quickly. Don't react aggressively.

5.31 Mark one answer

An elderly person's driving ability could be affected because they may be unable to

☐ obtain car insurance
☐ understand road signs
☐ react very quickly
☐ give signals correctly

Be tolerant of older drivers. Poor eyesight and hearing could affect the speed with which they react to a hazard and may cause them to be hesitant.

5.32 Mark one answer

You have just passed these warning lights. What hazard would you expect to see next?

☐ A level crossing with no barrier
☐ An ambulance station
☐ A school crossing patrol
☐ An opening bridge

These lights warn that children may be crossing the road to a nearby school. Slow down so that you're ready to stop if necessary.

5.33 Mark one answer

You are planning a long journey. Do you need to plan rest stops?

☐ Yes, you should plan to stop every half an hour
☐ Yes, regular stops help concentration
☐ No, you will be less tired if you get there as soon as possible
☐ No, only fuel stops will be needed

Try to plan your journey so that you can take rest stops. It's recommended that you take a break of at least 15 minutes after every two hours of driving. This should help to maintain your concentration.

5.34 Mark one answer

A driver does something that upsets you. You should

☐ try not to react
☐ let them know how you feel
☐ flash your headlights several times
☐ sound your horn

There are times when other road users make a misjudgement or mistake. When this happens try not to get annoyed and don't react by showing anger. Sounding your horn, flashing your headlights or shouting won't help the situation. Good anticipation will help to prevent these incidents becoming collisions.

5.35 Mark one answer

The red lights are flashing. What should you do when approaching this level crossing?

☐ Go through quickly
☐ Go through carefully
☐ Stop before the barrier
☐ Switch on hazard warning lights

At level crossings the red lights flash before and when the barrier is down. At most crossings an amber light will precede the red lights. You must stop behind the white line unless you have already crossed it when the amber light comes on. NEVER zigzag around half-barriers.

5.36 Mark one answer

You are approaching crossroads. The traffic lights have failed. What should you do?

☐ Brake and stop only for large vehicles
☐ Brake sharply to a stop before looking
☐ Be prepared to brake sharply to a stop
☐ Be prepared to stop for any traffic

When approaching a junction where the traffic lights have failed, you should proceed with caution. Treat the situation as an unmarked junction and be prepared to stop.

5.37 Mark one answer

What should the driver of the red car (arrowed) do?

☐ Wave the pedestrians who are waiting to cross
☐ Wait for the pedestrian in the road to cross
☐ Quickly drive behind the pedestrian in the road
☐ Tell the pedestrian in the road she should not have crossed

Some people might take longer to cross the road. They may be older or have a disability. Be patient and don't hurry them by showing your impatience. They might have poor eyesight or not be able to hear traffic approaching. If pedestrians are standing at the side of the road, don't signal or wave them to cross. Other road users may not have seen your signal and this could lead the pedestrians into a hazardous situation.

5.38 Mark one answer

You are following a slower-moving vehicle on a narrow country road. There is a junction just ahead on the right. What should you do?

☐ Overtake after checking your mirrors and signalling
☐ Stay behind until you are past the junction
☐ Accelerate quickly to pass before the junction
☐ Slow down and prepare to overtake on the left

You should never overtake as you approach a junction. If a vehicle emerged from the junction while you were overtaking, a dangerous situation could develop very quickly.

5.39 Mark one answer

What should you do as you approach this overhead bridge?

☐ Move out to the centre of the road before going through
☐ Find another route, this is only for high vehicles
☐ Be prepared to give way to large vehicles in the middle of the road
☐ Move across to the right-hand side before going through

Oncoming large vehicles may need to move to the middle of the road so that they can pass safely under the bridge. There will not be enough room for you to continue and you should be ready to stop and wait.

5.40 Mark one answer

Why are mirrors often slightly curved (convex)?

☐ They give a wider field of vision
☐ They totally cover blind spots
☐ They make it easier to judge the speed of following traffic
☐ They make following traffic look bigger

Although a convex mirror gives a wide view of the scene behind, you should be aware that it will not show you everything behind or to the side of the vehicle. Before you move off you will need to check over your shoulder to look for anything not visible in the mirrors.

5.41 Mark one answer

You see this sign on the rear of a slow-moving lorry that you want to pass. It is travelling in the middle lane of a three-lane motorway. You should

☐ cautiously approach the lorry then pass on either side
☐ follow the lorry until you can leave the motorway
☐ wait on the hard shoulder until the lorry has stopped
☐ approach with care and keep to the left of the lorry

This sign is found on slow-moving or stationary works vehicles. If you wish to overtake, do so on the left, as indicated.
Be aware that there might be workmen in the area.

5.42 Mark one answer

You think the driver of the vehicle in front has forgotten to cancel their right indicator. You should

☐ flash your lights to alert the driver
☐ sound your horn before overtaking
☐ overtake on the left if there is room
☐ stay behind and not overtake

The driver may be unsure of the location of a junction and turn suddenly. Be cautious and don't attempt to overtake.

5.43 Mark one answer

What is the main hazard the driver of the red car (arrowed) should be aware of?

☐ Glare from the sun may affect the driver's vision
☐ The black car may stop suddenly
☐ The bus may move out into the road
☐ Oncoming vehicles will assume the driver is turning right

If you can do so safely give way to buses signalling to move off at bus stops. Try to anticipate the actions of other road users around you. The driver of the red car should be prepared for the bus pulling out.

As you approach a bus stop look to see how many passengers are waiting to board. If the last one has just got on, the bus is likely to move off.

5.44 Mark one answer

This yellow sign on a vehicle indicates this is

☐ a broken-down vehicle
☐ a school bus
☐ an ice cream van
☐ a private ambulance

Buses which carry children to and from school may stop at places other than scheduled bus stops. Be aware that they might pull over at any time to allow children to get on or off. This will normally be when traffic is heavy during rush hour.

5.45 Mark two answers

What TWO main hazards should you be aware of when going along this street?

☐ Glare from the sun
☐ Car doors opening suddenly
☐ Lack of road markings
☐ The headlights on parked cars being switched on
☐ Large goods vehicles
☐ Children running out from between vehicles

On roads where there are many parked vehicles you should take extra care. You might not be able to see children between parked cars and they may run out into the road without looking.

People may open car doors without realising the hazard this can create. You will also need to look well down the road for oncoming traffic.

5.46 Mark one answer

What is the main hazard you should be aware of when following this cyclist?

☐ The cyclist may move to the left and dismount
☐ The cyclist may swerve out into the road
☐ The contents of the cyclist's carrier may fall onto the road
☐ The cyclist may wish to turn right at the end of the road

When following a cyclist be aware that they have to deal with the hazards around them.

They may wobble or swerve to avoid a pothole in the road or see a potential hazard and change direction suddenly.

Don't follow them too closely or rev your engine impatiently.

5.47 Mark one answer

A driver's behaviour has upset you. It may help if you

☐ stop and take a break
☐ shout abusive language
☐ gesture to them with your hand
☐ follow their car, flashing your headlights

Tiredness may make you more irritable than you would be normally. You might react differently to situations because of it.

If you feel yourself becoming tense, take a break.

5.48 Mark one answer

In areas where there are 'traffic calming' measures you should

☐ travel at a reduced speed
☐ always travel at the speed limit
☐ position in the centre of the road
☐ only slow down if pedestrians are near

Traffic calming measures such as road humps, chicanes and narrowings are intended to slow you down. Maintain a reduced speed until you reach the end of these features. They are there to protect pedestrians. Kill your speed!

5.49 Mark two answers

When approaching this hazard why should you slow down?

☐ Because of the bend
☐ Because it's hard to see to the right
☐ Because of approaching traffic
☐ Because of animals crossing
☐ Because of the level crossing

There are two hazards clearly signed in this picture. You should be preparing for the bend by slowing down and selecting the correct gear. You might also have to stop at the level crossing, so be alert and be prepared to stop if necessary.

5.50 Mark one answer

Why are place names painted on the road surface?

☐ To restrict the flow of traffic
☐ To warn you of oncoming traffic
☐ To enable you to change lanes early
☐ To prevent you changing lanes

The names of towns and cities may be painted on the road at busy junctions and complex road systems. Their purpose is to let you move into the correct lane in good time, allowing traffic to flow more freely.

5.51 Mark one answer

Some two-way roads are divided into three lanes. Why are these particularly dangerous?

☐ Traffic in both directions can use the middle lane to overtake
☐ Traffic can travel faster in poor weather conditions
☐ Traffic can overtake on the left
☐ Traffic uses the middle lane for emergencies only

If you intend to overtake you must consider that approaching traffic could be planning the same manoeuvre. When you have considered the situation and have decided it is safe, indicate your intentions early. This will show the approaching traffic that you intend to pull out.

5.52 Mark one answer

You are on a dual carriageway. Ahead you see a vehicle with an amber flashing light. What could this be?

☐ An ambulance
☐ A fire engine
☐ A doctor on call
☐ A disabled person's vehicle

An amber flashing light on a vehicle indicates that it is slow-moving. Battery powered vehicles used by disabled people are limited to 8 mph. It's not advisable for them to be used on dual carriageways where the speed limit exceeds 50 mph. If they are then an amber flashing light must be used.

5.53 Mark one answer

What does this signal from a police officer mean to oncoming traffic?

☐ Go ahead
☐ Stop
☐ Turn left
☐ Turn right

Police officers may need to direct traffic, for example, at a junction where the traffic lights have broken down. Check your copy of *The Highway Code* for the signals that they use.

5.54 Mark two answers

Why should you be especially cautious when going past this stationary bus?

☐ There is traffic approaching in the distance
☐ The driver may open the door
☐ It may suddenly move off
☐ People may cross the road in front of it
☐ There are bicycles parked on the pavement

A stationary bus at a bus stop can hide pedestrians just in front of it who might be about to cross the road. Only go past at a speed that will enable you to stop safely if you need to.

5.55 Mark three answers

Overtaking is a major cause of collisions. In which THREE of these situations should you NOT overtake?

☐ If you are turning left shortly afterwards
☐ When you are in a one-way street
☐ When you are approaching a junction
☐ If you are travelling up a long hill
☐ When your view ahead is blocked

You should not overtake unless it is really necessary. Arriving safely is more important than taking risks. Also look out for road signs and markings that show it is illegal or would be unsafe to overtake. In many cases overtaking is unlikely to significantly improve journey times.

5.56 Mark three answers

Which THREE result from drinking alcohol?

☐ Less control
☐ A false sense of confidence
☐ Faster reactions
☐ Poor judgement of speed
☐ Greater awareness of danger

You must understand the serious dangers of mixing alcohol with driving or riding.

Alcohol will severely reduce your ability to drive or ride safely. Just one drink could put you over the limit. Don't risk people's lives –

DON'T DRINK AND DRIVE OR RIDE!

vulnerable road users

6.1 Mark one answer
You should not ride too closely behind a lorry because

☐ you will breathe in the lorry's exhaust fumes
☐ wind from the lorry will slow you down
☐ drivers behind you may not be able to see you
☐ it will reduce your view ahead

If you're following too close behind a large vehicle your view beyond it will be restricted. Drop back. This will help you to see more of the road ahead. It will also help the driver of the large vehicle to see you in the mirror and gives you a safe separation distance in which to take avoiding action if a hazardous situation arises.

6.2 Mark three answers
You are riding on a country lane. You see cattle on the road. You should

☐ slow down
☐ stop if necessary
☐ give plenty of room
☐ rev your engine
☐ sound your horn
☐ ride up close behind them

Try not to startle the animals. They can be easily frightened by noise or by traffic passing too closely.

6.3 Mark one answer
A learner driver has begun to emerge into your path from a side road on the left. You should

☐ be ready to slow down and stop
☐ let them emerge then ride close behind
☐ turn into the side road
☐ brake hard, then wave them out

If you see another vehicle begin to emerge into your path you should ride defensively.
Always be ready to slow down or stop if necessary.

6.4 Mark one answer
The vehicle ahead is being driven by a learner. You should

☐ keep calm and be patient
☐ ride up close behind
☐ put your headlight on full beam
☐ sound your horn and overtake

Learners might take longer to react to traffic situations. Don't unnerve them by riding up close behind or showing signs of impatience.

6.5 Mark one answer
You are riding in fast-flowing traffic. The vehicle behind is following too closely. You should

☐ slow down gradually to increase the gap in front of you
☐ slow down as quickly as possible by braking
☐ accelerate to get away from the vehicle behind you
☐ apply the brakes sharply to warn the driver behind

It is dangerous for vehicles to travel too close together. Visibility is reduced and there is a higher risk of collision if a vehicle brakes suddenly to avoid a hazard. By increasing the separation distance between you and the vehicle in front, you have a greater safety margin. It also gives space for the vehicles behind to overtake you if they wish.

6.6 Mark one answer
You are riding towards a zebra crossing. Waiting to cross is a person in a wheelchair. You should

☐ continue on your way
☐ wave to the person to cross
☐ wave to the person to wait
☐ be prepared to stop

As you would with an able-bodied person, you should prepare to slow down and stop.
Don't wave them across, as other traffic may not stop.

6.7 Mark one answer
Why should you allow extra room when overtaking another motorcyclist on a windy day?

☐ The rider may turn off suddenly to get out of the wind
☐ The rider may be blown across in front of you
☐ The rider may stop suddenly
☐ The rider may be travelling faster than normal

On a windy day, be aware that the blustery conditions might blow you or other motorcyclists out of position. Think about this before deciding to overtake.

6.8 Mark two answers

You have stopped at a pelican crossing. A disabled person is crossing slowly in front of you. The lights have now changed to green. You should

☐ allow the person to cross
☐ ride in front of the person
☐ ride behind the person
☐ sound your horn
☐ be patient
☐ edge forward slowly

At a pelican crossing the green light means you may proceed as long as the crossing is clear. If someone hasn't finished crossing, be patient and wait for them.

6.9 Mark one answer

Where should you take particular care to look out for other motorcyclists and cyclists?

☐ On dual carriageways
☐ At junctions
☐ At zebra crossings
☐ On one-way streets

Other motorcyclists and cyclists may be difficult to see on the road, particularly at junctions. If your view is blocked by other traffic you may not be able to see them approaching.

6.10 Mark one answer

Why is it vital for a rider to make a 'lifesaver' check before turning right?

☐ To check for any overtaking traffic
☐ To confirm that they are about to turn
☐ To make sure the side road is clear
☐ To check that the rear indicator is flashing

The 'lifesaver' glance makes you aware of what is happening behind and alongside you before altering your course. This glance must be timed so that you still have time to react if it isn't safe to carry out your manoeuvre.

6.11 Mark two answers

You are about to overtake horse riders. Which TWO of the following could scare the horses?

☐ Sounding your horn
☐ Giving arm signals
☐ Riding slowly
☐ Revving your engine

When passing horses allow them plenty of space and slow down. Animals can be frightened by sudden or loud noises, so don't sound your horn or rev the engine.

6.12 Mark one answer

What is a main cause of road traffic incidents among young and new motorcyclists?

☐ Using borrowed equipment
☐ Lack of experience and judgement
☐ Riding in bad weather conditions
☐ Riding on country roads

Young and inexperienced motorcyclists are far more likely to be involved in incidents than more experienced riders. Reasons for this include natural exuberance, showing off, competitive behaviour and over confidence. Don't overestimate your abilities and never ride too fast for the conditions.

6.13 Mark one answer

Which of the following is applicable to young motorcyclists?

☐ They are normally better than experienced riders
☐ They are usually less likely to have a crash
☐ They are often over-confident of their own ability
☐ They are more likely to get cheaper insurance

Young and inexperienced motorcyclists often have more confidence than ability. It takes time to gain experience and become a good rider. Make sure you have the right attitude and put safety first.

289

6.14   Mark one answer

The road outside this school is marked with yellow zigzag lines. What do these lines mean?

☐ You may park on the lines when dropping off school children
☐ You may park on the lines when picking up school children
☐ You should not wait or park your motorcycle here
☐ You must stay with your motorcycle if you park here

Parking here will block the view of the school gates, endangering the lives of children on their way to and from school.

6.15   Mark one answer

Which sign means that there may be people walking along the road?

☐   ☐

☐   ☐

Always check the road signs. Triangular signs are warning signs and they'll keep you informed of hazards ahead and help you to anticipate any problems. There are a number of different signs showing pedestrians. Learn the meaning of each one.

6.16   Mark one answer

You are turning left at a junction. Pedestrians have started to cross the road. You should

☐ go on, giving them plenty of room
☐ stop and wave at them to cross
☐ blow your horn and proceed
☐ give way to them

If you're turning into a side road, pedestrians already crossing the road have priority and you should give way to them.

Don't wave them across the road, sound your horn, flash your lights or give any other misleading signal. Other road users may misinterpret your signal and this may lead the pedestrians into a dangerous situation. If a pedestrian is slow or indecisive be patient and wait. Don't hurry them across by revving your engine.

6.17   Mark one answer

You are turning left from a main road into a side road. People are already crossing the road into which you are turning. You should

☐ continue, as it is your right of way
☐ signal to them to continue crossing
☐ wait and allow them to cross
☐ sound your horn to warn them of your presence

Always check the road into which you are turning. Approaching at the correct speed will allow you enough time to observe and react.

Give way to any pedestrians already crossing the road.

6.18 Mark one answer

You are at a road junction, turning into a minor road. There are pedestrians crossing the minor road. You should

☐ stop and wave the pedestrians across
☐ sound your horn to let the pedestrians know that you are there
☐ give way to the pedestrians who are already crossing
☐ carry on; the pedestrians should give way to you

Always look into the road into which you are turning. If there are pedestrians crossing, give way to them, but don't wave or signal to them to cross. Signal your intention to turn as you approach.

6.19 Mark one answer

You are turning left into a side road. What hazards should you be especially aware of?

☐ One way street
☐ Pedestrians
☐ Traffic congestion
☐ Parked vehicles

Make sure that you have reduced your speed and are in the correct gear for the turn. Look into the road before you turn and always give way to any pedestrians who are crossing.

6.20 Mark one answer

You intend to turn right into a side road. Just before turning you should check for motorcyclists who might be

☐ overtaking on your left
☐ following you closely
☐ emerging from the side road
☐ overtaking on your right

Never attempt to change direction to the right without first checking your right-hand mirror. A motorcyclist might not have seen your signal and could be hidden by the car behind you. This action should become a matter of routine.

6.21 Mark one answer

A toucan crossing is different from other crossings because

☐ moped riders can use it
☐ it is controlled by a traffic warden
☐ it is controlled by two flashing lights
☐ cyclists can use it

Toucan crossings are shared by pedestrians and cyclists and they are shown the green light together. Cyclists are permitted to cycle across.
The signals are push-button operated and there is no flashing amber phase.

6.22 Mark one answer

How will a school crossing patrol signal you to stop?

☐ By pointing to children on the opposite pavement
☐ By displaying a red light
☐ By displaying a stop sign
☐ By giving you an arm signal

If a school crossing patrol steps out into the road with a stop sign you must stop.
Don't wave anyone across the road and don't get impatient or rev your engine.

6.23 Mark one answer

Where would you see this sign?

☐ In the window of a car taking children to school
☐ At the side of the road
☐ At playground areas
☐ On the rear of a school bus or coach

Vehicles that are used to carry children to and from school will be travelling at busy times of the day. If you're following a vehicle with this sign be prepared for it to make frequent stops. It might pick up or set down passengers in places other than normal bus stops.

6.24 Mark one answer

Which sign tells you that pedestrians may be walking in the road as there is no pavement?

☐   ☐

☐   ☐

Give pedestrians who are walking at the side of the road plenty of room when you pass them. They may turn around when they hear your engine and unintentionally step into the path of your vehicle.

6.25 Mark one answer

What does this sign mean?

☐ No route for pedestrians and cyclists
☐ A route for pedestrians only
☐ A route for cyclists only
☐ A route for pedestrians and cyclists

This sign shows a shared route for pedestrians and cyclists: when it ends, the cyclists will be rejoining the main road.

6.26 Mark one answer

You see a pedestrian with a white stick and red band. This means that the person is

☐ physically disabled
☐ deaf only
☐ blind only
☐ deaf and blind

If someone is deaf as well as blind, they may be carrying a white stick with a red reflective band. You can't see if a pedestrian is deaf. Don't assume everyone can hear you approaching.

6.27 Mark one answer

What action would you take when elderly people are crossing the road?

☐ Wave them across so they know that you have seen them
☐ Be patient and allow them to cross in their own time
☐ Rev the engine to let them know that you are waiting
☐ Tap the horn in case they are hard of hearing

Be aware that older people might take a long time to cross the road. They might also be hard of hearing and not hear you approaching. Don't hurry older people across the road by getting too close to them or revving your engine.

6.28 Mark one answer

You see two elderly pedestrians about to cross the road ahead. You should

☐ expect them to wait for you to pass
☐ speed up to get past them quickly
☐ stop and wave them across the road
☐ be careful, they may misjudge your speed

Older people may have impaired hearing, vision, concentration and judgement. They may also walk slowly and so could take a long time to cross the road.

6.29 Mark one answer

You are coming up to a roundabout. A cyclist is signalling to turn right. What should you do?

☐ Overtake on the right
☐ Give a horn warning
☐ Signal the cyclist to move across
☐ Give the cyclist plenty of room

If you're following a cyclist who's signalling to turn right at a roundabout leave plenty of room. Give them space and time to get into the correct lane.

6.30 Mark two answers

Which TWO should you allow extra room when overtaking?

☐ Motorcycles
☐ Tractors
☐ Bicycles
☐ Road-sweeping vehicles

Don't pass riders too closely as this may cause them to lose balance. Always leave as much room as you would for a car, and don't cut in.

6.31 Mark one answer

Why should you look particularly for motorcyclists and cyclists at junctions?

☐ They may want to turn into the side road
☐ They may slow down to let you turn
☐ They are harder to see
☐ They might not see you turn

Cyclists and motorcyclists are smaller than other vehicles and so are more difficult to see. They can easily become hidden from your view by cars parked near a junction.

6.32 Mark one answer

You are waiting to come out of a side road. Why should you watch carefully for motorcycles?

☐ Motorcycles are usually faster than cars
☐ Police patrols often use motorcycles
☐ Motorcycles are small and hard to see
☐ Motorcycles have right of way

If you're waiting to emerge from a side road watch out for motorcycles: they're small and can be difficult to see. Be especially careful if there are parked vehicles restricting your view, there might be a motorcycle approaching.
IF YOU DON'T KNOW, DON'T GO.

6.33 Mark one answer

In daylight, an approaching motorcyclist is using a dipped headlight. Why?

☐ So that the rider can be seen more easily
☐ To stop the battery overcharging
☐ To improve the rider's vision
☐ The rider is inviting you to proceed

A motorcycle can be lost from sight behind another vehicle. The use of the headlight helps to make it more conspicuous and therefore more easily seen.

6.34 Mark one answer

Motorcyclists should wear bright clothing mainly because

☐ they must do so by law
☐ it helps keep them cool in summer
☐ the colours are popular
☐ drivers often do not see them

Motorcycles are small vehicles and can be difficult to see. If the rider wears bright clothing it can make it easier for other road users to see them approaching, especially at junctions.

6.35 Mark one answer

There is a slow-moving motorcyclist ahead of you. You are unsure what the rider is going to do. You should

☐ pass on the left
☐ pass on the right
☐ stay behind
☐ move closer

If a motorcyclist is travelling slowly it may be that they are looking for a turning or entrance. Be patient and stay behind them in case they need to make a sudden change of direction.

6.36 Mark one answer

Motorcyclists will often look round over their right shoulder just before turning right. This is because

☐ they need to listen for following traffic
☐ motorcycles do not have mirrors
☐ looking around helps them balance as they turn
☐ they need to check for traffic in their blind area

If you see a motorcyclist take a quick glance over their shoulder, this could mean they are about to change direction.
Recognising a clue like this helps you to be prepared and take appropriate action, making you safer on the road.

6.37 Mark three answers

At road junctions which of the following are most vulnerable?

☐ Cyclists
☐ Motorcyclists
☐ Pedestrians
☐ Car drivers
☐ Lorry drivers

Pedestrians and riders on two wheels can be harder to see than other road users.
Make sure you keep a look-out for them, especially at junctions. Good effective observation, coupled with appropriate action, can save lives.

6.38 Mark one answer

Motorcyclists are particularly vulnerable

☐ when moving off
☐ on dual carriageways
☐ when approaching junctions
☐ on motorways

Another road user failing to see a motorcyclist is a major cause of collisions at junctions. Wherever streams of traffic join or cross there's the potential for this type of incident to occur.

6.39 Mark two answers

You are approaching a roundabout. There are horses just ahead of you. You should

☐ be prepared to stop
☐ treat them like any other vehicle
☐ give them plenty of room
☐ accelerate past as quickly as possible
☐ sound your horn as a warning

Horse riders often keep to the outside of the roundabout even if they are turning right. Give them plenty of room and remember that they may have to cross lanes of traffic.

6.40 Mark one answer

As you approach a pelican crossing the lights change to green. Elderly people are halfway across. You should

☐ wave them to cross as quickly as they can
☐ rev your engine to make them hurry
☐ flash your lights in case they have not heard you
☐ wait because they will take longer to cross

Even if the lights turn to green, wait for them to clear the crossing. Allow them to cross the road in their own time, and don't try to hurry them by revving your engine.

6.41 Mark one answer

There are flashing amber lights under a school warning sign. What action should you take?

☐ Reduce speed until you are clear of the area
☐ Keep up your speed and sound the horn
☐ Increase your speed to clear the area quickly
☐ Wait at the lights until they change to green

The flashing amber lights are switched on to warn you that children may be crossing near a school. Slow down and take extra care as you may have to stop.

6.42 Mark one answer

These road markings must be kept clear to allow

∿-SCHOOL KEEP CLEAR-∿

☐ school children to be dropped off
☐ for teachers to park
☐ school children to be picked up
☐ a clear view of the crossing area

The markings are there to show that the area must be kept clear to allow an unrestricted view for

• approaching drivers and riders

• children wanting to cross the road.

6.43 Mark one answer

Where would you see this sign?

☐ Near a school crossing
☐ At a playground entrance
☐ On a school bus
☐ At a 'pedestrians only' area

Watch out for children crossing the road from the other side of the bus.

6.44 Mark one answer

You are following two cyclists. They approach a roundabout in the left-hand lane. In which direction should you expect the cyclists to go?

☐ Left
☐ Right
☐ Any direction
☐ Straight ahead

Cyclists approaching a roundabout in the left-hand lane may be turning right but may not have been able to get into the correct lane due to the heavy traffic. They may also feel safer keeping to the left all the way round the roundabout. Be aware of them and give them plenty of room.

6.45 Mark one answer

You are travelling behind a moped. You want to turn left just ahead. You should

☐ overtake the moped before the junction
☐ pull alongside the moped and stay level until just before the junction
☐ sound your horn as a warning and pull in front of the moped
☐ stay behind until the moped has passed the junction

Passing the moped and turning into the junction could mean that you cut across the front of the rider. This might force them to slow down, stop or even lose control.

Slow down and stay behind the moped until it has passed the junction and you can then turn safely.

6.46 Mark one answer

You see a horse rider as you approach a roundabout. They are signalling right but keeping well to the left. You should

☐ proceed as normal
☐ keep close to them
☐ cut in front of them
☐ stay well back

Allow the horse rider to enter and exit the roundabout in their own time. They may feel safer keeping to the left all the way around the roundabout. Don't get up close behind or alongside them. This is very likely to upset the horse and create a dangerous situation.

6.47 Mark one answer

How would you react to drivers who appear to be inexperienced?

☐ Sound your horn to warn them of your presence
☐ Be patient and prepare for them to react more slowly
☐ Flash your headlights to indicate that it is safe for them to proceed
☐ Overtake them as soon as possible

Learners might not have confidence when they first start to drive. Allow them plenty of room and don't react adversely to their hesitation. We all learn from experience, but new drivers will have had less practice in dealing with all the situations that might occur.

6.48 Mark one answer

You are following a learner driver who stalls at a junction. You should

☐ be patient as you expect them to make mistakes
☐ stay very close behind and flash your headlights
☐ start to rev your engine if they take too long to restart
☐ immediately steer around them and drive on

Learning is a process of practice and experience. Try to understand this and tolerate those who are at the beginning of this process.

6.49 Mark one answer

You are on a country road. What should you expect to see coming towards you on YOUR side of the road?

☐ Motorcycles
☐ Bicycles
☐ Pedestrians
☐ Horse riders

On a quiet country road always be aware that there may be a hazard just around the next bend, such as a slow-moving vehicle or pedestrians. Pedestrians are advised to walk on the right-hand side of the road if there is no pavement, so they may be walking towards you on your side of the road.

6.50 Mark one answer

You are turning left into a side road. Pedestrians are crossing the road near the junction. You must

☐ wave them on
☐ sound your horn
☐ switch on your hazard lights
☐ wait for them to cross

Check that it's clear before you turn into a junction. If there are pedestrians crossing they have priority, so let them cross in their own time.

6.51 Mark one answer

You are following a car driven by an elderly driver. You should

☐ expect the driver to drive badly
☐ flash your lights and overtake
☐ be aware that the driver's reactions may not be as fast as yours
☐ stay very close behind but be careful

You must show consideration to other road users. The reactions of older drivers may be slower and they might need more time to deal with a situation. Be tolerant and don't lose patience or show your annoyance.

6.52 Mark one answer

You are following a cyclist. You wish to turn left just ahead. You should

☐ overtake the cyclist before the junction
☐ pull alongside the cyclist and stay level until after the junction
☐ hold back until the cyclist has passed the junction
☐ go around the cyclist on the junction

Make allowances for cyclists. Allow them plenty of room. Don't try to overtake and then immediately turn left. Be patient and stay behind them until they have passed the junction.

6.53 Mark one answer

A horse rider is in the left-hand lane approaching a roundabout. You should expect the rider to

☐ go in any direction
☐ turn right
☐ turn left
☐ go ahead

Horses and their riders will move more slowly than other road users. They might not have time to cut across heavy traffic to take up positions in the offside lane. For this reason a horse and rider may approach a roundabout in the left-hand lane, even though they're turning right.

6.54 Mark one answer

Powered vehicles used by disabled people are small and hard to see. How do they give early warning when on a dual carriageway?

☐ They will have a flashing red light
☐ They will have a flashing green light
☐ They will have a flashing blue light
☐ They will have a flashing amber light.

Powered vehicles used by disabled people are small, low, hard to see and travel very slowly. On a dual carriageway a flashing amber light will warn other road users.

6.55 Mark one answer

You should never attempt to overtake a cyclist

☐ just before you turn left
☐ on a left hand bend
☐ on a one-way street
☐ on a dual carriageway

If you want to turn left and there's a cyclist in front of you, hold back. Wait until the cyclist has passed the junction and then turn left behind them.

6.56 Mark one answer

Ahead of you there is a moving vehicle with a flashing amber beacon. This means it is

☐ slow moving
☐ broken down
☐ a doctor's car
☐ a school crossing patrol

As you approach the vehicle, assess the situation. Due to its slow progress you will need to judge whether it is safe to overtake.

6.57 Mark one answer

What does this sign mean?

☐ Contraflow pedal cycle lane
☐ With-flow pedal cycle lane
☐ Pedal cycles and buses only
☐ No pedal cycles or buses

The picture of a cycle will also usually be painted on the road, sometimes with a different coloured surface. Leave these clear for cyclists and don't pass too closely when you overtake.

6.58 Mark one answer

You notice horse riders in front. What should you do FIRST?

☐ Pull out to the middle of the road
☐ Slow down and be ready to stop
☐ Accelerate around them
☐ Signal right

Be particularly careful when approaching horse riders – slow down and be prepared to stop. Always pass wide and slowly and look out for signals given by horse riders.
   Horses are unpredictable: always treat them as potential hazards and take great care when passing them.

6.59 Mark one answer

You must not stop on these road markings because you may obstruct

☐ children's view of the crossing area
☐ teachers' access to the school
☐ delivery vehicles' access to the school
☐ emergency vehicles' access to the school

These markings are found on the road outside schools. DO NOT stop (even to set down or pick up children) or park on them.
   The markings are to make sure that drivers, riders, children and other pedestrians have a clear view.

6.60 Mark one answer
The left-hand pavement is closed due to street repairs. What should you do?

☐ Watch out for pedestrians walking in the road
☐ Use your right-hand mirror more often
☐ Speed up to get past the roadworks quicker
☐ Position close to the left-hand kerb

Where street repairs have closed off pavements, proceed carefully and slowly as pedestrians might have to walk in the road.

6.61 Mark one answer
You are following a motorcyclist on an uneven road. You should

☐ allow less room so you can be seen in their mirrors
☐ overtake immediately
☐ allow extra room in case they swerve to avoid potholes
☐ allow the same room as normal because road surfaces do not affect motorcyclists

Potholes and bumps in the road can unbalance a motorcyclist. For this reason the rider might swerve to avoid an uneven road surface. Watch out at places where this is likely to occur.

6.62 Mark one answer
What does this sign tell you?

☐ No cycling
☐ Cycle route ahead
☐ Cycle parking only
☐ End of cycle route

With people's concern today for the environment, cycle routes are being created in our towns and cities. These are usually defined by road markings and signs.
    Respect the presence of cyclists on the road and give them plenty of room if you need to pass.

6.63 Mark one answer
You are approaching this roundabout and see the cyclist signal right. Why is the cyclist keeping to the left?

☐ It is a quicker route for the cyclist
☐ The cyclist is going to turn left instead
☐ The cyclist thinks *The Highway Code* does not apply to bicycles
☐ The cyclist is slower and more vulnerable

Cycling in today's heavy traffic can be hazardous. Some cyclists may not feel happy about crossing the path of traffic to take up a position in an outside lane. Be aware of this and understand that, although in the left-hand lane, the cyclist might be turning right.

6.64 Mark one answer
You are approaching this crossing. You should

☐ prepare to slow down and stop
☐ stop and wave the pedestrians across
☐ speed up and pass by quickly
☐ continue unless the pedestrians step out

Be courteous and prepare to stop. Do not wave people across as this could be dangerous if another vehicle is approaching the crossing.

6.65 Mark one answer

You see a pedestrian with a dog. The dog has a yellow or burgundy coat. This especially warns you that the pedestrian is

☐ elderly
☐ dog training
☐ colour blind
☐ deaf

Take extra care as the pedestrian may not be aware of vehicles approaching.

6.66 Mark one answer

At toucan crossings

☐ you only stop if someone is waiting to cross
☐ cyclists are not permitted
☐ there is a continuously flashing amber beacon
☐ pedestrians and cyclists may cross

There are some crossings where cycle routes lead the cyclists to cross at the same place as pedestrians. These are called toucan crossings. Always look out for cyclists, as they're likely to be approaching faster than pedestrians.

6.67 Mark one answer

Some junctions controlled by traffic lights have a marked area between two stop lines. What is this for?

☐ To allow taxis to position in front of other traffic
☐ To allow people with disabilities to cross the road
☐ To allow cyclists and pedestrians to cross the road together
☐ To allow cyclists to position in front of other traffic

These are known as advanced stop lines.
When the lights are red (or about to become red) you should stop at the first white line. However, if you have crossed that line as the lights change you must stop at the second line even if it means you are in the area reserved for cyclists.

6.68 Mark one answer

At some traffic lights there are advance stop lines and a marked area. What are these for?

☐ To allow cyclists to position in front of other traffic
☐ To let pedestrians cross when the lights change
☐ To prevent traffic from jumping the lights
☐ To let passengers get off a bus which is queuing

You should always stop at the first white line. Avoid going into the marked area which is reserved for cyclists only. However, if you have crossed the first white line at the time the signal changes to red you must stop at the second line even if you are in the marked area.

6.69 Mark one answer

When you are overtaking a cyclist you should leave as much room as you would give to a car. What is the main reason for this?

☐ The cyclist might speed up
☐ The cyclist might get off the bike
☐ The cyclist might swerve
☐ The cyclist might have to make a left turn

Before overtaking assess the situation.
Look well ahead to see if the cyclist will need to change direction. Be especially aware of the cyclist approaching parked vehicles as they will need to alter course.
Do not pass too closely or cut in sharply.

6.70 Mark three answers

Which THREE should you do when passing sheep on a road?

☐ Allow plenty of room
☐ Go very slowly
☐ Pass quickly but quietly
☐ Be ready to stop
☐ Briefly sound your horn

Slow down and be ready to stop if you see animals in the road ahead. Animals are easily frightened by noise and vehicles passing too close to them. Stop if signalled to do so by the person in charge.

6.71 Mark one answer

At night you see a pedestrian wearing reflective clothing and carrying a bright red light. What does this mean?

☐ You are approaching roadworks
☐ You are approaching an organised walk
☐ You are approaching a slow-moving vehicle
☐ You are approaching a traffic danger spot

The people on the walk should be keeping to the left, but don't assume this. Pass slowly, make sure you have time to do so safely. Be aware that the pedestrians have their backs to you and may not know that you're there.

6.72 Mark one answer

You have just passed your test. How can you reduce your risk of being involved in a collision?

☐ By always staying close to the vehicle in front
☐ By never going over 40 mph
☐ By staying only in the left-hand lane on all roads
☐ By taking further training

New drivers and riders are often involved in a collision or incident early in their driving career. Due to a lack of experience they may not react to hazards as quickly as more experienced road users. Approved training courses are offered by driver and rider training schools. The Pass Plus scheme has been created by DSA for new drivers who would like to improve their basic skills and safely widen their driving experience.

other types of vehicles

7.1 Mark one answer

You are riding behind a long vehicle. There is a mini-roundabout ahead. The vehicle is signalling left, but positioned to the right. You should

☐ sound your horn
☐ overtake on the left
☐ keep well back
☐ flash your headlights

The long vehicle needs more room than other vehicles in order to make the left turn.

Don't overtake on the left – the driver will not expect you to be there and may not see you. Staying well back will also give you a better view around the vehicle.

7.2 Mark two answers

Why should you be careful when riding on roads where electric trams operate?

☐ They cannot steer to avoid you
☐ They move quickly and quietly
☐ They are noisy and slow
☐ They can steer to avoid you
☐ They give off harmful exhaust fumes

Electric trams run on rails and cannot steer to avoid you. Keep a lookout for trams as they move very quietly and can appear suddenly.

7.3 Mark one answer

You are about to overtake a slow-moving motorcyclist. Which one of these signs would make you take special care?

☐   ☐

☐   ☐

In windy weather, watch out for motorcyclists and also cyclists as they can be blown sideways into your path. When you pass them, leave plenty of room and check their position in your mirror before pulling back in.

7.4 Mark one answer

You are waiting to emerge left from a minor road. A large vehicle is approaching from the right. You have time to turn, but you should wait. Why?

☐ The large vehicle can easily hide an overtaking vehicle
☐ The large vehicle can turn suddenly
☐ The large vehicle is difficult to steer in a straight line
☐ The large vehicle can easily hide vehicles from the left

Large vehicles can hide other vehicles that are overtaking, especially motorcycles which may be filtering past queuing traffic.

You need to be aware of the possibility of hidden vehicles and not assume that it is safe to emerge.

7.5 Mark one answer

You are following a long vehicle. It approaches a crossroads and signals left, but moves out to the right. You should

☐ get closer in order to pass it quickly
☐ stay well back and give it room
☐ assume the signal is wrong and it is really turning right
☐ overtake as it starts to slow down

A lorry may swing out to the right as it approaches a left turn. This is to allow the rear wheels to clear the kerb as it turns.

Don't try to filter through if you see a gap on the nearside.

7.6 Mark one answer

You are following a long vehicle approaching a crossroads. The driver signals right but moves close to the left-hand kerb. What should you do?

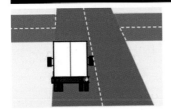

☐ Warn the driver of the wrong signal
☐ Wait behind the long vehicle
☐ Report the driver to the police
☐ Overtake on the right-hand side

When a long vehicle is going to turn right it may need to keep close to the left-hand kerb. This is to prevent the rear end of the trailer cutting the corner. You need to be aware of how long vehicles behave in such situations. Don't overtake the lorry because it could turn as you're alongside. Stay behind and wait for it to turn.

7.7 Mark one answer

You are approaching a mini-roundabout. The long vehicle in front is signalling left but positioned over to the right. You should

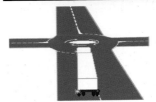

☐ sound your horn
☐ overtake on the left
☐ follow the same course as the lorry
☐ keep well back

At mini-roundabouts there isn't much room for a long vehicle to manoeuvre. It will have to swing out wide so that it can complete the turn safely. Keep well back and don't try to move up alongside it.

7.8 Mark one answer

Before overtaking a large vehicle you should keep well back. Why is this?

☐ To give acceleration space to overtake quickly on blind bends
☐ To get the best view of the road ahead
☐ To leave a gap in case the vehicle stops and rolls back
☐ To offer other drivers a safe gap if they want to overtake you

When following a large vehicle keep well back. If you're too close you won't be able to see the road ahead and the driver of the long vehicle might not be able to see you in their mirrors.

7.9 Mark two answers

You are travelling behind a bus that pulls up at a bus stop. What should you do?

☐ Accelerate past the bus sounding your horn
☐ Watch carefully for pedestrians
☐ Be ready to give way to the bus
☐ Pull in closely behind the bus

There might be pedestrians crossing from in front of the bus. Look out for them if you intend to pass. Consider staying back and waiting.

How many people are waiting to get on the bus? Check the queue if you can. The bus might move off straight away if there is no one waiting to get on.

If a bus is signalling to pull out, give it priority as long as it is safe to do so.

301

7.10   Mark one answer

You are following a large lorry on a wet road. Spray makes it difficult to see. You should

☐ drop back until you can see better
☐ put your headlights on full beam
☐ keep close to the lorry, away from the spray
☐ speed up and overtake quickly

Large vehicles may throw up a lot of spray when the roads are wet. This will make it difficult for you to see ahead. Dropping back further will

• move you out of the spray and allow you to see further

• increase your separation distance. It takes longer to stop when the roads are wet and you need to allow more room.

Don't

• follow the vehicle in front too closely

• overtake, unless you can see and are sure that the way ahead is clear.

7.11   Mark one answer

You are following a large articulated vehicle. It is going to turn left into a narrow road. What action should you take?

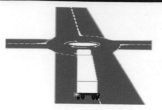

☐ Move out and overtake on the right
☐ Pass on the left as the vehicle moves out
☐ Be prepared to stop behind
☐ Overtake quickly before the lorry moves out

Lorries are larger and longer than other vehicles and this can affect their position when approaching junctions. When turning left they may move out to the right so that they don't cut in and mount the kerb with the rear wheels.

7.12   Mark one answer

You keep well back while waiting to overtake a large vehicle. A car fills the gap. You should

☐ sound your horn
☐ drop back further
☐ flash your headlights
☐ start to overtake

It's very frustrating when your separation distance is shortened by another vehicle.
  React positively, stay calm and drop further back.

7.13   Mark one answer

You are following a long lorry. The driver signals to turn left into a narrow road. What should you do?

☐ Overtake on the left before the lorry reaches the junction
☐ Overtake on the right as soon as the lorry slows down
☐ Do not overtake unless you can see there is no oncoming traffic
☐ Do not overtake, stay well back and be prepared to stop.

When turning into narrow roads articulated and long vehicles will need more room.
  Initially they will need to swing out in the opposite direction to which they intend to turn. They could mask another vehicle turning out of the same junction. DON'T be tempted to overtake them or pass on the inside.

7.14   Mark one answer

When you approach a bus signalling to move off from a bus stop you should

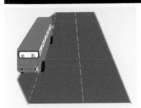

☐ get past before it moves
☐ allow it to pull away, if it is safe to do so
☐ flash your headlights as you approach
☐ signal left and wave the bus on

Try to give way to buses if you can do so safely, especially when they signal to pull away from bus stops. Look out for people who've stepped off the bus or are running to catch it, and may try to cross the road without looking. Don't try to accelerate past before it moves away or flash your lights as other road users may be misled by this signal.

7.15   Mark one answer

You wish to overtake a long, slow-moving vehicle on a busy road. You should

☐ follow it closely and keep moving out to see the road ahead
☐ flash your headlights for the oncoming traffic to give way
☐ stay behind until the driver waves you past
☐ keep well back until you can see that it is clear

If you want to overtake a long vehicle, stay well back so that you can get a better view of the road ahead. The closer you get the less you will be able to see of the road ahead. Be patient, overtaking calls for sound judgement. DON'T take a gamble, only overtake when you are certain that you can complete the manoeuvre safely.

7.16   Mark one answer

Which of these is LEAST likely to be affected by crosswinds?

☐ Cyclists
☐ Motorcyclists
☐ High-sided vehicles
☐ Cars

Although cars are the least likely to be affected, crosswinds can take anyone by surprise. This is most likely to happen after overtaking a large vehicle, when passing gaps between hedges or buildings, and on exposed sections of road.

7.17   Mark one answer

What should you do as you approach this lorry?

☐ Slow down and be prepared to wait
☐ Make the lorry wait for you
☐ Flash your lights at the lorry
☐ Move to the right-hand side of the road

When turning, long vehicles need much more room on the road than other vehicles. At junctions they may take up the whole of the road space, so be patient and allow them the room they need.

7.18   Mark one answer

You are following a large vehicle approaching crossroads. The driver signals to turn left. What should you do?

☐ Overtake if you can leave plenty of room
☐ Overtake only if there are no oncoming vehicles
☐ Do not overtake until the vehicle begins to turn
☐ Do not overtake when at or approaching a junction

Hold back and wait until the vehicle has turned before proceeding. Do not overtake because the vehicle turning left could hide a vehicle emerging from the same junction.

7.19   Mark one answer

Powered vehicles, such as wheelchairs or scooters, used by disabled people have a maximum speed of

☐ 8 mph
☐ 12 mph
☐ 16 mph
☐ 20 mph

These are small battery powered vehicles and include wheelchairs and mobility scooters. Some are designed for use on the pavement only and have an upper speed limit of 4 mph (6 km/h). Others can go on the road as well and have a speed limit of 8 mph (12 km/h). They are now very common and are generally used by the elderly, disabled or infirm. Take great care as they are extremely vulnerable because of their low speed and small size.

7.20   Mark one answer
Why is it more difficult to overtake a large vehicle than a car?

☐ It takes longer to pass one
☐ They may suddenly pull up
☐ Their brakes are not as good
☐ They climb hills more slowly

Depending on relevant speed, it will usually take you longer to pass a lorry than other vehicles. Some hazards to watch for include oncoming traffic, junctions ahead, bends or dips which could restrict your view, and signs or road markings that prohibit overtaking. Make sure you can see that it's safe to complete the manoeuvre before you start to overtake.

7.21   Mark one answer
In front of you is a class 3 powered vehicle (powered wheelchair) driven by a disabled person. These vehicles have a maximum speed of

☐ 8 mph (12 km/h)
☐ 18 mph (29 km/h)
☐ 28 mph (45 km/h)
☐ 38 mph (61 km/h)

These vehicles are battery powered and very vulnerable due to their slow speed, small size and low height. Some are designed for pavement and road use and have a maximum speed of 8 mph (12 km/h). Others are for pavement use only and are restricted to 4 mph (6 km/h). Take extra care and be patient if you are following one. Allow plenty of room when overtaking and do not go past unless you can do so safely.

motorcycle handling

8.1
Mark two answers

As a safety measure before starting your engine, you should

- [ ] push the motorcycle forward to check the rear wheel turns freely
- [ ] engage first gear and apply the rear brake
- [ ] engage first gear and apply the front brake
- [ ] glance at the neutral light on your instrument panel

Before starting the engine you should ensure the motorcycle is in neutral. This can be done by, moving the motorcycle to check that the rear wheel turns freely and making sure the neutral warning light is lit when the ignition is turned on.

8.2
Mark two answers

You are approaching this junction. As the motorcyclist you should

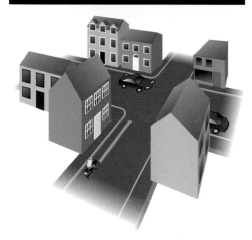

- [ ] prepare to slow down
- [ ] sound your horn
- [ ] keep near the left kerb
- [ ] speed up to clear the junction
- [ ] stop, as the car has right of way

Look out for road signs indicating side roads, even if you aren't turning off. A driver who is emerging might not be able to see you due to parked cars or heavy traffic.

Always be prepared, and stop if necessary.

Remember, no one has priority at unmarked crossroads.

8.3
Mark one answer

What can you do to improve your safety on the road as a motorcyclist?

- [ ] Anticipate the actions of others
- [ ] Stay just above the speed limits
- [ ] Keep positioned close to the kerbs
- [ ] Remain well below speed limits

Always ride defensively. This means looking and planning ahead as well as anticipating the actions of other road users.

8.4
Mark three answers

Which THREE of these can cause skidding?

- [ ] Braking too gently
- [ ] Leaning too far over when cornering
- [ ] Staying upright when cornering
- [ ] Braking too hard
- [ ] Changing direction suddenly

In order to keep control of your motorcycle and prevent skidding you must plan well ahead to prevent harsh, late braking. Try to avoid braking while changing direction, as this reduces the tyres' grip on the road.

Take the road and weather conditions into consideration and adjust your speed if necessary.

8.5
Mark two answers

It is very cold and the road looks wet. You cannot hear any road noise. You should

- [ ] continue riding at the same speed
- [ ] ride slower in as high a gear as possible
- [ ] ride in as low a gear as possible
- [ ] keep revving your engine
- [ ] slow down as there may be black ice

Rain freezing on roads is called black ice. It can be hard to see. Indications of black ice are when you can't hear tyre noise and the steering becomes very light. You need to keep your speed down and avoid harsh steering, braking and acceleration. Riding in as high a gear as possible will help to reduce the risk of wheel-spin.

8.6 Mark one answer

When riding a motorcycle you should wear full protective clothing

☐ at all times
☐ only on faster, open roads
☐ just on long journeys
☐ only during bad weather

Protective clothing is designed to protect you from the cold and wet and also gives some protection from injury.

8.7 Mark two answers

You have to make a journey in fog. What are the TWO most important things you should do before you set out?

☐ Fill up with fuel
☐ Make sure that you have a warm drink with you
☐ Check that your lights are working
☐ Check the battery
☐ Make sure that your visor is clean

When you're riding a motorcycle, keep your visor as clean as possible to give you a clear view of the road. It's a good idea to carry a clean, damp cloth in a polythene bag for this purpose.

You need to ensure that your lights are clean and can be seen clearly by other road users. This is especially important when visibility is reduced, for example in fog or heavy rain.

8.8 Mark one answer

The best place to park your motorcycle is

☐ on soft tarmac
☐ on bumpy ground
☐ on grass
☐ on firm, level ground

Parking your motorcycle on soft ground might cause the stand to sink and the bike to fall over. The ground should also be level to ensure that the bike is stable. Where off-road parking or motorcycle parking areas are available, use them.

8.9 Mark one answer

When riding in windy conditions, you should

☐ stay close to large vehicles
☐ keep your speed up
☐ keep your speed down
☐ stay close to the gutter

Strong winds can blow motorcycles off course and even across the road. In windy conditions you need to, slow down, avoid riding on exposed roads and watch for gaps in buildings and hedges where you may be affected by a sudden blast of wind.

8.10 Mark one answer

In normal riding your position on the road should be

☐ about a foot from the kerb
☐ about central in your lane
☐ on the right of your lane
☐ near the centre of the road

If you're riding a motorcycle it's very important to ride where other road users can see you. In normal weather you should ride in the centre of your lane. This will help you to avoid uneven road surfaces in the gutter and allow others to overtake on the right if they wish.

8.11 Mark one answer

Your motorcycle is parked on a two-way road. You should get on from the

☐ right and apply the rear brake
☐ left and leave the brakes alone
☐ left and apply the front brake
☐ right and leave the brakes alone

When you get onto a motorcycle you should get on from the left side to avoid putting yourself in danger from passing traffic. Also apply the front brake to prevent the motorcycle rolling either forwards or backwards.

8.12 Mark one answer

To gain basic skills in how to ride a motorcycle you should

☐ practise off-road with an approved training body
☐ ride on the road on the first dry day
☐ practise off-road in a public park or in a quiet cul-de-sac
☐ ride on the road as soon as possible

All new motorcyclists must complete a course of basic training with an approved training body before going on the road.

This training is given on a site which has been authorised by the Driving Standards Agency as being suitable for off-road training.

8.13   Mark one answer
You should not ride with your clutch lever pulled in for longer than necessary because it

☐ increases wear on the gearbox
☐ increases petrol consumption
☐ reduces your control of the motorcycle
☐ reduces the grip of the tyres

Riding with the clutch lever pulled in is known as coasting. It gives you less steering control, reduces traction, and can cause you to pick up speed. When you're travelling downhill your motorcycle will pick up speed quickly. If you are coasting the engine won't be able to assist the braking.

8.14   Mark one answer
You are approaching a road with a surface of loose chippings. What should you do?

☐ Ride normally
☐ Speed up
☐ Slow down
☐ Stop suddenly

The handling of your motorcycle will be greatly affected by the road surface. Look well ahead and be especially alert if the road looks uneven or has loose chippings.
  Slow down in good time as braking harshly in these conditions will cause you to skid.
  Avoid making sudden changes of direction for the same reason.

8.15   Mark one answer
It rains after a long dry, hot spell. This may cause the road surface to

☐ be unusually slippery
☐ give better grip
☐ become covered in grit
☐ melt and break up

Oil and other substances build up on the road surface during long dry spells and when it rains this surface becomes very slippery.

8.16   Mark three answers
The main causes of a motorcycle skidding are

☐ heavy and sharp braking
☐ excessive acceleration
☐ leaning too far when cornering
☐ riding in wet weather
☐ riding in the winter

Skids are a lot easier to get into than they are to get out of.
  Riding at a speed that suits the conditions, looking ahead for hazards and braking in good time will all help you to avoid skidding or losing control of your vehicle.

8.17   Mark one answer
To stop your motorcycle quickly in an emergency you should apply

☐ the rear brake only
☐ the front brake only
☐ the front brake just before the rear
☐ the rear brake just before the front

You should plan ahead to avoid the need to stop suddenly. But if an emergency should arise you must be able to stop safely.
  Applying the correct amount of braking effort to each wheel will help you to stop safely and in control.

8.18   Mark one answer
You leave the choke on for too long. This causes the engine to run too fast. When is this likely to make your motorcycle most difficult to control?

☐ Accelerating
☐ Going uphill
☐ Slowing down
☐ On motorways

Forgetting to switch the choke off will cause the engine to run too fast. This makes it difficult to control the motorcycle, especially when slowing down, for example when approaching junctions and bends.

8.19 Mark one answer

You should NOT look down at the front wheel when riding because it can

☐ make your steering lighter
☐ improve your balance
☐ use less fuel
☐ upset your balance

When riding look ahead and around you, but don't look down at the front wheel as this can severely upset your balance.

8.20 Mark one answer

In normal riding conditions you should brake

☐ by using the rear brake first and then the front
☐ when the motorcycle is being turned or ridden through a bend
☐ by pulling in the clutch before using the front brake
☐ when the motorcycle is upright and moving in a straight line

A motorcycle is most stable when it's upright and moving in a straight line. This is the best time to brake. Normally both brakes should be used, with the front brake being applied just before the rear.

8.21 Mark three answers

Which THREE of the following will affect your stopping distance?

☐ How fast you are going
☐ The tyres on your motorcycle
☐ The time of day
☐ The weather
☐ The street lighting

There are several factors that can affect the distance it takes to stop your motorcycle. In wet weather you should double the separation distance from the vehicle in front. Your tyres will have less grip on the road and you therefore need to allow more time to stop. Always ride in accordance with the conditions.

8.22 Mark one answer

You are on a motorway at night. You MUST have your headlights switched on unless

☐ there are vehicles close in front of you
☐ you are travelling below 50 mph
☐ the motorway is lit
☐ your motorcycle is broken down on the hard shoulder

Always use your headlights at night on a motorway unless you have stopped on the hard shoulder. If you have to use the hard shoulder, switch off the headlights but leave the parking lights on so that other road users can see your motorcycle.

8.23 Mark one answer

You have to park on the road in fog. You should

☐ leave parking lights on
☐ leave no lights on
☐ leave dipped headlights on
☐ leave main beam headlights on

If you have to park on the road in foggy conditions it's important that your motorcycle can be seen by other road users. Try to find a place to park off the road. If this isn't possible leave your motorcycle facing in the same direction as the traffic. Make sure that your lights are clean and that you leave your parking lights on.

8.24 Mark one answer

You ride over broken glass and get a sudden puncture. What should you do?

☐ Close the throttle and roll to a stop
☐ Brake to a stop as quickly as possible
☐ Release your grip on the handlebars
☐ Steer from side to side to keep your balance

Your motorcycle will be very unstable if a tyre bursts. Try to keep a straight course and stop as gently as possible.

8.25 Mark one answer

You are riding in wet weather. You see diesel fuel on the road. What should you do?

☐ Swerve to avoid the area
☐ Accelerate through quickly
☐ Brake sharply to a stop
☐ Slow down in good time

Spilt diesel will show up in wet weather as a rainbow-coloured pattern on the road.
   You should try to avoid riding over this area if you can. Slow down in good time but don't swerve suddenly or change direction without taking proper observation.

8.26 Mark one answer

Spilt fuel on the road can be very dangerous for you as a motorcyclist. How can this hazard be seen?

- ☐ By a rainbow pattern on the surface
- ☐ By a series of skid marks
- ☐ By a pitted road surface
- ☐ By a highly polished surface

This rainbow-coloured pattern can be seen much more easily on a wet road. You should avoid riding over these areas if possible. If you have to go over them do so with extreme caution.

8.27 Mark one answer

You leave the choke on for too long. This could make the engine run faster than normal. This will make your motorcycle

- ☐ handle much better
- ☐ corner much safer
- ☐ stop much more quickly
- ☐ more difficult to control

Leaving the choke on for longer than necessary will usually make the engine run too fast. This can lead to loss of control, which is especially dangerous when approaching junctions and bends in the road and whenever you need to slow down.

8.28 Mark four answers

Which FOUR types of road surface increase the risk of skidding for motorcyclists?

- ☐ White lines
- ☐ Dry tarmac
- ☐ Tar banding
- ☐ Yellow grid lines
- ☐ Loose chippings

When riding it's important to look out for slippery surfaces. These include, potholes, drain covers (especially in the wet), oily and greasy surfaces, road markings, tram tracks, wet mud and leaves. You will then have more time to brake or change course if you need to.

8.29 Mark one answer

You are riding on a wet road. When braking you should

- ☐ apply the rear brake well before the front
- ☐ apply the front brake just before the rear
- ☐ avoid using the front brake at all
- ☐ avoid using the rear brake at all

On wet roads you will need to be especially careful: brake earlier and more smoothly.

Always try to brake when the motorcycle is upright. This is particularly important in wet conditions.

8.30 Mark one answer

The road is wet. You are passing a line of queuing traffic and riding on the painted road markings. You should take extra care, particularly when

- ☐ signalling
- ☐ braking
- ☐ carrying a passenger
- ☐ checking your mirrors

Take extra care when braking or cornering on wet roads and try to avoid slippery objects, such as drain covers and painted road markings.

8.31 Mark one answer

You are going ahead and will have to cross tram lines. Why should you be especially careful ?

- ☐ Tram lines are always 'live'
- ☐ Trams will be stopping here
- ☐ Pedestrians will be crossing here
- ☐ The steel rails can be slippery

These rails can affect your steering and be a hazard when braking. The smooth surface of the rails makes them slippery and dangerous for motorcyclists, especially when wet. Try to cross them at right angles.

8.32 Mark one answer

You have to brake sharply and your motorcycle starts to skid. You should

- ☐ continue braking and select a low gear
- ☐ apply the brakes harder for better grip
- ☐ select neutral and use the front brake only
- ☐ release the brakes and reapply

If you skid as a result of braking harshly you need to ease off the brakes to stop the skid. Then reapply them progressively to stop.

8.33 Mark one answer

You see a rainbow-coloured pattern across the road. What will this warn you of?

☐ A soft uneven road surface
☐ A polished road surface
☐ Fuel spilt on the road
☐ Water on the road

If fuel, especially diesel, is spilt on the road it will make the surface very slippery. In wet weather this can be seen as a rainbow-coloured pattern on the road.

8.34 Mark one answer

Traction Control Systems (TCS) are fitted to some motorcycles. What does this help to prevent?

☐ Wheelspin when accelerating
☐ Skidding when braking too hard
☐ Uneven front tyre wear
☐ Uneven rear tyre wear

Traction Control Systems (TCS) help to prevent the rear wheel from spinning, especially when accelerating on a slippery surface.

8.35 Mark one answer

Braking too hard has caused both wheels to skid. What should you do?

☐ Release both brakes together
☐ Release the front then the rear brake
☐ Release the front brake only
☐ Release the rear brake only

Braking too hard will cause a skid. Release the brakes immediately to allow the wheels to turn, then reapply them as firmly as the road surface and conditions will allow.

8.36 Mark one answer

Your motorcycle does NOT have linked brakes. What should you do when braking to a normal stop?

☐ Only apply the front brake
☐ Rely just on the rear brake
☐ Apply both brakes smoothly
☐ Apply either of the brakes gently

In normal riding you should always use both brakes. Braking when the motorcycle is upright and travelling in a straight line helps you to keep control. If your motorcycle has linked brakes refer to the owners' manual.

8.37 Mark one answer

You are sitting on a stationary motorcycle and checking your riding position. You should be able to

☐ just touch the ground with your toes
☐ place both feet on the ground
☐ operate the centre stand
☐ adjust your mirrors by stretching

When sitting astride a stationary motorcycle you should be able to place both feet on the ground to support yourself and your machine.

8.38 Mark one answer

It has rained after a long dry spell. You should be very careful because the road surface will be unusually

☐ rough
☐ dry
☐ sticky
☐ slippery

During a long hot, dry spell the road surface will become coated with rubber and dust. When it rains after this the road surface will be unusually slippery. Take extra care, particularly at junctions, bends and roundabouts, and allow double the usual stopping distance.

8.39 Mark one answer

Riding with the side stand down could cause you to crash. This is most likely to happen when

☐ going uphill
☐ accelerating
☐ braking
☐ cornering

Cornering with the side stand down could lead to a serious crash. Most motorcycles have a device that stops the engine if you try to ride off with the side stand down, but don't rely on this.

8.40 Mark one answer

You are entering a bend. Your side stand is not fully raised. This could

☐ cause you to crash
☐ improve your balance
☐ alter the motorcycle's centre of gravity
☐ make the motorcycle more stable

If the stand isn't fully up it could dig into the road and cause a serious crash. Always check that it is fully raised before moving off. Most side stands have a safety device or cut-out switch, but do NOT rely on this.
CHECK FOR YOURSELF!

8.41 Mark three answers

In which THREE of these situations may you overtake another vehicle on the left?

☐ When you are in a one-way street
☐ When approaching a motorway slip road where you will be turning off
☐ When the vehicle in front is signalling to turn right
☐ When a slower vehicle is travelling in the right-hand lane of a dual carriageway
☐ In slow-moving traffic queues when traffic in the right-hand lane is moving more slowly

At certain times of the day, traffic might be heavy. If traffic is moving slowly in queues and vehicles in the right-hand lane are moving more slowly, you may overtake on the left. Don't keep changing lanes to try and beat the queue.

8.42 Mark one answer

You are travelling in very heavy rain. Your overall stopping distance is likely to be

☐ doubled
☐ halved
☐ up to ten times greater
☐ no different

As well as visibility being reduced, the road will be extremely wet. This will reduce the grip the tyres have on the road and increase the distance it takes to stop.
Double your separation distance.

8.43 Mark two answers

Which TWO of the following are correct? When overtaking at night you should

☐ wait until a bend so that you can see the oncoming headlights
☐ sound your horn twice before moving out
☐ be careful because you can see less
☐ beware of bends in the road ahead
☐ put headlights on full beam

Only overtake the vehicle in front if it's really necessary. At night the risks are increased due to the poor visibility. Don't overtake if there's a possibility of

• road junctions

• bends ahead

• the brow of a bridge or hill, except on a dual carriageway

• pedestrian crossings

• double white lines ahead

• vehicles changing direction

• any other potential hazard.

8.44 Mark one answer

When may you wait in a box junction?

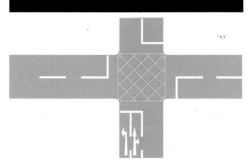

☐ When you are stationary in a queue of traffic
☐ When approaching a pelican crossing
☐ When approaching a zebra crossing
☐ When oncoming traffic prevents you turning right

The purpose of a box junction is to keep the junction clear by preventing vehicles from stopping in the path of crossing traffic.
You must not enter a box junction unless your exit is clear. But, you may enter the box and wait if you want to turn right and are only prevented from doing so by oncoming traffic.

8.45 Mark one answer
Which of these plates normally appear with this road sign?

☐ **Humps for ½ mile**

☐ **Low Bridge**

☐ **Hump Bridge**

☐ **Soft Verge**

Road humps are used to slow down the traffic. They are found in places where there are often pedestrians, such as

• in shopping areas

• near schools

• in residential areas.

Watch out for people close to the kerb or crossing the road.

8.46 Mark one answer
Traffic calming measures are used to

☐ stop road rage
☐ help overtaking
☐ slow traffic down
☐ help parking

Traffic calming measures are used to make the roads safer for vulnerable road users, such as cyclists, pedestrians and children.
  These can be designed as chicanes, road humps or other obstacles that encourage drivers and riders to slow down.

8.47 Mark one answer
You are on a motorway in fog. The left-hand edge of the motorway can be identified by reflective studs. What colour are they?

☐ Green
☐ Amber
☐ Red
☐ White

Be especially careful if you're on a motorway in fog. Reflective studs are used to help you in poor visibility. Different colours are used so that you'll know which lane you are in. These are

• red on the left-hand side of the road

• white between lanes

• amber on the right-hand edge of the carriageway

• green between the carriageway and slip roads.

8.48 Mark two answers
A rumble device is designed to

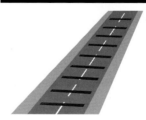

☐ give directions
☐ prevent cattle escaping
☐ alert you to low tyre pressure
☐ alert you to a hazard
☐ encourage you to reduce speed

A rumble device usually consists of raised markings or strips across the road. It gives an audible, visual and tactile warning of a hazard. These strips are found in places where traffic has constantly ignored warning or restriction signs. They are there for a good reason. Slow down and be ready to deal with a hazard.

8.49 Mark one answer

You have to make a journey in foggy conditions. You should

☐ follow other vehicles' tail lights closely
☐ avoid using dipped headlights
☐ leave plenty of time for your journey
☐ keep two seconds behind other vehicles

If you're planning to make a journey when it's foggy, listen to the weather reports on the radio or television. Don't travel if visibility is very poor or your trip isn't necessary.

If you do travel, leave plenty of time for your journey. If someone is expecting you at the other end, let them know that you'll be taking longer than normal to arrive.

8.50 Mark one answer

You are overtaking a car at night. You must be sure that

☐ you flash your headlights before overtaking
☐ you select a higher gear
☐ you have switched your lights to full beam before overtaking
☐ you do not dazzle other road users

To prevent your lights from dazzling the driver of the car in front, wait until you've overtaken before switching to full beam.

8.51 Mark one answer

You are on a road which has speed humps. A driver in front is travelling slower than you. You should

☐ sound your horn
☐ overtake as soon as you can
☐ flash your headlights
☐ slow down and stay behind

Be patient and stay behind the car in front.

Normally you should not overtake other vehicles in traffic-calmed areas. If you overtake here your speed may exceed that which is safe along that road, defeating the purpose of the traffic calming measures.

8.52 Mark one answer

You see these markings on the road. Why are they there?

☐ To show a safe distance between vehicles
☐ To keep the area clear of traffic
☐ To make you aware of your speed
☐ To warn you to change direction

These lines may be painted on the road on the approach to a roundabout, village or a particular hazard. The lines are raised and painted yellow and their purpose is to make you aware of your speed. Reduce your speed in good time so that you avoid having to brake harshly over the last few metres before reaching the junction.

8.53 Mark three answers

Areas reserved for trams may have

☐ metal studs around them
☐ white line markings
☐ zigzag markings
☐ a different coloured surface
☐ yellow hatch markings
☐ a different surface texture

Trams can run on roads used by other vehicles and pedestrians. The part of the road used by the trams is known as the reserved area and this should be kept clear.

It has a coloured surface and is usually edged with white road markings. It might also have different surface texture.

8.54 Mark one answer

You see a vehicle coming towards you on a single-track road. You should

☐ go back to the main road
☐ do an emergency stop
☐ stop at a passing place
☐ put on your hazard warning lights

You must take extra care when on single track roads. You may not be able to see around bends due to high hedges or fences. Proceed with caution and expect to meet oncoming vehicles around the next bend. If you do, pull into or opposite a passing place.

8.55   Mark one answer

The road is wet. Why might a motorcyclist steer round drain covers on a bend?

☐ To avoid puncturing the tyres on the edge of the drain covers

☐ To prevent the motorcycle sliding on the metal drain covers

☐ To help judge the bend using the drain covers as marker points

☐ To avoid splashing pedestrians on the pavement

Other drivers or riders may have to change course due to the size or characteristics of their vehicle. Understanding this will help you to anticipate their actions.

Motorcyclists and cyclists will be checking the road ahead for uneven or slippery surfaces, especially in wet weather. They may need to move across their lane to avoid surface hazards such as potholes and drain covers.

8.56   Mark one answer

After this hazard you should test your brakes. Why is this?

☐ You will be on a slippery road
☐ Your brakes will be soaking wet
☐ You will be going down a long hill
☐ You will have just crossed a long bridge

A ford is a crossing over a stream that's shallow enough to go through. After you've gone through a ford or deep puddle the water will affect your brakes. To dry them out apply a light brake pressure while moving slowly. Don't travel at normal speeds until you are sure your brakes are working properly again.

8.57   Mark one answer

Why should you always reduce your speed when travelling in fog?

☐ The brakes do not work as well
☐ You will be dazzled by other headlights
☐ The engine will take longer to warm up
☐ It is more difficult to see events ahead

You won't be able to see as far ahead in fog as you can on a clear day. You will need to reduce your speed so that, if a hazard looms out of the fog, you have the time and space to take avoiding action.

Travelling in fog is hazardous. If you can, try and delay your journey until it has cleared.

motorway rules

9.1 Mark one answer
On a motorway you may ONLY stop on the hard shoulder

☐ in an emergency
☐ If you feel tired and need to rest
☐ if you go past the exit that you wanted to take
☐ to pick up a hitchhiker

You must not stop on the hard shoulder except in an emergency. Never use it to, have a rest or a picnic, pick up hitchhikers, answer a mobile phone, or check a road map. You must not travel back along the hard shoulder if you go past your intended exit.

9.2 Mark one answer
You are intending to leave the motorway at the next exit. Before you reach the exit you should normally position your motorcycle

☐ in the middle lane
☐ in the left-hand lane
☐ on the hard shoulder
☐ in any lane

You'll see the first advance warning sign for a junction one mile from the exit. If you're travelling at 60 mph you'll only have about 50 seconds before you reach the countdown markers. Move in to the left-hand lane in good time if you're not there already. Don't cut across traffic at the last moment.

9.3 Mark one answer
You are joining a motorway from a slip road. You should

☐ adjust your speed to the speed of the traffic on the motorway
☐ accelerate as quickly as you can and ride straight out
☐ ride onto the hard shoulder until a gap appears
☐ expect drivers on the motorway to give way to you

Give way to the traffic already on the motorway and join it where there's a suitable gap in the traffic. Don't expect traffic on the motorway to give way to you, but try to avoid stopping at the end of the slip road.

9.4 Mark one answer
A motorcycle is not allowed on a motorway if it has an engine size smaller than

☐ 50 cc
☐ 125 cc
☐ 150 cc
☐ 250 cc

Very small motorcycles are not allowed to use motorways due to their restricted speed, as this may cause a hazard to other vehicles.

9.5 Mark one answer
To ride on a motorway your motorcycle must be

☐ 50 cc or more
☐ 100 cc or more
☐ 125 cc or more
☐ 250 cc or more

Traffic on motorways travels at high speeds. Vehicles need to be capable of keeping up with the flow of traffic. For this reason low-powered vehicles are prohibited.

9.6 Mark one answer
On a three-lane motorway why should you normally ride in the left-hand lane?

☐ The left-hand lane is only for lorries and motorcycles
☐ The left-hand lane should only be used by smaller vehicles
☐ The lanes on the right are for overtaking
☐ Motorcycles are not allowed in the far right-hand lane

Change lanes only if necessary. When you do change lanes make sure you observe, signal and manoeuvre in good time. Always remember your 'lifesaver' check. This is a final, quick rearward glance before you pull out.

9.7 Mark one answer
You are riding at 70 mph on a three-lane motorway. There is no traffic ahead. Which lane should you use?

☐ Any lane
☐ Middle lane
☐ Right-hand lane
☐ Left-hand lane

Use the left-hand lane if it's free, regardless of the speed you're travelling.

9.8   Mark one answer   NI EXEMPT

You are riding on a motorway. Unless signs show otherwise you must NOT exceed

☐ 50 mph
☐ 60 mph
☐ 70 mph
☐ 80 mph

Ride in accordance with the conditions.
   Bad weather or heavy traffic may mean you have to lower your speed.

9.9   Mark one answer

Why is it particularly important to carry out a check of your motorcycle before making a long motorway journey?

☐ You will have to do more harsh braking on motorways
☐ Motorway service stations do not deal with breakdowns
☐ The road surface will wear down the tyres faster
☐ Continuous high speeds may increase the risk of your motorcycle breaking down

Before starting a motorway journey, make sure your motorcycle can cope with the demands of high-speed riding. Things you need to check include, oil, water and tyres.
   When you're travelling a long way it's a good idea to plan rest stops in advance.

9.10   Mark one answer

When joining a motorway you must always

☐ use the hard shoulder
☐ stop at the end of the acceleration lane
☐ come to a stop before joining the motorway
☐ give way to traffic already on the motorway

You should give way to traffic already on the motorway. Where possible they may move over to let you in but don't force your way into the traffic stream. The traffic may be travelling at high speed so you should match your speed to fit in.

9.11   Mark one answer

What is the national speed limit for cars and motorcycles in the centre lane of a three-lane motorway?

☐ 40 mph
☐ 50 mph
☐ 60 mph
☐ 70 mph

Unless shown otherwise, the speed limit on a motorway applies to all the lanes. Look out for any signs of speed limit changes due to roadworks or traffic flow control.

9.12   Mark one answer

What is the national speed limit on motorways for cars and motorcycles?

☐ 30 mph
☐ 50 mph
☐ 60 mph
☐ 70 mph

Travelling at the national speed limit doesn't allow you to hog the right-hand lane.
   Always use the left-hand lane whenever possible. When leaving a motorway get into the left-hand lane well before your exit.
   Reduce your speed on the slip road and look out for sharp bends or curves and traffic queuing at roundabouts.

9.13   Mark one answer

The left-hand lane on a three-lane motorway is for use by

☐ any vehicle
☐ large vehicles only
☐ emergency vehicles only
☐ slow vehicles only

On a motorway all traffic should use the left-hand lane unless overtaking. Use the centre or right-hand lanes if you need to overtake. If you're overtaking a number of slower vehicles move back to the left-hand lane when you're safely past. Check your mirrors frequently and don't stay in the middle or right-hand lane if the left-hand lane is free.

9.14 Mark one answer

Which of these IS NOT allowed to travel in the right-hand lane of a three-lane motorway?

☐ A small delivery van
☐ A motorcycle
☐ A vehicle towing a trailer
☐ A motorcycle and side-car

A vehicle with a trailer is restricted to 60 mph. For this reason it isn't allowed in the right-hand lane as it might hold up the faster-moving traffic that wishes to overtake in that lane.

9.15 Mark one answer

You break down on a motorway. You need to call for help. Why may it be better to use an emergency roadside telephone rather than a mobile phone?

☐ It connects you to a local garage
☐ Using a mobile phone will distract other drivers
☐ It allows easy location by the emergency services
☐ Mobile phones do not work on motorways

On a motorway it is best to use a roadside emergency telephone so that the emergency services are able to locate you easily. The nearest telephone is shown by an arrow on marker posts at the edge of the hard shoulder. If you use a mobile, they will need to know your exact location.

Before you call, find out the number on the nearest marker post. This number will identify your exact location.

9.16 Mark one answer

After a breakdown you need to rejoin the main carriageway of a motorway from the hard shoulder. You should

☐ move out onto the carriageway then build up your speed
☐ move out onto the carriageway using your hazard lights
☐ gain speed on the hard shoulder before moving out onto the carriageway
☐ wait on the hard shoulder until someone flashes their headlights at you

Wait for a safe gap in the traffic before you move out. Indicate your intention and use the hard shoulder to gain speed but don't force your way into the traffic.

9.17 Mark one answer

A crawler lane on a motorway is found

☐ on a steep gradient
☐ before a service area
☐ before a junction
☐ along the hard shoulder

Slow-moving, large vehicles might slow down the progress of other traffic. On a steep gradient this extra lane is provided for these slow-moving vehicles to allow the faster-moving traffic to flow more easily.

9.18 Mark one answer

What do these motorway signs show?

☐ They are countdown markers to a bridge
☐ They are distance markers to the next telephone
☐ They are countdown markers to the next exit
☐ They warn of a police control ahead

The exit from a motorway is indicated by countdown markers. These are positioned 90 metres (100 yards) apart, the first being 270 metres (300 yards) from the start of the slip road. Move into the left-hand lane well before you reach the start of the slip road.

9.19   Mark one answer

On a motorway the amber reflective studs can be found between

☐ the hard shoulder and the carriageway
☐ the acceleration lane and the carriageway
☐ the central reservation and the carriageway
☐ each pair of the lanes

On motorways reflective studs are located into the road to help you in the dark and in conditions of poor visibility. Amber-coloured studs are found on the right-hand edge of the main carriageway, next to the central reservation.

9.20   Mark one answer

What colour are the reflective studs between the lanes on a motorway?

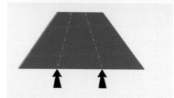

☐ Green
☐ Amber
☐ White
☐ Red

White studs are found between the lanes on motorways. The light from your headlights is reflected back and this is especially useful in bad weather, when visibility is restricted.

9.21   Mark one answer

What colour are the reflective studs between a motorway and its slip road?

☐ Amber
☐ White
☐ Green
☐ Red

The studs between the carriageway and the hard shoulder are normally red. These change to green where there is a slip road.

They will help you identify slip roads when visibility is poor or when it is dark.

9.22   Mark one answer

You have broken down on a motorway. To find the nearest emergency telephone you should always walk

☐ with the traffic flow
☐ facing oncoming traffic
☐ in the direction shown on the marker posts
☐ in the direction of the nearest exit

Along the hard shoulder there are marker posts at 100-metre intervals. These will direct you to the nearest emergency telephone.

9.23   Mark one answer

You are joining a motorway. Why is it important to make full use of the slip road?

☐ Because there is space available to turn round if you need to
☐ To allow you direct access to the overtaking lanes
☐ To build up a speed similar to traffic on the motorway
☐ Because you can continue on the hard shoulder

Try to join the motorway without affecting the progress of the traffic already travelling on it. Always give way to traffic already on the motorway. At busy times you may have to slow down to merge into slow-moving traffic.

9.24   Mark one answer

How should you use the emergency telephone on a motorway?

☐ Stay close to the carriageway
☐ Face the oncoming traffic
☐ Keep your back to the traffic
☐ Stand on the hard shoulder

Traffic is passing you at speed. If the draught from a large lorry catches you by surprise it could blow you off balance and even onto the carriageway. By facing the oncoming traffic you can see approaching lorries and so be prepared for their draught.

You are also in a position to see other hazards approaching.

9.25 Mark one answer

You are on a motorway. What colour are the reflective studs on the left of the carriageway?

- ☐ Green
- ☐ Red
- ☐ White
- ☐ Amber

Red studs are placed between the edge of the carriageway and the hard shoulder.
  Where slip roads leave or join the motorway the studs are green.

9.26 Mark one answer

On a three-lane motorway which lane should you normally use?

- ☐ Left
- ☐ Right
- ☐ Centre
- ☐ Either the right or centre

On a three-lane motorway you should travel in the left-hand lane unless you're overtaking. This applies regardless of the speed at which you're travelling.

9.27 Mark one answer

When going through a contraflow system on a motorway you should

- ☐ ensure that you do not exceed 30 mph
- ☐ keep a good distance from the vehicle ahead
- ☐ switch lanes to keep the traffic flowing
- ☐ stay close to the vehicle ahead to reduce queues

There's likely to be a speed restriction in force. Keep to this. Don't

- switch lanes

- get too close to traffic in front of you.

Be aware there will be no permanent barrier between you and the oncoming traffic.

9.28 Mark one answer

You are on a three-lane motorway. There are red reflective studs on your left and white ones to your right. Where are you?

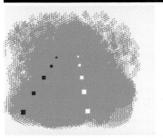

- ☐ In the right-hand lane
- ☐ In the middle lane
- ☐ On the hard shoulder
- ☐ In the left-hand lane

The colours of the reflective studs on the motorway and their locations are

- red – between the hard shoulder and the carriageway

- white – lane markings

- amber – between the edge of the carriageway and the central reservation

- green – along slip road exits and entrances

- bright green/yellow – roadworks and contraflow systems.

9.29 Mark one answer

You are approaching roadworks on a motorway. What should you do?

- ☐ Speed up to clear the area quickly
- ☐ Always use the hard shoulder
- ☐ Obey all speed limits
- ☐ Stay very close to the vehicle in front

Collisions can often happen at roadworks.
  Be aware of the speed limits, slow down in good time and keep your distance from the vehicle in front.

9.30 Mark four answers

Which FOUR of these must NOT use motorways?

☐ Learner car drivers
☐ Motorcycles over 50cc
☐ Double-deck buses
☐ Farm tractors
☐ Horse riders
☐ Cyclists

In addition, motorways MUST NOT be used by pedestrians, motorcycles under 50 cc, certain slow-moving vehicles without permission, and invalid carriages weighing less than 254 kg (560 lbs).

9.31 Mark four answers

Which FOUR of these must NOT use motorways?

☐ Learner car drivers
☐ Motorcycles over 50cc
☐ Double-deck buses
☐ Farm tractors
☐ Learner motorcyclists
☐ Cyclists

Learner car drivers and motorcyclists are not allowed on the motorway until they have passed their practical test.
Motorways have rules that you need to know before you venture out for the first time. When you've passed your practical test it's a good idea to have some lessons on motorways. Check with your instructor about this.

9.32 Mark one answer

Immediately after joining a motorway you should normally

☐ try to overtake
☐ re-adjust your mirrors
☐ position your vehicle in the centre lane
☐ keep in the left-hand lane

Stay in the left-hand lane long enough to get used to the higher speeds of motorway traffic.

9.33 Mark one answer

What is the right-hand lane used for on a three-lane motorway?

☐ Emergency vehicles only
☐ Overtaking
☐ Vehicles towing trailers
☐ Coaches only

You should keep to the left and only use the right-hand lane if you're passing slower-moving traffic.

9.34 Mark one answer

What should you use the hard shoulder of a motorway for?

☐ Stopping in an emergency
☐ Leaving the motorway
☐ Stopping when you are tired
☐ Joining the motorway

Don't use the hard shoulder for stopping unless it is an emergency. If you want to stop for any other reason go to the next exit or service station.

9.35 Mark one answer

You are in the right-hand lane on a motorway. You see these overhead signs. This means

☐ move to the left and reduce your speed to 50 mph
☐ there are roadworks 50 metres (55 yards) ahead
☐ use the hard shoulder until you have passed the hazard
☐ leave the motorway at the next exit

You MUST obey this sign. There might not be any visible signs of a problem ahead.
However, there might be queuing traffic or another hazard which you cannot yet see.

9.36 Mark one answer
You are allowed to stop on a motorway when you

☐ need to walk and get fresh air
☐ wish to pick up hitchhikers
☐ are told to do so by flashing red lights
☐ need to use a mobile telephone

You MUST stop if there are red lights flashing above every lane on the motorway.
However, if any of the other lanes do not show flashing red lights or red cross you may move into that lane and continue if it is safe to do so.

9.37 Mark one answer
You are travelling along the left-hand lane of a three-lane motorway. Traffic is joining from a slip road. You should

☐ race the other vehicles
☐ move to another lane
☐ maintain a steady speed
☐ switch on your hazard flashers

You should move to another lane if it is safe to do so. This can greatly assist the flow of traffic joining the motorway, especially at peak times.

9.38 Mark one answer
A basic rule when on motorways is

☐ use the lane that has least traffic
☐ keep to the left-hand lane unless overtaking
☐ overtake on the side that is clearest
☐ try to keep above 50 mph to prevent congestion

You should normally travel in the left-hand lane unless you are overtaking a slower-moving vehicle. When you are past that vehicle move back into the left-hand lane as soon as it's safe to do so. Don't cut across in front of the vehicle that you're overtaking.

9.39 Mark one answer
On motorways you should never overtake on the left unless

☐ you can see well ahead that the hard shoulder is clear
☐ the traffic in the right-hand lane is signalling right
☐ you warn drivers behind by signalling left
☐ there is a queue of slow-moving traffic to your right that is moving more slowly than you are

Only overtake on the left if traffic is moving slowly in queues and the traffic on your right is moving more slowly than the traffic in your lane.

9.40 Mark one answer — NI EXEMPT
Motorway emergency telephones are usually linked to the police. In some areas they are now linked to

☐ the Highways Agency Control Centre
☐ the Driver Vehicle Licensing Agency
☐ the Driving Standards Agency
☐ the local Vehicle Registration Office

In some areas motorway telephones are now linked to a Highways Agency Control Centre, instead of the police. Highways Agency Traffic Officers work in partnership with the police and assist at motorway emergencies and incidents. They are recognised by a high-visibility orange and yellow jacket and high-visibility vehicle with yellow and black chequered markings.

9.41 Mark one answer
An Emergency Refuge Area is an area

☐ on a motorway for use in cases of emergency or breakdown
☐ for use if you think you will be involved in a road rage incident
☐ on a motorway for a police patrol to park and watch traffic
☐ for construction and road workers to store emergency equipment

Emergency Refuge Areas may be found at the side of the hard shoulder about 500 metres apart. If you break down you should use them rather than the hard shoulder if you are able. When re-joining the motorway you must remember to take extra care especially when the hard shoulder is being used as a running lane within an Active Traffic Management area. Try to match your speed to that of traffic in the lane you are joining.

9.42 Mark one answer
What is an Emergency Refuge Area on a motorway for?

☐ An area to park in when you want to use a mobile phone
☐ To use in cases of emergency or breakdown
☐ For an emergency recovery vehicle to park in a contra-flow system
☐ To drive in when there is queuing traffic ahead

In cases of breakdown or emergency try to get your vehicle into an Emergency Refuge Area. This is safer than just stopping on the hard shoulder as it gives you greater distance from the main carriageway. If you are able to re-join the motorway you must take extra care, especially when the hard shoulder is being used as a running lane.

9.43   Mark one answer   NI EXEMPT
Highways Agency Traffic Officers

☐ will not be able to assist at a breakdown or emergency

☐ are not able to stop and direct anyone on a motorway

☐ will tow a broken down vehicle and it's passengers home

☐ are able to stop and direct anyone on a motorway

Highways Agency Traffic Officers (HATOs) are able to stop and direct traffic on most motorways and some 'A' class roads. They work in partnership with the police at motorway incidents and provide a highly-trained and visible service. Their role is to help keep traffic moving and make your journey as safe and reliable as possible.

They are recognised by an orange and yellow jacket and their vehicle has yellow and black markings.

9.44   Mark one answer   NI EXEMPT
You are on a motorway. A red cross is displayed above the hard shoulder. What does this mean?

☐ Pull up in this lane to answer your mobile phone

☐ Use this lane as a running lane

☐ This lane can be used if you need a rest

☐ You should not travel in this lane

Active Traffic Management schemes are being introduced on motorways. Within these areas at certain times the hard shoulder will be used as a running lane. A red cross above the hard shoulder shows that this lane should NOT be used, except for emergencies and breakdowns.

9.45   Mark one answer   NI EXEMPT
You are on a motorway in an Active Traffic Management (ATM) area. A mandatory speed limit is displayed above the hard shoulder. What does this mean?

☐ You should not travel in this lane

☐ The hard shoulder can be used as a running lane

☐ You can park on the hard shoulder if you feel tired

☐ You can pull up in this lane to answer a mobile phone

A mandatory speed limit sign above the hard shoulder shows that it can be used as a running lane between junctions. You must stay within the speed limit. Look out for vehicles that may have broken down and could be blocking the hard shoulder.

9.46   Mark one answer   NI EXEMPT
The aim of an Active Traffic Management scheme on a motorway is to

☐ prevent overtaking

☐ reduce rest stops

☐ prevent tailgating

☐ reduce congestion

Active Traffic Management schemes are intended to reduce congestion and make journey times more reliable. In these areas the hard shoulder may be used as a running lane to ease congestion at peak times or in the event of an incident. It may appear that you could travel faster for a short distance, but keeping traffic flow at a constant speed may improve your journey time.

9.47   Mark one answer   NI EXEMPT

You are in an Active Traffic Management area on a motorway. When the Actively Managed mode is operating

☐ speed limits are only advisory
☐ the national speed limit will apply
☐ the speed limit is always 30 mph
☐ all speed limit signals are set

When an Active Traffic Management (ATM) scheme is operating on a motorway you MUST follow the mandatory instructions shown on the gantries above each lane.
     This includes the hard shoulder.

9.48   Mark one answer   NI EXEMPT

You are travelling on a motorway. A red cross is shown above the hard shoulder. What does this mean?

☐ Use this lane as a rest area
☐ Use this as a normal running lane
☐ Do not use this lane to travel in
☐ National speed limit applies in this lane

When a red cross is shown above the hard shoulder it should only be used for breakdowns or emergencies. Within Active Traffic Management (ATM) areas the hard shoulder may sometimes be used as a running lane. Speed limit signs directly above the hard shoulder will show that it's open.

9.49   Mark one answer

Why can it be an advantage for traffic speed to stay constant over a longer distance?

☐ You will do more stop-start driving
☐ You will use far more fuel
☐ You will be able to use more direct routes
☐ Your overall journey time will normally improve

When traffic travels at a constant speed over a longer distance, journey times normally improve. You may feel that you could travel faster for short periods but this won't generally improve your overall journey time. Signs will show the maximum speed at which you should travel.

9.50   Mark one answer   NI EXEMPT

You should not normally travel on the hard shoulder of a motorway. When can you use it?

☐ When taking the next exit
☐ When traffic is stopped
☐ When signs direct you to
☐ When traffic is slow moving

Normally you should only use the hard shoulder for emergencies and breakdowns, and at roadworks when signs direct you to do so. Active Traffic Management (ATM) areas are being introduced to ease traffic congestion. In these areas the hard shoulder may be used as a running lane when speed limit signs are shown directly above.

9.51   Mark one answer

For what reason may you use the right-hand lane of a motorway?

☐ For keeping out of the way of lorries
☐ For travelling at more than 70 mph
☐ For turning right
☐ For overtaking other vehicles

The right-hand lane of the motorway is for overtaking.
     Sometimes you may be directed into a right-hand lane as a result of roadworks or a traffic incident. This will be indicated by signs or officers directing the traffic.

9.52   Mark one answer

On a motorway what is used to reduce traffic bunching?

☐ Variable speed limits
☐ Contraflow systems
☐ National speed limits
☐ Lane closures

Congestion can be reduced by keeping traffic at a constant speed. At busy times maximum speed limits are displayed on overhead gantries. These can be varied quickly depending on the amount of traffic.
     By keeping to a constant speed on busy sections of motorway overall journey times are normally improved.

9.53   Mark three answers
When should you stop on a motorway?

☐ If you have to read a map
☐ When you are tired and need a rest
☐ If red lights show above every lane
☐ When told to by the police
☐ If your mobile phone rings
☐ When signalled by a Highways Agency Traffic Officer

There are some occasions when you may have to stop on the carriageway of a motorway. These include when being signalled by the police or a Highways Agency Traffic Officer, when flashing red lights show above every lane and in traffic jams.

9.54   Mark one answer
When may you stop on a motorway?

☐ If you have to read a map
☐ When you are tired and need a rest
☐ If your mobile phone rings
☐ In an emergency or breakdown

You should not normally stop on a motorway but there may be occasions when you need to do so. If you are unfortunate enough to break down make every effort to pull up on the hard shoulder.

9.55   Mark one answer   NI EXEMPT
You are travelling on a motorway. Unless signs show a lower speed limit you must NOT exceed

☐ 50 mph
☐ 60 mph
☐ 70 mph
☐ 80 mph

The national speed limit for a car or motorcycle on the motorway is 70 mph.
   Lower speed limits may be in force, for example at roadworks, so look out for the signs. Variable speed limits operate in some areas to control very busy stretches of motorway. The speed limit may change depending on the volume of traffic.

9.56   Mark one answer
Motorway emergency telephones are usually linked to the police. In some areas they are now linked to

☐ the local ambulance service
☐ an Highways Agency control centre
☐ the local fire brigade
☐ a breakdown service control centre

The controller will ask you

• the make and colour of your vehicle

• whether you are a member of an emergency breakdown service

• the number shown on the emergency telephone casing

• whether you are travelling alone.

9.57   Mark one answer
You are on a motorway. There are red flashing lights above every lane. You must

☐ pull onto the hard shoulder
☐ slow down and watch for further signals
☐ leave at the next exit
☐ stop and wait

Red flashing lights above every lane mean you must not go on any further. You'll also see a red cross illuminated. Stop and wait.

Don't

• change lanes

• continue

• pull onto the hard shoulder (unless in an emergency).

9.58   Mark one answer   NI EXEMPT

You are on a three-lane motorway. A red cross is shown above the hard shoulder and mandatory speed limits above all other lanes. This means

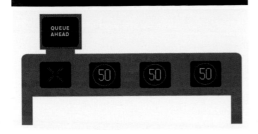

☐ the hard shoulder can be used as a rest area if you feel tired

☐ the hard shoulder is for emergency or breakdown use only

☐ the hard shoulder can be used as a normal running lane

☐ the hard shoulder has a speed limit of 50 mph

A red cross above the hard shoulder shows it is closed as a running lane and should only be used for emergencies or breakdowns. At busy times within an Active Traffic Management (ATM) area the hard shoulder may be used as a running lane.

This will be shown by a mandatory speed limit on the gantry above.

9.59   Mark one answer   NI EXEMPT

You are on a three-lane motorway and see this sign. It means you can use

☐ any lane except the hard shoulder

☐ the hard shoulder only

☐ the three right hand lanes only

☐ all the lanes including the hard shoulder

Mandatory speed limit signs above all lanes including the hard shoulder, show that you are in an Active Traffic Management (ATM) area. In this case you can use the hard shoulder as a running lane. You must stay within the speed limit shown. Look out for any vehicles that may have broken down and be blocking the hard shoulder.

9.60   Mark one answer

You are travelling on a motorway. You decide you need a rest. You should

☐ stop on the hard shoulder

☐ pull in at the nearest service area

☐ pull up on a slip road

☐ park on the central reservation

If you feel tired stop at the nearest service area. If it's too far away leave the motorway at the next exit and find a safe place to stop. You must not stop on the carriageway or hard shoulder of a motorway except in an emergency, in a traffic queue, when signalled to do so by a police or enforcement officer, or by traffic signals. Plan your journey so that you have regular rest stops.

9.61   Mark one answer

You are on a motorway. You become tired and decide you need to rest. What should you do?

☐ Stop on the hard shoulder

☐ Pull up on a slip road

☐ Park on the central reservation

☐ Leave at the next exit

Ideally you should plan your journey so that you have regular rest stops. If you do become tired leave at the next exit, or pull in at a service area if this is sooner.

10.1 Mark one answer

You are riding slowly in a town centre. Before turning left you should glance over your left shoulder to

☐ check for cyclists
☐ help keep your balance
☐ look for traffic signs
☐ check for potholes

When riding slowly you must remember cyclists. They can travel quickly and fit through surprisingly narrow spaces. Before you turn left in slow-moving traffic it's important to check that a cyclist isn't trying to overtake on your left.

10.2 Mark two answers

As a motorcycle rider which TWO lanes must you NOT use?

☐ Crawler lane
☐ Overtaking lane
☐ Acceleration lane
☐ Cycle lane
☐ Tram lane

In some towns motorcycles are permitted to use bus lanes. Check the signs carefully.

10.3 Mark one answer

What does this sign mean?

☐ No parking for solo motorcycles
☐ Parking for solo motorcycles
☐ Passing place for motorcycles
☐ Police motorcycles only

In some towns and cities there are special areas reserved for parking motorcycles.
Look out for these signs.

10.4 Mark one answer

**You are riding on a busy dual carriageway.
When changing lanes you should**

☐ rely totally on mirrors
☐ always increase your speed
☐ signal so others will give way
☐ use mirrors and shoulder checks

Before changing direction, as well as using your mirrors, you need to take a quick sideways glance to check for vehicles in any of your blind spots. These are areas behind and to the side of you which are not covered by the mirrors.

10.5 Mark one answer

You are looking for somewhere to park your motorcycle. The area is full EXCEPT for spaces marked 'disabled use'. You can

☐ use these spaces when elsewhere is full
☐ park if you stay with your motorcycle
☐ use these spaces, disabled or not
☐ not park there unless permitted

Don't be selfish. These spaces are intended for people with limited mobility.
Find somewhere else to park, even if it means that you have to walk further.

10.6 Mark one answer

You are on a road with passing places. It is only wide enough for one vehicle. There is a car coming towards you. What should you do?

☐ Pull into a passing place on your right
☐ Force the other driver to reverse
☐ Turn round and ride back to the main road
☐ Pull into a passing place on your left

If you meet another vehicle in a narrow road and the passing place is on your left, pull into it. If the passing place is on the right, wait opposite it.

10.7 Mark one answer

You are both turning right at this crossroads. It is safer to keep the car to your right so you can

☐ see approaching traffic
☐ keep close to the kerb
☐ keep clear of following traffic
☐ make oncoming vehicles stop

When turning right at this crossroads you should keep the oncoming car on your right. This will give you a clear view of the road ahead and any oncoming traffic.

10.8 Mark three answers

When filtering through slow-moving or stationary traffic you should

☐ watch for hidden vehicles emerging from side roads
☐ continually use your horn as a warning
☐ look for vehicles changing course suddenly
☐ always ride with your hazard lights on
☐ stand up on the footrests for a good view ahead
☐ look for pedestrians walking between vehicles

Other road users may not expect or look for motorcycles filtering through slow-moving or stationary traffic. Your view will be reduced by the vehicles around you.
    Watch out for, pedestrians walking between the vehicles, vehicles suddenly changing direction and vehicles pulling out of side roads.

10.9 Mark one answer

You are riding towards roadworks. The temporary traffic lights are at red. The road ahead is clear. What should you do?

☐ Ride on with extreme caution
☐ Ride on at normal speed
☐ Carry on if approaching cars have stopped
☐ Wait for the green light

You must obey all traffic signs and signals.
    Just because the lights are temporary it does not mean that you can disregard them.

10.10 Mark one answer

You intend to go abroad and will be riding on the right-hand side of the road. What should you fit to your motorcycle?

☐ Twin headlights
☐ Headlight deflectors
☐ Tinted yellow brake lights
☐ Tinted red indicator lenses

When abroad and riding on the right, deflectors are usually required to prevent your headlight dazzling approaching drivers.

10.11 Mark one answer

You want to tow a trailer with your motorcycle. Your engine must be more than

☐ 50 cc
☐ 125 cc
☐ 525 cc
☐ 1000 cc

You must remember that towing a trailer requires special care. You must obey the restrictions which apply to all vehicles towing trailers. Do not forget it is there, especially when negotiating bends and junctions.

10.12 Mark one answer

What is the national speed limit on a single carriageway?

☐ 40 mph
☐ 50 mph
☐ 60 mph
☐ 70 mph

You don't have to ride at the speed limit.
    Use your own judgement and ride at a speed that suits the prevailing road, weather and traffic conditions.

10.13 Mark three answers

On which THREE occasions MUST you stop your motorcycle?

☐ When involved in a collision
☐ At a red traffic light
☐ When signalled to do so by a police officer
☐ At a junction with double broken white lines
☐ At a clear pelican crossing when the amber light is flashing

Don't stop or hold up traffic unnecessarily.
    However there are occasions when you MUST stop by law. These include, when signalled to do so by a police officer, at a red traffic light and if you have a collision.
    There are many other instances where you may have to stop.

10.14 Mark one answer
What is the meaning of this sign?

☐ Local speed limit applies
☐ No waiting on the carriageway
☐ National speed limit applies
☐ No entry to vehicular traffic

This sign doesn't tell you the speed limit in figures. You should know the speed limit for the type of road that you're on. Study your copy of *The Highway Code*.

10.15 Mark one answer
What is the national speed limit for cars and motorcycles on a dual carriageway?

☐ 30 mph
☐ 50 mph
☐ 60 mph
☐ 70 mph

Ensure that you know the speed limit for the road that you're on. The speed limit on a dual carriageway or motorway is 70 mph for cars and motorcycles, unless there are signs to indicate otherwise. The speed limits for different types of vehicles are listed in *The Highway Code*.

10.16 Mark one answer
There are no speed limit signs on the road. How is a 30 mph limit indicated?

☐ By hazard warning lines
☐ By street lighting
☐ By pedestrian islands
☐ By double or single yellow lines

There is usually a 30 mph speed limit where there are street lights unless there are signs showing another limit.

10.17 Mark one answer
Where you see street lights but no speed limit signs the limit is usually

☐ 30 mph
☐ 40 mph
☐ 50 mph
☐ 60 mph

The presence of street lights generally shows that there is a 30 mph speed limit, unless signs tell you otherwise.

10.18 Mark one answer
What does this sign mean?

☐ Minimum speed 30 mph
☐ End of maximum speed
☐ End of minimum speed
☐ Maximum speed 30 mph

A red slash through this sign indicates that the restriction has ended. In this case the restriction was a minimum speed limit of 30 mph.

10.19 Mark one answer
There is a tractor ahead of you. You wish to overtake but you are NOT sure if it is safe to do so. You should

☐ follow another overtaking vehicle through
☐ sound your horn to the slow vehicle to pull over
☐ speed through but flash your lights to oncoming traffic
☐ not overtake if you are in doubt

Never overtake if you're not sure whether it's safe. Can you see far enough down the road to ensure that you can complete the manoeuvre safely? If the answer is no, DON'T GO.

10.20 Mark three answers
Which three of the following are most likely to take an unusual course at roundabouts?

☐ Horse riders
☐ Milk floats
☐ Delivery vans
☐ Long vehicles
☐ Estate cars
☐ Cyclists

Long vehicles might have to take a slightly different position when approaching the roundabout or going around it. This is to stop the rear of the vehicle cutting in and mounting the kerb.

Horse riders and cyclists might stay in the left-hand lane although they are turning right. Be aware of this and allow them room.

10.21 Mark one answer
On a clearway you must not stop

☐ at any time
☐ when it is busy
☐ in the rush hour
☐ during daylight hours

Clearways are in place so that traffic can flow without the obstruction of parked vehicles. Just one parked vehicle will cause an obstruction for all other traffic. You MUST NOT stop where a clearway is in force, not even to pick up or set down passengers.

10.22 Mark one answer
What is the meaning of this sign?

☐ No entry
☐ Waiting restrictions
☐ National speed limit
☐ School crossing patrol

This sign indicates that there are waiting restrictions. It is normally accompanied by details of when restrictions are in force.

Details of most signs which are in common use are shown in *The Highway Code* and a more comprehensive selection is available in *Know Your Traffic Signs*.

10.23 Mark one answer
You can park on the right-hand side of a road at night

☐ in a one-way street
☐ with your sidelights on
☐ more than 10 metres (32 feet) from a junction
☐ under a lamp-post

Red rear reflectors show up when headlights shine on them. These are useful when you are parked at night but will only reflect if you park in the same direction as the traffic flow. Normally you should park on the left, but if you're in a one-way street you may also park on the right-hand side.

10.24 Mark one answer
On a three-lane dual carriageway the right-hand lane can be used for

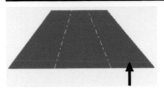

☐ overtaking only, never turning right
☐ overtaking or turning right
☐ fast-moving traffic only
☐ turning right only, never overtaking

You should normally use the left-hand lane on any dual carriageway unless you are overtaking or turning right.

When overtaking on a dual carriageway, look for vehicles ahead that are turning right. They're likely to be slowing or stopped. You need to see them in good time so that you can take appropriate action.

10.25 Mark one answer
You are approaching a busy junction. There are several lanes with road markings. At the last moment you realise that you are in the wrong lane. You should

☐ continue in that lane
☐ force your way across
☐ stop until the area has cleared
☐ use clear arm signals to cut across

There are times where road markings can be obscured by queuing traffic, or you might be unsure which lane you need to be in.

If you realise that you're in the wrong lane, don't cut across lanes or bully other drivers to let you in. Follow the lane you're in and find somewhere safe to turn around if you need to.

10.26 Mark one answer
Where may you overtake on a one-way street?

☐ Only on the left-hand side
☐ Overtaking is not allowed
☐ Only on the right-hand side
☐ Either on the right or the left

You can overtake other traffic on either side when travelling in a one-way street. Make full use of your mirrors and ensure that it's clear all around before you attempt to overtake. Look for signs and road markings and use the most suitable lane for your destination.

10.27 Mark one answer

When going straight ahead at a roundabout you should

☐ indicate left before leaving the roundabout
☐ not indicate at any time
☐ indicate right when approaching the roundabout
☐ indicate left when approaching the roundabout

When you want to go straight on at a roundabout, don't signal as you approach it, but indicate left just after you pass the exit before the one you wish to take.

10.28 Mark one answer

Which vehicle might have to use a different course to normal at roundabouts?

☐ Sports car
☐ Van
☐ Estate car
☐ Long vehicle

A long vehicle may have to straddle lanes either on or approaching a roundabout so that the rear wheels don't cut in over the kerb.

If you're following a long vehicle, stay well back and give it plenty of room.

10.29 Mark one answer

You may only enter a box junction when

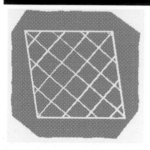

☐ there are less than two vehicles in front of you
☐ the traffic lights show green
☐ your exit road is clear
☐ you need to turn left

Yellow box junctions are marked on the road to prevent the road becoming blocked. Don't enter one unless your exit road is clear. You may only wait in the yellow box if your exit road is clear but oncoming traffic is preventing you from completing the turn.

10.30 Mark one answer

You may wait in a yellow box junction when

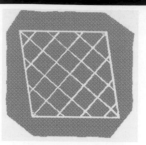

☐ oncoming traffic is preventing you from turning right
☐ you are in a queue of traffic turning left
☐ you are in a queue of traffic to go ahead
☐ you are on a roundabout

The purpose of this road marking is to keep the junction clear of queuing traffic.

You may only wait in the marked area when you're turning right and your exit lane is clear but you can't complete the turn because of oncoming traffic.

10.31 Mark three answers

You MUST stop when signalled to do so by which THREE of these?

☐ A police officer
☐ A pedestrian
☐ A school crossing patrol
☐ A bus driver
☐ A red traffic light

Looking well ahead and 'reading' the road will help you to anticipate hazards. This will enable you to stop safely at traffic lights or if ordered to do so by an authorised person.

10.32 Mark one answer

Someone is waiting to cross at a zebra crossing. They are standing on the pavement. You should normally

☐ go on quickly before they step onto the crossing
☐ stop before you reach the zigzag lines and let them cross
☐ stop, let them cross, wait patiently
☐ ignore them as they are still on the pavement

By standing on the pavement, the pedestrian is showing an intention to cross.

If you are looking well down the road you will give yourself enough time to slow down and stop safely. Don't forget to check your mirrors before slowing down.

10.33 Mark one answer

At toucan crossings, apart from pedestrians you should be aware of

☐ emergency vehicles emerging
☐ buses pulling out
☐ trams crossing in front
☐ cyclists riding across

The use of cycles is being encouraged and more toucan crossings are being installed.

These crossings enable pedestrians and cyclists to cross the path of other traffic.

Watch out as cyclists will approach the crossing faster than pedestrians.

10.34 Mark two answers

Who can use a toucan crossing?

☐ Trains
☐ Cyclists
☐ Buses
☐ Pedestrians
☐ Trams

Toucan crossings are similar to pelican crossings but there is no flashing amber phase. Cyclists share the crossing with pedestrians and are allowed to cycle across when the green cycle symbol is shown.

10.35 Mark one answer

At a pelican crossing, what does a flashing amber light mean?

☐ You must not move off until the lights stop flashing
☐ You must give way to pedestrians still on the crossing
☐ You can move off, even if pedestrians are still on the crossing
☐ You must stop because the lights are about to change to red

If there is no-one on the crossing when the amber light is flashing, you may proceed over the crossing. You don't need to wait for the green light to show.

10.36 Mark one answer

You are waiting at a pelican crossing. The red light changes to flashing amber. This means you must

☐ wait for pedestrians on the crossing to clear
☐ move off immediately without any hesitation
☐ wait for the green light before moving off
☐ get ready and go when the continuous amber light shows

This light allows time for the pedestrians already on the crossing to get to the other side in their own time, without being rushed. Don't rev your engine or start to move off while they are still crossing.

10.37 Mark one answer

When can you park on the left opposite these road markings?

☐ If the line nearest to you is broken
☐ When there are no yellow lines
☐ To pick up or set down passengers
☐ During daylight hours only

You MUST NOT park or stop on a road marked with double white lines (even where one of the lines is broken) except to pick up or set down passengers.

10.38 Mark one answer

You are intending to turn right at a crossroads. An oncoming driver is also turning right. It will normally be safer to

☐ keep the other vehicle to your RIGHT and turn behind it (offside to offside)
☐ keep the other vehicle to your LEFT and turn in front of it (nearside to nearside)
☐ carry on and turn at the next junction instead
☐ hold back and wait for the other driver to turn first

At some junctions the layout may make it difficult to turn offside to offside. If this is the case, be prepared to pass nearside to nearside, but take extra care as your view ahead will be obscured by the vehicle turning in front of you.

10.39 Mark one answer

You are on a road that has no traffic signs. There are street lights. What is the speed limit?

☐ 20 mph
☐ 30 mph
☐ 40 mph
☐ 60 mph

If you aren't sure of the speed limit a good indication is the presence of street lights. If there is street lighting the speed limit will be 30 mph unless otherwise indicated.

10.40 Mark three answers

You are going along a street with parked vehicles on the left-hand side. For which THREE reasons should you keep your speed down?

☐ So that oncoming traffic can see you more clearly
☐ You may set off car alarms
☐ Vehicles may be pulling out
☐ Drivers' doors may open
☐ Children may run out from between the vehicles

Travel slowly and carefully where there are parked vehicles in a built-up area.

Beware of

• vehicles pulling out, especially bicycles and other motorcycles

• pedestrians, especially children, who may run out from between cars

• drivers opening their doors.

10.41 Mark one answer

You meet an obstruction on your side of the road. You should

☐ carry on, you have priority
☐ give way to oncoming traffic
☐ wave oncoming vehicles through
☐ accelerate to get past first

Take care if you have to pass a parked vehicle on your side of the road. Give way to oncoming traffic if there isn't enough room for you both to continue safely.

10.42 Mark two answers

You are on a two-lane dual carriageway. For which TWO of the following would you use the right-hand lane?

☐ Turning right
☐ Normal progress
☐ Staying at the minimum allowed speed
☐ Constant high speed
☐ Overtaking slower traffic
☐ Mending punctures

Normally you should travel in the left-hand lane and only use the right-hand lane for overtaking or turning right. Move back into the left lane as soon as it's safe but don't cut in across the path of the vehicle you've just passed.

10.43 Mark one answer

Who has priority at an unmarked crossroads?

☐ The larger vehicle
☐ No one has priority
☐ The faster vehicle
☐ The smaller vehicle

Practise good observation in all directions before you emerge or make a turn.
  Proceed only when you're sure it's safe to do so.

10.44 Mark one answer   NI EXEMPT

What is the nearest you may park to a junction?

☐ 10 metres (32 feet)
☐ 12 metres (39 feet)
☐ 15 metres (49 feet)
☐ 20 metres (66 feet)

Don't park within 10 metres (32 feet) of a junction (unless in an authorised parking place). This is to allow drivers emerging from, or turning into, the junction a clear view of the road they are joining. It also allows them to see hazards such as pedestrians or cyclists at the junction.

10.45 Mark three answers   NI EXEMPT

In which THREE places must you NOT park?

☐ Near the brow of a hill
☐ At or near a bus stop
☐ Where there is no pavement
☐ Within 10 metres (32 feet) of a junction
☐ On a 40 mph road

Other traffic will have to pull out to pass you. They may have to use the other side of the road, and if you park near the brow of a hill, they may not be able to see oncoming traffic. It's important not to park at or near a bus stop as this could inconvenience passengers, and may put them at risk as they get on or off the bus.

  Parking near a junction could restrict the view for emerging vehicles.

10.46 Mark one answer

You are waiting at a level crossing. A train has passed but the lights keep flashing. You must

☐ carry on waiting
☐ phone the signal operator
☐ edge over the stop line and look for trains
☐ park and investigate

If the lights at a level crossing continue to flash after a train has passed, you should still wait as there might be another train coming. Time seems to pass slowly when you're held up in a queue. Be patient and wait until the lights stop flashing.

10.47 Mark one answer

At a crossroads there are no signs or road markings. Two vehicles approach. Which has priority?

☐ Neither of the vehicles
☐ The vehicle travelling the fastest
☐ Oncoming vehicles turning right
☐ Vehicles approaching from the right

At a crossroads where there are no 'give way' signs or road markings be very careful. No vehicle has priority, even if the sizes of the roads are different.

10.48 Mark one answer

What does this sign tell you?

☐ That it is a no-through road
☐ End of traffic calming zone
☐ Free parking zone ends
☐ No waiting zone ends

The blue and red circular sign on its own means that waiting restrictions are in force.
    This sign shows that you are leaving the controlled zone and waiting restrictions no longer apply.

10.49 Mark one answer

You are entering an area of roadworks. There is a temporary speed limit displayed. You should

☐ not exceed the speed limit
☐ obey the limit only during rush hour
☐ ignore the displayed limit
☐ obey the limit except at night

Where there are extra hazards such as roadworks, it's often necessary to slow traffic down by imposing a temporary speed limit. These speed limits aren't advisory, they must be obeyed.

10.50 Mark two answers

In which TWO places should you NOT park?

☐ Near a school entrance
☐ Near a police station
☐ In a side road
☐ At a bus stop
☐ In a one-way street

It may be tempting to park where you shouldn't while you run a quick errand.
    Careless parking is a selfish act and could endanger other road users.

10.51 Mark one answer

You are travelling on a well-lit road at night in a built-up area. By using dipped headlights you will be able to

☐ see further along the road
☐ go at a much faster speed
☐ switch to main beam quickly
☐ be easily seen by others

You may be difficult to see when you're travelling at night, even on a well-lit road. If you use dipped headlights rather than sidelights other road users will see you more easily.

10.52 Mark one answer

The dual carriageway you are turning right onto has a very narrow central reservation. What should you do?

☐ Proceed to the central reservation and wait
☐ Wait until the road is clear in both directions
☐ Stop in the first lane so that other vehicles give way
☐ Emerge slightly to show your intentions

When the central reservation is narrow you should treat a dual carriageway as one road. Wait until the road is clear in both directions before emerging to turn right. If you try to treat it as two separate roads and wait in the middle, you are likely to cause an obstruction and possibly a collision.

10.53 Mark one answer

What is the national speed limit on a single carriageway road for cars and motorcycles?

☐ 30 mph
☐ 50 mph
☐ 60 mph
☐ 70 mph

Exceeding the speed limit is dangerous and can result in you receiving penalty points on your licence. It isn't worth it. You should know the speed limit for the road that you're on by observing the road signs.

Different speed limits apply if you are towing a trailer.

10.54 Mark one answer

You park at night on a road with a 40 mph speed limit. You should park

☐ facing the traffic
☐ with parking lights on
☐ with dipped headlights on
☐ near a street light

You MUST use parking lights when parking at night on a road or lay-by with a speed limit greater than 30 mph. You MUST also park in the direction of the traffic flow and not close to a junction.

10.55 Mark one answer

You will see these red and white markers when approaching

☐ the end of a motorway
☐ a concealed level crossing
☐ a concealed speed limit sign
☐ the end of a dual carriageway

If there is a bend just before the level crossing you may not be able to see the level crossing barriers or waiting traffic.

These signs give you an early warning that you may find these hazards just around the bend.

10.56 Mark one answer   NI EXEMPT

You are travelling on a motorway. You MUST stop when signalled to do so by which of these?

☐ Flashing amber lights above your lane
☐ A Highways Agency Traffic Officer
☐ Pedestrians on the hard shoulder
☐ A driver who has broken down

You will find Highways Agency Traffic Officers on many of Britain's motorways.

They work in partnership with the police, helping to keep traffic moving and to make your journey as safe as possible. It is an offence not to comply with the directions given by a Traffic Officer.

10.57 Mark one answer

At a busy unmarked crossroads, which of the following has priority?

☐ Vehicles going straight ahead
☐ Vehicles turning right
☐ None of the vehicles
☐ The vehicles that arrived first

If there are no road signs or markings do not assume that you have priority.

Remember that other drivers may assume they have the right to go. No type of vehicle has priority but it's courteous to give way to large vehicles. Also look out in particular for cyclists and motorcyclists.

10.58 Mark one answer

You are going straight ahead at a roundabout. How should you signal?

☐ Signal right on the approach and then left to leave the roundabout
☐ Signal left after you leave the roundabout and enter the new road
☐ Signal right on the approach to the roundabout and keep the signal on
☐ Signal left just after you pass the exit before the one you will take

To go straight ahead at a roundabout you should normally approach in the left-hand lane. You will not normally need to signal, but look out for the road markings. At some roundabouts the left lane on approach is marked as 'left turn only', so make sure you use the correct lane to go ahead. Signal before you leave as other road users need to know your intentions.

road and traffic signs

11.1 Mark one answer

How should you give an arm signal to turn left?

☐   ☐

☐   ☐

Arm signals can be effective during daylight, especially when you're wearing bright clothing. Practise giving arm signals when you're learning. You need to be able to keep full control of your motorcycle with one hand off the handlebars.

11.2 Mark one answer

You are giving an arm signal ready to turn left. Why should you NOT continue with the arm signal while you turn?

☐ Because you might hit a pedestrian on the corner
☐ Because you will have less steering control
☐ Because you will need to keep the clutch applied
☐ Because other motorists will think that you are stopping on the corner

Consider giving an arm signal if it will help other road users. Situations where you might do this include, approaching a pedestrian crossing, in bright sunshine when your indicators may be difficult to see, when your indicators may be obscured in a traffic queue and where your indicators could cause confusion, such as when pulling up close to a side road. Don't maintain an arm signal when turning.

Maintain full control by keeping both hands on the handlebars when you turn.

11.3 Mark one answer

This sign is of particular importance to motorcyclists. It means

☐ side winds
☐ airport
☐ slippery road
☐ service area

Strong crosswinds can suddenly blow you off course. Keep your speed down when it's very windy, especially on exposed roads.

11.4 Mark one answer

Which one of these signs are you allowed to ride past on a solo motorcycle?

☐   ☐

☐   ☐

Most regulatory signs are circular, a red circle tells you what you must NOT do.

11.5 Mark one answer

Which of these signals should you give when slowing or stopping your motorcycle?

Arm signals can be given to reinforce your flashing indicators, especially if the indicator signal could cause confusion, for example if you intend to pull up close to a side road.

11.6 Mark one answer

When drivers flash their headlights at you it means

☐ that there is a radar speed trap ahead
☐ that they are giving way to you
☐ that they are warning you of their presence
☐ that there is something wrong with your motorcycle

A driver flashing their headlights has the same meaning as sounding the horn, it's a warning of their presence.

11.7 Mark one answer

Why should you make sure that you cancel your indicators after turning?

☐ To avoid flattening the battery
☐ To avoid misleading other road users
☐ To avoid dazzling other road users
☐ To avoid damage to the indicator relay

Always check that you have cancelled your indicators after turning. Failing to cancel your indicators could lead to a serious or even fatal collision. Other road users may pull out in front of you if they think you are going to turn off before you reach them.

11.8 Mark one answer

Your indicators are difficult to see due to bright sunshine. When using them you should

☐ also give an arm signal
☐ sound your horn
☐ flash your headlight
☐ keep both hands on the handlebars

Arm signals should be used to confirm your intentions when you aren't sure that your indicators can be seen by other road users.

Use the signals shown in *The Highway Code* and return your hand to the handlebars before you turn.

11.9 Mark one answer

You are riding on a motorway. There is a slow-moving vehicle ahead. On the back you see this sign. What should you do?

☐ Pass on the right
☐ Pass on the left
☐ Leave at the next exit
☐ Drive no further

If this vehicle is in your lane you will have to move to the left. Use your mirrors and signal if necessary. When it's safe move into the lane on your left. You should always look well ahead so that you can spot such hazards early, giving yourself time to react safely.

11.10 Mark one answer

You MUST obey signs giving orders. These signs are mostly in

☐ green rectangles
☐ red triangles
☐ blue rectangles
☐ red circles

There are three basic types of traffic sign, those that warn, inform or give orders.

Generally, triangular signs warn, rectangular ones give information or directions, and circular signs usually give orders. An exception is the eight-sided 'STOP' sign.

11.11 Mark one answer
Traffic signs giving orders are generally which shape?

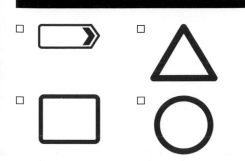

□
□
□
□

Road signs in the shape of a circle give orders. Those with a red circle are mostly prohibitive. The 'stop' sign is octagonal to give it greater prominence. Signs giving orders MUST always be obeyed.

11.12 Mark one answer
Which type of sign tells you NOT to do something?

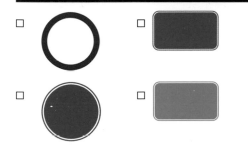

□
□
□
□

Signs in the shape of a circle give orders. A sign with a red circle means that you aren't allowed to do something. Study *Know Your Traffic Signs* to ensure that you understand what the different traffic signs mean.

11.13 Mark one answer
What does this sign mean?

□ Maximum speed limit with traffic calming
□ Minimum speed limit with traffic calming
□ '20 cars only' parking zone
□ Only 20 cars allowed at any one time

If you're in places where there are likely to be pedestrians such as outside schools, near parks, residential areas and shopping areas, you should be extra-cautious and keep your speed down.

Many local authorities have taken measures to slow traffic down by creating traffic calming measures such as speed humps.

They are there for a reason; slow down.

11.14 Mark one answer
Which sign means no motor vehicles are allowed?

□   □

□   □

You would generally see this sign at the approach to a pedestrian-only zone.

11.15 Mark one answer

Which of these signs means no motor vehicles?

If you are driving a motor vehicle or riding a motorcycle you MUST NOT travel past this sign. This area has been designated for use by pedestrians.

11.16 Mark one answer

What does this sign mean?

- ☐ New speed limit 20 mph
- ☐ No vehicles over 30 tonnes
- ☐ Minimum speed limit 30 mph
- ☐ End of 20 mph zone

Where you see this sign the 20 mph restriction ends. Check all around for possible hazards and only increase your speed if it's safe to do so.

11.17 Mark one answer

What does this sign mean?

- ☐ No overtaking
- ☐ No motor vehicles
- ☐ Clearway (no stopping)
- ☐ Cars and motorcycles only

A sign will indicate which types of vehicles are prohibited from certain roads. Make sure that you know which signs apply to the vehicle you're using.

11.18 Mark one answer

What does this sign mean?

- ☐ No parking
- ☐ No road markings
- ☐ No through road
- ☐ No entry

'No entry' signs are used in places such as one-way streets to prevent vehicles driving against the traffic. To ignore one would be dangerous, both for yourself and other road users, as well as being against the law.

11.19 Mark one answer

What does this sign mean?

- ☐ Bend to the right
- ☐ Road on the right closed
- ☐ No traffic from the right
- ☐ No right turn

The 'no right turn' sign may be used to warn road users that there is a 'no entry' prohibition on a road to the right ahead.

11.20 Mark one answer

Which sign means 'no entry'?

Look out for traffic signs. Disobeying or not seeing a sign could be dangerous. It may also be an offence for which you could be prosecuted.

11.21 Mark one answer

What does this sign mean?

☐ Route for trams only
☐ Route for buses only
☐ Parking for buses only
☐ Parking for trams only

Avoid blocking tram routes. Trams are fixed on their route and can't manoeuvre around other vehicles and pedestrians. Modern trams travel quickly and are quiet so you might not hear them approaching.

11.22 Mark one answer

Which type of vehicle does this sign apply to?

☐ Wide vehicles
☐ Long vehicles
☐ High vehicles
☐ Heavy vehicles

The triangular shapes above and below the dimensions indicate a height restriction that applies to the road ahead.

11.23 Mark one answer

Which sign means NO motor vehicles allowed?

☐   ☐

☐   ☐

This sign is used to enable pedestrians to walk free from traffic. It's often found in shopping areas.

11.24 Mark one answer

What does this sign mean?

☐ You have priority
☐ No motor vehicles
☐ Two-way traffic
☐ No overtaking

Road signs that prohibit overtaking are placed in locations where passing the vehicle in front is dangerous. If you see this sign don't attempt to overtake. The sign is there for a reason and you must obey it.

11.25 Mark one answer

What does this sign mean?

☐ Keep in one lane
☐ Give way to oncoming traffic
☐ Do not overtake
☐ Form two lanes

If you're behind a slow-moving vehicle be patient. Wait until the restriction no longer applies and you can overtake safely.

11.26 Mark one answer

Which sign means no overtaking?

☐   ☐

☐   ☐

This sign indicates that overtaking here is not allowed and you could face prosecution if you ignore this prohibition.

11.27 Mark one answer
What does this sign mean?

☐ Waiting restrictions apply
☐ Waiting permitted
☐ National speed limit applies
☐ Clearway (no stopping)

There will be a plate or additional sign to tell you when the restrictions apply.

11.28 Mark one answer
What does this sign mean?

☐ End of restricted speed area
☐ End of restricted parking area
☐ End of clearway
☐ End of cycle route

Even though you have left the restricted area, make sure that you park where you won't endanger other road users or cause an obstruction.

11.29 Mark one answer
Which sign means 'no stopping'?

Stopping where this clearway restriction applies is likely to cause congestion. Allow the traffic to flow by obeying the signs.

11.30 Mark one answer
What does this sign mean?

☐ Roundabout
☐ Crossroads
☐ No stopping
☐ No entry

This sign is in place to ensure a clear route for traffic. Don't stop except in an emergency.

11.31 Mark one answer
You see this sign ahead. It means

☐ national speed limit applies
☐ waiting restrictions apply
☐ no stopping
☐ no entry

Clearways are stretches of road where you aren't allowed to stop unless in an emergency. You'll see this sign. Stopping where these restrictions apply may be dangerous and likely to cause an obstruction. Restrictions might apply for several miles and this may be indicated on the sign.

11.32 Mark one answer
What does this sign mean?

☐ Distance to parking place ahead
☐ Distance to public telephone ahead
☐ Distance to public house ahead
☐ Distance to passing place ahead

If you intend to stop and rest, this sign allows you time to reduce speed and pull over safely.

11.33 Mark one answer
What does this sign mean?

☐ Vehicles may not park on the verge or footway
☐ Vehicles may park on the left-hand side of the road only
☐ Vehicles may park fully on the verge or footway
☐ Vehicles may park on the right-hand side of the road only

In order to keep roads free from parked cars, there are some areas where you're allowed to park on the verge. Only do this where you see the sign. Parking on verges or footways anywhere else could lead to a fine.

11.34 Mark one answer
What does this traffic sign mean?

☐ No overtaking allowed
☐ Give priority to oncoming traffic
☐ Two way traffic
☐ One-way traffic only

Priority signs are normally shown where the road is narrow and there isn't enough room for two vehicles to pass. These can be at narrow bridges, road works and where there's a width restriction.

Make sure that you know who has priority, don't force your way through. Show courtesy and consideration to other road users.

11.35 Mark one answer
What is the meaning of this traffic sign?

☐ End of two-way road
☐ Give priority to vehicles coming towards you
☐ You have priority over vehicles coming towards you
☐ Bus lane ahead

Don't force your way through. Show courtesy and consideration to other road users. Although you have priority, make sure oncoming traffic is going to give way before you continue.

11.36 Mark one answer
What does this sign mean?

☐ No overtaking
☐ You are entering a one-way street
☐ Two-way traffic ahead
☐ You have priority over vehicles from the opposite direction

Don't force your way through if oncoming vehicles fail to give way. If necessary, slow down and give way to avoid confrontation or a collision.

11.37 Mark one answer
What shape is a STOP sign at a junction?

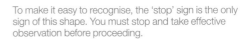

To make it easy to recognise, the 'stop' sign is the only sign of this shape. You must stop and take effective observation before proceeding.

341

11.38 Mark one answer

At a junction you see this sign partly covered by snow. What does it mean?

☐ Cross roads
☐ Give way
☐ Stop
☐ Turn right

The STOP sign is the only road sign that is octagonal. This is so that it can be recognised and obeyed even if it is obscured, for example by snow.

11.39 Mark one answer

What does this sign mean?

☐ Service area 30 miles ahead
☐ Maximum speed 30 mph
☐ Minimum speed 30 mph
☐ Lay-by 30 miles ahead

This sign is shown where slow-moving vehicles would impede the flow of traffic, for example in tunnels. However, if you need to slow down or even stop to avoid an incident or potential collision, you should do so.

11.40 Mark one answer

What does this sign mean?

☐ Give way to oncoming vehicles
☐ Approaching traffic passes you on both sides
☐ Turn off at the next available junction
☐ Pass either side to get to the same destination

These signs are often seen in one-way streets that have more than one lane.

When you see this sign, use the route that's the most convenient and doesn't require a late change of direction.

11.41 Mark one answer

What does this sign mean?

☐ Route for trams
☐ Give way to trams
☐ Route for buses
☐ Give way to buses

Take extra care when you encounter trams.

Look out for road markings and signs that alert you to them. Modern trams are very quiet and you may not hear them approaching.

11.42 Mark one answer

What does a circular traffic sign with a blue background do?

☐ Give warning of a motorway ahead
☐ Give directions to a car park
☐ Give motorway information
☐ Give an instruction

Signs with blue circles give a positive instruction. These are often found in urban areas and include signs for mini-roundabouts and directional arrows.

11.43 Mark one answer

Where would you see a contraflow bus and cycle lane?

☐ On a dual carriageway
☐ On a roundabout
☐ On an urban motorway
☐ On a one-way street

In a contraflow lane the traffic permitted to use it travels in the opposite direction to traffic in the other lanes on the road.

11.44 Mark one answer
What does this sign mean?

☐ Bus station on the right
☐ Contraflow bus lane
☐ With-flow bus lane
☐ Give way to buses

There will also be markings on the road surface to indicate the bus lane. You must not use this lane for parking or overtaking.

11.45 Mark one answer
What does a sign with a brown background show?

☐ Tourist directions
☐ Primary roads
☐ Motorway routes
☐ Minor routes

Signs with a brown background give directions to places of interest. They will often be seen on a motorway directing you along the easiest route to the attraction.

11.46 Mark one answer
This sign means

☐ tourist attraction
☐ beware of trains
☐ level crossing
☐ beware of trams

These signs indicate places of interest and are designed to guide you by the easiest route. They are particularly useful if you are unfamiliar with the area.

11.47 Mark one answer
What are triangular signs for?

☐ To give warnings
☐ To give information
☐ To give orders
☐ To give directions

This type of sign will warn you of hazards ahead.

Make sure you look at each sign that you pass on the road, so that you do not miss any vital instructions or information.

11.48 Mark one answer
What does this sign mean?

☐ Turn left ahead
☐ T-junction
☐ No through road
☐ Give way

This type of sign will warn you of hazards ahead. Make sure you look at each sign and road markings that you pass, so that you do not miss any vital instructions or information. This particular sign shows there is a T-junction with priority over vehicles from the right.

11.49 Mark one answer
What does this sign mean?

☐ Multi-exit roundabout
☐ Risk of ice
☐ Six roads converge
☐ Place of historical interest

It will take up to ten times longer to stop when it's icy. Where there is a risk of icy conditions you need to be aware of this and take extra care. If you think the road may be icy, don't brake or steer harshly as your tyres could lose their grip on the road.

11.50 Mark one answer
What does this sign mean?

☐ Crossroads
☐ Level crossing with gate
☐ Level crossing without gate
☐ Ahead only

The priority through the junction is shown by the broader line. You need to be aware of the hazard posed by traffic crossing or pulling out onto a major road.

11.51 Mark one answer
What does this sign mean?

☐ Ring road
☐ Mini-roundabout
☐ No vehicles
☐ Roundabout

As you approach a roundabout look well ahead and check all signs. Decide which exit you wish to take and move into the correct position as you approach the roundabout, signalling as required.

11.52 Mark four answers
Which FOUR of these would be indicated by a triangular road sign?

☐ Road narrows
☐ Ahead only
☐ Low bridge
☐ Minimum speed
☐ Children crossing
☐ T-junction

Warning signs are there to make you aware of potential hazards on the road ahead. Act on the signs so you are prepared and can take whatever action is necessary.

11.53 Mark one answer
What does this sign mean?

☐ Cyclists must dismount
☐ Cycles are not allowed
☐ Cycle route ahead
☐ Cycle in single file

Where there's a cycle route ahead, a sign will show a bicycle in a red warning triangle. Watch out for children on bicycles and cyclists rejoining the main road.

11.54 Mark one answer

Which sign means that pedestrians may be walking along the road?

When you pass pedestrians in the road, leave plenty of room. You might have to use the right-hand side of the road, so look well ahead, as well as in your mirrors, before pulling out. Take great care if there is a bend in the road obscuring your view ahead.

11.55 Mark one answer

Which of these signs means there is a double bend ahead?

Triangular signs give you a warning of hazards ahead. They are there to give you time to prepare for the hazard, for example by adjusting your speed.

11.56 Mark one answer

What does this sign mean?

☐ Wait at the barriers
☐ Wait at the crossroads
☐ Give way to trams
☐ Give way to farm vehicles

Obey the 'give way' signs. Trams are unable to steer around you if you misjudge when it is safe to enter the junction.

11.57 Mark one answer

What does this sign mean?

☐ Humpback bridge
☐ Humps in the road
☐ Entrance to tunnel
☐ Soft verges

These have been put in place to slow the traffic down. They're usually found in residential areas. Slow down to an appropriate speed.

theory questions

11.58 Mark one answer

Which of these signs means the end of a dual carriageway?

If you're overtaking make sure you move back safely into the left-hand lane before you reach the end of the dual carriageway.

11.59 Mark one answer

What does this sign mean?

☐ End of dual carriageway
☐ Tall bridge
☐ Road narrows
☐ End of narrow bridge

Don't leave moving into the left-hand lane until the last moment. Plan ahead and don't rely on other traffic letting you in.

11.60 Mark one answer

What does this sign mean?

☐ Crosswinds
☐ Road noise
☐ Airport
☐ Adverse camber

A warning sign with a picture of a windsock will indicate there may be strong crosswinds. This sign is often found on exposed roads.

11.61 Mark one answer

What does this traffic sign mean?

☐ Slippery road ahead
☐ Tyres liable to punctures ahead
☐ Danger ahead
☐ Service area ahead

This sign is there to alert you to the likelihood of danger ahead. It may be accompanied by a plate indicating the type of hazard. Be ready to reduce your speed and take avoiding action.

11.62 Mark one answer

You are about to overtake when you see this sign. You should

☐ overtake the other driver as quickly as possible
☐ move to the right to get a better view
☐ switch your headlights on before overtaking
☐ hold back until you can see clearly ahead

You won't be able to see any hazards that might be hidden in the dip. As well as oncoming traffic the dip may conceal

• cyclists

• horse riders

• parked vehicles

• pedestrians in the road.

11.63 Mark one answer
What does this sign mean?

☐ Level crossing with gate or barrier
☐ Gated road ahead
☐ Level crossing without gate or barrier
☐ Cattle grid ahead

Some crossings have gates but no attendant or signals. You should stop, look both ways, listen and make sure that there is no train approaching. If there is a telephone, contact the signal operator to make sure that it's safe to cross.

11.64 Mark one answer
What does this sign mean?

☐ No trams ahead
☐ Oncoming trams
☐ Trams crossing ahead
☐ Trams only

This sign warns you to beware of trams. If you don't usually drive in a town where there are trams, remember to look out for them at junctions and look for tram rails, signs and signals.

11.65 Mark one answer
What does this sign mean?

☐ Adverse camber
☐ Steep hill downwards
☐ Uneven road
☐ Steep hill upwards

This sign will give you an early warning that the road ahead will slope downhill. Prepare to alter your speed and gear. Looking at the sign from left to right will show you whether the road slopes uphill or downhill.

11.66 Mark one answer
What does this sign mean?

☐ Uneven road surface
☐ Bridge over the road
☐ Road ahead ends
☐ Water across the road

This sign is found where a shallow stream crosses the road. Heavy rainfall could increase the flow of water. If the water looks too deep or the stream has spread over a large distance, stop and find another route.

11.67 Mark one answer
What does this sign mean?

☐ Turn left for parking area
☐ No through road on the left
☐ No entry for traffic turning left
☐ Turn left for ferry terminal

If you intend to take a left turn, this sign shows you that you can't get through to another route using the left-turn junction ahead.

11.68 Mark one answer
What does this sign mean?

☐ T-junction
☐ No through road
☐ Telephone box ahead
☐ Toilet ahead

You will not be able to find a through route to another road. Use this road only for access.

11.69 Mark one answer
Which sign means 'no through road'?

This sign is found at the entrance to a road that can only be used for access.

11.70 Mark one answer
Which is the sign for a ring road?

Ring roads are designed to relieve congestion in towns and city centres.

11.71 Mark one answer
What does this sign mean?

☐ The right-hand lane ahead is narrow
☐ Right-hand lane for buses only
☐ Right-hand lane for turning right
☐ The right-hand lane is closed

Yellow and black temporary signs may be used to inform you of roadworks or lane restrictions. Look well ahead. If you have to change lanes, do so in good time.

11.72 Mark one answer
What does this sign mean?

☐ Change to the left lane
☐ Leave at the next exit
☐ Contraflow system
☐ One-way street

If you use the right-hand lane in a contraflow system, you'll be travelling with no permanent barrier between you and the oncoming traffic. Observe speed limits and keep a good distance from the vehicle ahead.

11.73 Mark one answer
What does this sign mean?

☐ Leave motorway at next exit
☐ Lane for heavy and slow vehicles
☐ All lorries use the hard shoulder
☐ Rest area for lorries

Where there's a long, steep, uphill gradient on a motorway, a crawler lane may be provided. This helps the traffic to flow by diverting the slower heavy vehicles into a dedicated lane on the left.

11.74 Mark one answer
A red traffic light means

☐ you should stop unless turning left
☐ stop, if you are able to brake safely
☐ you must stop and wait behind the stop line
☐ proceed with caution

Make sure you learn and understand the sequence of traffic lights. Whatever light appears you will then know what light is going to appear next and be able to take the appropriate action. For example if amber is showing on its own you'll know that red will appear next, giving you ample time to slow and stop safely.

11.75 Mark one answer
At traffic lights, amber on its own means

☐ prepare to go
☐ go if the way is clear
☐ go if no pedestrians are crossing
☐ stop at the stop line

When amber is showing on its own red will appear next. The amber light means STOP, unless you have already crossed the stop line or you are so close to it that pulling up might cause a collision.

11.76 Mark one answer
You are at a junction controlled by traffic lights. When should you NOT proceed at green?

☐ When pedestrians are waiting to cross
☐ When your exit from the junction is blocked
☐ When you think the lights may be about to change
☐ When you intend to turn right

As you approach the lights look into the road you wish to take. Only proceed if your exit road is clear. If the road is blocked hold back, even if you have to wait for the next green signal.

11.77 Mark one answer
You are in the left-hand lane at traffic lights. You are waiting to turn left. At which of these traffic lights must you NOT move on?

☐   ☐

☐   ☐

At some junctions there may be a separate signal for different lanes. These are called 'filter' lights. They're designed to help traffic flow at major junctions. Make sure that you're in the correct lane and proceed if the way is clear and the green light shows for your lane.

11.78 Mark one answer
What does this sign mean?

☐ Traffic lights out of order
☐ Amber signal out of order
☐ Temporary traffic lights ahead
☐ New traffic lights ahead

Where traffic lights are out of order you might see this sign. Proceed with caution as nobody has priority at the junction.

11.79 Mark one answer
When traffic lights are out of order, who has priority?

☐ Traffic going straight on
☐ Traffic turning right
☐ Nobody
☐ Traffic turning left

When traffic lights are out of order you should treat the junction as an unmarked crossroads. Be cautious as you may need to give way or stop. Keep a look out for traffic attempting to cross the junction at speed.

11.80 Mark three answers
These flashing red lights mean STOP. In which THREE of the following places could you find them?

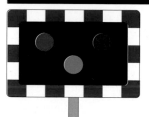

☐ Pelican crossings
☐ Lifting bridges
☐ Zebra crossings
☐ Level crossings
☐ Motorway exits
☐ Fire stations

You must always stop when the red lights are flashing, whether or not the way seems to be clear.

11.81 Mark one answer
What do these zigzag lines at pedestrian crossings mean?

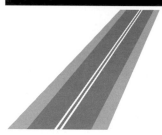

☐ No parking at any time
☐ Parking allowed only for a short time
☐ Slow down to 20 mph
☐ Sounding horns is not allowed

The approach to, and exit from, a pedestrian crossing is marked with zigzag lines. You must not park on them or overtake the leading vehicle when approaching the crossing. Parking here would block the view for pedestrians and the approaching traffic.

11.82 Mark one answer
When may you cross a double solid white line in the middle of the road?

☐ To pass traffic that is queuing back at a junction
☐ To pass a car signalling to turn left ahead
☐ To pass a road maintenance vehicle travelling at 10 mph or less
☐ To pass a vehicle that is towing a trailer

You may cross the solid white line to pass a stationary vehicle, pedal cycle, horse or road maintenance vehicle if they are travelling at 10 mph or less. You may also cross the solid line to enter into a side road or access a property.

11.83 Mark one answer
What does this road marking mean?

☐ Do not cross the line
☐ No stopping allowed
☐ You are approaching a hazard
☐ No overtaking allowed

Road markings will warn you of a hazard ahead. A single, broken line along the centre of the road, with long markings and short gaps, is a hazard warning line. Don't cross it unless you can see that the road is clear well ahead.

11.84 Mark one answer
Where would you see this road marking?

☐ At traffic lights
☐ On road humps
☐ Near a level crossing
☐ At a box junction

Due to the dark colour of the road, changes in level aren't easily seen. White triangles painted on the road surface give you an indication of where there are road humps.

11.85 Mark one answer
Which is a hazard warning line?

☐   ☐

☐   ☐

You need to know the difference between the normal centre line and a hazard warning line. If there is a hazard ahead, the markings are longer and the gaps shorter.
This gives you advanced warning of an unspecified hazard ahead.

11.86 Mark one answer
At this junction there is a stop sign with a solid white line on the road surface. Why is there a stop sign here?

☐ Speed on the major road is de-restricted
☐ It is a busy junction
☐ Visibility along the major road is restricted
☐ There are hazard warning lines in the centre of the road

If your view is restricted at a road junction you must stop. There may also be a 'stop' sign. Don't emerge until you're sure there's no traffic approaching.
IF YOU DON'T KNOW, DON'T GO.

11.87 Mark one answer

You see this line across the road at the entrance to a roundabout. What does it mean?

☐ Give way to traffic from the right
☐ Traffic from the left has right of way
☐ You have right of way
☐ Stop at the line

Slow down as you approach the roundabout and check for traffic from the right. If you need to stop and give way, stay behind the broken line until it is safe to emerge onto the roundabout.

11.88 Mark one answer

How will a police officer in a patrol vehicle normally get you to stop?

☐ Flash the headlights, indicate left and point to the left
☐ Wait until you stop, then approach you
☐ Use the siren, overtake, cut in front and stop
☐ Pull alongside you, use the siren and wave you to stop

You must obey signals given by the police.
   If a police officer in a patrol vehicle wants you to pull over they will indicate this without causing danger to you or other traffic.

11.89 Mark one answer

You approach a junction. The traffic lights are not working. A police officer gives this signal. You should

☐ turn left only
☐ turn right only
☐ stop level with the officer's arm
☐ stop at the stop line

If a police officer or traffic warden is directing traffic you must obey them. They will use the arm signals shown in *The Highway Code*. Learn what these mean and act accordingly.

11.90 Mark one answer

The driver of the car in front is giving this arm signal. What does it mean?

☐ The driver is slowing down
☐ The driver intends to turn right
☐ The driver wishes to overtake
☐ The driver intends to turn left

There might be an occasion where another driver uses an arm signal. This may be because the vehicle's indicators are obscured by other traffic. In order for such signals to be effective all drivers should know the meaning of them. Be aware that the 'left turn' signal might look similar to the 'slowing down' signal.

11.91 Mark one answer

Where would you see these road markings?

☐ At a level crossing
☐ On a motorway slip road
☐ At a pedestrian crossing
☐ On a single-track road

When driving on a motorway or slip road, you must not enter into an area marked with chevrons and bordered by a solid white line for any reason, except in an emergency.

11.92 Mark one answer

What does this motorway sign mean?

☐ Change to the lane on your left
☐ Leave the motorway at the next exit
☐ Change to the opposite carriageway
☐ Pull up on the hard shoulder

On the motorway, signs sometimes show temporary warnings due to traffic or weather conditions. They may be used to indicate

• lane closures

• temporary speed limits

• weather warnings.

11.93 Mark one answer

What does this motorway sign mean?

☐ Temporary minimum speed 50 mph
☐ No services for 50 miles
☐ Obstruction 50 metres (164 feet) ahead
☐ Temporary maximum speed 50 mph

Look out for signs above your lane or on the central reservation. These will give you important information or warnings about the road ahead. Due to the high speed of motorway traffic these signs may light up some distance from any hazard. Don't ignore the signs just because the road looks clear to you.

11.94 Mark one answer

What does this sign mean?

☐ Through traffic to use left lane
☐ Right-hand lane T-junction only
☐ Right-hand lane closed ahead
☐ 11 tonne weight limit

You should move into the lanes as directed by the sign. Here the right-hand lane is closed and the left-hand and centre lanes are available. Merging in turn is recommended when it's safe and traffic is going slowly, for example at road works or a road traffic incident. When vehicles are travelling at speed this is not advisable and you should move into the appropriate lane in good time.

11.95 Mark one answer

On a motorway this sign means

☐ move over onto the hard shoulder
☐ overtaking on the left only
☐ leave the motorway at the next exit
☐ move to the lane on your left

It is important to know and obey temporary signs on the motorway: they are there for a reason. You may not be able to see the hazard straight away, as the signs give warnings well in advance, due to the speed of traffic on the motorway.

11.96 Mark one answer

What does '25' mean on this motorway sign?

Nottingham
A46
25

- ☐ The distance to the nearest town
- ☐ The route number of the road
- ☐ The number of the next junction
- ☐ The speed limit on the slip road

Before you set out on your journey use a road map to plan your route. When you see advance warning of your junction, make sure you get into the correct lane in plenty of time. Last-minute harsh braking and cutting across lanes at speed is extremely hazardous.

11.97 Mark one answer

The right-hand lane of a three-lane motorway is

- ☐ for lorries only
- ☐ an overtaking lane
- ☐ the right-turn lane
- ☐ an acceleration lane

You should stay in the left-hand lane of a motorway unless overtaking. The right-hand lane of a motorway is an overtaking lane and not a 'fast lane'.

After overtaking, move back to the left when it is safe to do so.

11.98 Mark one answer

Where can you find reflective amber studs on a motorway?

- ☐ Separating the slip road from the motorway
- ☐ On the left-hand edge of the road
- ☐ On the right-hand edge of the road
- ☐ Separating the lanes

At night or in poor visibility reflective studs on the road help you to judge your position on the carriageway.

11.99 Mark one answer

Where on a motorway would you find green reflective studs?

- ☐ Separating driving lanes
- ☐ Between the hard shoulder and the carriageway
- ☐ At slip road entrances and exits
- ☐ Between the carriageway and the central reservation

Knowing the colours of the reflective studs on the road will help you judge your position, especially at night, in foggy conditions or when visibility is poor.

11.100 Mark one answer

You are travelling along a motorway. You see this sign. You should

- ☐ leave the motorway at the next exit
- ☐ turn left immediately
- ☐ change lane
- ☐ move onto the hard shoulder

You'll see this sign if the motorway is closed ahead. Pull into the nearside lane as soon as it is safe to do so. Don't leave it to the last moment.

11.101 Mark one answer

What does this sign mean?

- ☐ No motor vehicles
- ☐ End of motorway
- ☐ No through road
- ☐ End of bus lane

When you leave the motorway make sure that you check your speedometer. You may be going faster than you realise. Slow down and look out for speed limit signs.

11.102 Mark one answer

Which of these signs means that the national speed limit applies?

You should know the speed limit for the road on which you are travelling, and the vehicle that you are driving. The different speed limits are shown in *The Highway Code*.

11.103 Mark one answer

What is the maximum speed on a single carriageway road?

- ☐ 50 mph
- ☐ 60 mph
- ☐ 40 mph
- ☐ 70 mph

If you're travelling on a dual carriageway that becomes a single carriageway road, reduce your speed gradually so that you aren't exceeding the limit as you enter.

Thoro might not be a sign to remind you of the limit, so make sure you know what the speed limits are for different types of roads and vehicles.

11.104 Mark one answer

What does this sign mean?

- ☐ End of motorway
- ☐ End of restriction
- ☐ Lane ends ahead
- ☐ Free recovery ends

Temporary restrictions on motorways are shown on signs which have flashing amber lights. At the end of the restriction you will see this sign without any flashing lights.

11.105 Mark one answer

This sign is advising you to

- ☐ follow the route diversion
- ☐ follow the signs to the picnic area
- ☐ give way to pedestrians
- ☐ give way to cyclists

When a diversion route has been put in place, drivers are advised to follow a symbol which may be a triangle, square, circle or diamond shape on a yellow background.

11.106 Mark one answer

Why would this temporary speed limit sign be shown?

- ☐ To warn of the end of the motorway
- ☐ To warn you of a low bridge
- ☐ To warn you of a junction ahead
- ☐ To warn of road works ahead

In the interests of road safety, temporary speed limits are imposed at all major road works. Signs like this, giving advanced warning of the speed limit, are normally placed about three quarters of a mile ahead of where the speed limit comes into force.

11.107 Mark one answer

This traffic sign means there is

- ☐ a compulsory maximum speed limit
- ☐ an advisory maximum speed limit
- ☐ a compulsory minimum speed limit
- ☐ an advised separation distance

The sign gives you an early warning of a speed restriction. If you are travelling at a higher speed, slow down in good time. You could come across queuing traffic due to roadworks or a temporary obstruction.

11.108 Mark one answer

You see this sign at a crossroads. You should

- ☐ maintain the same speed
- ☐ carry on with great care
- ☐ find another route
- ☐ telephone the police

When traffic lights are out of order treat the junction as an unmarked crossroad. Be very careful as no one has priority and be prepared to stop.

11.109 Mark one answer

You are signalling to turn right in busy traffic. How would you confirm your intention safely?

- ☐ Sound the horn
- ☐ Give an arm signal
- ☐ Flash your headlights
- ☐ Position over the centre line

In some situations you may feel your indicators cannot be seen by other road users. If you think you need to make your intention more clearly seen, give the arm signal shown in *The Highway Code*.

11.110 Mark one answer

What does this sign mean?

- ☐ Motorcycles only
- ☐ No cars
- ☐ Cars only
- ☐ No motorcycles

You must comply with all traffic signs and be especially aware of those signs which apply specifically to the type of vehicle you are using.

11.111 Mark one answer

You are on a motorway. You see this sign on a lorry that has stopped in the right-hand lane. You should

- ☐ move into the right-hand lane
- ☐ stop behind the flashing lights
- ☐ pass the lorry on the left
- ☐ leave the motorway at the next exit

Sometimes work is carried out on the motorway without closing the lanes. When this happens, signs are mounted on the back of lorries to warn other road users of roadworks ahead.

11.112 Mark one answer

You are on a motorway. Red flashing lights appear above your lane only. What should you do?

- ☐ Continue in that lane and look for further information
- ☐ Move into another lane in good time
- ☐ Pull onto the hard shoulder
- ☐ Stop and wait for an instruction to proceed

Flashing red lights above your lane show that your lane is closed. You should move into another lane as soon as you can do so safely.

11.113 Mark one answer

A red traffic light means

☐ you must stop behind the white stop line
☐ you may go straight on if there is no other traffic
☐ you may turn left if it is safe to do so
☐ you must slow down and prepare to stop if traffic
has started to cross

The white line is generally positioned so that pedestrians have room to cross in front of waiting traffic. Don't move off while pedestrians are crossing, even if the lights change to green.

11.114 Mark one answer

The driver of this car is giving an arm signal. What are they about to do?

☐ Turn to the right
☐ Turn to the left
☐ Go straight ahead
☐ Let pedestrians cross

In some situations drivers may need to give arm signals, in addition to indicators, to make their intentions clear. For arm signals to be effective, all road users should know their meaning.

11.115 Mark one answer

When may you sound the horn?

☐ To give you right of way
☐ To attract a friend's attention
☐ To warn others of your presence
☐ To make slower drivers move over

Never sound the horn aggressively. You MUST NOT sound it when driving in a built-up area between 11.30 pm and 7.00 am or when you are stationary, an exception to this is when another road user poses a danger. Do not scare animals by sounding your horn.

11.116 Mark one answer

You must not use your horn when you are stationary

☐ unless a moving vehicle may cause you danger
☐ at any time whatsoever
☐ unless it is used only briefly
☐ except for signalling that you have just arrived

When stationary only sound your horn if you think there is a risk of danger from another road user. Don't use it just to attract someone's attention. This causes unnecessary noise and could be misleading.

11.117 Mark one answer

What does this sign mean?

☐ You can park on the days and times shown
☐ No parking on the days and times shown
☐ No parking at all from Monday to Friday
☐ End of the urban clearway restrictions

Urban clearways are provided to keep traffic flowing at busy times. You may stop only briefly to set down or pick up passengers. Times of operation will vary from place to place so always check the signs.

11.118 Mark one answer

What does this sign mean?

☐ Quayside or river bank
☐ Steep hill downwards
☐ Uneven road surface
☐ Road liable to flooding

You should be careful in these locations as the road surface is likely to be wet and slippery. There may be a steep drop to the water, and there may not be a barrier along the edge of the road.

11.119 Mark one answer

Which sign means you have priority over oncoming vehicles?

☐

☐

☐

☐

Even though you have priority, be prepared to give way if other drivers don't. This will help to avoid congestion, confrontation or even a collision.

11.120 Mark one answer

A white line like this along the centre of the road is a

☐ bus lane marking
☐ hazard warning
☐ give way marking
☐ lane marking

The centre of the road is usually marked by a broken white line, with lines that are shorter than the gaps. When the lines become longer than the gaps this is a hazard warning line. Look well ahead for these, especially when you are planning to overtake or turn off.

11.121 Mark one answer

What is the reason for the yellow criss-cross lines painted on the road here?

☐ To mark out an area for trams only
☐ To prevent queuing traffic from blocking the junction on the left
☐ To mark the entrance lane to a car park
☐ To warn you of the tram lines crossing the road

Yellow 'box junctions' like this are often used where it's busy. Their purpose is to keep the junction clear for crossing traffic.

Don't enter the painted area unless your exit is clear. The exception to this is when you are turning right and are only prevented from doing so by oncoming traffic or by other vehicles waiting to turn right.

11.122 Mark one answer

What is the reason for the area marked in red and white along the centre of this road?

☐ It is to separate traffic flowing in opposite directions
☐ It marks an area to be used by overtaking motorcyclists
☐ It is a temporary marking to warn of the roadworks
☐ It is separating the two sides of the dual carriageway

Areas of 'hatched markings' such as these are to separate traffic streams which could be a danger to each other. They are often seen on bends or where the road becomes narrow. If the area is bordered by a solid white line, you must not enter it except in an emergency.

11.123 Mark one answer

Other drivers may sometimes flash their headlights at you. In which situation are they allowed to do this?

☐ To warn of a radar speed trap ahead
☐ To show that they are giving way to you
☐ To warn you of their presence
☐ To let you know there is a fault with your vehicle

If other drivers flash their headlights this isn't a signal to show priority. The flashing of headlights has the same meaning as sounding the horn, it's a warning of their presence.

11.124 Mark one answer

In some narrow residential streets you may find a speed limit of

☐ 20 mph
☐ 25 mph
☐ 35 mph
☐ 40 mph

In some built-up areas, you may find the speed limit reduced to 20 mph. Driving at a slower speed will help give you the time and space to see and deal safely with hazards such as pedestrians and parked cars.

11.125 Mark one answer

At a junction you see this signal. It means

☐ cars must stop
☐ trams must stop
☐ both trams and cars must stop
☐ both trams and cars can continue

The white light shows that trams must stop, but the green light shows that other vehicles may go if the way is clear. You may not live in an area where there are trams but you should still learn the signs. You never know when you may go to a town with trams.

11.126 Mark one answer

Where would you find these road markings?

☐ At a railway crossing
☐ At a junction
☐ On a motorway
☐ On a pedestrian crossing

These markings show the direction in which the traffic should go at a mini-roundabout.

11.127 Mark one answer

There is a police car following you. The police officer flashes the headlights and points to the left. What should you do?

☐ Turn left at the next junction
☐ Pull up on the left
☐ Stop immediately
☐ Move over to the left

You must pull up on the left as soon as it's safe to do so and switch off your engine.

11.128 Mark one answer

You see this amber traffic light ahead. Which light or lights, will come on next?

☐ Red alone
☐ Red and amber together
☐ Green and amber together
☐ Green alone

At junctions controlled by traffic lights you must stop behind the white line until the lights change to green. Red and amber lights showing together also mean stop.

You may proceed when the light is green unless your exit road is blocked or pedestrians are crossing in front of you.

If you're approaching traffic lights that are visible from a distance and the light has been green for some time they are likely to change. Be ready to slow down and stop.

11.129 Mark one answer

This broken white line painted in the centre of the road means

☐ oncoming vehicles have priority over you
☐ you should give priority to oncoming vehicles
☐ there is a hazard ahead of you
☐ the area is a national speed limit zone

A long white line with short gaps means that you are approaching a hazard. If you do need to cross it, make sure that the road is clear well ahead.

11.130 Mark one answer

You see this signal overhead on the motorway. What does it mean?

☐ Leave the motorway at the next exit
☐ All vehicles use the hard shoulder
☐ Sharp bend to the left ahead
☐ Stop, all lanes ahead closed

You will see this sign if there has been an incident ahead and the motorway is closed.
   You MUST obey the sign. Make sure that you prepare to leave as soon as you see the warning sign.
   Don't pull over at the last moment or cut across other traffic.

11.131 Mark one answer

What is the purpose of these yellow criss-cross lines on the road?

☐ To make you more aware of the traffic lights
☐ To guide you into position as you turn
☐ To prevent the junction becoming blocked
☐ To show you where to stop when the lights change

You MUST NOT enter a box junction until your exit road or lane is clear. The exception to this is if you want to turn right and are only prevented from doing so by oncoming traffic or by other vehicles waiting to turn right.

11.132 Mark one answer

What MUST you do when you see this sign?

☐ Stop, only if traffic is approaching
☐ Stop, even if the road is clear
☐ Stop, only if children are waiting to cross
☐ Stop, only if a red light is showing

STOP signs are situated at junctions where visibility is restricted or there is heavy traffic.
   They MUST be obeyed. You MUST stop.
   Take good all-round observation before moving off.

11.133 Mark one answer

Which shape is used for a 'give way' sign?

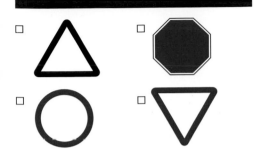

☐   ☐

☐   ☐

Other warning signs are the same shape and colour, but the 'give way' sign triangle points downwards. When you see this sign you MUST give way to traffic on the road which you are about to enter.

11.134 Mark one answer

What does this sign mean?

☐ Buses turning
☐ Ring road
☐ Mini-roundabout
☐ Keep right

When you see this sign, look out for any direction signs and judge whether you need to signal your intentions. Do this in good time so that other road users approaching the roundabout know what you're planning to do.

11.135 Mark one answer

What does this sign mean?

☐ Two-way traffic straight ahead
☐ Two-way traffic crosses a one-way road
☐ Two-way traffic over a bridge
☐ Two-way traffic crosses a two-way road

Be prepared for traffic approaching from junctions on either side of you. Try to avoid unnecessary changing of lanes just before the junction.

11.136 Mark one answer

What does this sign mean?

☐ Two-way traffic ahead across a one-way road
☐ Traffic approaching you has priority
☐ Two-way traffic straight ahead
☐ Motorway contraflow system ahead

This sign may be at the end of a dual carriageway or a one-way street. It is there to warn you of oncoming traffic.

11.137 Mark one answer

What does this sign mean?

☐ Hump-back bridge
☐ Traffic calming hump
☐ Low bridge
☐ Uneven road

You will need to slow down. At humpback bridges your view ahead will be restricted and the road will often be narrow on the bridge. If the bridge is very steep or your view is restricted sound your horn to warn others of your approach. Going too fast over the bridge is highly dangerous to other road users and could even cause your wheels to leave the road, with a resulting loss of control.

11.138 Mark one answer

Which of the following signs informs you that you are coming to a 'no through road'?

This sign is found at the entrance to a road that can only be used for access.

11.139 Mark one answer

What does this sign mean?

☐ Direction to park-and-ride car park
☐ No parking for buses or coaches
☐ Directions to bus and coach park
☐ Parking area for cars and coaches

To ease the congestion in town centres, some cities and towns provide park-and-ride schemes. These allow you to park in a designated area and ride by bus into the centre.

Park-and-ride schemes are usually cheaper and easier than car parking in the town centre.

11.140 Mark one answer

You are approaching traffic lights. Red and amber are showing. This means

☐ pass the lights if the road is clear
☐ there is a fault with the lights – take care
☐ wait for the green light before you cross the stop line
☐ the lights are about to change to red

Be aware that other traffic might still be clearing the junction. Make sure the way is clear before continuing.

11.141 Mark one answer

This marking appears on the road just before a

☐ 'no entry' sign
☐ 'give way' sign
☐ 'stop' sign
☐ 'no through road' sign

Where you see this road marking you should give way to traffic on the main road.

It might not be used at junctions where there is relatively little traffic. However, if there is a double broken line across the junction the 'give way' rules still apply.

11.142 Mark one answer

At a railway level crossing the red light signal continues to flash after a train has gone by. What should you do?

☐ Phone the signal operator
☐ Alert drivers behind you
☐ Wait
☐ Proceed with caution

You MUST always obey red flashing stop lights. If a train passes but the lights continue to flash, another train will be passing soon. Cross only when the lights go off and the barriers open.

11.143 Mark one answer

You are in a tunnel and you see this sign. What does it mean?

☐ Direction to emergency pedestrian exit
☐ Beware of pedestrians, no footpath ahead
☐ No access for pedestrians
☐ Beware of pedestrians crossing ahead

If you have to leave your vehicle in a tunnel and leave by an emergency exit, do so as quickly as you can. Follow the signs directing you to the nearest exit point. If there are several people using the exit, don't panic but try to leave in a calm and orderly manner.

11.144 Mark one answer

Which of these signs shows that you are entering a one-way system?

If the road has two lanes you can use either lane and overtake on either side. Use the lane that's more convenient for your destination unless signs or road markings indicate otherwise.

11.145 Mark one answer

What does this sign mean?

☐ With-flow bus and cycle lane
☐ Contraflow bus and cycle lane
☐ No buses and cycles allowed
☐ No waiting for buses and cycles

Buses and cycles can travel in this lane. In this case they will flow in the same direction as other traffic. If it's busy they may be passing you on the left, so watch out for them. Times on the sign will show its hours of operation. No times shown, or no sign at all, means it's 24 hours. In some areas other vehicles, such as taxis and motorcycles, are allowed to use bus lanes.
The sign will show these.

11.146 Mark one answer

Which of these signs warns you of a zebra crossing?

Look well ahead and check the pavements and surrounding areas for pedestrians.
Look for anyone walking towards the crossing. Check your mirrors for traffic behind, in case you have to slow down or stop.

11.147 Mark one answer

What does this sign mean?

☐ No footpath
☐ No pedestrians
☐ Zebra crossing
☐ School crossing

You need to be aware of the various signs that relate to pedestrians. Some of the signs look similar but have very different meanings. Make sure you know what they all mean and be ready for any potential hazard.

11.148 Mark one answer

What does this sign mean?

☐ School crossing patrol
☐ No pedestrians allowed
☐ Pedestrian zone – no vehicles
☐ Zebra crossing ahead

Look well ahead and be ready to stop for any pedestrians crossing, or about to cross, the road. Also check the pavements for anyone who looks like they might step or run into the road.

11.149 Mark one answer

Which sign means there will be two-way traffic crossing your route ahead?

☐

☐

☐

☐

This sign is found in or at the end of a one-way system. It warns you that traffic will be crossing your path from both directions.

11.150 Mark one answer

Which arm signal tells you that the car you are following is going to pull up?

☐

☐

☐

☐

There may be occasions when drivers need to give an arm signal to confirm an indicator. This could include in bright sunshine, at a complex road layout, when stopping at a pedestrian crossing or when turning right just after passing a parked vehicle. You should understand what each arm signal means. If you give arm signals, make them clear, correct and decisive.

11.151 Mark one answer

Which of these signs means turn left ahead?

☐

☐

☐

☐

Blue circles tell you what you must do and this sign gives a clear instruction to turn left ahead. You should be looking out for signs at all times and know what they mean.

11.152 Mark one answer

Which sign shows that traffic can only travel in one direction on the road you're on?

☐

☐

☐

☐

This sign means that traffic can only travel in one direction. The others show different priorities on a two-way road.

11.153 Mark one answer

You have just driven past this sign. You should be aware that

☐ it is a single track road
☐ you cannot stop on this road
☐ there is only one lane in use
☐ all traffic is going one way

In a one-way system traffic may be passing you on either side. Always be aware of all traffic signs and understand their meaning. Look well ahead and react to them in good time.

11.154 Mark one answer

You are approaching a red traffic light. What will the signal show next?

☐ Red and amber
☐ Green alone
☐ Amber alone
☐ Green and amber

If you know which light is going to show next you can plan your approach accordingly. This can help prevent excessive braking or hesitation at the junction.

11.155 Mark one answer

What does this sign mean?

☐ Low bridge ahead
☐ Tunnel ahead
☐ Ancient monument ahead
☐ Traffic danger spot ahead

When approaching a tunnel switch on your dipped headlights. Be aware that your eyes might need to adjust to the sudden darkness. You may need to reduce your speed.

documents

12.1   Mark three answers

Which of the following information is found on your motorcycle registration document?

☐ Make and model
☐ Service history record
☐ Ignition key security number
☐ Engine size and number
☐ Purchase price
☐ Year of first registration

Each motorcycle has a registration document which describes the vehicle's make, model and other details; it also gives details of the registered keeper. If you buy a new motorcycle the dealer will register your motorcycle with the licensing authority, who will send the registration document to you.

12.2   Mark one answer   NI EXEMPT

Compulsory Basic Training (CBT) can only be carried out by

☐ any ADI (Approved Driving Instructor)
☐ any road safety officer
☐ any DSA (Driving Standards Agency) approved training body
☐ any motorcycle main dealer

CBT courses can only be given by training bodies that are approved by DSA. The standard of training is monitored by DSA examiners. The course is designed to give you basic skills before going on the road.

12.3   Mark one answer

Before riding anyone else's motorcycle you should make sure that

☐ the owner has third party insurance cover
☐ your own motorcycle has insurance cover
☐ the motorcycle is insured for your use
☐ the owner has the insurance documents with them

If you borrow a motorcycle you must make sure that you are insured. Find out yourself.
Don't take anyone else's word for it.

12.4   Mark one answer

Vehicle excise duty is often called 'Road Tax' or 'The Tax Disc'. You must

☐ keep it with your registration document
☐ display it clearly on your motorcycle
☐ keep it concealed safely in your motorcycle
☐ carry it on you at all times

You must display a current, valid tax disc on your vehicle. It can't be transferred from one vehicle to another. A vehicle that is exempt from duty must display a valid nil licence instead.

12.5   Mark one answer   NI EXEMPT

Motorcycles must FIRST have an MOT test certificate when they are

☐ one year old
☐ three years old
☐ five years old
☐ seven years old

Any motorcycle you ride must be in good condition and roadworthy. If it's over three years old it must have a valid MOT test certificate.

12.6   Mark three answers

Which THREE pieces of information are found on a registration document?

☐ Registered keeper
☐ Make of the motorcycle
☐ Service history details
☐ Date of the MOT
☐ Type of insurance cover
☐ Engine size

Every motorcycle used on the road has a registration document issued by the Driver and Vehicle Licensing Agency (DVLA) or Driver and Vehicle Agency (DVA) in Northern Ireland. It is used to record any change of ownership and gives, date of first registration, registration number, previous keeper, registered keeper, make of motorcycle, engine size and frame number, year of manufacture and colour.

12.7 Mark three answers

You have a duty to contact the licensing authority when

☐ you go abroad on holiday
☐ you change your motorcycle
☐ you change your name
☐ your job status is changed
☐ your permanent address changes
☐ your job involves travelling abroad

The licensing authority will need to keep their records up to date. They send out a reminder when your road tax is due and need your current address for this purpose.

Every motorcycle in the country is registered, so it is possible to trace its history.

12.8 Mark two answers

Your motorcycle is insured third party only. This covers

☐ damage to your motorcycle
☐ damage to other vehicles
☐ injury to yourself
☐ injury to others
☐ all damage and injury

Third party insurance cover is usually cheaper than fully comprehensive.

However, it does not cover any damage to your own motorcycle or property and it does not provide cover if your motorcycle is stolen.

12.9 Mark one answer

What is the legal minimum insurance cover you must have to ride on public roads?

☐ Third party, fire and theft
☐ Fully comprehensive
☐ Third party only
☐ Personal injury cover

The minimum insurance cover required by law is third party only. This covers other people and vehicles involved in a collision, but not you or your vehicle. Also basic third party insurance won't cover you for theft or fire damage. Make sure you carefully read and understand your policy.

12.10 Mark one answer

A Vehicle Registration Document will show

☐ the service history
☐ the year of first registration
☐ the purchase price
☐ the tyre sizes

A Vehicle Registration Document contains a number of details that are unique to a particular vehicle. You must notify DVLA (or DVA in Northern Ireland) of any changes to, for example, the registered keeper, registration number or any modifications to the vehicle.

12.11 Mark one answer

What is the purpose of having a vehicle test certificate (MOT)?

☐ To make sure your motorcycle is roadworthy
☐ To certify how many miles per gallon it does
☐ To prove you own the motorcycle
☐ To allow you to park in restricted areas

It is your responsibility to make sure that any motorcycle you ride is in a roadworthy condition. Any faults that develop should be promptly corrected. If your motorcycle fails an MOT test, it should not be used on the road unless you're taking it to have the faults repaired or for a previously arranged retest.

12.12 Mark one answer   NI EXEMPT

Before taking a practical motorcycle test you need

☐ a full moped licence
☐ a full car licence
☐ a CBT (Compulsory Basic Training) certificate
☐ 12 months riding experience

The purpose of a CBT (Compulsory Basic Training) course is to teach you basic theory and practical skills before riding on the road, on your own, for the first time.

They can only be given by Approved Training Bodies (ATBs).

12.13 Mark three answers

You must notify the licensing authority when

☐ your health affects your riding
☐ your eyesight does not meet a set standard
☐ you intend lending your motorcycle
☐ your motorcycle requires an MOT certificate
☐ you change your motorcycle

The Driver and Vehicle Licensing Agency (DVLA) hold the records of all vehicles, drivers and riders in Great Britain (DVA in Northern Ireland). They need to know of any change in circumstances so they can keep their records up to date. Your health might affect your ability to ride safely. Don't put yourself or other road users at risk.

12.14 Mark two answers

You have just passed your practical motorcycle test. This is your first full licence. Within two years you get six penalty points. You will have to

☐ retake only your theory test
☐ retake your theory and practical tests
☐ retake only your practical test
☐ reapply for your full licence immediately
☐ reapply for your provisional licence

If, during your first two years of holding a full licence, the number of points on your licence reaches six or more, your licence will be revoked. This includes offences you committed before you passed your test.
   You may ride only as a learner until you pass both the theory and practical tests again.

12.15 Mark three answers

You hold a provisional motorcycle licence. This means you must NOT

☐ exceed 30 mph
☐ ride on a motorway
☐ ride after dark
☐ carry a pillion passenger
☐ ride without 'L' plates displayed

Provisional entitlement means that restrictions apply to your use of motorcycles. The requirements are there to protect you and other road users. Make sure you are aware of all the restrictions that apply before you ride your motorcycle on the road.

12.16 Mark one answer

A full category A1 licence will allow you to ride a motorcycle up to

☐ 125 cc
☐ 250 cc
☐ 350 cc
☐ 425 cc

When you pass your test on a motorcycle between 75 cc and 125 cc you will be issued with a full light motorcycle licence of category A1. You will then be allowed to ride any motorcycle up to 125 cc and with a power output of 11 Kw (14.6 bhp).

12.17 Mark one answer   NI EXEMPT

You want a licence to ride a large motorcycle via Direct Access. You will

☐ not require L-plates if you have passed a car test
☐ require L-plates only when learning on your own machine
☐ require L-plates while learning with a qualified instructor
☐ not require L-plates if you have passed a moped test

While training through the Direct Access scheme you must be accompanied by an instructor on another motorcycle and be in radio contact. You must display L-plates on your motorcycle and follow all normal learner restrictions.

12.18 Mark three answers   NI EXEMPT

A motorcyclist may only carry a pillion passenger when

☐ the rider has successfully completed CBT (Compulsory Basic Training)
☐ the rider holds a full licence for the category of motorcycle
☐ the motorcycle is fitted with rear footrests
☐ the rider has a full car licence and is over 21
☐ there is a proper passenger seat fitted
☐ there is no sidecar fitted to the machine

Before carrying a passenger on a motorcycle the rider must hold a full licence for the category being ridden. They must also ensure that a proper passenger seat and footrests are fitted.

12.19 Mark one answer NI EXEMPT

You have a CBT (Compulsory Basic Training) certificate. How long is it valid?

☐ one year
☐ two years
☐ three years
☐ four years

All new learner motorcycle and moped riders must complete a Compulsory Basic Training (CBT) course before riding on the road. This can only be given by an Approved Training Body (ATB). If you don't pass your practical test within two years you will need to retake and pass CBT to continue riding.

12.20 Mark one answer

Your road tax disc is due to expire. To renew it you may need a renewal form, the fee, and valid MOT (if required). What else will you need?

☐ Proof of purchase receipt
☐ Compulsory Basic Training certificate
☐ A valid certificate of insurance
☐ A complete service record

You will normally be sent a reminder automatically by the DVLA (DVA in Northern Ireland) close to the time of renewal. Make sure that all your documentation is correct, up to date and valid. You can renew, by post, in person, by phone or online.

12.21 Mark one answer

You want to carry a pillion passenger on your motorcycle. To do this

☐ your motorcycle must be larger than 125 cc
☐ they must be a full motorcycle licence-holder
☐ you must have passed your test for a full motorcycle licence
☐ you must have three years motorcycle riding experience

As a learner motorcyclist you are not allowed to carry a pillion passenger, even if they hold a full motorcycle licence. You MUST NOT carry a pillion, or tow a trailer, until you have passed your test.

12.22 Mark one answer

A friend asks you to give them a lift on your motorcycle. What conditions apply?

☐ Your motorcycle must be larger than 125 cc
☐ You must have three years motorcycle riding experience
☐ The pillion must be a full motorcycle licence-holder
☐ You must have passed your test for a full motorcycle licence

By law, you can only carry a pillion passenger after you have gained a full motorcycle licence. Even if they hold a full licence it makes no difference. As a learner you are also restricted from towing a trailer.

12.23 Mark one answer

Your motorcycle insurance policy has an excess of £100. What does this mean?

☐ The insurance company will pay the first £100 of any claim
☐ You will be paid £100 if you do not have a crash
☐ Your motorcycle is insured for a value of £100 if it is stolen
☐ You will have to pay the first £100 of any claim

This is a method used by insurance companies to keep annual premiums down. Generally, the higher the excess you choose to pay, the lower the annual premium you will be charged.

12.24 Mark one answer

An MOT certificate is normally valid for

☐ three years after the date it was issued
☐ 10,000 miles
☐ one year after the date it was issued
☐ 30,000 miles

Make a note of the date that your MOT certificate expires. Some garages remind you that your vehicle is due an MOT but not all do. You may take your vehicle for MOT up to to one month in advance and have the certificate post dated.

12.25 Mark one answer

A cover note is a document issued before you receive your

☐ driving licence
☐ insurance certificate
☐ registration document
☐ MOT certificate

Sometimes an insurance company will issue a temporary insurance certificate called a cover note. It gives you the same insurance cover as your certificate, but lasts for a limited period, usually one month.

369

12.26 Mark two answers

You have just passed your practical test. You do not hold a full licence in another category. Within two years you get six penalty points on your licence. What will you have to do?

☐ Retake only your theory test
☐ Retake your theory and practical tests
☐ Retake only your practical test
☐ Reapply for your full licence immediately
☐ Reapply for your provisional licence

If you accumulate six or more penalty points within two years of gaining your first full licence it will be revoked. The six or more points include any gained due to offences you committed before passing your test. If this happens you may only drive as a learner until you pass both the theory and practical tests again.

12.27 Mark one answer

How long will a Statutory Off Road Notification (SORN) last for?

☐ 12 months
☐ 24 months
☐ 3 years
☐ 10 years

A SORN declaration allows you to keep a vehicle off road and untaxed for 12 months. If you want to keep your vehicle off road beyond that you must send a further SORN form to DVLA, or DVA in Northern Ireland. If the vehicle is sold SORN will end and the new owner becomes responsible immediately.

12.28 Mark one answer   NI EXEMPT

What is a Statutory Off Road Notification (SORN) declaration?

☐ A notification to tell VOSA that a vehicle does not have a current MOT
☐ Information kept by the police about the owner of the vehicle
☐ A notification to tell DVLA that a vehicle is not being used on the road
☐ Information held by insurance companies to check the vehicle is insured

If you want to keep a vehicle off the public road you must declare SORN. It is an offence not to do so. You then won't have to pay road tax. If you don't renew the SORN declaration or re-license the vehicle, you will incur a penalty.

12.29 Mark one answer   NI EXEMPT

A Statutory Off Road Notification (SORN) declaration is

☐ to tell DVLA that your vehicle is being used on the road but the MOT has expired
☐ to tell DVLA that you no longer own the vehicle
☐ to tell DVLA that your vehicle is not being used on the road
☐ to tell DVLA that you are buying a personal number plate

This will enable you to keep a vehicle off the public road for 12 months without having to pay road tax. You must send a further SORN declaration after 12 months.

12.30 Mark one answer

A Statutory Off Road Notification (SORN) is valid

☐ for as long as the vehicle has an MOT
☐ for 12 months only
☐ only if the vehicle is more than 3 years old
☐ provided the vehicle is insured

If you want to keep a vehicle off the public road you must declare SORN. It is an offence not to do so. You then won't have to pay road tax for that vehicle. You will incur a penalty after 12 months if you don't renew the SORN declaration, or re-license the vehicle. If you sell the vehicle the SORN declaration ends and the new owner should declare SORN or re-license the vehicle.

12.31 Mark one answer

A Statutory Off Road Notification (SORN) will last

☐ for the life of the vehicle
☐ for as long as you own the vehicle
☐ for 12 months only
☐ until the vehicle warranty expires

If you are keeping a vehicle, or vehicles, off road and don't want to pay road tax you must declare SORN. You must still do this even if the vehicle is incapable of being used, for example it may be under restoration or being stored. After 12 months you must send another SORN declaration or re-license your vehicle. You will be fined if you don't do this. The SORN will end if you sell the vehicle and the new owner will be responsible immediately.

12.32 Mark one answer

What is the maximum specified fine for driving without insurance?

☐ £50
☐ £500
☐ £1000
☐ £5000

It is a serious offence to drive without insurance. As well as a heavy fine you may be disqualified or incur penalty points.

12.33 Mark one answer

Who is legally responsible for ensuring that a Vehicle Registration Certificate (V5C) is updated?

☐ The registered vehicle keeper
☐ The vehicle manufacturer
☐ Your insurance company
☐ The licensing authority

It is your legal responsibility to keep the details of your Vehicle Registration Certificate (V5C) up to date. You should tell the licensing authority of any changes.

These include your name, address, or vehicle details. If you don't do this you may have problems when you sell your vehicle.

12.34 Mark one answer

For which of these MUST you show your insurance certificate?

☐ When making a SORN declaration
☐ When buying or selling a vehicle
☐ When a police officer asks you for it
☐ When having an MOT inspection

You MUST be able to produce your valid insurance certificate when requested by a police officer. If you can't do this immediately you may be asked to take it to a police station. Other documents you may be asked to produce are your driving licence and MOT certificate.

12.35 Mark one answer

You must have valid insurance before you can

☐ make a SORN declaration
☐ buy or sell a vehicle
☐ apply for a driving licence
☐ obtain a tax disc

You MUST have valid insurance before you can apply for a tax disc. Your vehicle will also need to have a valid MOT certificate, if applicable. You can apply on-line, at certain post offices or by post. It is illegal and can be dangerous to drive without valid insurance or an MOT.

12.36 Mark one answer

Your vehicle needs a current MOT certificate. Until you have one you will NOT be able to

☐ renew your driving licence
☐ change your insurance company
☐ renew your road tax disc
☐ notify a change of address

If your vehicle is required to have an MOT certificate you will need to make sure this is current before you are able to renew your tax disc (also known as vehicle excise duty). You can renew online, by phone or by post.

12.37 Mark three answers

Which THREE of these do you need before you can use a vehicle on the road legally?

☐ A valid driving licence
☐ A valid tax disc clearly displayed
☐ Proof of your identity
☐ Proper insurance cover
☐ Breakdown cover
☐ A vehicle handbook

Using a vehicle on the road illegally carries a heavy fine and can lead to penalty points on your licence. Things you MUST have include a valid driving licence, a current valid tax disc, and proper insurance cover.

12.38 Mark one answer

When you apply to renew your Vehicle Excise Duty (tax disc) you must have

☐ valid insurance
☐ the old tax disc
☐ the handbook
☐ a valid driving licence

Tax discs can be renewed at post offices, vehicle registration offices, online, or by post. When applying make sure you have all the relevant valid documents, including MOT where applicable.

12.39 Mark one answer

A police officer asks to see your documents. You do not have them with you. You may be asked to take them to a police station within

☐ 5 days
☐ 7 days
☐ 14 days
☐ 21 days

You don't have to carry the documents for your vehicle around with you. If a police officer asks to see them and you don't have them with you, you may be asked to produce them at a police station within seven days.

12.40 Mark one answer

When you apply to renew your vehicle excise licence (tax disc) what must you have?

☐ Valid insurance
☐ The old tax disc
☐ The vehicle handbook
☐ A valid driving licence

Tax discs can be renewed online, at most post offices, your nearest vehicle registration office or by post to the licensing authority. Make sure you have or take all the relevant documents with your application.

12.41 Mark one answer

When should you update your Vehicle Registration Certificate?

☐ When you pass your driving test
☐ When you move house
☐ When your vehicle needs an MOT
☐ When you have a collision

As the registered keeper of a vehicle it is up to you to inform DVLA (DVA in Northern Ireland) of any changes in your vehicle or personal details, for example, change of name or address. You do this by completing the relevant section of the Registration Certificate and sending it to them.

incidents, accidents and emergencies

13.1 Mark one answer

Your motorcycle has broken down on a motorway. How will you know the direction of the nearest emergency telephone?

☐ By walking with the flow of traffic
☐ By following an arrow on a marker post
☐ By walking against the flow of traffic
☐ By remembering where the last phone was

If you break down on a motorway pull onto the hard shoulder and stop as far over to the left as you can. Switch on hazard lights (if fitted) and go to the nearest emergency telephone. Marker posts spaced every 100 metres will show you where the nearest telephone is.

13.2 Mark one answer

You should use the engine cut-out switch to

☐ stop the engine in an emergency
☐ stop the engine on short journeys
☐ save wear on the ignition switch
☐ start the engine if you lose the key

Most motorcycles are fitted with an engine cut out switch. This is designed to stop the engine in an emergency and so reduce the risk of fire.

13.3 Mark one answer

You are riding on a motorway. The car in front switches on its hazard warning lights whilst moving. This means

☐ they are going to take the next exit
☐ there is a danger ahead
☐ there is a police car in the left lane
☐ they are trying to change lanes

When riding on a motorway, or a dual carriageway subject to a national speed limit, vehicles may switch on their hazard warning lights to warn following traffic of an obstruction ahead.

13.4 Mark three answers

You have broken down on a motorway. When you use the emergency telephone you will be asked

☐ for the number on the telephone that you are using
☐ for your driving licence details
☐ for the name of your vehicle insurance company
☐ for details of yourself and your motorcycle
☐ whether you belong to a motoring organisation

Have these details ready before you phone and be sure to give the correct information.

For your own safety face the traffic when you speak on the telephone.

13.5 Mark one answer

You are on a motorway. When can you use hazard warning lights?

☐ When a vehicle is following too closely
☐ When you slow down quickly because of danger ahead
☐ When you are being towed by another vehicle
☐ When riding on the hard shoulder

Hazard lights will warn the traffic behind you that there is a potential hazard ahead.

Don't forget to turn them off again when your signal has been seen.

13.6 Mark one answer

Your motorcycle breaks down in a tunnel. What should you do?

☐ Stay with your motorcycle and wait for the Police
☐ Stand in the lane behind your motorcycle to warn others
☐ Stand in front of your motorcycle to warn oncoming drivers
☐ Switch on hazard lights then go and call for help immediately

Any broken down vehicle in a tunnel can cause serious congestion and danger to other traffic and drivers. If you break down you should get help without delay. Switch on your hazard warning lights and then go to an emergency telephone point to call for help.

13.7 Mark one answer

You are riding through a tunnel. Your motorcycle breaks down. What should you do?

☐ Switch on hazard warning lights
☐ Remain on your motorcycle
☐ Wait for the police to find you
☐ Rely on CCTV cameras seeing you

If your motorcycle breaks down in a tunnel it could present a danger to other traffic.

First switch on your hazard warning lights and then call for help from an emergency telephone point. Don't rely on being found by the police or being seen by a CCTV camera.

13.8 Mark one answer

You are travelling on a motorway. A bag falls from your motorcycle. There are valuables in the bag. What should you do?

☐ Go back carefully and collect the bag as quickly as possible
☐ Stop wherever you are and pick up the bag, but only when there is a safe gap
☐ Stop on the hard shoulder and use the emergency telephone to inform the authorities
☐ Stop on the hard shoulder and then retrieve the bag yourself

You must never walk on a motorway, however important you think retrieving your property may be. Your bag might be creating a hazard but not as great a hazard as you would be.

13.9 Mark one answer

You are on a motorway. Luggage falls from your motorcycle. What should you do?

☐ Stop at the next emergency telephone and report the hazard
☐ Stop on the motorway and put on hazard lights while you pick it up
☐ Walk back up the motorway to pick it up
☐ Pull up on the hard shoulder and wave traffic down

If any of your luggage falls onto the road, pull onto the hard shoulder near an emergency telephone and phone for assistance. Don't stop on the carriageway or attempt to retrieve anything.

13.10 Mark four answers

You are in collision with another vehicle. Someone is injured. Your motorcycle is damaged. Which FOUR of the following should you find out?

☐ Whether the driver owns the other vehicle involved
☐ The other driver's name, address and telephone number
☐ The make and registration number of the other vehicle
☐ The occupation of the other driver
☐ The details of the other driver's vehicle insurance
☐ Whether the other driver is licensed to drive

If you are involved in a collision where someone is injured, your first priority is to warn other traffic and call the emergency services.

When exchanging details, make sure you have all the information you need before you leave the scene. Don't ride your motorcycle if it is unroadworthy.

13.11 Mark one answer

You see a car on the hard shoulder of a motorway with a HELP pennant displayed. This means the driver is most likely to be

☐ a disabled person
☐ first aid trained
☐ a foreign visitor
☐ a rescue patrol person

If a disabled driver's vehicle breaks down and they are unable to walk to an emergency phone, they are advised to stay in their car and switch on the hazard warning lights. They may also display a 'Help' pennant in their vehicle.

13.12 Mark two answers

For which TWO should you use hazard warning lights?

☐ When you slow down quickly on a motorway because of a hazard ahead
☐ When you have broken down
☐ When you wish to stop on double yellow lines
☐ When you need to park on the pavement

Hazard warning lights are fitted to all modern cars and some motorcycles. They should only be used to warn other road users of a hazard ahead.

13.13 Mark one answer

When are you allowed to use hazard warning lights?

☐ When stopped and temporarily obstructing traffic
☐ When travelling during darkness without headlights
☐ When parked for shopping on double yellow lines
☐ When travelling slowly because you are lost

You must not use hazard warning lights when moving, except when slowing suddenly on a motorway or unrestricted dual carriageway to warn the traffic behind.
　Never use hazard warning lights to excuse dangerous or illegal parking.

13.14 Mark one answer

You are going through a congested tunnel and have to stop. What should you do?

☐ Pull up very close to the vehicle in front to save space
☐ Ignore any message signs as they are never up to date
☐ Keep a safe distance from the vehicle in front
☐ Make a U-turn and find another route

It's important to keep a safe distance from the vehicle in front at all times. This still applies in congested tunnels even if you are moving very slowly or have stopped. If the vehicle in front breaks down you may need room to manoeuvre past it.

13.15 Mark one answer

On the motorway, the hard shoulder should be used

☐ to answer a mobile phone
☐ when an emergency arises
☐ for a short rest when tired
☐ to check a road atlas

Pull onto the hard shoulder and use the emergency telephone to report your problem. This lets the emergency services know your exact location so they can send help. Never cross the carriageway to use the telephone on the other side.

13.16 Mark one answer

You arrive at the scene of a crash. Someone is bleeding badly from an arm wound. There is nothing embedded in it. What should you do?

☐ Apply pressure over the wound and keep the arm down
☐ Dab the wound
☐ Get them a drink
☐ Apply pressure over the wound and raise the arm

If possible, lay the casualty down. Check for anything that may be in the wound.
　Apply firm pressure to the wound using clean material, without pressing on anything which might be in it. Raising the arm above the level of the heart will also help to stem the flow of blood.

13.17 Mark one answer

You are at an incident where a casualty is unconscious. Their breathing should be checked. This should be done for at least

☐ 2 seconds
☐ 10 seconds
☐ 1 minute
☐ 2 minutes

Once the airway is open, check breathing.
　Listen and feel for breath. Do this by placing your cheek over their mouth and nose, and look to see if the chest rises.
　This should be done for up to 10 seconds.

13.18 Mark one answer

Following a collision someone has suffered a burn. The burn needs to be cooled. What is the shortest time it should be cooled for?

☐ 5 minutes
☐ 10 minutes
☐ 15 minutes
☐ 20 minutes

Check the casualty for shock and if possible try to cool the burn for at least ten minutes. Use a clean, cold non-toxic liquid preferably water.

13.19 Mark one answer

After a collision someone has suffered a burn. The burn needs to be cooled. What is the shortest time it should be cooled for?

☐ 30 seconds
☐ 60 seconds
☐ 5 minutes
☐ 10 minutes

It's important to cool a burn for at least ten minutes. Use a clean, cold non-toxic liquid preferably water. Bear in mind the person may also be in shock.

13.20 Mark one answer

A casualty is not breathing normally. Chest compressions should be given. At what rate?

☐ 50 per minute
☐ 100 per minute
☐ 200 per minute
☐ 250 per minute

If a casualty is not breathing normally chest compressions may be needed to maintain circulation. Place two hands on the centre of the chest and press down about 4–5 centimetres, at the rate of 100 per minute.

13.21 Mark one answer

A person has been injured. They may be suffering from shock. What are the warning signs to look for?

☐ Flushed complexion
☐ Warm dry skin
☐ Slow pulse
☐ Pale grey skin

The effects of shock may not be immediately obvious. Warning signs are rapid pulse, sweating, pale grey skin and rapid shallow breathing.

13.22 Mark one answer

You suspect that an injured person may be suffering from shock. What are the warning signs to look for?

☐ Warm dry skin
☐ Sweating
☐ Slow pulse
☐ Skin rash

Sometimes you may not realise that someone is in shock. The signs to look for are rapid pulse, sweating, pale grey skin and rapid shallow breathing.

13.23 Mark one answer

An injured person has been placed in the recovery position. They are unconscious but breathing normally. What else should be done?

☐ Press firmly between the shoulders
☐ Place their arms by their side
☐ Give them a hot sweet drink
☐ Check the airway is clear

After a casualty has been placed in the recovery position, their airway should be checked to make sure it's clear. Don't leave them alone until medical help arrives.

Where possible do NOT move a casualty unless there's further danger.

13.24 Mark one answer

An injured motorcyclist is lying unconscious in the road. You should always

☐ remove the safety helmet
☐ seek medical assistance
☐ move the person off the road
☐ remove the leather jacket

If someone has been injured, the sooner proper medical attention is given the better.

Send someone to phone for help or go yourself. An injured person should only be moved if they're in further danger. An injured motorcyclist's helmet should NOT be removed unless it is essential.

13.25 Mark one answer

You are on a motorway. A large box falls onto the road from a lorry. The lorry does not stop. You should

☐ go to the next emergency telephone and report the hazard
☐ catch up with the lorry and try to get the driver's attention
☐ stop close to the box until the police arrive
☐ pull over to the hard shoulder, then remove the box

Lorry drivers can be unaware of objects falling from their vehicles. If you see something fall onto a motorway look to see if the driver pulls over. If they don't stop, do not attempt to retrieve it yourself. Pull on to the hard shoulder near an emergency telephone and report the hazard. You will be connected to the police or a Highways Agency control centre.

13.26 Mark one answer

You are going through a long tunnel. What will warn you of congestion or an incident ahead?

☐ Hazard warning lines
☐ Other drivers flashing their lights
☐ Variable message signs
☐ Areas marked with hatch markings

Follow the instructions given by the signs or by tunnel officials.

In congested tunnels a minor incident can soon turn into a major one with serious or even fatal results.

13.27 Mark one answer

An adult casualty is not breathing. To maintain circulation, compressions should be given. What is the correct depth to press?

☐ 1 to 2 centimetres
☐ 4 to 5 centimetres
☐ 10 to 15 centimetres
☐ 15 to 20 centimetres

An adult casualty is not breathing normally.

To maintain circulation place two hands on the centre of the chest. Then press down 4 to 5 centimetres at a rate of 100 times per minute.

13.28 Mark two answers

You are the first to arrive at the scene of a crash. Which TWO of these should you do?

☐ Leave as soon as another motorist arrives
☐ Make sure engines are switched off
☐ Drag all casualties away from the vehicles
☐ Call the emergency services promptly

At a crash scene you can help in practical ways, even if you aren't trained in first aid.

Make sure you do not put yourself or anyone else in danger. The safest way to warn other traffic is by switching on your hazard warning lights.

13.29 Mark one answer

At the scene of a traffic incident you should

☐ not put yourself at risk
☐ go to those casualties who are screaming
☐ pull everybody out of their vehicles
☐ leave vehicle engines switched on

It's important that people at the scene of a collision do not create further risk to themselves or others. If the incident is on a motorway or major road, traffic will be approaching at speed. Do not put yourself at risk when trying to help casualties or warning other road users.

13.30 Mark three answers

You are the first person to arrive at an incident where people are badly injured. Which THREE should you do?

☐ Switch on your own hazard warning lights
☐ Make sure that someone telephones for an ambulance
☐ Try and get people who are injured to drink something
☐ Move the people who are injured clear of their vehicles
☐ Get people who are not injured clear of the scene

If you're the first to arrive at a crash scene the first concerns are the risk of further collision and fire. Ensuring that vehicle engines are switched off will reduce the risk of fire. Use hazard warning lights so that other traffic knows there's a need for caution. Make sure the emergency services are contacted, don't assume this has already been done.

13.31 Mark one answer

You arrive at the scene of a motorcycle crash. The rider is injured. When should the helmet be removed?

☐ Only when it is essential
☐ Always straight away
☐ Only when the motorcyclist asks
☐ Always, unless they are in shock

DO NOT remove a motorcyclist's helmet unless it is essential. Remember they may be suffering from shock. Don't give them anything to eat or drink but do reassure them confidently.

13.32 Mark three answers

You arrive at a serious motorcycle crash. The motorcyclist is unconscious and bleeding. Your THREE main priorities should be to

☐ try to stop the bleeding
☐ make a list of witnesses
☐ check their breathing
☐ take the numbers of other vehicles
☐ sweep up any loose debris
☐ check their airways

Further collisions and fire are the main dangers immediately after a crash. If possible get others to assist you and make the area safe. Help those involved and remember DR ABC, Danger, Response, Airway, Breathing, Compressions. This will help when dealing with any injuries.

13.33 Mark one answer

You arrive at an incident. A motorcyclist is unconscious. Your FIRST priority is the casualty's

☐ breathing
☐ bleeding
☐ broken bones
☐ bruising

At the scene of an incident always be aware of danger from further collisions or fire. The first priority when dealing with an unconscious person is to ensure they can breathe. This may involve clearing their airway if you can see an obstruction, or if they're having difficulty breathing.

13.34 Mark three answers

At an incident a casualty is unconscious. Which THREE of these should you check urgently?

☐ Circulation
☐ Airway
☐ Shock
☐ Breathing
☐ Broken bones

Remember DR ABC. An unconscious casualty may have difficulty breathing.

Check that their airway is clear by tilting the head back gently and unblock it if necessary. Then make sure they are breathing. If there is bleeding, stem the flow by placing clean material over any wounds but without pressing on any objects in the wound. Compressions may need to be given to maintain circulation.

13.35 Mark three answers

You arrive at the scene of an incident. It has just happened and someone is unconscious. Which THREE of these should be given urgent priority to help them?

☐ Clear the airway and keep it open
☐ Try to get them to drink water
☐ Check that they are breathing
☐ Look for any witnesses
☐ Stop any heavy bleeding
☐ Take the numbers of vehicles involved

Make sure that the emergency services are called immediately. Once first aid has been given, stay with the casualty.

13.36 Mark three answers

At an incident someone is unconscious. Your THREE main priorities should be to

☐ sweep up the broken glass
☐ take the names of witnesses
☐ count the number of vehicles involved
☐ check the airway is clear
☐ make sure they are breathing
☐ stop any heavy bleeding

Remember this procedure by saying DR ABC. This stands for Danger, Response, Airway, Breathing, Compressions.

13.37 Mark three answers

You have stopped at an incident to give help. Which THREE things should you do?

☐ Keep injured people warm and comfortable
☐ Keep injured people calm by talking to them reassuringly
☐ Keep injured people on the move by walking them around
☐ Give injured people a warm drink
☐ Make sure that injured people are not left alone

There are a number of things you can do to help, even without expert training. Be aware of further danger and fire, make sure the area is safe. People may be in shock.

Don't give them anything to eat or drink.

Keep them warm and comfortable and reassure them. Don't move injured people unless there is a risk of further danger.

13.38 Mark three answers

You arrive at an incident. It has just happened and someone is injured. Which THREE should be given urgent priority?

☐ Stop any severe bleeding
☐ Give them a warm drink
☐ Check they are breathing
☐ Take numbers of vehicles involved
☐ Look for witnesses
☐ Clear their airway and keep it open

The first priority with a casualty is to make sure their airway is clear and they are breathing. Any wounds should be checked for objects and then bleeding stemmed using clean material. Ensure the emergency services are called, they are the experts. If you're not first aid trained consider getting training. It might save a life.

13.39 Mark one answer

Which of the following should you NOT do at the scene of a collision?

☐ Warn other traffic by switching on your hazard warning lights
☐ Call the emergency services immediately
☐ Offer someone a cigarette to calm them down
☐ Ask drivers to switch off their engines

Keeping casualties or witnesses calm is important, but never offer a cigarette because of the risk of fire. Bear in mind they may be in shock. Don't offer an injured person anything to eat or drink. They may have internal injuries or need surgery.

13.40 Mark two answers

There has been a collision. A driver is suffering from shock. What TWO of these should you do?

☐ Give them a drink
☐ Reassure them
☐ Not leave them alone
☐ Offer them a cigarette
☐ Ask who caused the incident

Be aware they could have an injury that is not immediately obvious. Ensure the emergency services are called. Reassure and stay with them until the experts arrive.

13.41 Mark one answer

You have to treat someone for shock at the scene of an incident. You should

☐ reassure them constantly
☐ walk them around to calm them down
☐ give them something cold to drink
☐ cool them down as soon as possible

Stay with the casualty and talk to them quietly and firmly to calm and reassure them. Avoid moving them unnecessarily in case they are injured. Keep them warm, but don't give them anything to eat or drink.

13.42 Mark one answer

You arrive at the scene of a motorcycle crash. No other vehicle is involved. The rider is unconscious and lying in the middle of the road. The FIRST thing you should do is

☐ move the rider out of the road
☐ warn other traffic
☐ clear the road of debris
☐ give the rider reassurance

The motorcyclist is in an extremely vulnerable position, exposed to further danger from traffic. Approaching vehicles need advance warning in order to slow down and safely take avoiding action or stop. Don't put yourself or anyone else at risk. Use the hazard warning lights on your vehicle to alert other road users to the danger.

13.43 Mark one answer

At an incident a small child is not breathing. To restore normal breathing you should breathe into their mouth

☐ sharply
☐ gently
☐ heavily
☐ rapidly

If a young child has stopped breathing, first check that the airway is clear. Then give compressions to the chest using one hand (two fingers for an infant) and begin mouth-to-mouth resuscitation. Breathe very gently and continue the procedure until they can breathe without help.

13.44 Mark three answers

At an incident a casualty is not breathing. To start the process to restore normal breathing you should

☐ tilt their head forward
☐ clear the airway
☐ turn them on their side
☐ tilt their head back gently
☐ pinch the nostrils together
☐ put their arms across their chest

It's important to ensure that the airways are clear before you start mouth-to-mouth resuscitation. Gently tilt their head back and use your finger to check for and remove any obvious obstruction in the mouth.

13.45 Mark one answer

You arrive at an incident. There has been an engine fire and someone's hands and arms have been burnt. You should NOT

☐ douse the burn thoroughly with clean cool non-toxic liquid
☐ lay the casualty down on the ground
☐ remove anything sticking to the burn
☐ reassure them confidently and repeatedly

This could cause further damage and infection to the wound. Your first priority is to cool the burn with a clean, cool, non-toxic liquid, preferably water. Don't forget the casualty may be in shock.

13.46 Mark one answer

You arrive at an incident where someone is suffering from severe burns. You should

☐ apply lotions to the injury
☐ burst any blisters
☐ remove anything stuck to the burns
☐ douse the burns with clean cool non-toxic liquid

Use a liquid that is clean, cold and non-toxic, preferably water. Its coolness will help take the heat out of the burn and relieve the pain. Keep the wound doused for at least ten minutes. If blisters appear don't attempt to burst them as this could lead to infection.

13.47 Mark two answers

You arrive at an incident. A pedestrian has a severe bleeding leg wound. It is not broken and there is nothing in the wound. What TWO of these should you do?

☐ Dab the wound to stop bleeding
☐ Keep both legs flat on the ground
☐ Apply firm pressure to the wound
☐ Raise the leg to lessen bleeding
☐ Fetch them a warm drink

First check for anything that may be in the wound such as glass. If there's nothing in it apply a pad of clean cloth or bandage.
  Raising the leg will lessen the flow of blood.
  Don't tie anything tightly round the leg. This will restrict circulation and can result in long-term injury.

13.48 Mark one answer

At an incident a casualty is unconscious but still breathing. You should only move them if

☐ an ambulance is on its way
☐ bystanders advise you to
☐ there is further danger
☐ bystanders will help you to

Do not move a casualty unless there is further danger, for example, from other traffic or fire. They may have unseen or internal injuries. Moving them unnecessarily could cause further injury. Do NOT remove a motorcyclists helmet unless it's essential.

13.49 Mark one answer

At a collision you suspect a casualty has back injuries. The area is safe. You should

☐ offer them a drink
☐ not move them
☐ raise their legs
☐ not call an ambulance

Talk to the casualty and keep them calm.
  Do not attempt to move them as this could cause further injury. Call an ambulance at the first opportunity.

13.50 Mark one answer

At an incident it is important to look after any casualties. When the area is safe, you should

☐ get them out of the vehicle
☐ give them a drink
☐ give them something to eat
☐ keep them in the vehicle

When the area is safe and there's no danger from other traffic or fire it's better not to move casualties. Moving them may cause further injury.

13.51 Mark one answer

A tanker is involved in a collision. Which sign shows that it is carrying dangerous goods?

☐

☐

☐

☐

There will be an orange label on the side and rear of the tanker. Look at this carefully and report what it says when you phone the emergency services. Details of hazard warning plates are given in *The Highway Code*.

13.52 Mark three answers

You are involved in a collision. Because of this which THREE of these documents may the police ask you to produce?

☐ Vehicle registration document
☐ Driving licence
☐ Theory test certificate
☐ Insurance certificate
☐ MOT test certificate
☐ Vehicle service record

You MUST stop if you have been involved in a collision which results in injury or damage. The police may ask to see your documents at the time or later at a police station.

13.53 Mark one answer

After a collision someone is unconscious in their vehicle. When should you call the emergency services?

☐ Only as a last resort
☐ As soon as possible
☐ After you have woken them up
☐ After checking for broken bones

It is important to make sure that emergency services arrive on the scene as soon as possible. When a person is unconscious, they could have serious injuries that are not immediately obvious.

13.54 Mark one answer

A casualty has an injured arm. They can move it freely but it is bleeding. Why should you get them to keep it in a raised position?

☐ Because it will ease the pain
☐ It will help them to be seen more easily
☐ To stop them touching other people
☐ It will help to reduce the blood flow

If a casualty is bleeding heavily, raise the limb to a higher position. This will help to reduce the blood flow. Before raising the limb you should make sure that it is not broken.

13.55 Mark one answer

You are going through a tunnel. What systems are provided to warn of any incidents, collisions or congestion?

☐ Double white centre lines
☐ Variable message signs
☐ Chevron 'distance markers'
☐ Rumble strips

Take notice of any instructions given on variable message signs or by tunnel officials. They will warn you of any incidents or congestion ahead and advise you what to do.

13.56 Mark one answer

A collision has just happened. An injured person is lying in a busy road. What is the FIRST thing you should do to help?

☐ Treat the person for shock
☐ Warn other traffic
☐ Place them in the recovery position
☐ Make sure the injured person is kept warm

The most immediate danger is further collisions and fire. You could warn other traffic by displaying an advance warning triangle or sign (but not on a motorway), switching on hazard warning lights or by any other means that does not put you or others at risk.

13.57 Mark two answers

At an incident a casualty has stopped breathing. You should

☐ remove anything that is blocking the mouth
☐ keep the head tilted forwards as far as possible
☐ raise the legs to help with circulation
☐ try to give the casualty something to drink
☐ tilt the head back gently to clear the airway

Unblocking the airway and gently tilting the head back will help the casualty to breathe.

They will then be in the correct position if mouth-to-mouth resuscitation is required.

Don't move a casualty unless there's further danger.

13.58 Mark four answers

You are at the scene of an incident. Someone is suffering from shock. You should

☐ reassure them constantly
☐ offer them a cigarette
☐ keep them warm
☐ avoid moving them if possible
☐ avoid leaving them alone
☐ give them a warm drink

The signs of shock may not be immediately obvious. Prompt treatment can help to minimise the effects. Lay the casualty down, loosen tight clothing, call an ambulance and check their breathing and pulse.

13.59 Mark one answer

There has been a collision. A motorcyclist is lying injured and unconscious. Unless it's essential, why should you usually NOT attempt to remove their helmet?

☐ Because they may not want you to
☐ This could result in more serious injury
☐ They will get too cold if you do this
☐ Because you could scratch the helmet

When someone is injured, any movement which is not absolutely necessary should be avoided since it could make injuries worse. Unless it is essential, it's generally safer to leave a motorcyclist's helmet in place.

motorcycle loading

14.1 Mark one answer

If a trailer swerves or snakes when you are towing it you should

☐ ease off the throttle and reduce your speed
☐ let go of the handlebars and let it correct itself
☐ brake hard and hold the brake on
☐ increase your speed as quickly as possible

Don't be tempted to use harsh braking to stop swerving or snaking as this won't help the situation. You should reduce your speed by easing off the throttle.

14.2 Mark two answers

When riding with a sidecar attached for the first time you should

☐ keep your speed down
☐ be able to stop more quickly
☐ accelerate quickly round bends
☐ approach corners more carefully

A motorcycle with a sidecar will feel very different to ride than a solo motorcycle.
Keep your speed down until you get used to the outfit, especially when negotiating bends and junctions.

14.3 Mark three answers

When carrying extra weight on a motorcycle, you may need to make adjustments to the

☐ headlight
☐ gears
☐ suspension
☐ tyres
☐ footrests

Carrying extra weight such as luggage or a pillion passenger, will probably affect the aim of the headlight. Adjust this so that it does not dazzle other road users. The feel and balance will also be affected so you may need to adjust the suspension and tyre pressures to help overcome this.

14.4 Mark one answer　　　NI EXEMPT

To obtain the full category 'A' licence through the accelerated or direct access scheme, your motorcycle must be

☐ solo with maximum power 25kw (33 bhp)
☐ solo with maximum power of 11kw (14.6 bhp)
☐ fitted with a sidecar and have minimum power of 35kw (46.6 bhp)
☐ solo with minimum power of 35 kw (46.6 bhp)

From the age of 21 you may take a category A test via the Direct or Accelerated Access schemes. The motorcycle you use for your practical test under the Direct or Accelerated Access scheme is one that has an engine with a minimum power output of 35 kw (46.6 bhp).

14.5 Mark one answer

Any load that is carried on a luggage rack MUST be

☐ securely fastened when riding
☐ carried only when strictly necessary
☐ visible when you are riding
☐ covered with plastic sheeting

Don't risk losing any luggage while riding: it could fall into the path of following vehicles and cause danger. It is an offence to travel with an insecure load.

14.6 Mark one answer

Pillion passengers should

☐ have a provisional motorcycle licence
☐ be lighter than the rider
☐ always wear a helmet
☐ signal for the rider

Pillion passengers must sit astride the machine on a proper passenger seat and rear footrests should be fitted. They must wear a safety helmet which is correctly fastened.

14.7   Mark one answer
Pillion passengers should

☐ give the rider directions
☐ lean with the rider when going round bends
☐ check the road behind for the rider
☐ give arm signals for the rider

When riding with a pillion passenger, your motorcycle may feel unbalanced and the acceleration and braking distance may also be affected. Make sure your passenger knows they must lean with you while cornering. If they don't, they could cause the motorcycle to become unstable and difficult to control.

14.8   Mark one answer
When you are going around a corner your pillion passenger should

☐ give arm signals for you
☐ check behind for other vehicles
☐ lean with you on bends
☐ lean to one side to see ahead

A pillion passenger should not give signals or look round for you.
If your passenger has never been on a motorcycle before, make sure they know that they need to lean with you while going around bends.

14.9   Mark one answer
Which of these may need to be adjusted when carrying a pillion passenger?

☐ Indicators
☐ Exhaust
☐ Fairing
☐ Headlight

Your headlight must be properly adjusted to avoid dazzling other road users. You will probably need to do this when carrying a heavy load or the extra weight of a pillion passenger. You may also need to adjust suspension and tyre pressures.

14.10   Mark one answer
You are towing a trailer with your motorcycle. You should remember that your

☐ stopping distance may increase
☐ fuel consumption will improve
☐ tyre grip will increase
☐ stability will improve

When you tow a trailer remember that you must obey the relevant speed limits. Ensure that the trailer is hitched correctly and that any load in the trailer is secure. You should also bear in mind that your stopping distance may increase.

14.11   Mark one answer
Heavy loads in a motorcycle top box may

☐ improve stability
☐ cause low-speed wobble
☐ cause a puncture
☐ improve braking

Carrying heavy loads in your top box could make your motorcycle unstable because the weight is high up and at the very back of the machine. Take extra care.

14.12   Mark one answer
Who is responsible for making sure that a motorcycle is not overloaded?

☐ The rider of the motorcycle
☐ The owner of the items being carried
☐ The licensing authority
☐ The owner of the motorcycle

Correct loading is the responsibility of the rider. Overloading a motorcycle can seriously affect the control and handling. It could result in a crash with serious or even fatal consequences.

14.13   Mark one answer
Before fitting a sidecar to a motorcycle you should

☐ have the wheels balanced
☐ have the engine tuned
☐ pass the extended bike test
☐ check that the motorcycle is suitable

Make sure that the sidecar is fixed securely and properly aligned. If your motorcycle is registered on or after 1 August 1981 the sidecar must be fitted on the left-hand side of the motorcycle.

14.14 Mark one answer

You are using throw-over saddlebags. Why is it important to make sure they are evenly loaded?

☐ They will be uncomfortable for you to sit on
☐ They will slow your motorcycle down
☐ They could make your motorcycle unstable
☐ They will be uncomfortable for a pillion passenger to sit on

Panniers or saddlebags should be loaded so that you carry about the same weight in each bag. Uneven loading could affect your balance, especially when cornering.

14.15 Mark one answer

You are carrying a bulky tank bag. What could this affect?

☐ Your ability to steer
☐ Your ability to accelerate
☐ Your view ahead
☐ Your insurance premium

If your tank bag is too bulky it could get in the way of your arms or restrict the movement of the handlebars.

14.16 Mark one answer   NI EXEMPT

To carry a pillion passenger you must

☐ hold a full car licence
☐ hold a full motorcycle licence
☐ be over the age of 21
☐ be over the age of 25

The law requires you to have a full licence for the category of motorcycle you are riding before you can carry a pillion passenger.

14.17 Mark one answer

When carrying a heavy load on your luggage rack, you may need to adjust your

☐ carburettor
☐ fuel tap
☐ seating position
☐ tyre pressures

The load will increase the overall weight that your motorcycle is carrying. You may need to adjust your tyre pressures according to the manufacturer's instructions to allow for this. You may also need to adjust your headlight beam alignment.

14.18 Mark one answer

You are carrying a pillion passenger. When following other traffic, which of the following should you do?

☐ Keep to your normal following distance
☐ Get your passenger to keep checking behind
☐ Keep further back than you normally would
☐ Get your passenger to signal for you

The extra weight of a passenger may increase your stopping distance. Allow for this when following another vehicle by increasing the separation distance.

14.19 Mark one answer

You should only carry a child as a pillion passenger when

☐ they are over 14 years old
☐ they are over 16 years old
☐ they can reach the floor from the seat
☐ they can reach the handholds and footrests

Any passenger you carry must be able to reach footrests and handholds properly to remain safe on your machine. Ensure they are wearing protective weatherproof kit and a properly fitting helmet.

14.20 Mark one answer

You have fitted a sidecar to your motorcycle. You should make sure that the sidecar

☐ has a registration plate
☐ is correctly aligned
☐ has a waterproof cover
☐ has a solid cover

If the sidecar is not correctly aligned to the mounting points it will result in the outfit being difficult to control and even dangerous.
   Riding with a sidecar attached requires a different technique to riding a solo motorcycle and you should keep your speed down while learning this skill.

14.21 Mark one answer

You are riding a motorcycle and sidecar. The extra weight

☐ will allow you to corner more quickly
☐ will allow you to brake later for hazards
☐ may increase your stopping distance
☐ will improve your fuel consumption

You will need to adapt your riding technique when riding a motorcycle fitted with a sidecar. The extra weight will affect the handling and may increase your overall stopping distance.

14.22 Mark one answer

You are carrying a pillion passenger. To allow for the extra weight which of the following is most likely to need adjustment?

☐ Preload on the front forks
☐ Preload on the rear shock absorber(s)
☐ The balance of the rear wheel
☐ The front and rear wheel alignment

When carrying a passenger or other extra weight, you may need to make adjustments, particularly to the rear shock absorber(s), tyre pressures and headlight alignment. Check your owner's handbook for details.

14.23 Mark one answer

A trailer on a motorcycle must be no wider than

☐ 0.5 metres (1 foot 8 inches)
☐ 1 metre (3 feet 3 inches)
☐ 1.5 metres (4 feet 11 inches)
☐ 2 metres (6 feet 6 inches)

When you're towing a trailer you must remember that you may not be able to filter through traffic. Don't forget that the trailer is there, especially when riding round bends and negotiating junctions.

14.24 Mark one answer

You want to tow a trailer with your motorcycle. Which one applies?

☐ The motorcycle should be attached to a sidecar
☐ The trailer should weigh more than the motorcycle
☐ The trailer should be fitted with brakes
☐ The trailer should NOT be more than 1 metre (3 feet 3 inches) wide

To tow a trailer behind a motorcycle you must have, a full motorcycle licence and a motorcycle with an engine larger than 125 cc. Motorcycle trailers must not exceed 1 metre (3 feet 3 inches) in width.

14.25 Mark one answer

You have a sidecar fitted to your motorcycle. What effect will it have?

☐ Reduce stability
☐ Make steering lighter
☐ Increase stopping distance
☐ Increase fuel economy

If you want to fit a sidecar to your motorcycle make sure that your motorcycle is suitable to cope with the extra load.
Make sure that the sidecar is fixed correctly and properly aligned. A sidecar will alter the handling considerably. Give yourself time to adjust to the different characteristics.

14.26 Mark three answers

Which THREE must a learner motorcyclist under 21 NOT do?

☐ Ride a motorcycle with an engine capacity greater than 125 cc
☐ Pull a trailer
☐ Carry a pillion passenger
☐ Ride faster than 30 mph
☐ Use the right-hand lane on dual carriageways

Learner motorcyclists are not allowed to pull a trailer or carry a pillion passenger. In addition, if you are a learner motorcyclist under 21, you may not ride a motorcycle on the road with an engine capacity of more than 125 cc.

14.27 Mark one answer

Carrying a heavy load in your top box may

☐ cause high speed-weave
☐ cause a puncture
☐ use less fuel
☐ improve stability

Carrying a heavy weight high up and at the very back of the motorcycle can make it unstable, especially when travelling at high speeds.

14.28 Mark two answers

You want to tow a trailer behind your motorcycle. You should

☐ display a 'long vehicle' sign
☐ fit a larger battery
☐ have a full motorcycle licence
☐ ensure that your engine is more than 125 cc
☐ ensure that your motorcycle has shaft drive

When you tow a trailer your stopping distance will be increased. Any load on the trailer must be secure and the trailer must be fitted to the motorcycle correctly. You must obey the lower speed limit restrictions that apply to vehicles with trailers. Any trailer towed by a motorcycle must be no wider than 1 metre. The laden weight should be no greater than 150 kg or two-thirds of the kerbside weight of the motorcycle, whichever is less.

14.29 Mark two answers

To carry a pillion passenger your motorcycle should be fitted with

☐ rear footrests
☐ an engine of 250 cc or over
☐ a top box
☐ a grab handle
☐ a proper pillion seat

When carrying a pillion there are certain things they should NOT do. Before carrying a pillion tell them NOT to, give hand signals, lean away from the rider when cornering, fidget or move around, put their feet down to try and support the machine when you stop, or wear long, loose items that might get caught in the rear wheel or drive chain.

14.30 Mark three answers

Your motorcycle is fitted with a top box. It is unwise to carry a heavy load in the top box because it may

☐ reduce stability
☐ improve stability
☐ make turning easier
☐ cause high-speed weave
☐ cause low-speed wobble
☐ increase fuel economy

Carrying a heavy weight high up and at the very back of the motorcycle can cause problems in maintaining control.

14.31 Mark one answer

You hold a provisional motorcycle licence. Are you allowed to carry a pillion passenger?

☐ Only if the passenger holds a full licence
☐ Not at any time
☐ Not unless you are undergoing training
☐ Only if the passenger is under 21

You are not allowed to carry a pillion passenger until you hold a full motorcycle licence. This allows you to gain riding experience. Even when you've passed, don't carry a passenger if you are not confident of being able to do so safely. You are responsible for their safety.

14.32 Mark one answer

Overloading your motorcycle can seriously affect the

☐ gearbox
☐ weather protection
☐ handling
☐ battery life

Any load will affect the handling of your motorcycle by changing its centre of gravity. Try to keep any load as low as possible. When using panniers spread the weight evenly. Avoid carrying heavy items in a top box, as this could make your steering dangerously light.

14.33 Mark two answers

You are towing a small trailer on a busy three-lane motorway. All the lanes are open. You must

☐ not exceed 60 mph
☐ not overtake
☐ have a stabiliser fitted
☐ use only the left and centre lanes

You should be aware of the motorway regulations for vehicles towing trailers.

These state that a vehicle towing a trailer must not

• use the right-hand lane of a three-lane motorway unless directed to do so, for example, at roadworks or due to a lane closure

• exceed 60 mph.

answers

Section One
Alertness

1.1	Take a 'lifesaver' glance over your shoulder
1.2	A final, rearward glance before changing direction
1.3	Slow down before the bend
1.4	slow down or stop
1.5	extend the mirror arms
1.6	have parked in a safe place
1.7	As soon as the other vehicle passes you
1.8	look over your shoulder for a final check
1.9	lose concentration
1.10	Slow down and stop
1.11	moving off
1.12	changing direction
1.13	changing lanes
1.14	To give you the best view of the road behind
1.15	a final rearward glance
1.16	Never, you should always look for yourself
1.17	Check for yourself before pulling out
1.18	Use your mirrors
1.19	Mirrors may not cover blind spots
	Drivers behind you would be warned
1.20	Make a 'lifesaver' check
1.21	Check that the central reservation is wide enough
1.22	be sure you know where all controls and switches are
1.23	take a 'lifesaver' glance over your left shoulder
1.24	take a 'lifesaver' glance over your left shoulder
1.25	Take a 'lifesaver' glance over your left shoulder
1.26	Before moving into the left lane
1.27	concentrate on what is happening ahead
1.28	look over your shoulder for a final check
1.29	slow down
	consider using your horn
	beware of pedestrians
1.30	Approaching a dip in the road
1.31	overtaking drivers to move back to the left
1.32	pull up in a suitable place
1.33	To make you aware of your speed
1.34	be ready to stop
1.35	Use the mirrors
1.36	allows the driver to see you in the mirrors
1.37	To assess how your actions will affect following traffic
1.38	Stop and then move forward slowly and carefully for a proper view

Section Two
Attitude

2.1	slow down and prepare to stop
2.2	well back so that you can see past the vehicle
2.3	slow down and be ready to stop
2.4	the pedestrians have reached a safe position
2.5	pull in safely when you can, to let vehicles behind you overtake
2.6	the driver ahead to see you in their mirrors
	you to be seen by traffic that is emerging from junctions ahead
2.7	showing off and being competitive
2.8	give way to pedestrians already on the crossing
2.9	there may be another vehicle coming
2.10	following another vehicle too closely
2.11	your view ahead is reduced

2.12	four seconds
2.13	Slow down
2.14	Bomb disposal
	Blood transfusion
	Police patrol
2.15	Coastguard
	Bomb disposal
	Mountain rescue
2.16	pull over as soon as safely possible to let it pass
2.17	Doctor's car
2.18	doctor on an emergency call
2.19	tram drivers
2.20	Cycles
2.21	To alert others to your presence
2.22	in the right-hand lane
2.23	To help other road users know what you intend to do
2.24	Toucan
2.25	allow the vehicle to overtake
2.26	to let them know that you are there
2.27	Slow down and look both ways
2.28	give way to pedestrians who are crossing
2.29	to keep a safe gap from the vehicle in front
2.30	Steady amber
2.31	Slow down, gradually increasing the gap between you and the vehicle in front
2.32	A doctor is answering an emergency call
2.33	slow down and give way if it is safe to do so

Section Three
Safety and your motorcycle

3.1	the rear wheel to lock
3.2	To keep the machine roadworthy
3.3	Carefully, until the shiny surface is worn off
3.4	be seen more easily by other motorists
3.5	continue to wear protective clothing
3.6	It helps other road users to see you
3.7	To be seen better at night
3.8	Touring
3.9	replace it
3.10	1 mm
3.11	Using a dipped headlight
	Wearing a fluorescent jacket
	Wearing a white helmet
3.12	stop as quickly as possible and try to find the cause
3.13	be correctly inflated
	have sufficient tread depth
3.14	a locked wheel
3.15	cause much more engine wear
3.16	Slow gently to a stop
3.17	have lower exhaust emissions
3.18	Soapy water
3.19	Stop as soon as possible and wipe it
3.20	Boots
3.21	Velcro tab
3.22	Use more fuel
3.23	Reflective clothing
	A white helmet
3.24	exhaust emissions
3.25	rear wheel
3.26	Your wheel alignment
3.27	Between 1 and 2 times
3.28	The rear wheel alignment

3.29	Worn steering head bearings
3.30	Yes, oil could drip onto your tyre
3.31	Dripping oil could reduce the grip of your tyre
3.32	Your brakes could be affected by dripping oil
3.33	Incorrect rear wheel alignment
3.34	Your motorcycle could be unstable on bends
3.35	Replace the tyre before riding the motorcycle
3.36	By checking the vehicle owner's manual
3.37	oiled
3.38	increased tyre wear
3.39	Instability when cornering
3.40	Stability
3.41	Because it gives best protection from the weather
3.42	use the steering lock
3.43	give extra security
3.44	Leave it in a low gear
3.45	stop the engine in an emergency
3.46	Maintain a reduced speed throughout
3.47	Before a long journey
3.48	Take it to a local authority site
3.49	Check out any strong smell of petrol
3.50	Wearing a black helmet
3.51	the helmet is not fastened correctly
3.52	When carrying a passenger
	When carrying a load
	When riding at high speeds
3.53	Number plate
	Headlight
3.54	stop the engine in an emergency
3.55	rear wheel alignment
3.56	It may be damaged
3.57	Tread less than 1 mm deep
	A large bulge in the wall
	A recut tread
	Exposed ply or cord
3.58	by regular adjustment when necessary
	by oiling cables and pivots regularly
3.59	better fuel economy
	cleaner exhaust emissions
3.60	lock the rear wheel
3.61	In poor visibility
3.62	carrying a pillion passenger
3.63	Oil leaks
3.64	Not on any occasion
3.65	Use the engine cut-out switch
3.66	ride with your headlight on
	wear reflective clothing
3.67	Braking
	Steering
3.68	between 11.30 pm and 7 am in a built-up area
3.69	reduces noise pollution
	uses electricity
	reduces town traffic
3.70	they use electric power
3.71	help the traffic flow
3.72	traffic calming measures
3.73	toxic exhaust gases
3.74	exhaust fumes cleaner
3.75	When tyres are cold
3.76	Between 11.30 pm and 7 am
3.77	under-inflated
3.78	Take it to a local authority site
	Take it to a garage
3.79	Harsh braking and accelerating
3.80	Distilled water
3.81	Where the speed limit exceeds 30 mph
3.82	air pollution
	damage to buildings
	using up of natural resources

3.83	The braking system
	Wheel alignment
	The suspension
3.84	Just above the cell plates
3.85	left with parking lights on
3.86	Look at a map
3.87	a motoring organisation
3.88	Use a route planner on the internet
3.89	Print or write down the route
3.90	You will have an easier journey
3.91	you will have a more pleasant journey
3.92	it will help to ease congestion
3.93	you are less likely to be delayed
3.94	Your original route may be blocked
3.95	Your first route may be blocked
3.96	allow plenty of time for your journey
3.97	increased fuel consumption
3.98	20%
3.99	Brake fluid level

Section Four
Safety margins

4.1	with a passenger
4.2	Use both brakes
4.3	ease off the throttle
4.4	think if you need to ride at all
4.5	It helps other road users to see you
4.6	visibility is 100 metres (328 feet) or less
4.7	at night when street lighting is poor
	on motorways during darkness
	at times of poor visibility
4.8	make it hard to see unlit objects
4.9	Keep the engine running fast to keep water out of the exhaust
	Ride slowly and test your brakes when you are out of the water
4.10	brakes
4.11	slowly in a low gear
4.12	use tinted glasses, lenses or visors
4.13	Use your dipped headlight
	Keep your visor or goggles clear
4.14	The painted lines may be slippery
4.15	wear reflective clothing
4.16	Wear suitable clothing
4.17	ride with your headlight on dipped beam
	wear reflective clothing
4.18	in the rain
4.19	Potholes
	Drain covers
	Oil patches
	Loose gravel
4.20	It can make the surface slippery
	It can reduce tyre grip
4.21	Traffic could be emerging and may not see you
4.22	Heavy braking
4.23	Keep your speed down
4.24	Ease off the throttle smoothly
4.25	Ride slowly, braking lightly
4.26	switch on your dipped headlights
	be aware of others not using their headlights
4.27	the separation distance when riding in good conditions
4.28	the painted area
4.29	overtaking a large vehicle
	riding in exposed places
4.30	A bus may have left patches of oil
4.31	38 metres (125 feet)
4.32	Ease off the throttle

389

4.33	ten times the normal distance		**5.33**	Yes, regular stops help concentration
4.34	ten times		**5.34**	try not to react
4.35	passing pedal cyclists		**5.35**	Stop before the barrier
4.36	To improve your view of the road		**5.36**	Be prepared to stop for any traffic
4.37	go slowly while gently applying the brakes		**5.37**	Wait for the pedestrian in the road to cross
4.38	The grip of the tyres		**5.38**	Stay behind until you are past the junction
	The braking		**5.39**	Be prepared to give way to large vehicles in the middle of the road
4.39	On an open stretch of road		**5.40**	They give a wider field of vision
4.40	96 metres (315 feet)		**5.41**	approach with care and keep to the left of the lorry
4.41	73 metres (240 feet)		**5.42**	stay behind and not overtake
4.42	Drop back to regain a safe distance		**5.43**	The bus may move out into the road
4.43	53 metres (175 feet)		**5.44**	a school bus
4.44	36 metres (118 feet)		**5.45**	Car doors opening suddenly
4.45	Pass wide			Children running out from between vehicles
4.46	Allow extra room		**5.46**	The cyclist may swerve out into the road
4.47	38 metres (125 feet)		**5.47**	stop and take a break
4.48	Increase your distance from the vehicle in front		**5.48**	travel at a reduced speed
4.49	Reduce your speed and increase the gap in front		**5.49**	Because of the bend
4.50	reduce speed in good time choose an appropriate lane in good time			Because of the level crossing
	keep the correct separation distance		**5.50**	To enable you to change lanes early
			5.51	Traffic in both directions can use the middle lane to overtake

Section Five
Hazard awareness

			5.52	A disabled person's vehicle
			5.53	Stop
5.1	You may lose concentration		**5.54**	It may suddenly move off
	Your reaction times may be slower			People may cross the road in front of it
5.2	By signalling with your right arm		**5.55**	If you are turning left shortly afterwards
5.3	find a way of getting home without riding			When you are approaching a junction
5.4	Reduced co-ordination			When your view ahead is blocked
	Increased confidence		**5.56**	Less control
	Poor judgement			A false sense of confidence
5.5	At all times when riding			Poor judgement of speed
5.6	slow down your reactions to hazards			
	worsen your judgement of speed			
	give a false sense of confidence			

Section Six
Vulnerable road users

5.7	Tinted		**6.1**	it will reduce your view ahead
5.8	When riding on a motorway to warn traffic behind of a hazard ahead		**6.2**	slow down
				stop if necessary
5.9	Using ear plugs			give plenty of room
5.10	Wear ear plugs		**6.3**	be ready to slow down and stop
5.11	To help to prevent ear damage		**6.4**	keep calm and be patient
5.12	Stick to non-alcoholic drinks		**6.5**	slow down gradually to increase the gap in front of you
5.13	Your insurance may become invalid		**6.6**	be prepared to stop
5.14	To check for overtaking vehicles		**6.7**	The rider may be blown across in front of you
5.15	Ask your doctor		**6.8**	allow the person to cross
	Check the medicine label			be patient
5.16	When your motorcycle has broken down and is causing an obstruction		**6.9**	At junctions
			6.10	To check for any overtaking traffic
5.17	A soft road surface		**6.11**	Sounding your horn
5.18	Traffic emerging			Revving your engine
5.19	On a large goods vehicle		**6.12**	Lack of experience and judgement
	On a builder's skip placed on the road		**6.13**	They are often over-confident of their own ability
5.20	The cyclist crossing the road		**6.14**	You should not wait or park your motorcycle here
5.21	The parked car (arrowed A)		**6.15**	
5.22	Slow down and get ready to stop			
5.23	Pedestrians stepping out between cars			
	Doors opening on parked cars			
	Cars leaving parking spaces			
5.24	bend sharply to the left			
5.25	slow down and allow the cyclist to turn			
5.26	There is reduced visibility			
5.27	buses			
5.28	Lorry		**6.16**	give way to them
5.29	behind the line, then edge forward to see clearly		**6.17**	wait and allow them to cross
5.30	ignore the error and stay calm		**6.18**	give way to the pedestrians who are already crossing
5.31	react very quickly		**6.19**	Pedestrians
5.32	A school crossing patrol		**6.20**	overtaking on your right
			6.21	cyclists can use it

6.22   By displaying a stop sign
6.23   On the rear of a school bus or coach
6.24

6.25   A route for pedestrians and cyclists
6.26   deaf and blind
6.27   Be patient and allow them to cross in their own time
6.28   be careful, they may misjudge your speed
6.29   Give the cyclist plenty of room
6.30   Motorcycles
         Bicycles
6.31   They are harder to see
6.32   Motorcycles are small and hard to see
6.33   So that the rider can be seen more easily
6.34   drivers often do not see them
6.35   stay behind
6.36   they need to check for traffic in their blind area
6.37   Cyclists
         Motorcyclists
         Pedestrians
6.38   when approaching junctions
6.39   be prepared to stop
         give them plenty of room
6.40   wait because they will take longer to cross
6.41   Reduce speed until you are clear of the area
6.42   a clear view of the crossing area
6.43   On a school bus
6.44   Any direction
6.45   stay behind until the moped has passed the junction
6.46   stay well back
6.47   Be patient and prepare for them to react more slowly
6.48   be patient as you expect them to make mistakes
6.49   Pedestrians
6.50   wait for them to cross
6.51   be aware that the driver's reactions may not be as fast as yours
6.52   hold back until the cyclist has passed the junction
6.53   go in any direction
6.54   They will have a flashing amber light
6.55   just before you turn left
6.56   slow moving
6.57   With-flow pedal cycle lane
6.58   Slow down and be ready to stop
6.59   children's view of the crossing area
6.60   Watch out for pedestrians walking in the road
6.61   allow extra room in case they swerve to avoid potholes
6.62   Cycle route ahead
6.63   The cyclist is slower and more vulnerable
6.64   prepare to slow down and stop
6.65   deaf
6.66   pedestrians and cyclists may cross
6.67   To allow cyclists to position in front of other traffic
6.68   To allow cyclists to position in front of other traffic
6.69   The cyclist might swerve
6.70   Allow plenty of room
         Go very slowly
         Be ready to stop
6.71   You are approaching an organised walk
6.72   By taking further training

Section Seven
Other types of vehicle

7.1   keep well back
7.2   They cannot steer to avoid you
         They move quickly and quietly
7.3

7.4   The large vehicle can easily hide an overtaking vehicle
7.5   stay well back and give it room
7.6   Wait behind the long vehicle
7.7   keep well back
7.8   To get the best view of the road ahead
7.9   Watch carefully for pedestrians
         Be ready to give way to the bus
7.10   drop back until you can see better
7.11   Be prepared to stop behind
7.12   drop back further
7.13   Do not overtake, stay well back and be prepared to stop
7.14   allow it to pull away, if it is safe to do so
7.15   keep well back until you can see that it is clear
7.16   Cars
7.17   Slow down and be prepared to wait
7.18   Do not overtake when at or approaching a junction
7.19   8 mph
7.20   It takes longer to pass one
7.21   8 mph (12 km/h)

Section Eight
Motorcycle handling

8.1   push the motorcycle forward to check the rear wheel turns freely
         glance at the neutral light on your instrument panel
8.2   prepare to slow down
         sound your horn
8.3   Anticipate the actions of others
8.4   Leaning too far over when cornering
         Braking too hard
         Changing direction suddenly
8.5   ride slower in as high a gear as possible
         slow down as there may be black ice
8.6   at all times
8.7   Check that your lights are working
         Make sure that your visor is clean
8.8   on firm, level ground
8.9   keep your speed down
8.10   about central in your lane
8.11   left and apply the front brake
8.12   practise off-road with an approved training body
8.13   reduces your control of the motorcycle
8.14   Slow down
8.15   be unusually slippery
8.16   heavy and sharp braking
         excessive acceleration
         leaning too far when cornering
8.17   the front brake just before the rear
8.18   Slowing down
8.19   upset your balance
8.20   when the motorcycle is upright and moving in a straight line
8.21   How fast you are going
         The tyres on your motorcycle
         The weather

8.22	your motorcycle is broken down on the hard shoulder
8.23	leave parking lights on
8.24	Close the throttle and roll to a stop
8.25	Slow down in good time
8.26	By a rainbow pattern on the surface
8.27	more difficult to control
8.28	White lines
	Tar banding
	Yellow grid lines
	Loose chippings
8.29	apply the front brake just before the rear
8.30	braking
8.31	The steel rails can be slippery
8.32	release the brakes and reapply
8.33	Fuel spilt on the road
8.34	Wheelspin when accelerating
8.35	Release both brakes together
8.36	Apply both brakes smoothly
8.37	place both feet on the ground
8.38	slippery
8.39	cornering
8.40	cause you to crash
8.41	When you are in a one-way street
	When the vehicle in front is signalling to turn right
	In slow-moving traffic queues when traffic in the right-hand lane is moving more slowly
8.42	doubled
8.43	be careful because you can see less
	beware of bends in the road ahead
8.44	When oncoming traffic prevents you turning right
8.45	**Humps for ½ mile**
8.46	slow traffic down
8.47	Red
8.48	alert you to a hazard
	encourage you to reduce speed
8.49	leave plenty of time for your journey
8.50	you do not dazzle other road users
8.51	slow down and stay behind
8.52	To make you aware of your speed
8.53	white line markings
	a different coloured surface
	a different surface texture
8.54	stop at a passing place
8.55	To prevent the motorcycle sliding on the metal drain covers
8.56	Your brakes will be soaking wet
8.57	It is more difficult to see events ahead

Section Nine
Motorway rules

9.1	in an emergency
9.2	in the left-hand lane
9.3	adjust your speed to the speed of the traffic on the motorway
9.4	50 cc
9.5	50 cc or more
9.6	The lanes on the right are for overtaking
9.7	Left-hand lane
9.8	70 mph
9.9	Continuous high speeds may increase the risk of your motorcycle breaking down
9.10	give way to traffic already on the motorway
9.11	70 mph
9.12	70 mph
9.13	any vehicle

9.14	A vehicle towing a trailer
9.15	It allows easy location by the emergency services
9.16	gain speed on the hard shoulder before moving out onto the carriageway
9.17	on a steep gradient
9.18	They are countdown markers to the next exit
9.19	the central reservation and the carriageway
9.20	White
9.21	Green
9.22	in the direction shown on the marker posts
9.23	To build up a speed similar to traffic on the motorway
9.24	Face the oncoming traffic
9.25	Red
9.26	Left
9.27	keep a good distance from the vehicle ahead
9.28	In the left-hand lane
9.29	Obey all speed limits
9.30	Learner car drivers
	Farm tractors
	Horse riders
	Cyclists
9.31	Learner car drivers
	Farm tractors
	Learner motorcyclists
	Cyclists
9.32	keep in the left-hand lane
9.33	Overtaking
9.34	Stopping in an emergency
9.35	move to the left and reduce your speed to 50 mph
9.36	are told to do so by flashing red lights
9.37	move to another lane
9.38	keep to the left-hand lane unless overtaking
9.39	there is a queue of slow-moving traffic to your right that is moving more slowly than you are
9.40	the Highways Agency Control Centre
9.41	on a motorway for use in cases of emergency or breakdown
9.42	To use in cases of emergency or breakdown
9.43	are able to stop and direct anyone on a motorway
9.44	You should not travel in this lane
9.45	The hard shoulder can be used as a running lane
9.46	reduce congestion
9.47	all speed limit signals are set
9.48	Do not use this lane to travel in
9.49	Your overall journey time will normally improve
9.50	When signs direct you to
9.51	For overtaking other vehicles
9.52	Variable speed limits
9.53	If red lights show above every lane
	When told to by the police
	When signalled by a Highways Agency Traffic Officer
9.54	In an emergency or breakdown
9.55	70 mph
9.56	an Highways Agency control centre
9.57	stop and wait
9.58	the hard shoulder is for emergency or breakdown use only
9.59	all the lanes including the hard shoulder
9.60	pull in at the nearest service area
9.61	Leave at the next exit

Section Ten
Rules of the road

10.1	check for cyclists
10.2	Cycle lane
	Tram lane
10.3	Parking for solo motorcycles

10.4 use mirrors and shoulder checks
10.5 not park there unless permitted
10.6 Pull into a passing place on your left
10.7 see approaching traffic
10.8 watch for hidden vehicles emerging from side roads
look for vehicles changing course suddenly
look for pedestrians walking between vehicles
10.9 Wait for the green light
10.10 Headlight deflectors
10.11 125 cc
10.12 60 mph
10.13 When involved in a collision
At a red traffic light
When signalled to do so by a police officer
10.14 National speed limit applies
10.15 70 mph
10.16 By street lighting
10.17 30 mph
10.18 End of minimum speed
10.19 not overtake if you are in doubt
10.20 Horse riders
Long vehicles
Cyclists
10.21 at any time
10.22 Waiting restrictions
10.23 in a one-way street
10.24 overtaking or turning right
10.25 continue in that lane
10.26 Either on the right or the left
10.27 indicate left before leaving the roundabout
10.28 Long vehicle
10.29 your exit road is clear
10.30 oncoming traffic is preventing you from turning right
10.31 A police officer
A school crossing patrol
A red traffic light
10.32 stop, let them cross, wait patiently
10.33 cyclists riding across
10.34 Cyclists
Pedestrians
10.35 You must give way to pedestrians still on the crossing
10.36 wait for pedestrians on the crossing to clear
10.37 To pick up or set down passengers
10.38 keep the other vehicle to your RIGHT and turn behind it (offside to offside)
10.39 30 mph
10.40 Vehicles may be pulling out
Drivers' doors may open
Children may run out from between the vehicles
10.41 give way to oncoming traffic
10.42 Turning right
Overtaking slower traffic
10.43 No one has priority
10.44 10 metres (32 feet)
10.45 Near the brow of a hill
At or near a bus stop
Within 10 metres (32 feet) of a junction
10.46 carry on waiting
10.47 Neither of the vehicles
10.48 No waiting zone ends
10.49 not exceed the speed limit
10.50 Near a school entrance
At a bus stop
10.51 be easily seen by others
10.52 Wait until the road is clear in both directions
10.53 60 mph
10.54 with parking lights on
10.55 a concealed level crossing

10.56 A Highways Agency Traffic Officer
10.57 None of the vehicles
10.58 Signal left just after you pass the exit before the one you will take

Section Eleven
Road and traffic signs

11.1

11.2 Because you will have less steering control
11.3 side winds
11.4

11.5

11.6 that they are warning you of their presence
11.7 To avoid misleading other road users
11.8 also give an arm signal
11.9 Pass on the left
11.10 red circles
11.11

11.12

11.13 Maximum speed limit with traffic calming
11.14

11.15

11.16 End of 20 mph zone
11.17 No motor vehicles
11.18 No entry
11.19 No right turn

11.20

11.21 Route for trams only
11.22 High vehicles
11.23

11.24 No overtaking
11.25 Do not overtake
11.26

11.27 Waiting restrictions apply
11.28 End of restricted parking area
11.29

11.30 No stopping
11.31 no stopping
11.32 Distance to parking place ahead
11.33 Vehicles may park fully on the verge or footway
11.34 Give priority to oncoming traffic
11.35 You have priority over vehicles coming towards you
11.36 You have priority over vehicles from the opposite direction
11.37

11.38 Stop
11.39 Minimum speed 30 mph
11.40 Pass either side to get to the same destination
11.41 Route for trams
11.42 Give an instruction
11.43 On a one-way street
11.44 Contraflow bus lane
11.45 Tourist directions
11.46 tourist attraction
11.47 To give warnings
11.48 T-junction
11.49 Risk of ice
11.50 Crossroads
11.51 Roundabout
11.52 Road narrows
Low bridge
Children crossing
T-junction
11.53 Cycle route ahead

11.54

11.55

11.56 Give way to trams
11.57 Humps in the road
11.58

11.59 End of dual carriageway
11.60 Crosswinds
11.61 Danger ahead
11.62 hold back until you can see clearly ahead
11.63 Level crossing with gate or barrier
11.64 Trams crossing ahead
11.65 Steep hill downwards
11.66 Water across the road
11.67 No through road on the left
11.68 No through road
11.69

11.70

11.71 The right-hand lane is closed
11.72 Contraflow system
11.73 Lane for heavy and slow vehicles
11.74 you must stop and wait behind the stop line
11.75 stop at the stop line
11.76 When your exit from the junction is blocked
11.77

11.78 Traffic lights out of order
11.79 Nobody
11.80 Lifting bridges
Level crossings
Fire stations
11.81 No parking at any time
11.82 To pass a road maintenance vehicle travelling at 10 mph or less
11.83 You are approaching a hazard

11.84 On road humps
11.85

11.86 Visibility along the major road is restricted
11.87 Give way to traffic from the right
11.88 Flash the headlights, indicate left and point to the left
11.89 stop at the stop line
11.90 The driver intends to turn left
11.91 On a motorway slip road
11.92 Change to the lane on your left
11.93 Temporary maximum speed 50 mph
11.94 Right-hand lane closed ahead
11.95 move to the lane on your left
11.96 The number of the next junction
11.97 an overtaking lane
11.98 On the right-hand edge of the road
11.99 At slip road entrances and exits
11.100 leave the motorway at the next exit
11.101 End of motorway

11.102
11.103 60 mph
11.104 End of restriction
11.105 follow the route diversion
11.106 To warn of road works ahead
11.107 a compulsory maximum speed limit
11.108 carry on with great care
11.109 Give an arm signal
11.110 No motorcycles
11.111 pass the lorry on the left
11.112 Move into another lane in good time
11.113 you must stop behind the white stop line
11.114 Turn to the left
11.115 To warn others of your presence
11.116 unless a moving vehicle may cause you danger
11.117 No parking on the days and times shown
11.118 Quayside or river bank
11.119

11.120 hazard warning
11.121 To prevent queuing traffic from blocking the junction on the left
11.122 It is to separate traffic flowing in opposite directions
11.123 To warn you of their presence
11.124 20 mph
11.125 trams must stop
11.126 At a junction
11.127 Pull up on the left
11.128 Red alone
11.129 there is a hazard ahead of you
11.130 Leave the motorway at the next exit
11.131 To prevent the junction becoming blocked
11.132 Stop, even if the road is clear

11.133

11.134 Mini-roundabout
11.135 Two-way traffic crosses a one-way road
11.136 Two-way traffic straight ahead
11.137 Hump-back bridge

11.138
11.139 Direction to park-and-ride car park
11.140 wait for the green light before you cross the stop line
11.141 'give way' sign
11.142 Wait
11.143 Direction to emergency pedestrian exit

11.144
11.145 With-flow bus and cycle lane
11.146

11.147 Zebra crossing
11.148 Zebra crossing ahead
11.149

11.150

11.151

11.152
11.153 all traffic is going one way
11.154 Red and amber
11.155 Tunnel ahead

395

Section Twelve
Documents

12.1 Make and model
Engine size and number
Year of first registration
12.2 any DSA (Driving Standards Agency) approved training body
12.3 the motorcycle is insured for your use
12.4 display it clearly on your motorcycle
12.5 three years old
12.6 Registered keeper
Make of the motorcycle
Engine size
12.7 you change your motorcycle
you change your name
your permanent address changes
12.8 damage to other vehicles
injury to others
12.9 Third party only
12.10 the year of first registration
12.11 To make sure your motorcycle is roadworthy
12.12 a CBT (Compulsory Basic Training) certificate
12.13 your health affects your riding
your eyesight does not meet a set standard
you change your motorcycle
12.14 retake your theory and practical tests
reapply for your provisional licence
12.15 ride on a motorway
carry a pillion passenger
ride without 'L' plates displayed
12.16 125 cc
12.17 require L-plates while learning with a qualified instructor
12.18 the rider holds a full licence for the category of motorcycle
the motorcycle is fitted with rear footrests
there is a proper passenger seat fitted
12.19 two years
12.20 A valid certificate of insurance
12.21 you must have passed your test for a full motorcycle licence
12.22 You must have passed your test for a full motorcycle licence
12.23 You will have to pay the first £100 of any claim
12.24 one year after the date it was issued
12.25 insurance certificate
12.26 Retake your theory and practical tests
Reapply for your provisional licence
12.27 12 months
12.28 A notification to tell DVLA that a vehicle is not being used on the road
12.29 to tell DVLA that your vehicle is not being used on the road
12.30 for 12 months only
12.31 for 12 months only
12.32 £5000
12.33 The registered vehicle keeper
12.34 When a police officer asks you for it
12.35 obtain a tax disc
12.36 renew your road tax disc
12.37 A valid driving licence
A valid tax disc clearly displayed
Proper insurance cover
12.38 valid insurance
12.39 7 days
12.40 Valid insurance
12.41 When you move house

Section Thirteen
Incidents, accidents and emergencies

13.1 By following an arrow on a marker post
13.2 stop the engine in an emergency
13.3 there is a danger ahead
13.4 for the number on the telephone that you are using
for details of yourself and your motorcycle
whether you belong to a motoring organisation
13.5 When you slow down quickly because of danger ahead
13.6 Switch on hazard lights then go and call for help immediately
13.7 Switch on hazard warning lights
13.8 Stop on the hard shoulder and use the emergency telephone to inform the authorities
13.9 Stop at the next emergency telephone and report the hazard
13.10 Whether the driver owns the other vehicle involved
The other driver's name, address and telephone number
The make and registration number of the other vehicle
The details of the other driver's vehicle insurance
13.11 a disabled person
13.12 When you slow down quickly on a motorway because of a hazard ahead
When you have broken down
13.13 When stopped and temporarily obstructing traffic
13.14 Keep a safe distance from the vehicle in front
13.15 when an emergency arises
13.16 Apply pressure over the wound and raise the arm
13.17 10 seconds
13.18 10 minutes
13.19 10 minutes
13.20 100 per minute
13.21 Pale grey skin
13.22 Sweating
13.23 Check the airway is clear
13.24 seek medical assistance
13.25 go to the next emergency telephone and report the hazard
13.26 Variable message signs
13.27 4 to 5 centimetres
13.28 Make sure engines are switched off
Call the emergency services promptly
13.29 not put yourself at risk
13.30 Switch on your own hazard warning lights
Make sure that someone telephones for an ambulance
Get people who are not injured clear of the scene
13.31 Only when it is essential
13.32 try to stop the bleeding
check their breathing
check their airways
13.33 breathing
13.34 Circulation
Airway
Breathing
13.35 Clear the airway and keep it open
Check that they are breathing
Stop any heavy bleeding
13.36 check the airway is clear
make sure they are breathing stop any heavy bleeding
13.37 Keep injured people warm and comfortable
Keep injured people calm by talking to them reassuringly
Make sure that injured people are not left alone
13.38 Stop any severe bleeding
Check they are breathing
Clear their airway and keep it open
13.39 Offer someone a cigarette to calm them down

13.40 Reassure them
Not leave them alone
13.41 reassure them constantly
13.42 warn other traffic
13.43 gently
13.44 clear the airway
tilt their head back gently
pinch the nostrils together
13.45 remove anything sticking to the burn
13.46 douse the burns with clean cool non-toxic liquid
13.47 Apply firm pressure to the wound
Raise the leg to lessen bleeding
13.48 there is further danger
13.49 not move them
13.50 keep them in the vehicle
13.51

13.52 Driving licence
Insurance certificate
MOT test certificate
13.53 As soon as possible
13.54 It will help to reduce the blood flow
13.55 Variable message signs
13.56 Warn other traffic
13.57 remove anything that is blocking the mouth
tilt the head back gently to clear the airway
13.58 reassure them constantly
keep them warm
avoid moving them if possible
avoid leaving them alone
13.59 This could result in more serious injury

Section Fourteen
Motorcycle loading

14.1 ease off the throttle and reduce your speed
14.2 keep your speed down
approach corners more carefully
14.3 headlight
suspension
tyres
14.4 solo with minimum power of 35 kw (46.6 bhp)
14.5 securely fastened when riding
14.6 always wear a helmet
14.7 lean with the rider when going round bends
14.8 lean with you on bends
14.9 Headlight
14.10 stopping distance may increase
14.11 cause low-speed wobble
14.12 The rider of the motorcycle
14.13 check that the motorcycle is suitable
14.14 They could make your motorcycle unstable
14.15 Your ability to steer
14.16 hold a full motorcycle licence
14.17 tyre pressures
14.18 Keep further back than you normally would
14.19 they can reach the handholds and footrests
14.20 is correctly aligned
14.21 may increase your stopping distance
14.22 Preload on the rear shock absorber(s)
14.23 1 metre (3 feet 3 inches)
14.24 The trailer should NOT be more than 1 metre
(3 feet 3 inches) wide
14.25 Increase stopping distance
14.26 Ride a motorcycle with an engine capacity greater than
125 cc
Pull a trailer
Carry a pillion passenger
14.27 cause high speed-weave
14.28 have a full motorcycle licence
ensure that your engine is more than 125 cc
14.29 rear footrests
a proper pillion seat
14.30 reduce stability
cause high-speed weave
cause low-speed wobble
14.31 Not at any time
14.32 handling
14.33 not exceed 60 mph
use only the left and centre lanes

index

Author	Robert Davies
Project Manager	Louise McIntyre
Design and Page Build	Lee Parsons
	James Robertson
	Dominic Stickland
Technical Advisors	Elliot Bloy
	of Dorsetbiker Ltd
Photographer	Jim Godden
Copy Editor	John Hardaker

Photo credits:
Freefoto.com	p176
Tramlink Croydon Ltd	p172, 173
Watsonian-Squire	p15 (right) p207

The author and publishers would also like to thank the
following companies:
  Bransons of Yeovil
  Quickstart Motorcycle Training